SHAKESPEARE, VIOLENCE AND EARLY MODERN EUROPE

Shakespeare, Violence and Early Modern Europe broadens our understanding of the final years of the last Tudor monarch, revealing the
truly international context in which they must be understood.
Uncovering the extent to which Shakespeare's dramatic art inter-
sected with European politics, Andrew Hiscock brings together
close readings of the history plays, compelling insights into late
Elizabethan political culture and renewed attention to neglected
continental accounts of Elizabeth I. With a fresh perspective, the
book charts the profound influence that Shakespeare and ambitious
courtiers had upon succeeding generations of European writers,
dramatists and audiences following the turn of the sixteenth century.
Informed by early modern and contemporary cultural debate, this
book demonstrates how the study of early modern violence can
illuminate ongoing crises of interpretation concerning brutality, victimisation and complicity today.

ANDREW HISCOCK is Dean and Professor of Early Modern
Literature at Bangor University, Wales, and Research Fellow at the
Institut de Recherche sur la Renaissance, l'Âge Classique et les
Lumières, Université Paul-Valéry, Montpellier 3. He is a Fellow of
the English Association and has published widely on English and
French early modern literature. He is series co-editor for the *Arden
Early Modern Drama Guides* and a trustee of the Modern Humanities
Research Association. His monographs include *Reading Memory in
Early Modern Literature* (Cambridge University Press, 2011) and *The
Uses of this World: Thinking Space in Shakespeare, Marlowe, Cary and
Jonson* (University of Wales Press, 2004).

T0371534

SHAKESPEARE, VIOLENCE AND EARLY MODERN EUROPE

ANDREW HISCOCK

Bangor University

CAMBRIDGE
UNIVERSITY PRESS

Shaftesbury Road, Cambridge CB2 8EA, United Kingdom

One Liberty Plaza, 20th Floor, New York, NY 10006, USA

477 Williamstown Road, Port Melbourne, VIC 3207, Australia

314–321, 3rd Floor, Plot 3, Splendor Forum, Jasola District Centre, New Delhi – 110025, India

103 Penang Road, #05–06/07, Visioncrest Commercial, Singapore 238467

Cambridge University Press is part of Cambridge University Press & Assessment,
a department of the University of Cambridge.

We share the University's mission to contribute to society through the pursuit of
education, learning and research at the highest international levels of excellence.

www.cambridge.org
Information on this title: www.cambridge.org/9781108821995

DOI: 10.1017/9781108909464

© Andrew Hiscock 2022

This publication is in copyright. Subject to statutory exception and to the provisions
of relevant collective licensing agreements, no reproduction of any part may take
place without the written permission of Cambridge University Press & Assessment.

First published 2022
First paperback edition 2023

A catalogue record for this publication is available from the British Library

Library of Congress Cataloging-in-Publication data
NAMES: Hiscock, Andrew, 1962– author.
TITLE: Shakespeare, violence and early modern Europe / Andrew Hiscock.
DESCRIPTION: Cambridge ; New York, NY : Cambridge University Press, 2022. | Includes
bibliographical references and index.
IDENTIFIERS: LCCN 2021039277 (print) | LCCN 2021039278 (ebook) | ISBN 9781108830188
(hardback) | ISBN 9781108909464 (ebook)
SUBJECTS: LCSH: Shakespeare, William, 1564–1616 – Histories. | Shakespeare, William,
1564–1616 – Influence. | Violence in literature. | Kings and rulers in literature. | English drama –
Early modern and Elizabethan, 1500–1600 – History and criticism. | Theater – Political aspects –
England. | Theater – Political aspects – Europe. | England – In literature. | England – Foreign
public opinion, European. | Great Britain – Politics and government – 1558–1603. | BISAC:
LITERARY CRITICISM / European / English, Irish, Scottish, Welsh
CLASSIFICATION: LCC PR2982 .H487 2022 (print) | LCC PR2982 (ebook) |
DDC 822.3/3–dc23/eng/20211013
LC record available at https://lccn.loc.gov/2021039277
LC ebook record available at https://lccn.loc.gov/2021039278

ISBN   978-1-108-83018-8   Hardback
ISBN   978-1-108-82199-5   Paperback

Cambridge University Press & Assessment has no responsibility for the persistence
or accuracy of URLs for external or third-party internet websites referred to in this
publication and does not guarantee that any content on such websites is, or will
remain, accurate or appropriate.

For Siân

Contents

Acknowledgements

This body of research has had an unexpectedly long gestation period, but it has enabled me to renew friendships, to forge friendships and to accumulate debts of gratitude with colleagues around the world. The advice and support of Emily Hockley, George Laver and Nicola Maclean, and previously of Sarah Stanton, at Cambridge University Press have been invaluable. Their responses to this project, along with those of Jayavel Radhakrishnan and Helen B. Cooper, have been unfailingly attentive and remain very much appreciated. The detailed responses of the Press's readers enormously enriched the remit of this work. In addition, the project would never have been possible without the awards of research leave linked to the department of English Literature at Bangor University, Wales, and the Institut de Recherches sur la Renaissance, l'Âge Classique et les Lumières (IRCL), Université Paul-Valéry Montpellier 3. I wish to thank my colleagues in the respective university research offices (Florent Goiffon, Vanessa Kuhner-Blaha, Christophe Remond and Cornelia Thomas) and also *all* my early modernist and medievalist colleagues at both institutions, both past and present, for their continued interest and support in this project. I would especially wish to thank Nathalie Vienne-Guerrin, the former director of IRCL, for welcoming me so generously to the research centre in Montpellier during my sabbatical there.

My gratitude goes also to the attentive and patient staff at: Bangor University Libraries; the libraries of Université Paul-Valéry, Montpellier 3; the British Library; the Bodleian Library; the National Archives, London; the Folger Shakespeare Library; New York Public Libraries; Columbia University Libraries; Bibliothèque Nationale de France (BNF) – François Mitterand; Richelieu-Louvois Bibliothèque (BNF); Département des Arts du Spectacle (BNF); Bibliothèque-musée de l'Opéra (BNF); Maison Jean Vilar (BNF), Avignon; Médiathèque Émile Zola, Montpellier; Biblioteca Casanatense, Rome; The Venerable English College, Rome; Biblioteca Nazionale di Roma; Archivum Romanum Societatis Iesu, Rome; Biblioteca Nacional de

España, Madrid; Biblioteca de Catalunya, Barcelona; and the Municipal Library of Borsele, Heinkenszand, the Netherlands. I would also like to record my appreciation to the Bayerische Staatsbibliothek, Munich for its generous permission to reproduce the cover image for this volume. In addition, I would like to thank the following editors and academic presses where earlier versions of some of the research in this volume appeared: '"More Warlike than politique": Shakespeare and the Theatre of War', *Shakespeare* 7.2. (2011), 221–47; '"*Achilles alter*": The Heroic Lives and Afterlives of Robert Devereux, 2nd Earl of Essex', in A. Connolly and L. Hopkins (eds.), *Essex. The Life and Times of an Elizabethan Courtier* (Manchester: Manchester University Press, 2013), pp. 101–32; '"Most fond and fruitlesse warre": Ralegh and the call to arms', in Christopher M. Armitage (ed.), *Literary and Visual Ralegh* (Manchester: Manchester University Press, 2013), pp. 257–83; 'Shakespeare and the fortunes of war and memory', *Actes des Congrès de la Société Française Shakespeare*, 30 (2013), 11–26; '"Shakspeare, s'avançant": A Bard, the Nineteenth Century and a Tale of Two Cities' Theatres', *Shakespeare* 13.4 (2017), 333–50.

As may be imagined given the international remit of this project, my enquiries have been many and various over the years. Apart from the advice of colleagues at Bangor and at IRCL, this project has benefited immeasurably from the knowledge and attentive readings of Paul Hammer and John Lee and I owe them a great debt of thanks. I would also like to thank the colleagues below (in alphabetical order) for sharing so generously (and patiently) their knowledge and advice with me: Richard Andrews, Alfonso Ardito, Hubert Baudet, Daniele Comberiati, Line Cottegnies, Leo de Visser, John Drakakis, Richard Dutton, Bill Engel, Jane Everson, Judith Farre, Alison Findlay, Raffaella Fiorini, Richard Harp, Thomas Herron, Rui Carvalho Homem, Lisa Hopkins, Wim Hüsken, Giovanni Iamartino, Stefano Jossa, Pamela King, Stephen Longstaffe, Julia R. Lupton, Helena Miguélez-Carballeira, Efterpi Mitsi, Herbert Mouwen, Joan Oleza, Judith Owen, Sandrine Parageau, Marie-Claire Phélippeau, Anne Lake Prescott, Bart Ramakers, Purificación Ribes, Brian Richardson, Emiel Roodenburg, Laura Rorato, Maria Cristina Seccia, Charlotte Steenbrugge, Elsa Strietman, Christine Sukic, Jesús Tronch, Diane Watt, Maurice Whitehead.

Finally, I would like to thank my family, Siân, Bronwen and Huw, for their love and long-suffering support as this project was being prepared. I could not have done it without them.

Notes on Sources and References

The abbreviations used in the notes are as follows:

CLSP   Calendar of Letters and State Papers, Relating to English Affairs preserved in, or originally belonging to, the Archives of Simancas, vol. IV: Elizabeth, 1587–1603

CM Bath   Calendar of the Manuscripts of Marquis of Bath Preserved at Longleat, Wiltshire

CM Salisbury   Calendar of the Manuscripts of the Most. Hon. The Marquis of Salisbury, Preserved at Hatfield House, Hertfordshire

CSP   Calendar of State Papers

CSP Col.   Calendar of State Papers, Colonial series

CSP Dom.   Calendar of State Papers, Domestic series

CSP Salisbury   Calendar of State Papers of the Most Hon. Marquis of Salisbury, Preserved at Hatfield House, Hertfordshire

CSPM   Calendar of State Papers and Manuscripts

PRO   Public Record Office

RM Lord Lisle   Report on the Manuscripts of Lord De L'Isle & Dudley Preserved at Penshurst Place

RM Viscount Lisle   Report on the Manuscripts of the Right Honourable Viscount De L'Isle Preserved at Penshurst Place

Against each entry, the part and the date of publication for the papers are rendered in parentheses. With regard to published books and articles, full reference details are reprised at the beginning of each chapter. All references to Shakespearean texts are taken from the *New Cambridge Shakespeare* series. Unless otherwise indicated, translations of sources are my own.

Introduction

> Without the city are some theatres where English Actors represent almost every day Tragedies and Comedies to very numerous audiences; these are concluded with excellent music, variety of dances, and the excessive applause of those that are present ... There is still another place, built in the form of a Theatre, which serves for the baiting of Bulls and Bears, they are fastened behind, and then worried by great English bulldogs ... To this entertainment, there often follows that of whipping a blinded Bear, which is performed by five or six men, standing circularly with whips, which they exercise upon him without any mercy, as he cannot escape from them because of his chain; he defends himself with all his force and skill, throwing down all who come within his reach, and are not active enough to get out of it, and tearing the whips out of their hands, and breaking them.[1]

The German lawyer Paul Hentzner accompanied his tutee, a young nobleman from Silesia, on a three-year European tour beginning in 1597. An account of their journeying was published in 1612 as *Itinerarium Germaniae, Galliae, Angliae, Italiae, cum Indice Locorum, Rerum atque Verborum*. The travellers arrived in Elizabethan England in the autumn of 1598 and Hentzner took his usual meticulous notes on the customs of the country, making time and space here to consider the singular vigour with which the creative industries catered to London audiences. Appetites in the Tudor capital for spectacles of violent blood-letting were easily accommodated in the playhouse and, indeed, at the scaffold. However, there was also any number of historical and crime narratives at the booksellers relating grisly tales; and ancient texts in modern editions were widely accessible in school and university classrooms to tempt the palate, if scenes of butchery were sought. Facing impending doom on the battlefields of Bordeaux, Talbot confesses in *1 Henry VI* that he had originally sent for his son '[t]o tutor [him] in stratagems of war' (*VI*: IV.v.2); and, for those similarly inclined to travel for a more first-hand experience of hostilities, a constantly changing itinerary might be proposed, linked to sites of violent contest unfolding across the length and breadth of the early modern continent.

In *The ciuile wars betweene the howses of Lancaster and Yorke* (1609), Samuel Daniel dubbed war an 'impious good, and good impietie . . . foul refiner of a State'.[2] Whatever the ambiguities surrounding the undertaking, it remained a frequent resource of political government in the sixteenth and seventeenth centuries. Frank Tallett relates that this was 'a remarkably bellicose age . . . Between 1480 and 1700 England was involved in 29 wars, France in 34, Spain in 36 . . . in terms of its belligerency the seventeenth century was outstripped only by the twentieth'.[3] The present study turns to early modern England and attends most particularly to the palpable need expressed in both the playhouse *and* the wider political arena for the staging of theatres of conflict that might extend well beyond the realm's borders. Thus, a selection of 1590s history plays as well as political projects promoted by a number of elite figures at Elizabeth I's court are analysed as key interventions in the age's thoroughgoing cultural debate concerning the status and functions of violence.

'the mistress-court of mighty Europe'

There is every evidence that the states of early modern Europe were determined to incorporate Elizabeth's subjects into their vigorous politicking and zealous profession of arms. Philip II himself regularly gave testament of his resolve that England should not be excluded from the continent's brutal struggles to redefine *meum* and *tuum*, as he submitted in a letter dated 1590:

> Everybody knows about the great, continuous and unavoidable expenses that I have incurred for many years past to defend our holy Catholic faith and to conserve my kingdoms and lordships, and how they have grown immensely through the war with England and the developments in France; but I have not been able to avoid them, both because I have such a specific obligation to God and the world to act, and also because if the heretics were to prevail (which I hope God will not allow) it might open the door to worse damage and dangers, and to war at home.[4]

In England itself, history plays of the 1590s, such as those focusing on Henry IV, Henry V and Henry VI by Shakespeare (and his collaborators in the latter case), as well as the political ambitions of significant court favourites, such as Sir Walter Ralegh (1554–1618) and Robert Devereux, Earl of Essex (1565–1601), sought to focus the minds of native audiences upon armed conflict as an instrument of state policy. This investment in violence articulated regularly in the playhouses and in early modern court culture exposed for public scrutiny the motivations and protocols of those resorting to combat (*ius ad bellum*) as well as the conduct of those at arms (*ius in bello*) and those seeking modes of conflict resolution (*ius post bellum*). In each instance, the waging of hostilities was frequently linked with the overseeing of political continuity or change management, assertions of lordship and/or pressing crises responding to individual or collective insecurities.

After the devastations of the Black Death in the fourteenth century, Europe's population in total may well have numbered between 60–70 million in 1500 and perhaps 80–90 million by 1600. In addition, as John Merriman has stressed, '[i]n 1500, Europe was maze of about 1,500 fragmented states ... Europe's political fragmentation was accompanied by cultural fragmentation, reinforced by the many languages spoken.'[5] Assessing this complex early modern environment, Lisa Hopkins emphasises that 'Elizabeth ruled over less territory than any other monarch since 1066, in spite of the imperial rhetoric that characterized her reign.'[6] Nevertheless, a number of the island's monarchs down the centuries had recognised that the attentions of the continental nations needed to be seized if the realm were to realise its oft-mooted aspirations to imperial greatness. The consuming interest of the late Elizabethan history play and, indeed, of strategic political figures, such as Ralegh and Essex, that the kingdom renew itself politically by expanding its borders, means that the final discussions of this study inevitably turn to England's neighbouring states. Strikingly, when early modern Europe had its own writers attend to the late Tudor kingdom, the cultural driver of violence was radically reinterpreted for audiences across the continent, albeit not in ways that would have gratified any of the figures depicted.

More generally, in each of the chapters which follows, the emphasis remains upon how political and theatrical audiences of the period were repeatedly urged to scrutinise the assertion of English sovereignty in response to scenes of violence and trauma unfolding across the seas – played out before, what Exeter terms in *Henry V*, 'the mistress-court of mighty Europe' (*V*: II.iv.134). When this *mistress-court* produced its own fictions of Elizabeth's court culture in the later seventeenth and eighteenth centuries, the focus would remain on the internal, perceivedly erotic politics in operation during the final years of the Tudor century. Thus, if this study begins in the sixteenth century, it closes reflecting on some of the ways in which a whole succession of European generations chose to

remember the age of Elizabeth onstage at home and abroad. Indeed, by the
eighteenth century, the enthusiasm to revive the Shakespearean world for
new, European audiences was such that Catherine II (the Great) could be
found penning adaptations of the bard's plays transplanted to the eastern
limits of the continent and rendered in the Russian language.[7]

In the post-war period, a renewed understanding of the complex variety
of this early modern continent was ushered in with a whole host of ground-
breaking studies, such as Fernand Braudel's *La Méditerranée et le
monde méditerranéen à l'époque de Philippe II*, Roland Mousnier's *Les
XVI et XVII siècles*, Denys Hay's *Europe: The Emergence of an Idea*, John
Hale's *The Civilization of Europe in the Renaissance* and Susan Doran's
England and Europe 1485–1603.[8] Such studies continue to encourage readers
and critics to interrogate the intellectual shorthand involved when we press
the term 'Europe' into service. More recently, Gerard Delanty's *Inventing
Europe: Idea, Identity, Reality* and Heikki Mikkeli's *Europe as an Idea and
an Identity*, for example, have demonstrated that down the centuries
European nations have often been viewed as having a community of
interest because they: inhabited a geographical zone with climatic and
topographical resemblances; invested in a common intellectual tradition
(philosophical, linguistic, legal) from antiquity; belonged to supranational
communities of religious confession; and, at the end of the seventeenth
century with its greater interest in secular enquiry, participated in
a common European cultural discourse, debating *distinctive* political liber-
ties and achieving a *distinctive* societal sophistication.[9]

Certainly, such considerations of cultural origination and difference
exercised early modern Europe as much as they have more recent political
debate. Nonetheless, a central contention of this study is that in attending
to the often spectacular ambitions of some members of the Elizabethan
elite, it became impossible to conceive of England's political survival
without having a watchful eye beyond the borders of the kingdom.

Violence and Its Discontents: The Critical Debate

If, as Julius R. Ruff argues, '[v]iolence . . . was part of the discourse of early
modern interpersonal relations',[10] it was also inevitable that this field of
enquiry, particularly in the aftermath of two world wars, would come to
dominate many areas of cultural debate in the second half of the twentieth
century as greater and greater evidence of acts of inhumanity was
uncovered. Diverse social theorists, such as Hannah Arendt, Julien
Freund, Wolfgang Sofsky, Slavoj Žižek, Judith Butler, Paul Virilio and

Zygmunt Bauman, to name but a few, have all in their different ways pointed to the difficulties of defining the subject because its extensive proportions appear to exceed the grasp of critical discourse.[11] Nonetheless, the need to engage in such analysis remains pressing because of the very commonplace status which violence continues to claim in our everyday understanding of the world around us.[12] This is all the more urgent, as Véronique Le Goaziou stresses, because if in the past 'le violent a été l'Autre', in more recent times we have come to reconcile ourselves to the fact that 'le violent pouvait être une personne ordinaire, pouvait être nous-mêmes'.[13a]

If critical debate continues to emphasise that violence need not necessarily manifest itself solely in physical terms, Robert Paul Wolff is a representative voice in broadly defining the phenomenon as 'the illegitimate or unauthorized use of force to effect decisions against the will or desire of others'.[14] This focus on compelling trauma upon resisting subject(s) is further developed in a number of recent studies regarding the matrix of human relationships which frame the performance and reception of the act: thus, in addition to the author(s) and the victim(s), we are left to conjure with the roles of witness(es) and judge(s).[15] Nowhere, of course, is this more apparent than in Shakespearean performance, where all too often audiences (on- and off-stage) are forced to reflect upon their own ethical integrity – nay, complicity – in bearing witness to the unfolding cycles of horror: anticipating the tortures about to be enacted, Cornwall advises Edmund in *King Lear*, 'Leave [Gloucester] to my displeasure. Edmund, keep you our sister company. The revenges we are bound to take upon your traitorous father are not fit for your beholding' (III.vii.6–8). The prolific early modern author, Anthony Munday, argued that, unlike the evils committed which 'pollute the doers onlie', theatre audiences 'saie nought, but gladlie looke on, they al by sight and assent be actors'.[16] Conversely, more recently, W. J. T. Mitchell has pointed to the ways in which 'beholding' violence may bring with it self-protective 'processes of temporal and spatial displacement' or detachment that render the observer and/or interpreter 'neither a perpetrator nor a victim'.[17] This volatile state of attaching/detaching, acting/beholding, anticipating/judging is something with which Shakespearean audiences remained all too familiar. Moreover, as the stage is visited with one trauma after another, we

---

[a] 'the violent [one] has been the Other'; 'the violent [one] could be an ordinary person, could be ourselves'.

are presented with the thorny problematisation of violations in the past
and of failing political systems in the present.[18]

The construction of Self and Other through the enactment, narration
and remembering of violence remains as apposite to the analysis of the early
modern age as it does to our own. During the Elizabethan military
campaign in Ireland, it was reported in the autumn of 1599, to a highly
receptive Privy Council, that there had been

> Many execrable murders and cruelties upon the English, as well in the
> county of Limerick, as in the counties of Cork and Kerry, and elsewhere;
> infants taken from the nurse's breast and the brains dashed against the walls;
> the hearts plucked out of the body of the husband in the view of the wife,
> who was forced to yield the use of her apron to wipe off the blood from the
> murderers' fingers.[19]

In accounts of early (and late) modernity, it quickly becomes evident that
the appetite for violence during perceived states of emergency generates its
own forms of logic and craves extravagantly polarised accounts of moral
adversaries, of superlative victims and of fugitives bereft of succour.
Nonetheless, Burghley himself had protested earlier in the 1590s that 'It
is no marvel that the [Irish] people have rebellious hearts, for the Flemings
had not such cause to rebel by the oppressions of the Spaniards as it is
reported the Irish people have.'[20] State correspondence, legal records,
ballads, print culture, street entertaiments, rumour . . . all might respond
during the sixteenth and seventeenth centuries to this consuming interest
in brutality. However, as Emmanuel Bruno Jean-François has argued, such
narratives markedly fail to take account of the complexity, fragility and
reversibility of the relationships of persecutor, persecuted and beholder.[21]

Acknowledging a rich heritage of judicial debate surrounding the status
and function of violence in the twentieth century, Walter Benjamin
addressed this enquiry in terms of a breach, or the healing of a breach, in
a culture's moral and legal consensus: 'All violence as means is either law-
making or law-preserving. If it lays claim to neither of these predicates, it
forfeits all validity.'[22] It was this very question of legitimation that later
came to dominate Hannah Arendt's meditations on the practice.
Construing it as 'the severe frustration of the faculty of action' in failing
political states, Arendt contended that '[v]iolence can destroy power; it is
utterly incapable of creating it'.[23] In such ways, critical debate in the post-
war period urged us to interrogate at length whether the practice of
violence denoted an interruptive or provisional intervention, an engagement in deviance, and/or an ethical failure.[24] Subsequent generations of

thinkers have often remained less sanguine in their analyses than Arendt. They have exposed how contemporary society has vainly tried to comfort itself by asserting the diminishing purchase that violence has on our 'civilising' society and by refusing to consider the sobering functionality which the practice can assume in our collective lives. Querying the protocols concerning the battlefield's bodycount, Shakespeare's Fluellen submits 'Is it not lawful, an't please your majesty, to tell how many is killed?' (*V*: IV.viii.111–12).[25] Like many voices in this critical debate, Xavier Crettiez trains attention on the grim possibility that 'La violence rapporte à ceux qui la pratiquent' and may excite a 'plaisir individuel' for those who participate in (and witness) the practice.[26a] Indeed, Jean Baudrillard went further, insisting that rather than scorning brutality as a practice, 'il faut voir que c'est notre modernité elle-même, notre hypermodernité, qui produit ce type de violence, et ces effets spéciaux dont le terrorisme fait partie lui aussi'.[27b] In an apocalyptic conclusion which synchronises remarkably with the dramatic discourse of the Shakespearean history plays under discussion, Baudrillard envisaged a world saturated with hatred – a punishing investment from which we cannot desist and which provokes in us a vexed longing for the end of this world where such conditions of existence cease to obtain.

All such lines of reasoning seem to have haunted the development of human society since earliest times. In the *Confessions*, Augustine related how his friend Alypius had formerly become addicted to the 'immanissimis voluptatibus' of the Roman Games: 'ut enim vidit illum sanguinem, immanitatem simul ebibit et non se avertit, sed fixit aspectum et hauriebat furias et nesciebat, et delectabatur scelere certaminis et cruenta voluptate inebriabatur'.[c] Taking up specifically this intellectual challenge for early modern enquiry, Cynthia Marshall argues forcefully that 'We need a way to account for an audience's pleasure in projected suffering such as that portrayed in violent Renaissance literature. A focus on pleasure is far from denial of literature's seriousness: providing pleasure may well be the most subversive of tactics.'[28] Marshall's timely emphasis upon the role of the witness (or audience member) in the enactment of violence remains key

---

[a] 'Violence yields benefits to those who engage in it'; 'particular pleasure'.
[b] 'we must recognize that it is the very essence of our modernity, our hypermodernity, which produces this kind of violence and these particular effects in which terrorism also should be counted'.
[c] 'monstrous gratification', 'For when he saw that blood, he drank deep of its barbarity and did not turn himself away but fixed his gaze and drank in the torments and was unaware, and found gratification in the wickedness of the contest, and became drunk on the pleasures of blood' – Augustine, *Confessions*, ed. and trans. Carolyn J.-B. Hammond (Cambridge, MA: Harvard University Press/Loeb Classical Library, 2014), pp. 264–5 (VI.8.13).

and connects with a much broader emphasis in the present study concerning whether we are held in the (en)thrall of such traumatic experiences. The theorist Willem Schinkel makes the uncomfortable point that 'The love of fictional violence may be a love of *fictional* violence; it is also a *love of violence*.'[29]

Despite Thomas Lodge's contention in *A Fig for Momus* (1595) that 'All things are chang'd, the meanes, the men and armes,/Our strategems now differ from the old', the textual inheritance of antiquity continued to shape his age's cultural interrogation of warfare.[30] This is a theme regularly taken up by Shakespeare's Fluellen in *Henry V*. Indeed, at the beginning of the sixteenth century, when in *Dell'arte della guerra* (1519/20) Machiavelli turned to the subject of armed hostilities, he wrote for 'the satisfying of those who are louers of auncient actes'.[31] The key military tracts from antiquity, Vegetius's *De Re Militari* and Frontinus's *Strategemata*, had circulated in manuscript in the medieval period prior to wider dissemination by print culture in subsequent centuries. Moreover, as Robert Appelbaum has justly pointed out, there was a whole range of European publications that considered the relative merits of recourse to violence: from la Boétie's *Discours sur la servitude volontaire* (Latin: 1574; French: 1576), Hotman's *Franco-Gallia* (1573), de Bèze's *De jure magistratuum* (1574), Buchanan's *De jure regni apud scotos* (1579) and the *Vindiciae contra tyrannos* (1579) to Mariana's *De rege et regis institutione* (1598) and Naudé's *Considérations sur les coups d'états* (1639).[32] One of the first English-language interventions in Tudor print culture treating the ancients' arts of war was Alexander Barclay's translation of Sallust's *famous cronycle of the warre* (1522). This was followed in 1544 by Anthony Cope's rendering of Livy in *The historie of two noble capitaines of the worlde, Anniball and Scipio*. Notable examples of this genre from the second half of the century include Arthur Golding's *eyght bookes of . . . Caesar* (1565), Thomas North's rendering of Plutarch's *Lives* (1579) and Henry Savile's translations in the 1590s of the *Histories* and the *Life of Agricola* by Tacitus. Indeed, John Hooker's prefatory letter, dedicated to Ralegh, at the opening of Holinshed's *Second volume of Chronicles* (1586) reminded readers that Caesar himself 'in his wars searched the ancient bookes and histories of the citie of Rome: and did . . . thereby draw a paterne for his owne direction, both for his ciuill and his martiall affaires'.[33]

In the wake of Caesar's death and the flight of the conspirators to Asia, the most favoured ancient writer in the early modern period, Cicero, wrote in 44 BC to C. Cassius Longinus, one of the prime instigators of the initial conspiracy: 'quid enim est quod contra vim sine vi fieri possit?'[34a] This thorny dilemma continues to weigh heavily in more recent exchanges on the subject: René Girard, for example, insisted that 'On ne peut se passer de la violence pour mettre fin à la violence. Mais c'est précisément pour cela que la violence est interminable.'[35b] Indeed, following in the footsteps of classical forebears, the early modern age might associate the very act of cognition with the performance of violence. Trained in rhetorical argumentation, speakers seeking to flex their faculty of memory might summon up mentally a harrowing scene of trauma in order to excite their powers of recall: the destruction (slaughter, suicide, violation) of something/someone thus triggered the mind into effective oratory.[36] The present study considers how much more tremendous might be the result amongst the serried ranks of the audience in a theatre, or even that of the political nation when worked upon with powerful evocations of killing and mutilation. As we have seen, war all too frequently ravaged the landscape of early modern Europe, a phenomenon that Carl von Clausewitz encapsulated later as 'an art of violence intended to compel our opponent to fulfil our will'.[37] In the *Naturales Quaestiones*, responding keenly to the anti-Carthaginian sympathies of his fellow Romans, Seneca had composed an all too persuasive portrait of an *ungovernable* Hannibal, who 'as an old man ... did not stop searching for war in every corner of the world. So, he could endure being without a country, but he could not stand being without an enemy.'[38] Figures like Walter Ralegh would resist such characterisations in their own accounts of the Carthaginian general, but discussion returns repeatedly in this study to the enduring early modern fascination with those who command over scenes of butchery and those who recall them for wider consumption in times of crisis.

The central role of language in mythologies of belonging and alterity had been recognised in antiquity where the Athenian state demonised those who could not decipher the Ancient Greek language (*barbaros*) and who, thus, seemed to communicate with empty mouthings – 'bar bar'. Ralegh is not unrepresentative for the early modern period in rehearsing such expectations in his prose writings. When he sought to establish a portrait of the unharnessed belligerence of the Barbarian, he returned to the thematic emphases of ineloquence, nomadism, political anarchy and occult practices described in antiquity, most readily identifiable in

---

[a] 'What can be done against violence except by violence?' See 'Cicero to Cassius, Rome, soon after 2 October 44', in Cicero, *Letters to Friends*, III.144–5 (345 (XII.3)).

[b] 'Only violence can put an end to violence, and that is why violence is self-propagating.' See René Girard, *Violence and the Sacred*, trans. Patrick Gregory (London: Continuum, 2005), p. 27.

Herodotus's *Histories*, Pliny's *Natural History* and Strabo's *Geography*. Moreover, in Ralegh's own *History of the World* (1614) and in intrigues performed in the early modern playhouse, we bear witness repeatedly to the ways in which verbal violence precedes the enactment of physical trauma: Aumerle argues in *Richard II*, for example, 'let's fight with gentle words/Till time lend friends and friends their helpful swords' (III.iii.131–2). If Shakespearean scholarship has often devoted much time and energy to detailing the highly transformative role which language itself may assume in shaping our appreciation of stage action,[39] more troublingly, Slavoj Žižek has queried in a more general exploration of the subject, 'What if . . . humans exceed animals in their capacity for violence precisely because they *speak*?'[40]

   At the opening of *1 Henry IV*, the figures of perceivedly remote, barely legible Welshwomen butchering English male corpses are summoned up for consideration by audiences on- and off-stage. Such highly charged accounts seek to reproduce English moral and political purpose in opposition to fantasied narratives of blood-letting and disfigurement displaced onto a dangerously proximate, yet verbally opaque *Other*. Shakespeare's histories are fully implicated in probing the ways by which speech acts may figure forth and excite antagonisms, bloodlusts. Nonetheless, the soundscapes of such plays also test strategically the limits of their social visions: in the punishing political conditions of the histories, speaking is intimately linked to the processes of social incorporation and social haemorrhaging. If the French princess Katharine will declare her love for Henry V 'soundly', then the latter will grant her leave to speak 'brokenly with [her] English tongue' (*V*: V.ii.305). The Duchess of York declares more roundly in the earlier *Richard II*, 'The chopping French we do not understand' (V.iii.122). Theorising how such specifically linguistic modes of hierarchisation are imbricated in schema of social (dis)placement, Dick Hebdige has stressed that '[s]ubcultures [may be seen to] represent "noise" (as opposed to sound): interference in the orderly'.[41] In all kinds of ways, Shakespeare's histories engage with such thinking and turn to the fractious exchange of words, rather than to pitched battles, to problematise the filiation of political contest and cultural priority.

   If painfully attritional interactions between Self and Other often characterise the intrigues of Shakespeare's history plays, such powerplay can evolve equally perplexingly into even-handed combat between predators. In his seminal study *La violence et le sacré*, René Girard acknowledged that our enduring desires for morally polarised accounts of human interaction may all too often break down in performance, in the theatre of Greek tragedy (and beyond): 'S'il n'y a pas de différence entre les antagonistes tragiques, c'est parce que la violence les efface toutes.'[42][a] Here, the conflicted debates of the classical world speak directly to those of early (and late) modernity. In *De Ira* Seneca had argued with a remarkable absence of queasiness that '*nec ulla dura videtur curatio, cuius salutaris effectus est*'.[43][b] However, in the wake of two world wars and the ever-present threat of renewed hostilities, a number of contemporary theorists remained markedly unreceptive to such absolute reasoning. Notably, the moral philosophy of Emmanuel Lévinas continued to interrogate the inhumanity of violence by testing the bounds of human (ir)responsibility: 'D'où me vient ce choc quand je passe indifférent sous le regard d'Autrui? La relation avec Autrui, me met en question, me vide de moi-même et ne cesse de me vider en me découvrant des ressources toujours nouvelles.'[44][c]

Elsewhere, critical voices have continued to query the imperatives by which violence remains a freely exploitable and, indeed, highly sought-after resource. So often couched in highly emotive, ideologically driven terms, the narration of violent behaviours may serve the bidding of a host of differing political causes: empowerment, appropriation, invasion, colonisation. However, as Shakespeare's histories and the accounts of Elizabethan political ambitions demonstrate, such practices can also respond to additional needs, enabling social groups to access highly advantageous narratives of shared experience and shared identity.[45] Indeed, Shakespearean dramaturgy repeatedly investigates how appetites for brutality can transform mechanisms of social exchange and produce arresting practices for social advancement and power assertion.[46] In this way, habits of received thinking underpinning our declared abhorrence of violence may rely upon normative *fictions* of social contracts, upon grand narratives of human protection and progress. The evidence of our daily lives may suggest otherwise.[47] If we are accustomed to associating the commitment to violence with ethical, political and spiritual failure, equally telling is the way in which violent behaviours, expert or incompetent, are frequently proffered as stimulants – in auditoria and beyond.[48] The sociologist Mike Presdee submits wryly that 'To suggest that there is any connection between those who perpetrate violence and ourselves is of course unthinkable but it may be true.'[49] The destructive act,

---

[a] 'In Greek tragedy violence invariably effaces the differences between antagonists.' See Girard, *Violence and the Sacred*, trans. Gregory, p. 49.

[b] 'No treatment seems harsh if its result is salutary.'

[c] 'From where do I feel this shock when I pass with indifference beneath the gaze of the Other? The relation with the Other makes me question myself, drains me of my very self and keeps on draining me as it reveals to me ever renewing sources of energy.'

even when performed across great distances of time and space, may bring about catalytic reactions in the beholder and effects of rupture/parturition in the lives of all the parties concerned, including ourselves.

As the intrigue of *Richard III* unfolds, the seasoned killer (and player) Richard of Gloucester coaches Buckingham in the arts of murder and concealment: 'Come, cousin, canst thou quake, and change thy colour,/ Murder thy breath in the middle of a word' (III.v.1–2). It is this troubling creativity of violence which has come to dominate cultural debate in the modern period. In the 1970s, Edgar Morin argued influentially that 'le désordre n'est pas seulment dispersion, écume, bave et poussière du monde en gestation, il est aussi charpentier. L'univers ne s'est pas seulment con-struit malgré le désordre, il s'est aussi construit dans et par le désordre.'[50a] In his own consideration of 'the autopoesis or self-reproduction of violence', Willem Schinkel contends equally persuasively that 'The destructiveness of violence is but one aspect of violence. To focus exclu-sively on this aspect ignores the aspect of productivity of all violence.'[51] Evidence of such *generative* disorder may be highly localised, even com-monplace, in the routines through which we formulate our everyday selves, responding to the threats of violence, crime, antagonism. Indeed, many forms of violence (predatory, defensive, instrumental, physical, psycho-logical, judicial, pleasurable) impress themselves upon our attentions, delivering unexpected mechanisms for exchange and interaction. Mowbray in Shakespeare's *Richard II* anticipates eagerly the prospect of armed combat with Bolingbroke, declaring 'my dancing soul doth celebrate/This feast of battle with mine adversary' (I.iii.91–2). He thus indicates the potentially jubilant responses with which some early modern minds might greet the onset of hostilities.[52]

The early modern jurist Alberico Gentili, who dedicated his *De Iure Belli* to Robert Devereux, Earl of Essex, had insisted that 'Some men differ very little from the brutes. They have the human form, but in reality they are beasts and should be reckoned in the number of beasts.'[53] Perhaps one of the most striking aspects of the theorising of violence in both early and late modernity is the preoccupation not only with the practice as a mode of control, but the way in which it seeks to diminish the human-ness of its victims. Amongst post-war critical voices, Lévinas remains notable here in leading such enquiries: 'In horror a subject is stripped of his subjectivity, of his power to have private existence.'[54] Similarly minded, Judith Butler

---

[a] 'disorder is not merely the dispersal, the froth, the discharge, the dust of the growing world, it is also constructive. The universe is not only made inspite of disorder, it is also built out of and by disorder.'

has posited the existence of *ungrievable* lives: 'Those we kill are not quite human, and not quite alive, which means that we do not feel the same horror and outrage over the loss of their lives as we do over the loss of those lives that bear national or religious similarity to our own.'[55] However, it was perhaps Simone Weil who developed this line of thinking to its most dire conclusion, stressing that 'Force is that which makes a thing of whoever submits to it. Exercised to the extreme, it makes the human being a thing quite literally, that is, a dead body.'[56] Engaging firmly with these varied lines of critical vision on violence in terms of its spectatorial, intensely reversible, potentially pleasurable and yet radically traumatic character, the present study embraces Willem Schinkel's endeavours to 'define violence *ontologically* . . . as *reduction of being*'.[57]

The School and Theatre of War

Messires, what newes from Fraunce, can you tell? Still warres, warres.[58]

This query, voiced in John Eliot's *Ortho-epia Gallica* (1593), was widely taken up across Europe in the second half of the sixteenth century. Indeed, the international focus upon France as a prime arena for armed combat spoke to a much larger debate across the continent concerning the status and function of militarism and the proliferation of its theatres of war. A generation earlier, in his influential *Methodus ad facilem historiarum cognitionem* (1566), Jean Bodin had probed the age's unceasing preoccupation with conflict. Building upon climatic theorising inherited from antiquity, he insisted that the northern reaches of the planet (to which the British Isles belonged) were the domain of the god Mars and governed by the mores of the Scythians.[59] The responses of the military polemicist John Smythe certainly served to endorse such contentions about the islanders:

> I even from my very tender years have delighted to hear histories read that did treat of actions and deeds of arms . . . I did always delight and procure my tutors as much as I could to read unto me the commentaries of Julius Caesar and Sallust and other such books. And after that I came from school and went to the university . . . I gave myself to the reading of many other histories and books treating of matters of war and sciences tending to the same.[60]

Clearly, the proliferation of military literatures, technological manuals and published reportage by sixteenth-century combatants offered a constantly changing repertoire of knowledge and resources with which to articulate

the bellicose unruliness of the times. However, fully appreciating the
ravages wrought by the French Wars of Religion, Bodin did not underestimate the 'delight that souldiours take, is to forrage and spoyle the
country . . . massacre good and bad, young and old, all ages, and all sexes'.[61]

Parsimony, shortage of Crown funds and/or profound insufficiencies in
political initiative and state infrastructure often governed military restraint
in Elizabeth's own policy-making: Ralegh believed 'her majesty did all
by halves, and by petty invasions taught the Spaniard how to defend
himself'.[62] Her Stuart successor aspired above all to the titles of scholar-
king and *rex pacificus*, declaring in his accession year to Parliament, 'Peace
abroad with all Foreign *Neighbours*.'[63] Indeed, responding keenly to the
temper of the new monarch, the publication of *King James his welcome to
London* by one I. F. proclaimed that 'The souldier lets his weapons now to
rust:/Nor to the spilling of more blood dooth trust,/But pleaseth most in
peace.'[64] Nonetheless, as one century gave way to the next, other, equally
pressing voices, like Smythe's, were heard on a regular basis, lamenting the
state's failure to uphold the profession of arms. It was inevitable in such
a political climate that the estimation of the combatant would also be
brought into question.[65] Echoing Bodin, John Norden's *A pensiue soules
delight* (1615) insisted that 'Among all other professions in the world: none
is more dangerous then the militarie . . . no sort of people are more loosely,
lasciuiously, and barbarously giuen then they.'[66] Conversely, seeking to
redeem the figure of the man-at-arms in a 1578 dedicatory address, Henrie
Bynniman argued forcefully that, 'The greatest seruice that men can doe, is
to saue theyr Countrey from daunger. The *Romanes* gaue him a crowne
that saued one Citizen. Then how many crownes deserueth he, that
helpeth to saue a number?'[67] Elsewhere, in *The castle, or picture of policy*
(1581), William Blandie sought to conjure up the vision of a cohesive,
organic polity for his early modern reader, envisaging a continuous social
hierarchy in the shape of 'A *King*, A *Iusticer*, A *Souldiar*, A *Marchaunt*, An
Artificer, A *Tiller* of the ground' – to which the soldier would contribute
'puissance'.[68] Whatever the case, there would be no regular army established until the conflicts of the 1640s and early modern England continued
to debate back and forth the relative merits of those engaged in military
affairs.[69] This was a profession that had no institutions of formal training
or carefully monitored career structure.[70] Moreover, those experienced in
hostilities were mostly familiar with the settling of conflicts (of dynastic
ascendancy and lordship, religious division, political ambition and mercantile rivalries) in the company of strangers beyond the kingdom's shores.
Inevitably, such figures conversant with the mores of distant battlefields

and foreign societies might, on their return, remain distinctly suspect in the eyes of many.[71]

One of the projects cogitated by Ralegh's cousin, the military commander/explorer Sir Humphrey Gilbert, was the possibility of 'an Achademy in London for educacion of her Maiestes Wardes, and others the youth of nobility and gentlemen'. It seems that a significant part of the literacy curriculum in such an establishment would embrace 'Orations made in England, both politique and militare' as well as a thorough grounding in logistics 'towching warres'. In addition, on the staff there would be 'one perfect trained Sowldiour, who shall teach them to handle the Harquebuz, and to practize in the said Achademie all kindes of Skirmishinges, Imbatttelinges, and sondery kindes of marchinges'.[72] Gilbert's drafted project, of which there appears to have been no further sequel, constitutes but one in a whole series of interventions in print and manuscript culture during the Elizabethan and Jacobean periods addressing the perceived decay of military expertise in the island kingdom.

In 1285, the Statute of Winchester had specified the demand that adult men have arms at their disposal for the keeping of order.[73] However, by 1558, two Parliamentary Acts had responded to the need for a more coherent system with which to levy troops, organise regular musters and equip adequately such forces. These reforms brought forward in the reign of Mary were further refined in the Elizabethan period with the formalisation of militia companies, or 'trained bands', from 1573 onwards for service at home and overseas. Such bands were designed to be: overseen by county gentry, magistrates and Lords Lieutenant; brought together regularly for drills; and resourced by local taxes. By the 1590s, despite ongoing local problems of command, recruitment and equipment,[74] the system was well-established and experienced officers were often recruited to lead the companies to support the defence of the realm or the waging of hostilities beyond its borders. If Mark Fissel underlines that 'The militia were trained amateurs, not professional soldiers', Paul Hammer adds that the companies across the country were 'of distinctly variable quality'.[75] Even at the time, Smythe was contending

> that this new deformed *Milicia* and euill gouernment of our men of war, by suffering their soldiers for lacke of pay in those warres to go a robbing and spoyling the countrie people their friends ... hath brought many of them from good to euill, and made most of those that haue returned into *England* impudent roges and theeues, that were true men before they went ouer.[76]

As we witness in 2 *Henry IV*, the recruitment process might produce unimpressive results.[77] Indeed, the outcome might be perilous even on the Home Front. The mayor of Chester wrote to the Privy Council in October 1598 that almost 200 recruited soldiers of suspect provenance en route for Ireland 'fell into mutinie, refusinge to marche farther, threatninge their captaine to kill him and woundings somme of his officers so greevouslie as it is doubtfull whether they are livinge or dead'.[78]

A general muster of troops was required at least once every three years and, responding to this reorganisation of armed forces, writers of quite different persuasions were eager to publish advicebooks on how to strengthen the professionalisation of the military life. Many of these works paid particular attention to the precedents of antiquity and to more recent technological advances in European campaigns, as well as reviewing received thinking on strategy and the maintenance of discipline. Such matter seems to have been avidly read by those such as Shakespeare's Fluellen in *Henry V*, who hails Captain Jamy as one who 'will maintain his argument as well as any military man in the world, in the disciplines of the pristine wars of the Romans' (*V*: III.iii.24–6).[79] In a general account of the manifestations of violence, Arendt noted that 'one of the most obvious distinctions between power and violence is that power always stands in need of numbers, whereas violence up to a point can manage without them because it relies on implements'.[80] Such debates had their counterpart in the early modern public sphere where technology – notably, in the period, the longbow versus the firearm – exercised a great many minds.[81] Smythe remained a notable champion of the bowman: 'the great daunger . . . is to seeke to abolish and extinguish the notable exercise and vse of our Longbowes and Archerie'.[82] In the event, this publication would continue to generate a number of contrary responses in print. Two years later, for example, Humfrey Barwick's *breefe discourse* (1592) engaged sceptically and in some detail with Smythe's arguments, retorting, 'what, shall we refuse the Cannon and fall to the Ram againe [?]'[83] However, as Shakespeare's contemporary, George Peele, underlined in *The Battle of Alcazar* (1594), 'gold is the glue, sinewes, and strength of war' and thorny crises in the resourcing of military campaigns were regularly communicated in documents surviving from the period, including those of Shakespearean drama.[84]

At the beginning of the seventeenth century, Sir Clement Edmondes, 'remembrancer of the Citie of London', published *Obseruations vpon the fiue first bookes of Caesars commentaries setting fourth the practise of the art military . . . for the better direction of our moderne warres* (1601).[85] Such texts, circulating in the vernacular, existed quite independently of Latin editions of writers such as Caesar and Tacitus, which were being read throughout Europe in the libraries of Great Houses as well as in the classroom. Moreover, this was an age in which English chronicles multiplied and jostled for space in a fiercely competitive market. Daniel Woolf has counted 220 editions of 79 different chronicles between 1475 and 1699, and Patricia A. Cahill estimates that, 'Between 1575 and 1600, some fifty military treatises, both original works and translations of classical and continental texts, were published in London, and several went through multiple editions.'[86] In this way, English print culture witnessed a great burgeoning of interest in the justification, regulation and analysis of military hostilities in the closing decades of the sixteenth century – and the theatres acknowledged this rise in interest at the bookstalls.[87] In *Pierce Penniless* (1592), Thomas Nashe argued that the stage could be found to showcase 'a rare exercise of vertue . . . for the subiect of them (for the most part) it is borrowed out of our English Chronicles, wherein our forefathers valiant acts (that have lain long buried in rustie brasse, and worm-eaten bookes) are reuiued, and they themselues raised from the Graue of Obliuion'. He contended, 'what can be a sharper reproofe to these degenerate effeminate dayes of ours?'[88]

More generally, Elizabeth's administration understood thoroughly the propensity of historical works, ancient and modern, to gravitate towards potentially inflammatory discourses. Thus, Holinshed's *Chronicles* enjoyed the particular attentions of the censor, and after 1599 English histories required the assent of a Privy Councillor before publication. Things were little better with the advent of a new king. Following his accession, James attended most closely, amongst other things, to the activities of the Society of Antiquaries (which had been meeting since at least the 1570s) and its gatherings were brought to a halt abruptly in 1607. Later, in 1627, when Sir Robert Cotton published *A Short View of the Long Life and Reign of King Henry III*, he quickly incurred the wrath of the Caroline authorities. The narrative had treated rather prominently the delicate subject of the dealings of kings with their favourites. On being further questioned, Cotton insisted that the text had been written much earlier, in 1614, but the Earl of Buckingham advised that the library of such a dangerous man should be shut down for it had clearly prompted dangerous speculations.

It was certainly true that, as one century yielded to the next, opportunities were legion for London theatre audiences to reflect at length upon the waging of war as an ever increasing number of tragedies, histories, satires and, indeed, comedies invested in martial intrigues.[89] Apart from anonymous plays such as *The Troublesome Raigne of King John* (1591) and *The Famous Victories of Henry V* (1598), Peele's *Edward I* (1593), Marlowe's *Edward II* (1593) and Heywood's *Edward IV* (1598), there are many lost plays from this period, such as *Edward III* (1590?), *John of Gaunt* (1594) and *The Funeral of Richard Coeur de Lion* (1598) which surely responded to audience expectations for evocations of soldiery and combat. Furthermore, the memories of military commanders, such as Henry V, Talbot, Julius Caesar, Old Hamlet and the younger Antony, amongst many others, are often found to haunt Shakespeare's own theatrical worlds.

Shakespeare, Violence and Early Modern Europe

> ther is certyne generall speache of the King of Spain's preparation of
> a great navy, but whither no man knoweth, it is supposed to vs.
> Philip Gawdy to his father (October 1587)[90]

If, in our postmodern age of endlessly fracturing conflicts, Foucault advised (in a witty reversal of Clausewitz's formula) that 'politics is the continuation of war by other means', such conclusions may not have been wholly unfamiliar to those inhabiting an earlier modernity.[91] Jeremy Black justly underlines that 'violence was endemic in early modern Europe', and Susan Dwyer Amussen further refines this point, emphasising that 'violent punishment was an important component of the exercise of power in early modern England'.[92] The practice of violence was thus commonplace in European political operations, deployed to regulate allegiances towards the powers that be and to discipline populations at home and abroad on a regular basis. Yet if, drawing upon the critical lexis of Max Weber, Jan Glete argues that early modern state administrations began to seize 'an effective *monopoly of violence* within well-defined boundaries ... [becoming] a monopoly wielder of violence or seller of protection', Shakespeare's history plays unveil an environment in which no such monopolies of war or peace may yet be conclusively secured.[93]

The discussions that follow treat a number of early modern anxieties concerning not only the figures of the soldier and the commander in England's international military engagements, but also the conflicted relationship between violence and nation-building in the island kingdom. Such enquiries came to dominate Shakespeare's evolving conception of the history play in the 1590s and the meditations of key members of the court elite at the time. Chapter 1 focuses on the political and authorial undertakings of Sir Walter Ralegh, ranging from his participation in the French

Wars of Religion in the 1570s to his imprisonment and execution in the Tower and the posthumous reception of his writings. Ralegh remained not only a royal favourite during the final decades of the sixteenth century at the English court, but a recurring voice in the realm's political life, often associated with favouring vigorous military intervention in overseas theatres of war. His roles as polemicist and chronicler are explored, most particularly his oft-voiced desire to embed England more resolutely in a European theatre of hostilities in order to defend, what York terms in *2 Henry VI*, 'the honour of this warlike isle' (*VI²*: I.i.122).

Chapter 2 examines the *Henry VI* plays written in the opening years of the 1590s by Shakespeare (and his collaborators). Here, rather than reviving models of heroic virtue, these plays are characterised by the remorseless iteration of territorial and political loss. Equally importantly, the figure of the warlord comes to dominate these dramatic narratives, radically unsettling the customary privileges of sovereignty and the very possibility of political cohesion when a whole generation of elite figures has gained an expert training in sedition and slaughter. Strikingly, as Nicholas Grene has highlighted, in this unending depiction of torment and blood-letting what emerges is 'the complete lack of partisanship available to an audience'.[94] There can be no social closure in a dramatic world riven by duplicating cycles of violence – cycles triggered by those wishing to prosecute superlative political claims of lordship and/or superlative accounts of suffering from the past. However, in such competitive environments perhaps our sufferings need to be excessive: for, as Susan Sontag argued for more contemporary readers, 'It is intolerable to have one's own sufferings twinned with anybody else's.'[95]

As hostilities spill backwards and forwards across frontiers in these plays, both audience members and stage inhabitants are thwarted in any attempt to endorse claims to cultural or ethical priority. Indeed, these plays compel us to witness the ways in which violence forecloses possibilities of thought and resistance for its subjects, leaving them frequently with only stunted, brutalised opportunities for self-expression and engagement. If, in the twentieth century, certain radical thinkers, such as Albert Camus, sought to promote 'la dignité affirmée par la révolte',[a] the opportunities for such heroic potential remain most bleak throughout the three *Henry VI* plays, as rebellions triggered by Yorkists, Lancastrians and, notably, Jack Cade offer little apart from a theatre of destruction all too familiar to the early modern age.[96] The hunger for violent action thus brings with it no lasting solution.

---

[a] 'the dignity asserted by means of revolt'.

As Hannah Arendt argued centuries later, 'Violence does not promote causes, neither history nor revolution, neither progress nor reaction; but it can serve to dramatize grievances and bring them to public attention.'[97]

In such a fractious and volatile dramatic world, even inertia appears to offer no promise of comfort: as Slavoj Žižek has submitted, 'Sometimes doing nothing is the most violent thing to do.'[98] The Volscian servant in Shakespeare's *Coriolanus* exclaims 'let me have war, say I, it exceeds peace' (IV.v.220) and, in the closing years of Elizabeth's reign, Sir William Cornwallis advised that 'Warre is the remedy for a State surfetted with peace, it is a medicine for Common-wealths sicke of too much ease and tranquilitie.[99] In Chapter 3, Shakespeare's *Henry IV* plays are seen to invest fully in such debate where the dispensing of government is confused with the waging of war. In this instance, cross-national conflict is afforded a specifically British character, recalling in part Montaigne's distaste for civil wars in his own land: 'et le pis de ces guerres, c'est que les chartes sont si meslees, vostre ennemy n'estant distingué d'avecques vous d'aulcune marque apparente, ny de langage, ny de port, nourry en mesmes loix, mœurs et mesme air, qu'il est malaysé d'y eviter confusion et desordre.'[100][a] The international focus for combat, which becomes a consuming interest in the *Henry VI* and *Henry V* plays, is initially articulated here in terms of an island people united in a crusade against the Infidel in the Holy Lands. However, such concerns are swiftly occluded in the subsequent splintering of political allegiances across the isles. The ailing monarch and his player-prince exploit the resources of deception, (attempted) amnesia and the battlefield to affirm publicly the legitimacy of their rule, but the justness of their claims to political and dramatic primacy remains in question. It soon becomes evident that Falstaff's exploitation of the Lancastrians' many and various arenas of performance is an inevitable consequence of the flawed power relations being organised across the realm. Earlier in the sixteenth century, in 1514, Erasmus had submitted that 'If you look narrowly into the case, you will find that they are, chiefly, the private, sinister, and selfish motives of princes, which operate as the real causes of war.'[101] As becomes clear in Chapter 4, Shakespeare's *Henry V* fails to challenge the humanist's account. In this dramatic world, the monarch eclipses all other warlords, drawing his populace together in

---

[a] 'The worst of these wars is that the cards are so mixed up, with your enemy indistinguishable from yourself by any clear indication of language or deportment, being brought up under the same laws, manners and climate, that it is not easy to avoid confusion and disorder.' See Michel de Montaigne, *The Complete Essays*, trans. M. A. Screech (London: Penguin, 2003 rep.), p. 411 ('On conscience', II.v).

bloodthirsty foreign hostilities. Determined to rupture the decades-old cycles of internal violence in his kingdom, Harry attempts a brutal tactic for the construction of a group, nay national, identity. In the process, he radically undermines the potential of the successful military commander to win moral approval or enduring political settlement.

This sequence of three discussions focusing on Shakespearean dramaturgy and its vigorous depictions of violent hostilities is then united in Chapter 5 with the consideration of another of Elizabeth's court favourites: Robert Devereux, Earl of Essex. During his youth and on into adulthood, the earl maintained a vigorous reading programme of texts, both ancient and modern, scrutinising modes of government and effective (military) leadership. With decidedly mixed results, Essex sought to figure forth such reading in public performances both at home and abroad. This was to prove an intensely risky strategy in the fragile polity of an ageing queen. Such was the political crisis occasioned during the 1599 campaign led by Essex in Ireland that George Fenner wrote to his Venetian correspondent, 'it is forbidden, on pain of death, to write or speak of Irish affairs; what is brought by post is known only to the Council; but it is very sure that Tyrone's party has prevailed most'.[102]

The final chapters analyse Elizabethan political debate from an alternative perspective: that of the island's continental neighbours. Concentrating initially in Chapter 6 on native responses to Ralegh and Essex in the decades which followed their executions, discussion then examines the ways in which the experience of violence at the Elizabethan court was portrayed on European stages, ranging from a small village community in the Low Countries, to the court at Madrid, the Paris theatres, and *commedia* and opera performances in Italy. Rather than depicting a courtly environment of an island race riven by international ambitions, here we regularly enter much more claustrophobic dramatic worlds – worlds wholly dominated not by the quest for military advantage, but by erotic turmoil and thwarted desire. Finally, in the Conclusion, we turn briefly to the figure of Shakespeare himself as he appeared on British and European stages, drawn into his flux-ridden society and destined to become its most noted literary voice for generations to come.

The present discussion has sought to explore some of the intricate connections between disorderly subjects and decaying polities in early modern England and Europe, and to indicate that such enquiries were as urgent at the Elizabethan fin de siècle as they seem to have been from the outset of our own. Inevitably, any consideration of cultural debate in early modern England cannot be exhaustive. However, an exploration of aspiring warlords both within and without the Elizabethan playhouse offers an important angle of vision from which to probe the status and functions of violence in the social mechanisms of early modernity – and, it is hoped, goes some way towards shedding light on those of late modernity as well. Rather than solely unveiling the flaws of 400-year-old political systems, the discussions which follow urge us to interrogate, as Paul Virilio has proposed, 'où gît l'hostilité' – then and now.[103a] Indeed, if our encounters with an early modern past (particularly a past fractured by violence and trauma) lead effortlessly to a reinvestigation of the cultural present, these same encounters also compel us to pluralise our consumption of the past, to revisit its perplexing indeterminacy.

Emmanuel Lévinas contended that 'For an ethical sensibility – confirming itself, in the inhumanity of our time, against this inhumanity – the justification of the neighbour's pain is certainly the source of all immorality.'[104] The discussions that follow are wholly exercised by this urgent questioning of human responsibility in harrowing times of conflict and slaughter, then and now. The son of Norfolk gentry, Philip Gawdy, wrote to his father on 9th May 1588, the year of the Armada:

> Ther is dyvers speaches in the towne: some speake of warre, some of pease, but moste of the fyrst.[105]

---

[a] 'where hostility resides'.

'touching violence or punishments':
Walter Ralegh and the Economy of Aggression

> The necessity of War, which among human Actions is the most lawlesse, hath some kind of affinity, and neere resemblances with the necessity of Law. For there were no use at all, either of War or of Law, if every man had prudence to conceive how much of right were due both to and from himself, and were withall so punctually just, as to perform what he knew requisite, and to rest contented with his owne.[1]

This extract, thought to be from the last prose work that Walter Ralegh composed during his long period of enforced residence at the Tower of London (1603–16), is drawn from 'A Discovrse of the Originall and Fundamentall Cause of Naturall, Customary, Arbitrary, Voluntary and Necessary Warre. With the Mysery of Invasive Warre.' This brief treatise made its appearance on the bookstalls in 1650 in *Judicious and Select Essayes and Observations By that Renowned Knight Sir Walter Raleigh*, more than thirty years after the fallen courtier's execution in 1618. When the publication was issued, its mid-century readership had already been profoundly (and violently) exercised in a prolonged interrogation of the government of the realm and the parameters within which the law might be enforced. It is an indication of Ralegh's cultural capital during the Interregnum that the printer's prefatory address insisted '*Raleighs* very Name is Proclamation enough for the *Stationers* advantage'.[2] Indeed, even as early as 1628, the posthumous publication of *The Prerogative of Parliaments in England* had hailed the author provocatively on its title page as 'the worthy (much lacked and lamented) Sir Walter Raleigh Knight'.[3]

As was witnessed in the Introduction, a number of cultural theorists in the modern period, such as Walter Benjamin, shaped their accounts of the human commitment to armed conflict by reviewing legal principles that might be seen to support the creation and/or preservation of political hegemonies. Characteristically, in the early decades of the seventeenth century, Ralegh attended not only to the legal and military mechanisms through which the polity might choose to renew itself, but also to recurring testimonies regarding the collapse in political governance down the generations. Such enquiries might attract the attentions of hostile authorities in any age, and no more so than when penned by an eminent and attention-seeking prisoner, deemed legally dead after his trial in 1603, lingering year after year at His Majesty's pleasure in the Tower.

In the 1590s Sir Robert Naunton had been part of the secretariat of Robert Devereux, 2nd Earl of Essex, but later served under James I as secretary of state at the time of Buckingham's political rise to fortune. Inevitably shaped by these formative experiences in milieux all too frequently hostile to the Devon knight, his posthumously published *Fragmenta regalia* (1641) nonetheless contended that Ralegh 'had the adjuncts of some generall learning, which by diligence he enforced to a great augmentation, and perfection; for he was an indefatigable Reader, whether by Sea or Land'.[4] Indeed, during the course of his career, Ralegh offered ample proof that he was well versed in the writings of earlier authorities, notably: secular writers from antiquity such as Herodotus, Homer, Virgil, Seneca and Cicero; Scripture; and the Church Fathers, such as Augustine and Origen. Moreover, in direct comparison with near contemporaries such as Hugo Grotius, he chose to showcase his extensive reading when reviewing the human appetite for violence and the responses to it under the law, whether the latter be dispensed under political, ethical or theological terms. In *De Jure Belli ac Pacis* (1625)[5] Grotius scrutinised at great length the protocols for legitimate war-making that had been inherited in writings from the ancients and sought to offer a written *pouvoir constituant* for future practice. Ralegh's rather briefer and dispersed enquiries were equally eager to devote time and energy to a consideration of the juridical and moral legitimacy (or otherwise) of 'natural' war (occasioned by expanding demography), 'arbitrary' war (driven by motivations of terror, pre-emption, ambition and/or revenge) and 'civil' war (linked directly to the power hunger of strategically placed individuals). Like a number of the contributions in the *Judicious and Select Essayes*, his 'Discovrse of ... Warre' insisted that the only secure hopes for peace in this fallen world resided in a nation's affirmation of military strength. Equally importantly, it pondered anew the rationale and logistics for war-making per se. In the process, the *Essayes* also unveiled the perceived military weaknesses of the early Jacobean state and, more generally, the moral and affective weaknesses of a painfully flawed humanity that had down the centuries unfailingly sought redress in brutal conflict to remedy its misfortunes.

As an author exploiting a host of different genres throughout his career, Ralegh might voice widely differing attitudes to the waging of war, but he never shed the belief that it had an ongoing influence on the evolution of human life in society. A deep and sustained acquaintance with historical narratives of diverse origins convinced him that the temptation to visit aggression upon a perceived adversary, to resolve a perceived weakness or loss through combat with an antagonist, to inflict (in Schinkel's terms) a 'reduction of being' upon another, would never be repressed amongst the communities of his fellow, fallen creatures.[6] Ralegh's *History of the World* (1614) rolled from the presses in an incomplete state, halting in 146 BC at the point of the Second Macedonian War.[7] However, even in this published form, the *magnum opus* extended to nearly 1,500 folio pages. In general terms, the *History* exhibits a fascination with the unceasing tribulations in ancient times of erring races, lurching from the one declaration of hostilities to the next, and forever facing the terrifying prospect of wrath from a louring Godhead – 'the Author of all our tragedies'.[8] Thus, the *History*'s reader is urged remorselessly to focus upon the drama of mighty empires locked in vast military campaigns and the vicissitudes of conflict resolution. Ralegh demonstrated that his accounts of military triumphs and peripeteia among peoples distant in time and space needed to be pondered and renarrated because they constituted a (if not *the*) pre-eminent feature of the human *circuitus temporum* – a concept inherited from Greco-Roman culture and one which continued to shape the early modern consumption of history on page and stage. Indeed, mindful of such concerns, the chronicler gravitated in an account entitled 'Of our base and fraile bodies' to a text by Marius Victor, affirming that 'Diseases, famine, enemies, in us no change have wrought,/What erst we were, we are; still in the same snare caught.'[9]

'that beast (meaning Warre)'

In contrast to humanist scholars such as Machiavelli working a generation earlier, Ralegh never sought to divorce the examination of political strategy, war-making and human misgovernment from moral and eschatological concerns. Even when he concentrated in the *History* upon antique civilisations deeply revered in his own society, he related arresting scenes of butchery without allowing a more general narrative of cultural and ethical collapse to exceed his grasp. As narratives of civil broils and slaughter between nations succeeded one another, Ralegh remained at pains to problematise any desire for some positivist thesis by which with the passage of time humanity gradually disengaged from its blood lusts. Instead, in this voluminous tome, we are caught in what his contemporary Francis Bacon termed the ever 'turning wheels of vicissitude'.[10] Thus, during his review of the evidence for human sacrifice in antiquity, the prisoner in the Tower stressed that such practices could not be consigned to a distant past, for 'among the saluages in the West *Indies* these cruell offerings haue been practised of late ages: which, as it is a sufficient argument that *Satans* malice is onely couered and hidden by this subtilitie among ciuill people: so may it serue as a probable Coniecture of the barbarismes then reigning in *Greece*'.[11] Significantly, given the context of subsequent discussions devoted to Shakespearean history-making in the present study, Ralegh focuses provisionally in his own chronicle upon the failure of English medieval sovereigns to consolidate military triumphs on the European continent with a grand scheme of successful empire-building. He laments that

> our Kings were like to the race of the *Æacidæ*, of whom the old Poet *Ennius* gaue this note; *Belli potentes sunt magè quam sapienti potentes*; *They were more warlike than politique.* Who so notes their proceedings, may finde that none of them went to worke like a Conquerour: saue only King *Henrie* the fift, the course of whose victories, it pleased God to interrupt by his death.[12]

If, in this brief digression, the chronicler concentrates (as Shakespeare does in the 1590s) upon the political travails of English rulers during the later Middle Ages, he gives yet another demonstration of early modern historiography's fondness for penetrating the fastness of previous ages by exploiting the narrative resources of prolepsis and analogy. Jean Bodin had explored a similar enquiry in his *Methodus ad facilem historiarum cognitionem* (1566) when he pondered the close of the Hundred Years' War:

> At long last the French conspired together and won a rapid series of victories, driving the English from the whole territory of France. But when the foreign war was over, these people waged civil wars with such great cruelty that the things which are reported about the tragic ferocity of the Thebans seem child's play beside those which are narrated by Polydore [Vergil].[13]

Shakespeare selected a rather different trajectory (and textual genre) in seeking to place the medieval centuries, a period often represented in Tudor chronicles as one of seemingly unceasing blood-letting and division, before early modern eyes. However, his dramas (like Ralegh's *History* and Bodin's *Methodus*) clearly submit the 'politique' nature of military hostilities to most urgent interrogation – most especially when undertaken by beleaguered, ill-experienced and/or vainglorious leaders.

Begun in 1611, the *History of the World* was entered in the Stationers' Register on 15th April for that year and its labours had initially been dedicated to Prince Henry. Indeed, publication seems to have been held back by the prince's demand for a more comprehensive narrative of secular concerns. In the wake of the latter's death from typhoid in 1612, Ralegh sought out the patronage of his royal father, James VI/I. That the wisdom of such a course of action was misguided remained evident even to many contemporaries, as the chronicle did not stint in addressing some of the most thorny political questions in a manner little designed to please a monarch espousing absolutist claims for his sovereignty.[14] Published in 1614, the *History*'s circulation was curtailed by the authorities in the same year: on 22nd December the Archbishop of Canterbury ordered the Stationers' Company to call in and suppress all copies by royal command.[15] In the event, examples of the *History* had already circulated rather too widely by this stage and, if anything, an expression of hostility on the part of the Crown appears to have afforded it an added cachet for many Jacobean readers. Such was the appetite for its publication, two more editions rolled from the presses in 1617.[16] Indeed, readers eager for its narratives might lie far beyond the island's shores. As early as 1616, it was being reported to Benjamin Farie, the mercantile 'principal' in Siam, that one Captain Richard Cocks (based in a trading enterprise in Japan) 'is very desirous of a book that you have of Sir Walter Ralegh's, which if you would spare him, he would take it very kindly at the price, and any that may be had at Bantam, or where I shall come, I will buy for you'.[17] When he turned his attentions to temporal affairs, Ralegh could easily be given to admire those (like Hannibal) who resisted the imperial claims of the formidable and increasing power of Rome. Elsewhere, scorn was reserved for those who left their realms unprotected through policies of appeasement or poor military husbandry. More generally, there was always time to meditate competing views of a sovereign's powers *to bind and loose* the lives of others. In Book Two, for example, the reader is invited to consider

> whether the power of the humane Law bee without exception of any person, it is doubtfully disputed among those that haue written of this subiect, as well *Diuines* as *Lawyers*: and namely, whether soueraigne Princes bee compellable; yea, or no? . . . For as touching violence or punishments, no man is bound to giue a prejudiciall judgement against himselfe . . . And speaking of the supreme power of lawes, simply then is the Prince so much aboue the lawes, as the soule and body vnited, is aboue a dead and senseless carcasse . . . For Kings are made by God, and lawes diuine; and by humane lawes onely declared to bee Kings.[18]

Down the generations, while some readers might have been persuaded by the authority of such closing remarks, others seemed to have savoured the complexity of the process by which Ralegh's enquiries unfolded, taking in such questions as 'humane Law' and 'violence or punishments'. Oliver Cromwell notably recommended Ralegh's *History* as prime reading matter for his eldest son Richard, affirming that it was 'a body of History, and will add much more to your understanding than fragments of story'.[19] For Cromwell, as for many of his fellow countrymen, Ralegh was to become important not only as an invaluable chronicler of historical materials but, equally significantly, as a victim of a seemingly pathological enmity on the part of a Stuart king – a king who in his own lifetime coveted the title of *rex pacificus*.

In 1606 it was recorded that Lady Ralegh gained access to Hampton Court and 'kneeled to the K. but his M[a.] passed by her wth silence'.[20] Little had changed years later when the Venetian ambassador reported back to the Republic in 1614 that James's brother-in-law, Christian IV of Denmark, received a cool reception when he sought a meeting with the famous prisoner in the Tower during his visit to London: 'havendo dimandato il Cavr. Rale, che si trova in Torre, habbia il Re mostrato buona dispositione, ma rimesso al Consiglio, è ha portato sino all'ultimo giorno senza poi farne altro.'[21a] Gervase Markham celebrated the Stuart king as entering 'not with an Olive Branch in his hand, but with a whole Forrest of Olives round about him; for he brought not Peace to his Kingdome alone, but almost to all the Christian Kingdomes in Europe'. In *The Peace-Maker* (1618), Thomas Middleton paid due tribute to 'the Land of Peace under the King of Peace'.[22] Nevertheless, elsewhere, it was not only for Ralegh that this royal claim to the title of Peacemaker would become anathema. As the Jacobean reign drew to a close amid the upheavals of the Thirty Years' War, Thomas Scott's *Robert Earle of Essex his Ghost* (1624) also added its voice to the growing unrest in the nation regarding the Crown's foreign policies of neutrality and appeasement: 'Yea, and it seems your King himselfe, is much affected with the name of *PEACE*, alleadging, that he hath become a peaceable King from his Cradle; That *BEATI PACIFICI* is his happy destined *MOTTO*; and with such like self-pleasing songs, hath a long time sung a *Requiem* to himselfe, &c.'[23]

---

[a] 'When he asked for Sir [Walter] Ralegh, who is in the Tower, the king seemed well disposed, but referred it to the Council and put it off until the last day, without doing anything else afterwards.'

Like those dramatists serving the playhouses at the time, Ralegh was often minded to give an extended airing to oppositional lines of vision in a given enquiry. In the *History* he was mostly at pains after such excursuses to tender a more orthodox (though, given his preceding narratives, not necessarily more authoritative) conclusion. Such a modus operandi in his many and various activities clearly aroused suspicions, both at home and abroad. Even in the final decade of the sixteenth century, *An aduertisement written to a secretarie of my L. Treasurers of Ingland, by an Inglishe intelligencer* (1592)[24] was painting a highly imaginative image of Elizabeth's entourage, which included 'Sir Walter Rauleys schoole of Atheisme by the waye':

> How miserable a thing it is that her Maiestie descending of so noble progen-itours, should be brought to make lawes and proclamations in matters of Religion, according to these mens senses and opinions, & leauing all her olde nobility, and the auncient wisedome, grauitie, and learning which Ingland was wonte to haue, should rule her self by these new vpstarts.[25]

Moreover, at least one publication of the mid-seventeenth century of dubious provenance hailed the possibility of *Sir Walter Ralegh's Sceptick*: 'The Sceptick doth neither affirm, neither denie any Position: but doubt-eth of it, and opposeth his Reasons against that which is affirmed, or denied, to justifie his not Consenting.'[26]

Since the Early Tudor period, monarchs had remained richly sensitive to the political capital potentially available in the business of war-making *and* history-making. However, these were certainly not activities in which the authorities sought to promote the principle of indeterminacy. Aiming to train up a new generation in the profession of arms, Henry VII commis-sioned an English translation of Christine de Pisan's *Faits d'armes et de chevalerie* (completed in 1489) and Polydore Vergil's *Anglica Historia* (not published until 1534 in Basle). Furthermore, seeking precedents for successful English military campaigns on the continent, Henry VIII com-missioned an English translation of Tito Livio's *Vita Henrici Quinti* (1437) in 1513. Nonetheless, Elizabeth's administration would remain acutely watchful of these 'makers' of history and might have such productions submitted to the rigour of the censor.

James VI/I was similarly alert to the critiques historiography might offer of his own sovereignty, most especially when emanating from someone whom he perceived as an adversary. Indeed, there were any number of examples in Ralegh's *History* which might trigger profound anxieties at court. As we move from one grand narrative of empire to the next, Ralegh directs the reader's attention to the successor of the Babylonian sovereign

Semiramis, for example, and we learn that the contention that 'Ninias [was] esteemed no man of warre at all, but altogether feminine, and subiected to ease and delicacie' contained 'no probabilitie': 'Now because there was nothing performed by this Ninias of any moment . . . I will for this present passe [him] ouer.'[27] In such ways, the executive powers of monarchs were constantly being passed over in this seemingly endless sequence of politically charged *récits*. Equally strategically, Ralegh might be given to condemn rulers in living memory. Henry VIII, who had notably overlooked the legitimacy of the Stuart line in his reshaping in the 1540s of the English line of royal succession, could find himself the focus of some strident criticism:

> Now for King *Henry* the eight: if all the pictures and Patternes of a mercilesse Prince were lost in the World, they might all againe be painted to the life, out of the story of this King . . . yea, in his very death-bed, and when hee was at the point to haue given his accompt to GOD for the aboundance of bloud already spilt: He imprisoned the Duke of *Nofolke* the Father; and executed the Earle of *Surrey* the sonne.[28]

William Camden, another of Ralegh's eminent contemporaries devoting himself to the mapping of national histories, had declared in the preface to his *Britannia* that he had been urged by the geographer Abraham Ortelius to 'restore antiquity to Britaine, and Britain to his antiquity'.[29] Nevertheless, the narrative trajectories that Ralegh adopted in order to 'restore antiquity to Britaine' could not fail to engender grave anxieties on the part of the authorities. He continued to create textual spaces in which to stage himself from his chambers in the Tower as learned counsellor and to open up all manner of debate upon the vicious and/or flawed undertakings of kings and emperors:

> It is not my purpose to wrong the worth of any [kings], by denying the praise where it is due; or by preferring a lesse excellent. But he that can finde a King, religious, and zealous in Gods cause, without enforcement either of aduersitie, or of some regard of state; a procurer of the general peace and quiet; who not onely vseth his authoritie, but addes the trauell of his eloquence, in admonishing his Iudges to doe iustice; by the vigorous influence of whose Gouernment, ciuilitie is infused, euen into those places, that haue beene the dennes of sauage Robbers and Cutthrotes . . . he, I say, that can finde such a King, findeth an example, worthie to adde vnto vertue an honourable title, if it were formerly wanting.[30]

By 5th January 1615, John Chamberlain was writing to Sir Dudley Carleton, 'Sir Walter Raleighs booke is called in by the Kinges commaundment, for divers exceptions, but specially for beeing too sawcie in censuring princes. I heare he take y^t much to hart, for he thought he had won his spurres and pleased the King extraordinarilie.'[31]

'The ordinary Theme and Argument of History is War'

In 'The Discovrse of . . . Warre' Ralegh remained adamant that 'Warre cannot be without mutuall violence',[32] and the present study focuses precisely upon this recurring vision of human landscapes convulsed by acts of aggression. Like Shakespeare's history plays, Ralegh compels us not only to interrogate the precarious distribution of cultural power under monarchy, but also to attend to the hesitant spectacle of political authority in process. These key investigations, conducted in a host of different contexts, converged repeatedly on the pursuit of arms. Indeed, at the very outset of 'The Discovrse of . . . Warre', Ralegh gave superlative expression to his unstinting belief that any intellectual or political commitment to history, and indeed history-making, remained indivisible from the contemplation of internecine strife:

> The ordinary Theme and Argument of History is War . . . since in humane reason there hath no meanes been found of holding all mankind at peace within it self: It is needfull that against the wit and subtilty of man, we oppose not only the bruit force of our bodyes, (wherein many Beasts exceed us,) but helping our strength with art and wisedome, strive to excell our enemies in those points wherein man is excellent over other Creatures.[33]

Here, the essayist remains at pains to distinguish between the violence of individual criminal acts and that which is legitimised on the battlefield by those in authority. In direct comparison with more recent theorists, such as Schinkel, Ralegh also dwells at length upon the very intimate communion constituted by violence – the drawing of bodies into close, but adversarial proximity – because 'there hath no meanes been found of holding all mankind at peace within it self'. Violence thus emerges as a resource freely available to even the most perceivedly primitive of peoples, who had at their disposal only a stunted vocabulary of 'saluage' aggression. Conversely, Ralegh also explored how an investment in arms might be attributed with some fitting *dignitas* for a fallen race. He often considered the dynamic relationship which violence maintained with changing technologies: 'the sword, the Arrow, the Gun'.[34] Thus, on occasions, the meting out of violence upon and with 'the bruit force of our bodyes' may be eclipsed in his published writings by a more pressing concern with the growing sophistication of instruments of war and their requirements in terms of training and maintenance. Common justifications for armed conflict (*ius ad bellum*) were often linked in his discussions to human appetites (e.g. ambition, greed and revenge) as well as other sources, such as threatened danger, rebellion, female agency ('of old time ... Women have been the common Argument of these tragedies') and religion ('The right of St. Peter, that is the Popes Revenews and Authority').[35]

In the *History*, this ongoing concern with faultlines in the transactions of human society is counterpointed with arresting accounts of political resistance, peerless leadership, rigorously disciplined soldiery and/or the expert implementation of available technologies. The imprisoned historian can participate in such debates as the 'maker' of national histories but, like Shakespeare and his fellow playwrights, Ralegh can also problematise their terms of reference by building complex character profiles of military commanders. In *1 Henry VI*, Talbot rails that the unruly Pucelle, 'A witch, by fear, not force, like Hannibal,/Drives back our troops and conquers as she lists' (*VI*: I.v.21–2). The mythologies concerning Hannibal also came to constitute a key focus for Ralegh's *History*. It is surely significant that two of the most impressive engravings from this volume are devoted to the commander's notable victory over the Romans at the battle of Cannae in 216 BC during the Second Punic War. However, elsewhere, in the midst of the seemingly unremitting accounts of flawed leaders and fallen races, there are occasions when society's overdetermined reflexes of violence inflict needless sorrow on ancient peoples and corrupt the fortunes of generations to come.

In the discussion of the Carthaginian general Amilcar's heroic aspiration to imperial greatness for his nation, we also learn of the binding of his son, Hannibal, to an oath of hatred against the Romans. At such points, we may be reminded of Shakespeare's Richard II, who suspects that Bolingbroke initially acts against Mowbray 'on ancient malice', and later himself exhorts both men to 'reconcile/This low'ring tempest of your home-bred hate' which might overwhelm those 'yet unborn and unbegot' (I.i.9, I.iii.180–1, III.iii.87).[36] Unlike his Roman sources, Ralegh often refrains from stressing the Carthaginians' path to defeat, but his discussions remain fraught with contrary motions. The narrator may promote the waging of war as a rite of passage for leaders wishing to earn the attentions of posterity, yet elsewhere the Jacobean reader remains in no doubt of the lessons to be learned from Amilcar's legacy of hatred to his son:

it is inhumane, to bequeath hatred in this sort, as it were by Legacie, it cannot be denyed. Yet for mine owne part, I doe not much doubt, but that some of those Kings, with whom we are now in peace, haue received the like charge from their Predecessors, that as soone as their coffers shall be full, they shall declare themselues enemies to the people of *England*.[37]

Such debates would also become familiar for playhouse audiences as in the instance of Shakespeare's *Richard II* where the Bishop of Carlisle ponders the consequences of deposition: 'The woe's to come. The children yet unborn/Shall feel this day as sharp to them as thorn' (*Richard II*: IV.i.321–2).

As Ralegh's *History*'s extensive accounts of antiquity unfold, his narrators maintain a keen interest not only in the terrifying practices of physical, verbal and psychological violence, but also in how they relate to changing perspectives on the protocols of warfare. In the case of the mercenary campaigns against the Carthaginian empire, the decision of the Gaulish leader, Autaritus, to put his prisoners 'to horrible death, by torments', together with the stonings of the resisting forces and the forcible amputation of the hands of Carthaginian captives, is fiercely condemned. Notwithstanding our knowledge of the soldier Ralegh's own implication in scenes of violent blood-letting, the chronicler duly submits 'Of this crueltie I need say no more, than that it was execrable severitie.'[38]

One of the most famous examples from Ralegh's corpus of writing in which we are asked to attend to the heroic exemplarity of the commander occurs in *A report of the truth of the fight about the Isles of Açores, this last summer, betwixt the Revenge, one of her Majesty's Ships, and an Armada of the King of Spain* (1591).[39] Here, attempting to occlude the loss of a valuable vessel from her Majesty's fleet and a singular display of military incompetence (described as 'the greatnesse of [Grenville's] minde'), Ralegh endeavours to scotch rumours which 'are diuersly spred' across Europe and the 'vaine glorious vaunts' made by 'the Spaniardes according to their usual manner'.[40] Indeed, the narrator is as exercised by the need to create a model of heroic resistance to the ever encroaching powers of Philip II's empire ('A small troupe to man such a ship, and a weak garrison to resist so mighty an army'), as he is to villify the seemingly innumerable forces of continental Catholicism.[41] Even the 'base' men of war on the Spanish galleons are compelled to bear witness to the matchless fortitude of Sir Richard Grenville on the *Revenge*.[42] The figure of Grenville, who 'ended his life honourably in respect of the reputation wonne to his nation and country, and of the same to his posteritie, and that being dead, he hath not outliued his owne honour',[43] may thus be instructively placed in relief against the familiar discourse of the 'bloudy and iniurious designes' of Spain.[44] At such moments, Ralegh remained ready to invest in and enrich the pan-European Black Legend,[45] to demonise the brutality of Spanish colonial and military practices, while often strategically deflecting attentions from his own participation in ruthless campaigns in both the Old World and the New.[46]

The Initiation into Hostilities

As we have seen, Ralegh frequently encouraged his readers to reflect at great length upon the already well-worn mythologies surrounding redoubtable warriors, such as Hannibal. However, prompted by a good measure of very personal experience in the aftermath of Elizabeth's death, the captive scholar could not refrain from the conclusion that

> there is no Profession more vnprosperous than that of Men of Warre . . . For besides the enuie and jealousie of men; the spoyles, rapes, famine, slaughter of the innocent, [de]vastation, and burnings, with a world of miseries layed on the labouring man, are so hatefull to God, as with good reason did *Monluc* the Marshall of *France* confesse, That *were not the mercies of* God *infinite, and without restriction, it were in vaine for those of his profession to hope for any portion of them: seeing the cruelties, by them permitted and committed, were also infinite.*[47]

Deploying here a favoured technique of *enumeratio* to enhance the *auctoritas* of his textual voices, Ralegh draws attention to the unending cycles of slaughter that had wracked France during the Wars of Religion.

Persuasively, Benjamin Schmidt has argued that the battlefields of France in the second half of the sixteenth century were like a military 'finishing school' for English gentlemen.[48] As the second son of West Country gentry, Ralegh (unlike other court favourites, such as Robert Dudley, Earl of Leicester, or Robert Devereux, 2nd Earl of Essex) could count upon no mighty networks of connections to propel him upwards in late Elizabethan society or to support him during periods (sometimes extended) when he forfeited the favour of the Crown. Indeed, as Naunton affirmed, 'it was a long time before he could brag of more then he carried at his back'.[49] Burghley would shrewdly counsel his own son, 'Be sure to keep some great man thy friend . . . Otherwise, in this ambitious age, thou shalt remain as an hop without a pole, live in obscurity, and be made a football for every insulting companion.'[50] Even if Ralegh might look periodically to support from the Earls of Shrewsbury, from Henry

Percy (the wizard earl), 9th Earl of Northumberland and from Bess of Hardwick, for example, many of these high-ranking individuals were frequently negotiating their own difficult relations with the Crown. In fact, Percy was a long-term prisoner in the Tower at the same time as Ralegh himself.

However, as an ambitious second son, Ralegh did have some enduring connections upon which he might call for support. Rory Rapple has underlined that by the second half of the sixteenth century, 'England's martial reputation was at its lowest point since the reign of Henry VI';[51] and, as an adolescent, Ralegh was drawn into cross-Channel military ventures led by the Champernowne family, with whom he claimed ties of kinship on the side of his mother, Catherine. His cousin Gawain, or Gawin, had married Roberde, third daughter of the Huguenot military commander Gabriel de Lorges, Comte de Montgommery. By the late 1560s the teenage Ralegh had joined a military company captained by Gawain's brother, Henry, to strengthen the ailing forces of the French Protestants who were locked in cycles of civil disorders with their Catholic adversaries. Initiatives, such as those of the Champernownes, were mostly privately financed. Indeed, Thomas Churchyard recalled in *A generall rehearsall of warres* (1579) that in 1569, 'Henry Champernowne ... serued in the cause of the Protestantes of Fraunce, of his own proper charges in the second Ciuile warres, with xij. gentlemen or more. And in the thirde Ciuile warres after the battaile of [Jarnac], he serued with an hundred men of his owne proper costes.'[52]

Treating the same events in an entry for that year of 1569, Camden recorded much later in his *Annals* (first published 1615) that

> The Queene though she were embroyled with this rebellion at home, yet failed she not to relieve the Protestants of *France* ... she supplyed the Queene of Navarre with money, taking Iewels in pawne for the same: and permitted *Henry Champernoun* ... to leade into *France* a Troupe of a hundred voluntary Gentleman on horse-backe, who had in his colours written, *Finem det mihi virtus*, that is, Let virtue give me end. Amongst these voluntary Gentlemen were *Philip Butshide, Francis Barkley*, and *Walter Ralegh* a very young man, who now began first to be of any eminent note.[53]

As Rapple has underlined, there was a remarkable dearth of possibilities for social mobility in the second half of the sixteenth century: 'Whereas great opportunities to make fortunes in spite of the sequence of one's birth had arisen in the heyday of the dissolution of the monasteries, under Mary and Elizabeth that sort of bonanza would not repeat itself.'[54] More troubling, as Sir Thomas Smith pointed out in *De republica anglorum*, was that 'when [men of war] haue no externe seruice wherewith to occupie their buisie heads & handes accustomed to fight and quarell, [they] must needes seeke quarels and contentions amongest themselues'.[55] Indeed, this anxiety operates as one of the driving forces for the international ambitions of Shakespeare's Henry V.

Churchyard contended that Henry Champernowne was 'one desirous of renowme, and greedie of glorie gotten by seruice'. Furthermore, we learn that 'many of those gentlemen that he brought with hym, augmented so muche his fame, that to this daie his deedes and theirs, are moste noblie spoken of, greatly to the honour of all our Englishe Nation'.[56] As will become apparent in the unfolding of the present study, the Crown could take a lively interest in the trappings of chivalric adventuring with its Accession Day tilts and knightly performances at court, but the appetite for armed conflict shared by subjects (both high- and low-born) was repeatedly marked for export. J. H. Elliott has argued that 'those who fought in the Protestant ranks [of the French wars] all subscribed, even if only through the fact of comradeship in arms, to a common vision of the world. It was a world in which the Christian was engaged in ceaseless struggle against the power of Satan.'[57] Whatever the truth of the matter in individual cases, David J. B. Trim remains persuasive in his more general contention that the Elizabethan regime's,

> allowing [of] companies of volunteers to serve on the Continent, [of corsairs to] use English ports as bases, and sending [of] occasional sums of money or shipments of arms . . . may seem more suggestive of an approach governed by *realpolitik*, rather than religious fervour.[58]

Certainly, in later life Ralegh himself did not lose sight of the strategic importance that the French Wars of Religion represented for those of his generation as an initiation into the profession of arms. His *History* stressed that 'among all their warres, I finde not any, wherein [Roman] valour hath appeared, comparable to the English. If *my* judgement seeme ouerpartiall; our warres in *France* may helpe to make it good.'[59] Indeed, in the same section, the narrator would strike an even more markedly patriotic note, submitting, 'If therefore it be demanded, whether the *Macedonian*, or the *Roman*, were the best Warriour? I will answere: The *Englishman*.'[60]

If narratives of Elizabethan political intervention are inevitably dominated by accounts of conflict with the imperial forces of Philip II or the colonisation of Ireland, there is every evidence in the intellectual and artistic life of the period that the French wars were not eclipsed in the public mind as a consequence of these other, ongoing hostilities. Much has been justly made in literary and cultural histories of Philippe de Mornay's close relations with the Sidneys, the advances made by the Duc d'Anjou to the Virgin Queen, Francis Bacon's sojourn at the English Embassy at Paris and the participation of Robert Devereux in Henri IV's Normandy campaign of 1591. However, John Foxe's evocations of the Duc de Guise ('the greate Archenemy of God'[61]) in the *Acts and Monuments* were echoed in a number of ways in Anne Dowriche's *The French historie* (1589) and Marlowe's *Massacre at Paris* (1592) – and, in all likelihood, in Webster's later, lost tragedy *The Guise* (1615?).[62] Moreover, the publication of pamphlet literature, such as *An edict set forth by the French king, for appeasing of troubles in his kingdome* (1570), *A mervaylous discourse vpon the lyfe, deedes, and behaviours of Katherine de Medicis Queene mother* (1575), *A Catholicke apologie against the libels, declarations, aduices, and consultations made, written, and published by those of the League, perturbers of the quiet estate of the realme of France* (1585), *The contre-Guyse* (1589) and *The mutable and wauering estate of France* (1597) continued to focus minds upon broils unfolding across the Channel.

By 1570 Henry Champernowne was dead and buried in France. Decades later, composing his *History* in the Tower, Ralegh was still minded to recall his own service on the fields of France, here and there punctuating his narratives of the rise and fall of ancient empires with carefully chosen *aperçus*. During an account of the destruction of Persepolis by Alexander the Great, we learn that 'it was a true saying of *Coligni*, Admirall of *France; That whoso will shape that beast* (meaning Warre) *must begin with his belly*'. Similarly, when evoking the killing of Alexander the Great's general Eumenes, we learn that 'it was not ill answered, by *Gaspar de Collignie*, Admiral of *France* in our dayes, to one that foretold his death, which ensued soone after in the massacre of *Paris*; That rather than to leade againe an Armie of Voluntaries, he would die a thousand times.'[63] Elsewhere, it is the brutality and rampant blood-letting witnessed in France that Ralegh presses upon the attentions of his reader. He segues effortlessly in the midst of a much larger account of Alexander's encounters with the Persians to an account of the seemingly impenetrable entries of 'certaine Caues in *Languedoc*' where Catholics had taken refuge during the Wars of Religion. Unable to engage with their adversaries, the Protestant troops 'by certaine bundels of straw, let downe by an yron chaine, and a waighty stone in the middest, those [Catholics] that defended it, were so smothered, as they rendred themselues, with their plate, monie, and other goods therein hidden'.[64] In this instance, a brief insight from his youth can lead to a forthright appreciation by the ageing prisoner of the lessons of military strategy to be gleaned from such exploits:

> I remember these things, but to giue caution to those that shall in times to come inuade any part of those Countries, that they alwayes, before they passe into the Land, burne down the grasse and sedge to the East of them; they may otherwise, without any other enemy than a handfull of straw set on fire, die the death of hony-Bees, burnt out of the Hiue.[65]

(Another seasoned warrior, Talbot in *1 Henry VI*, similarly concludes that 'bees with smoke and doves with noisome stench/Are from their hives and houses driven away' (*VI*: I.v.23–4).)

Ralegh appears to have returned to England after the Peace of St. Germain was signed in 1570. By 1572 he had proceeded up to Oriel College, Oxford, whence he would eventually move onto the Inns of Chancery. Another tie (or memory of a tie) of kinship which may have been of some value at this time to the aspiring young man was that of his mother's elder sister, Katherine Ashley, the queen's governess from 1544 until her death in 1565.[66] Steven May observes that Ralegh was rather mystifyingly styling himself '*de Curia*' as early as 1577.[67] However, he seems not to have won royal favour of any note until the beginning of the next decade.[68] Certainly, by 1581 Rogers Manners was reporting that 'Mr Raleigh is in very good favour', and Thomas Morgan, an agent of Mary Stuart at this time, wrote about him some two years later, in 1583, as 'the Quene's dere minion, who daylye growth in creditt'.[69] By 1582 Ralegh appears to have departed for the Low Countries in the company attending François, Duc d'Anjou, which was part of a larger contingent under the command of Leicester. It was during this campaign that the young man was accorded the honour, on at least one occasion, of being a messenger between William of Orange and Elizabeth herself.

Thereafter, Ralegh became increasingly enmeshed in the bitterly competitive, but potentially highly lucrative arena of the court. In these years, we find him: granted a London residence at Durham House as well as estates originally belonging to Babington; making a profit on the sale of Crown leases relating to All Soul's College, Oxford; and holding some valuable patents to license the purchasing of wines and the exportation of broadcloth. By the middle of the decade he had been awarded the rangership of Gillingham Forest in Dorset and appointed Vice-Admiral of the West, Lord Lieutenant of Cornwall and Lord Warden of the Stannaries. At the beginning of 1585 he was knighted, and by the close of that year

Hilliard was painting the famous miniature of the court favourite. Both Ralegh and Essex had connections of service and/or kinship to Leicester and, like Leicester, were determined to rise in importance in the life of the nation by bidding for the attentions of the monarch. Naunton might be rather wide of the mark in arguing that Elizabeth 'took [Ralegh] for a kinde of Oracle'.[70] Nonetheless, the favourite was in receipt of Crown patronage and this, along with his choleric disposition, made him a number of enemies at court.[71] With his wonted acerbic wit, the Queen's godson, John Harington, noted in his epigrams concerning one 'Paulus' (often construed as Ralegh): 'Thus while he daubs his speech with flattery's plaster/And calls himself her slave, he grows our Master.'[72]

In the inevitable jockeying for position to win royal favour, one of the Devon knight's most notable rivals in the 1590s was often Essex himself: the earl might be found 'mightelie backt by the greatest in opposition to Sir Walter Ralegh, who had offended manie and was maligned of most'.[73] As May indicates, by 1587 Essex allegedly chose to inform his sovereign in the presence of his rival about 'that knave Raleigh', while the latter would subsequently scorn the 'meaner wit' of the earl. In the following year, Essex challenged his adversary to a duel.[74] Such courses of actions were perhaps inevitable in the intensely volatile court environment, particularly in these post-Armada years when the passing of hitherto key political players, such as Leicester, Hatton and Walsingham, unveiled great opportunities for a new generation of aspiring courtiers.

Prior to sailing on the unsuccessful Islands Voyage in 1597 to intercept Philip II's treasure ships, Ralegh paid tribute to the intrepid Essex: 'my Lord Generall hyme sealf will wrestell with the seas to his perrill or, constrayned to cum bake, be found utterly hartbroken'.[75] However, once again, Ralegh would soon find himself in strained relations with the earl: 'The Generall with the rest of the fleet came to an anchor before the Island, and hearing of Sir *Walter Raleighs* landing and losse, was highly displeased, as he had cause; it being directly and expressely forbidden upon pain of death to land forces.' Writing from the Essex camp, Sir Francis Vere later submitted that 'The Generall's goodnesse would not suffer him to take any extream course, but with a wise and noble admonition forgave the offence.'[76] Relations between the court favourites would remain precarious. By 1600, in the wake of his rival's disgrace after the earl's return from Ireland, Ralegh was counselling Cecil, 'His malice is fixt ... The less yow make hyme the less he shalbe able to harme yow and yours ... if [Essex] continew he wilbe able to break the branches and pull up the tree, root and all. Lose not your advantage: if yow do I rede your destiny.'[77]

Nonetheless, despite their very different ranks, personalities and experiences of elite life in Elizabeth's realm, both Essex and Ralegh often had quite similar political aims and were not uniformly at loggerheads. News of Devereux's marriage to Frances, Philip Sidney's widow, became public in the autumn of 1590 and incurred the expected wrath from the Crown. Ralegh secretly married Elizabeth Throckmorton, one of Elizabeth's ladies-in-waiting, in 1591 and, indeed, Essex stood as godfather to the Raleghs' newborn son, the Plantaganet-ly named Damerei, in April 1592.[78] It was in the summer of that year that the Ralegh couple was placed under house arrest and then temporarily sent to the Tower. Tellingly, the fallen courtier seems to have redeemed himself in his sovereign's eyes during a temporary release to oversee the division of the spoils from a captured Spanish ship, the *Madre de Dios*, delivering some £80,000 to the royal coffers. The couple was released, but Lady Ralegh was exiled from court. Ralegh himself would not be allowed to return fully to her Majesty's favour until 1597, but his political activities seem not to have been absolutely curtailed in this period: he was elected burgess of Mitchell in Cornwall in 1593, and returned as a Member of Parliament for Dorset in 1597 and for Cornwall in 1601.

Much more significant for his long-term preoccupation with the waging of war was Ralegh's military service in Ireland. Ralegh's half-brother, Humphrey Gilbert, had led ruthless campaigns across the Irish Sea. Indeed, such was the cruelty that he meted out to the native population that Ralegh submitted in a letter of 1581 to Walsingham that he had 'never heard nor read of any man more feared then he is among the Irish nation'.[79] Gilbert's first engagements proper with Ireland had been in the late 1560s and early 1570s when he was collaborating with Henry Champernowne in initiatives for the settlement of Munster and Ulster. Robert Devereux's father, Walter, was made 1st Earl of Essex in this new creation of the title, and led his own ruthless military campaigns focusing upon the Plantation of Ulster from 1573 onwards. Walter Devereux was named Earl Marshal of Ireland before he succumbed to dysentery and died in Dublin in 1576. Ralegh served as a captain in Ireland in the years 1580 and 1581 under the newly appointed Lord Deputy of Ireland, Lord Grey de Wilton. Elizabeth had been excluded from the Church by the Pope in 1570 and thereafter, as Rapple emphasises, 'throughout Europe Elizabeth was widely viewed as an illegitimate, lewd excommunicate'.[80] Authorised by Gregory XIII to assist the Fitzgerald rebellion and under the command of Colonel Sebastiano di San Guiseppi, Spanish and Italian troops found themselves besieged at Smerwick in County Kerry in September 1580. Hemmed in on the Dingle peninsula between English ships and Grey's army, the garrison yielded unconditionally after two days' bombardment. Once it was confirmed that all arms had been surrendered, the company of some five to six hundred men was viciously cut down by the English forces in an assault led by their captains. Grey wrote back to London

> I sent straight certin gentlemen in to see their weapons and armures layed downe & to gard ye munition & victaile there lefte for spoile. Then putt I in certeyn bandes who straight fell to execution. There were 600 slayne; munition & vittaile great store, though much wasted through the disorder of ye souldier, wch in y^t furie could not bee helped.[81]

Indeed, recollecting this event over a decade later, John Hooker reported that 'capteine Raleigh together with capteine macworth . . . entered into the castell & made a great slaughter, manie or the most of them being put to the sword'.[82] Ominously, the humanist scholar Hubert Languet wrote in the following month to his protégé, Philip Sidney, that 'There seems reason to fear, that the flame which burns in Ireland, may one day seize upon your own England; all men agree that you carry on the war there as if you desired to keep it alive rather than suppress it.'[83] Much later, in the *Annales*, Camden submitted that the appointed commanders through to the queen herself were horrified by the butchery committed at Smerwick:

> it was resolued (against the Deputies will,) who (full of mercy and compassion) wept for it, that all strangers, the Commanders excepted, should be put to the Sword; and the *Irish* to be hanged, which was presently executed. Neuerthelesse, the Queen, who from her heart detested to vse cruelty to those that yeelded, wished that the slaughter had not beene, and was with much difficultie appeased and satisfied about it.[84]

More generally, the Elizabethan regime was little given to expressions of queasiness concerning the brutal repression of Irish resistants and their allies. Violence was ruthlessly deployed both as a military strategy and as a deterrent by the occupying armies.

The atrocities of the Munster campaign and the siege of Smerwick were far from being isolated events in the account of Elizabethan dealings with Ireland. Just within the ten-year span preceding the slaughter at Smerwick, there had been massacres performed by the troops of Sir John Norris and Francis Drake at Rathlin Island (1575), and two years later at Mullaghmast by Elizabethan troops. As Clodagh Tait, David Edwards and Pádraig Lenihan have highlighted, one of the governing stimuli for such conduct may indeed have been that the members of the English military forces were often

> recent arrivals in Ireland, with few ties to the local areas in which they operated or to the people whom they fought: their own loved ones were in little danger of immediate revenge attacks ... As well as getting rid of troublesome enemies, the use of massacre, murder and martial law communicated messages of strength and intent.[85]

In this context, Malcolm Smuts argues equally incisively that

> English rule in Ireland [was] ... a colonial regime engaged in a brutal policy of conquest involving deliberately induced famines, massacres of women and children, and mass executions carried out under martial law ... Although he had killed 'four hundred fighting men' while chasing down the outlaw Rory O'More, Sir Henry Sidney complained, 'this [was] counted no war but a chastisement of vagabonds'.[86]

Unlike the insights in the *History* into the French Wars of Religion, Ralegh did not return in his subsequent writings to the gruesome environment of blood-letting in Ireland in which he was so centrally implicated. Whatever Camden's claims concerning the outrage of Elizabeth and her ministers at the massacre, it appears not to have marred the young man's capital at the seat of power. By the close of 1580 Ralegh was delivering papers taken from the Catholic forces at Smerwick back to London. Nevertheless, the young captain soon found himself on strained terms with his commanding officer: Wilton wrote to Walsingham, 'For myne owne parte I must be playne I nether lyke his carriage nor company.'[87]

In 1587, Ralegh would receive the extensive grant of some 42,000 acres in the Munster Plantation, and thereafter he always seems to have kept an eye on Elizabethan schemes for plantation in that land. In the next decade, at the news of the latest 'Irish combination', he wrote with his usual candour on 10th May 1595 from his Dorset home of Sherborne to Elizabeth's minister, Robert Cecil: 'Wee ar so busyed and dandled in thes French warrs, which ar endless, as wee forgett the defens next the hart. Her Majesty hath good cause to remember that a million hath been spent in Irland not many yeares since. A better kingdome would have bynn purchased att a less.'[88] Ireland did not offer the lure of gold for settlers but, in English eyes, it remained dangerously receptive to the influence of the Catholic powers in Europe and thus had to be 'secured'. This might need to be performed with military might, as was indeed reiterated by the royal advisers in Shakespeare's *Richard II* – 'Now for the rebels which stand out in Ireland./Expedient manage must be made, my liege/Ere further leisure yield them further means/For their advantage and your highness' loss' (I.iv.37–40). One recurring strategy to give warrant to the meting out of violence to the Irish population was to present a 'savage' society in which the experience of brutality was already a commonplace. The avenging Francisco in Webster's *The White Devil* (1612) confides, 'Like the wild Irish I'll ne'er think thee dead/Till I can play at football with thy head' (IV.i.136–7). Indeed, more generally, Elizabethan and Jacobean writers indicated no reluctance in furnishing their readers with such oppositional discourses of barbaric Others.[89] Ireland, fashioned thus with overdetermined markers widely available in English print culture, emerged as a particularly pressing source of concern because of its close proximity to the Tudor realm as a potentially contagious source of unruliness and sedition. Indeed, Ralegh cautioned the readers of his *History* that 'the *Irish* in former times alwaies liued in a subdiuided *Ciuill* warre'.[90]

By December 1581, the aspiring courtier was in London once again and his visits to Ireland thereafter were by no means frequent. However, in disgrace at court in 1589, it was reported that the Earl of Essex had 'chassed Mr Rauly from the coart and [had] confined him in to Irland'.[91] He remained at Youghal in the west of Ireland in 1589 and 1590, and appears to have renewed his acquaintance with Spenser during this sojourn. More generally, in his 1935 biography, Edward Thompson submitted that, given his participation in the bloodthirsty conflict of the 1580s, 'It is horrible to remember Raleigh in Ireland; it is horrible to remember *any* Elizabethan in Ireland.'[92] Furthermore, Vincent P. Carey records that as late as the nineteenth century in the Gaelic-speaking communities of the west, misbehaving children were chastened with '"cughat an Rawley", or watch out for the Ralegh'.[93]

The Atlantic World

For Ralegh, and for many of those associated with his ventures, both Ireland and the Americas in their different ways represented an engagement with the past: whether in terms of charting the unknown, encountering barbarism or gaining access to some seemingly pristine landscape. Thus, strategies of colonial appropriation in the present might not only enable the English nation to fulfil its political destiny, they also generated opportunities for the more technologically advanced English to re-enact militarily the empire-building of the peoples of antiquity.

In 1578 Humphrey Gilbert was awarded letters patent to 'discover searche finde out and viewe such remote heathen and barbarous landes countries and territories not actually possessed of any Christian prince or people' and would claim the territory of Newfoundland for his sovereign.[94] In the event, Gilbert lost his life on his final, fateful 1583 voyage to North America. Following Gilbert's death, Ralegh succeeded in securing the letters patent to explore lands for settlement further south than Newfoundland on the North American continent. The third volume of Holinshed's *Chronicles* (1586) recorded that, in the spring of 1585, 'maister Walter Raleigh esquier, a gentleman from his infancie brought vp and trained in martiall discipline, both by land and sea, and well inclined to all vertuous and honorable aduentures', prepared to send out his first ships for the purposes of claiming new lands for the Crown.[95] Thus, if in the 1580s Ralegh was recruiting settlers in the West Country to populate lands in the counties of Cork and Waterford, he was simultaneously funding voyages to found colonies in the New World. Indeed, Richard Hakluyt penned a dedicatory address to him, claiming that 'this your most honourable enterprise [of Virginia was] farre more certaine then that of Columbus'.[96] Whatever the nature of the resources at the commander's disposal, the perceived commonality of experience between the two environments across the Irish sea and the Atlantic meant that similar expectations and ambitions were often applied to both. Moreover, on occasions, we find similar names recurring in Ralegh's ventures in both locations. John White sailed with Grenville to North Carolina in 1585 and drew images of the Roanoke inhabitants for publication back in England, went on to become governor of the Roanoke Island colony that Ralegh sponsored, and then returned to work on Ralegh's Irish estates when the colony collapsed. Thomas Hariot, author of *A briefe and true report of the new found land of Virginia*, leased a family residence in Ireland, Molana Abbey, from Ralegh.[97] Furthermore, violent coercion and butchery were all too often a commonplace in both Elizabethan political projects of colonialisation. Seemingly echoing Ralegh's own sentiments, Hakluyt had stressed in his dedicatory letter that 'it is not to bee denied, but that one hundred men will doe more nowe among the naked and vnarmed people in *Virginea*, then one thousande were able then to doe in Irelande against that armed and warrelike nation'.[98]

More generally, as Ralegh and many of his contemporaries frequently observed, it might be exceedingly difficult to enlist the services of even 'one hundred men' – and how far the recruits might differ from the supposed mores of the demonised Other gave much pause for thought. Like those participating in the recruiting ventures staged in *2 Henry IV*, Ralegh shows himself well versed in the morally flawed nature of the troops who were often at the disposal of any commander. Indeed, the world-weary and often cynical timbre of the *History*'s narrative voices betrays some telling insights into the author's own military travails: 'We finde it in daily experience, that all discourse of magnanimitie, of Nationall Vertue, of Religion, of Libertie, and whatsoeuer else hath bin wont to moue and incourage vertuous men, hath no force at all with the common Souldier, in comparison of spoile and riches.'[99] Years later, on his return to England after his second voyage to Guiana in 1618, Ralegh would (strategically?) blame a great deal of the expedition's failure on the fact that he found himself with 'volunteers who for the most part had neither seen the sea nor the wars, who, some forty gentlemen excepted, were the very scum of the world; drunkards, blasphemers, and such others, as their fathers, brothers, and friends'.[100] Given that such examples of *vituperatio* were commonplace in the period, it is unsurprising that John Everard would rail in a sermon in that same year (1618) 'that amongst *Souldiers* violence, cruelty, rapes, delight in blood, blasphemy, and prophanenesse, are so frequent and ordinary, that they are now thought proper vnto the profession'.[101]

Although Ralegh never set foot in Virginia himself, his ships arrived at the island of Wokoken in July of 1584 and claimed the native American realm of Prince Wingina for his queen. The Roanoke settlement offered the promise of a New World base for piratical attacks on enemy shipping, as well as longer prospects of securing gains in terms of colonisation, trade and political allies. The sailing of the Spanish Armada inhibited provisions being sent to New World settlers owing to the Crown's need for all shipping to remain near at hand, but Ralegh was centrally involved in the sponsoring of voyages to engage in privateering and to assist (or refound) settlements both before and after 1588. In addition, even when back in England, Ralegh clearly fostered the age's inquisitive desires surrounding this 'New World'. When the German Lupold von Wedel visited Hampton Court in the 1580s, he recounted that a ship had just travelled from uncharted parts across the Atlantic:

> The master or captain of the ship, named Ralegh, had brought with him two men of the island whom we asked permission to see. Their faces as well as their whole bodies were very similar to those of the white Moors at home, they wear no shirts, only a piece of fur to cover the pudenda and the skins of wild animals to cover their shoulders. Here they are clad in brown taffeta.

Nobody could understand their language, and they had a very childish and wild appearance.[102]

In the event, Ralegh funded five expeditions to the colony during his lifetime and clearly continued to envisage his native land as a great imperial power in-the-making, if it would only seize its destiny. Even in 1602, in the final months before his downfall and arrest, he was writing, in prophetic mode, 'I shall yet see [Virginia] an English nation.'[103]

As early as 1577 the humanist scholar Hubert Languet had written to his protégé Philip Sidney,

> I fear England will be tempted by the thirst for gold, and rush forth in a body to the islands which Frobisher has lately discovered, and how much English blood do you suppose must be spilt in order that you may keep possession of them? There is not one of all our maritime nations which will not enter the lists against you for them.[104]

Ralegh's political career would be shaped by such concerns as those of Languet. *The discouerie of the large, rich, and bewtiful empire of Guiana* (1596) is a highly selective account of his own expedition across the Atlantic. His ships set sail from Plymouth in February 1585, enticed by the lucrative prospect of locating *El Dorado* and by the possibility of a new arena for English imperial expansion. Ralegh's narrator appears to arrive in the New World, like his Hispanic predecessors, seeking to reproduce Old World knowledge and to substantiate its myths: 'a Countrey that hath yet her Maydenhead, neuer sackt, turned, nor wrought'.[105] Again and again this new-found land is claimed with cultural markers easily identifiable for his Elizabethan readers: when the expedition's vessels came unexpectedly upon a river, for example, and 'bicause it had no name we called the riuer of the Red crosse, our selues being the first Christians that euer came therein'.[106] In such ways, Ralegh populates his landscape with familiar textual spaces (in this case, of Christ's sacrifice and also, perhaps, of Spenserian knights in search of epic deeds) in order to consolidate strategies for English identification and/or ownership.[107] Nonetheless, the very fact that Ralegh was publishing his account at all indicates a marked absence of royal patronage and of enthusiasm on the part of ministers for his imperial schemes. As a consequence, there was a need to levy a body of speculators and colonists in the wider nation with such publications.[108]

Whereas Mary B. Campbell has argued convincingly that 'America, to European history, was above all a challenge, a disruption, a catalyst of discontinuities',[109] Ralegh offers again and again clear and emphatic indications of how this discontinuity should be resolved. On encountering the

Spanish forces in Trinidad, he 'set upon the *Corp du guard* in the euening, and haueing put them to the sword, sent Captaine *Calfield* onwards with 60. soldiers, & my selfe followed with 40. more ... and at the instance of the Indians, I set their City of *S. Iosephs* on fire'.[110] Elsewhere, when an Indian Pilot and his brother find themselves hunted by a hostile tribe, Ralegh's company determines to capture an old man from the rival community, 'assuring him that if we had not our Pilot againe, we would presently cut off his head'.[111] More generally, Campbell has argued forcefully that 'Ralegh's intentions were no better than those of Cortés ... My point is that Ralegh's political ethics were about as low as those of any other Renaissance man of action' – and, indeed, it seems that the *Discouerie* was clearly designed to showcase the talents of such a 'man of action' for contemporaries.[112] Whatever the moral case that might be made against Ralegh, the *Discouerie* met with instant success in 1596 (in terms of sales). Two additional editions rolled from the presses in the same year, and it was subsequently translated into Latin, German and Dutch.

In direct comparison with Ralegh's other accounts of his nation's imperial project, this encounter narrative is deeply penetrated with the political insecurities of the English ruling elite and the rapacity of the growing community of speculators ever alert to the riches continually drawn across the Atlantic by the treasure ships of Philip II.[113] In his writings, the courtier is eager to legitimise the Elizabethans' claims to colonies overseas by calling to mind their dealings with this Atlantic world in the past. During the reign of Henry VII, English adventurers had competed with their Iberian rivals to survey the coast of the new lands: 'The west Indies were first offered Her Maiesties Grandfather by Columbus, a strounger, in whome there might be doubt of deceipt.'[114] The *impresa* of the Spanish royal house was *Non sufficit orbis* (The world does not suffice). Ralegh's *Discouerie* offered the opportunity to his fellow countrymen to redress what he perceived as the gross economic and political advantages which England's enemy had enjoyed as a consequence of its American possessions: 'It is [Spain's] Indian Golde that indaungereth and disturbeth all the nations of Europe, it purchaseth intelligence, creepeth into Councels, and setteth bound loyaltie at libertie, in the greatest Monarchies of Europe.'[115]

Indeed, in all his prose writings, Ralegh remained richly sensitive that the relation of brutish antagonists, savage customs and unharnessed appetites amongst populations distant in time and space could both horrify *and* seduce his various audiences – and he was not alone. The future Archbishop of Canterbury, George Abbot, particularly stressed in one of his sermons the impoverished faith of primitive peoples, drawing attention to 'Those Ethnickes who knew little or nothing of true pietie ... People ruder then the Greekes and more barbarous then the Romanes ... I meane the Westerne Indians, the dull people of America, who thought that thunder and lightning & tempest were sent by the Sunne.'[116] Most famously perhaps to more modern eyes, in his *Apologie for Poesie* Philip Sidney moved immediately from a consideration of 'our neighbour country Ireland, where truly learning goeth very bare' to the 'most barbarous and simple Indians'.[117] This kind of adversarial cognitive mapping may equally be witnessed throughout Ralegh's *History*, as in the following comparison of the Persians resisting Alexander the Great's advances and those of the Celts in North Wales resisting those of the Romans under the command of Julius Agricola: 'Yet the *Britaines* were men stout enough; the *Persians* were very dastards.'[118]

'I lost the love of many': Captivity in the Tower

Shakespeare's Duke of York acknowledges that '[a]s in a theatre the eyes of men/After a well-graced actor leaves the stage/Are idly bent on him that enters next' (*Richard II*: V.ii.23–5). The transition from one political dynasty to the next clearly constitutes a similarly theatrical watershed moment in the life of any nation. In his *Briefe Discourse, touching the happy vnion of the Kingdomes of England, and Scotland* (1603), Francis Bacon hailed the Stuart succession to the English Crown as 'a successe and euent aboue the course of *Nature*, to haue so great a change, with so great a quiet: forasmuch as suddayne and great mutations, as well in state as in *Nature*, are rarely without violence and perturbation'.[119] His fellow essayist Sir William Cornwallis was similarly minded in *The miraculous and happie vnion of England and Scotland* (1604), commending the fact that in this convergence of nations 'there were no threates, no violence, no swordes drawne of neither side'.[120]

However, at the beginning of his *History* Ralegh acknowledged that devotion to the past can assume a number of guises: 'I know that I lost the loue of many, for my fidelity towards Her, whom I must still honor in the dust; though further then the defence of her excellent person, I neuer persecuted any man.'[121] He had little cause to celebrate the changing fortunes of his realm and quickly found himself alienated with the advent of the new regime in 1603. In his *Instructions to his Sonne and to Posterity* (published posthumously in 1632), he advised that 'There is nothing more becoming a wise man then to make choice of Friends', yet he failed spectacularly to observe his own counsel and this rendered him danger-ously exposed at court. During Elizabeth's final years, the correspondence of partisan voices (such as Cecil and Henry Howard) with the Scottish monarch conjured up the dangerous figure of an unruly and froward Ralegh, deeply unreceptive to Stuart ambitions. Indeed, much later in the century, John Aubrey would report that

> at a consultation at Whitehall after Queen Elizabeth's death, [there was talk of] how matters were to be ordered and what ought to be done, Sir Walter Raleigh declared his opinion, 'twas the wisest way for them to keepe the Government in their owne hands and sett up a Commonwealth, and not to be subject to a needy, beggarly nation. It seems there were some of this cabal who kept this not so secret.[122]

Whatever the truth of the matter, in the years after James' accession, Ralegh would submit to the reader of his *History*, 'It is true, that there was neuer any Common weale or Kingdome in the world, wherein no man had cause to lament. Kings liue in the world, and not aboue it.'[123]

Painfully unaware of the identities of his adversaries, the hounded courtier wrote to Cecil himself, declaring 'I have been strangely practised against, and that others have their lives promised to accuse me.'[124] By way of confirmation of this growing tide of enmity towards the fallen knight, the godson of the late queen, Sir John Harington, confided at this time in a letter to the Bishop of Bath and Wells that

> The Spaniards beare no good wyll to Raleigh, and I doubte if some of the Englyshe have muche better affectione towarde hym ... Cecil dothe beare no love to Raleighe ... [Ralegh] seemeth wondrouslie fittede, both by arte and nature, to serve the State, especiallie as he is versede in forain matters ... In religion, he hathe showne, in pryvate talke, greate depthe and goode readynge, as I once experyencede at hys own howse, before manie lernede men. In good trothe, I pitie his state, and doubte the dyce not fairely thrown, if hys lyfe be the losyng-stake.[125]

In July 1603, on the basis of sometimes changeful testimonies that he was complicit in seditious plots against the Crown and in league with contin-ental powers, Ralegh found himself under house arrest and then in the Tower.[126] The Lieutenant, Sir John Peyton, wrote regarding his new charge that '[he] standeth still upon his innocency, but with a mind the most dejected that ever I saw'. In a later, second letter in the same month, he protested that 'I am exceedingly cumbered with him. Five or six times in a day he sendeth for me in such passions as I see his fortitude is [not] competent to support his grief.' However, his gaoler had his eye to his own fortunes as well as to the collapse of his prisoner's. In 1600, the ageing court favourite had assumed his duties as Governor of Jersey and visited the island in that year and in 1602. Peyton would remind Cecil in 1603 in a postscript to a more formal communication, 'PS. I beseech your lordship mediate the continuance of his Majesty's favours for the island of Jarsye, as a place of all others best agreeing with my desires.'[127]

With his star in spectacular descent, Ralegh sought to take his own life. Cecil reported to the Crown's ambassador in France that on July 27th, 'we came to him, and found him in some agony, seeming to be unable to endure his misfortunes, and protesting innocency, with carelessness of life. In that humour he had wounded himself under the right pap; but no way mortally, being in truth rather a cut than a stab.'[128] Whereas critics have speculated variously about the authenticity of this suicide attempt, it is clear that there were conflicting reports circulating even at the time. The Norfolk gentleman Philip Gawdy reported in a letter to his brother in August 1603: 'It is thought S' Walter Rauly will clear him selfe touching hanging worke, for my Lo. Cycill saide at fyrst that he was bedashed, but not bemudded, and yet the stabbing of him selfe with a knyfe sholde not well agree withe the other.'[129]

As we have seen, Ralegh had already encountered, and indeed partici-pated in, the spectacle of killing at various locations before he reached middle age. Moreover, he had been clearly given ample opportunity to ponder the profession of soldiery and the destruction of human life. When he later came to compose the *History* he addressed the question of suicide on a number of occasions. During an account of the kings of Tyre, he attended to Strato (seemingly, a figure like Sardanapalus – 'a man of ill liuing: and most voluptuous') who, when faced with the prospect of Persian enemy forces near at hand, determined 'to kill himselfe, but fainting in the exequution, his wife being present wrested the sword out of his hand and slew him: which done shee also therewith pierced her owne bodie, and died'.[130] Elsewhere, Demosthenes, finding his enemies 'threatned violence ... secretly took poison ... rather choosing to doe the last execution vpon himselfe, than to fall into the hands of such as hated him. Only this act of his (commendable, perhaps, in a Heathen man) argued some valour in him; who was otherwise too much a coward in battaile.'[131] Again and again in the *History*, the narrator is drawn every which way to give accounts of recorded suicides, to acknowledge Christian doctrine concerning self-slaughter and to give due and considered appreci-ation of the status of the practice amongst the ancients. These conflicted attitudes appear to have shaped his own conduct at a number of points in his life.

In the years after Elizabeth's death, Cecil remained unyielding in his enmity. The eminent counsellor wrote to a correspondent in August 1603, 'Whatever you heare of innocency know they are all in the King's mercy. For Sir W. Ralegh, his contempts are high.'[132] By November the prisoner protested in writing that he 'never invented treason, consented to treason, or performed treason against the King. Beseeches him to remember that he has loved him now for twenty years, for which his Majesty has yet given him no reward.'[133] His trial took place in the same month at Winchester. The defendant clearly gave a good account of himself ('*Your* words cannot condemn me; my innocency is my defence. I pray you go to your proofs') but, undaunted, the Crown Prosecutor, the formidable Sir Edward Coke, retorted, 'Nay I will prove all; thou art a monster; thou hast an English face, but a Spanish heart.'[134] Indeed, it seems that such was the virulence of Coke's attacks during the course of the trial that the 'standers by began to hyss and Mr Attorney to be something daunted'.[135] It was at this moment that Dudley Carleton chose to make the famously barbed comment that 'Never was a man so hated and so popular in so short a time.'[136] In the event, Ralegh was allowed to live on as a prisoner – though dead in the eyes of the Law.

As the government feared, the captive Ralegh did not fail to attract the sympathies of others. By 1605, a certain informant found himself at 'a fair in Sherborne, [and] one called him aside and told him that on the 6th of Nov. Sir Walter Ralegh should be in danger of his life; but notwithstanding, "he will escape, and come to greater matters than I will now speak of".'[137] Subsequently, Peyton's charge was taken up by Sir William Wade. This new, but equally restive Lieutenant of the Tower wrote to Cecil that his celebrated (and ever attention-seeking) player-prisoner 'shows himself upon the wall in his garden to the view of the people, who gaze upon him, and he stares at them'.[138]

The Final Performances

Ralegh's celebrity status as one of the Tower's most conspicuous residents for the majority of James's reign meant that he received a constant stream of visitors. These included American natives transplanted to the Old World and the king's son himself, Prince Henry. The latter is reported famously to have remarked that 'only my father would keep such a bird in a cage'.[139]

In 1607, Ralegh petitioned James I's consort, Anna of Denmark, to be allowed to join the Jamestown settlement. In the event, only his nephew, Ralph Gilbert, was permitted to represent the family on the voyage to America. Any anxieties concerning his own perceived dealings with Ralegh might have been allayed when Cecil received a letter from James in 1608. The minister was thanked for his 'remembrance of Robert Care [Carr] for yon [i.e. Ralegh's] manor of Sherburne, the more cause have I to conclude that your mind ever watched to seek out all advantages for my honour and contentment'. Cecil might also be consoled, his sovereign advised, that 'yon unhappy man [Ralegh] is the first and last that ever I heard complain of you since ye had this office'.[140] The prisoner was eventually released in March 1616 to serve his irascible *rex pacificus* on a last voyage to Guiana in search of gold. However, James tactically had the plans for the expedition shared with the Spanish ambassador, Diego Sarmiento de Acuña, Count of Gondomar.[141] Bitterly, Ralegh would later submit in a letter to Cecil's successor as Secretary of State, Sir Ralph Winwood, that,

> it pleased his majesty to value us at so little as to command me upon my allegiance to set down under my hand the country and the very river by which I was to enter it; to set down the number of my men, and burden of my ships, with what ordnance every ship carried. Which being made known to the Spanish ambassador, and by him in post to the king of Spain, a despatch was made by him and his letters sent from Madrid before my departure out of the Thames.[142]

His ships set out from Plymouth on 12th June 1617. Having arrived in the Canary Islands, they were given short shrift by the Governor of Lanzarote, who believed them all to be murderous Turks.[143] Nor was the case altered in the New World. Formerly, in 1595, an Arwacan pilot and his fellow countrymen feared 'that we would haue eaten them, or otherwise haue put them to some cruell death'.[144] The newly liberated Ralegh remained convinced that such expectations of English barbarism could only be attributable to rumours peddled by the hostile Spanish. In 1595, the latter had 'perswaded all the nations, that we were men eaters, and *Canibals*'.[145]

Matters turned from bad to worse in Guiana. Three ships led by Lawrence Keymis sailed up the Orinoco and made an assault on the Spanish forces garrisoned at San Thomé. In the ensuing conflict both the Spanish Governor and Ralegh's eldest son, Wat, were slain. Keymis sent expeditions hundreds of miles up river to ascertain the locations of gold and/or silver mines, but all in vain. The company returned to the ailing

Ralegh at the mouth of the Cayenne river, empty handed and having burnt San Thomé to the ground. Grieving at the news of the death of his son and keenly aware of the reception awaiting him in London, Ralegh was unyielding in his condemnation of Keymis. He wrote to his wife

> I rejected all … his arguments, and told him that I must leave him to himself to resolve it to the king and the state, he shut up himself into his cabin and shot himself with a pocket pistol, which broke one of his ribs, and finding that it had not prevailed, he thrust a long knife under his short ribs up to the handle, and died.[146]

The long-standing companion-explorer had thus succeeded where the master had failed in 1603. Ralegh wrote plaintively to Winwood, 'What shall become of me now I know not. I am unpardoned in England and my poor estate consumed; and whether any other prince or state will give me bread I know not.'[147]

Returning to England in June 1618, he was found to be in desperate spirits and taken by ship from Plymouth to London in the custody of Sir Lewis Stukeley. It was reported by 'a seruant of the saide Sir *Walter* named *Robine* … that his Master was out of his wittes, and that hee was naked in his shirt vpon all foure, scratching and biting the rushes vpon the Plankes'.[148] Beset initially by convulsions, his limbs began to produce all manner of boils. However, it appears that the desperate Ralegh had taken medicaments prepared by a French physician. The isolation that the sick patient was subsequently afforded gave him just enough time to pen a formal *Apology* concerning his past conduct.[149]

Ralegh was summoned to be cross-questioned by the king's ministers in September 1618, but the sentence was not in doubt. Further afield, opinions were clearly divided about the conduct of the Devon knight. The Earl of Leicester wrote to his wife, 'Sr. Wal. Ralegh remains still as hee did; thogh every day his tricks and falshoods are more and more discovered.'[150] However, by the time of the execution itself on 29th October, John Chamberlain noted that 'The people were much affected at the sight insomuch that one was heard say that we had not such another head to cut of.'[151] There were many differing accounts of Ralegh's scaffold speech amongst the crowd, which included Thomas Hariot. Most versions seem to have him speak of Essex. Chamberlain, for example, noted that Ralegh 'spake somwhat of the death of the earle of Essex and how sory he was for him, for though he was of a contrarie faction, yet he foresaw that those who estemed him then in that respect, wold cast him of as they did afterward'.[152]

Ultimately, in both life and in death, Ralegh remained a figure to be reckoned with, even beyond the shores of his native realm. Indeed, his execution only seems to have enhanced his international profile – exactly as his enemies feared. A Spanish agent in London wrote back to his master in code that 'The death of this man has produced a great commotion and fear here, and it is looked upon as a matter of the highest importance, owing to his being a person of great parts and experience, subtle, crafty, ingenious, and brave enough for anything.'[153] Nearly a month later, Chamberlain was still writing in animated fashion to Carleton on 21st November that

> We are so full still of Sir Walter Raleigh that almost every day brings foorth somwhat in this kind, besides divers ballets wherof some are called in, and the rest such poore stuffe as are not worth the overlooking. But when this heat is somwhat allayed, we shall have a declaration touching him, that shall contradict much of that he protested with so great assevereation, but the proofes had neede be very pregnant and demonstrative, or els they will hardly prevaile.[154]

As we have seen, Ralegh was well versed in the ways in which the body might risk (and succumb to) its own destruction. He wrote to Robert Cecil on 24th January 1597 at the time of Lady Cecil's death that 'there is no man sorry for death it sealf butt only for the tyme of death, every on[e] knowinge that it is a bonnd never forfeted to God'.[155] Harking back to late medieval modes of *ars moriendi* writing which enjoyed continued attention in the early modern period, such resignation had been in evidence since the very beginnings of Ralegh's very varied careers as a soldier, courtier and writer. Indeed, in the *History* he would submit authoritatively, '*I haue considered* (saith SALOMON) *all the workes that are vnder the Sunne, and behold, all is vanitie, and vexation of spirit:* but who beleeues it, till Death tells it vs? . . . It is therefore Death alone that can suddenly make man to know himselfe.'[156] It was this persisting and multifarious knowledge of violence and destruction that, as we shall see, continued to shape the cultural transactions of the age as a whole.

CHAPTER 2

'Undoing all, as all had never been':
The Play of Violence in Henry VI

But if your desire of fame and glory makes your present inactivity
irksome to you, place before you the example of the old Chandoses
and Talbots; you will obtain greater honour and glory by following
their steps, than if you could obtain all the wealth which the
Spaniards have brought over from their new world, on the strength
of which they have insulted all the nations of Europe, and so disgusted
them with their insolence, that they now feel and perhaps will soon
feel still more that they have erred in their reckoning.[1]

In the late 1570s, when Ralegh joined Champernowne's company across
the Channel, Hubert Languet was writing thus to the young Philip Sidney,
impressing upon his protégé the models (models unexpectedly espoused by
a humanist scholar) of warrior patriots from medieval scenes of conflict. In
their different ways, all three men sought to promote the Reformist cause
in Europe in the final decades of the sixteenth century, but, as we have seen,
Ralegh would be particularly exercised by the far-flung possessions of Spain
and the riches they surrendered to their colonial masters across the
Atlantic. Leading Elizabethan figures, such as Sidney, Ralegh and Robert
Devereux, Earl of Essex, would enter the fray against Catholic forces on the
battlefields of Western Europe as the Tudor century drew to a close. Sidney
met his death at Zutphen in the Low Countries in 1586. Conversely, both
Ralegh and Essex survived their service in the Protestant cause in the
French Wars of Religion.

When the author of *The History of the World* came to consider, much
later in life, the demise of the Roman commander Aemilius in the field
against his Punic adversaries, he could not refrain from returning attention
to 'the *English* vertue of the Lord John Talbot' which was 'more highly to
be honoured'.[2] Indeed, if Thomas Nashe is to be believed, the charismatic
appeal of Talbot continued to stir the imaginations of a goodly number of
those who packed the London playhouses. In *Pierce Penniless* (1592), he
enthused

55

How would it haue ioyed braue Talbot (the terror of the French) to thinke
that after he had lyne two hundred yeares in his Tombe, hee should
triumphe againe on the Stage, and haue his bones new embalmed with
the teares of ten thousand spectators at least.[3]

The present discussion reflects upon the ways in which Shakespeare's (and
his collaborators') *Henry VI* plays of the 1590s, plays which seek at the
outset to heroise the martial exploits of Talbot, may be seen to engage more
broadly with lively contemporaneous debates concerning the call to arms,
both past and present.[4] These dramatic narratives unmask the terrifyingly
indiscriminate manner in which brutality pollutes everyday lives and selves
and lays waste to any remains of human dignity to which those locked
within these flux-ridden worlds still aspire. As we have seen, the promotion
of the combatant's trade remained a thorny undertaking in this period. If,
in *The arte of warre* (1591), William Garrard concluded 'a Souldier must be
as well acquainted, and as able to beare continual trauail, as a Bird can
endure to flie, yea and to put on a resolute minde to beare all the miseries
and hazards of warlike affaires',[5] others might share Ralegh's sometimes
doleful accounts of English soldiery witnessed in the previous chapter.
Indeed, the queen's godson, Sir John Harington, noted in his recollections
of the 1599 Irish campaign that the English cavalry was not supported
by 'Roman citizens, but rascal soldiers, who, so their commanders had
been saved, had been worthy to have been half hanged for their rascal
cowardliness'.[6]

The *Henry VI* plays concentrate squarely upon the ways in which
violence not only corrupts all forms of social exchange, but blights the
ethical potential to which the human subject might lay claim. Forsaking
his mourning garb at the opening of *1 Henry VI*, Bedford proclaims,
'Wounds will I lend the French instead of eyes,/To weep their intermissive
miseries' (*VI*: I.i.87–8); and Talbot himself barks at the French, 'Your
hearts I'll stamp out with my horse's heels/And make a quagmire of
your mingled brains' (*VI*: I.iv.107–8). In this anguished dramatic vision
extending over three plays, all human life is remorselessly *made flesh*.
Furthermore, we are urged to attend to the ways in which slaughter (the
politics of control in extremis) comes to monopolise the imaginative
existence and affective allegiances of anyone wishing to secure the power
of command. Indeed, by *3 Henry VI*, this irrepressible appetite to communicate human creativity (in thought, word and deed) with a stunted
vocabulary of blood sports is still very far from being exhausted. Richard
of Gloucester submits, 'Why, I can smile, and murder whiles I smile'

(*VI*³: III.ii.182), and Clifford confides to his victim, the Yorkist child Rutland, 'if I digged up thy forefathers' graves/And hung their rotten coffins up in chains,/It could not slake mine ire, nor ease my heart' (*VI*³: I.iii.27–9).[7]

Shakespeare's dramatised investigations into the power to excite violence run the length of the *Henry VI* plays – plays which may be seen to describe a striking narrative arc from the political demise of one warlord in the shape of Henry V to that, *not of his son*, but of one whom Warwick terms, as the cycle nears its conclusion, 'our quondam queen', Margaret of Anjou (*VI*³: III.iii.153). In these dramatic worlds of collapsing governance, the only means by which to affirm selfhood, to win political recognition and to subjugate others is through the perplexingly creative power to violate, to unpick hitherto prevailing constructs of *vis* and *virtus*. Fully acknowledging these debased conditions of existence (in which he has participated so vigorously), the doomed Suffolk rails before his killers, 'Come, soldiers, show what cruelty ye can,/That this my death may never be forgot!' (*VI*²: IV.i.132–3).

Restoring History to the Nation

At the beginning of *Britannia* (first published in Latin in 1586), William Camden attended to the ways in which his native land had been characterised since antiquity by culturally freighted expectations of excentricity and exceptionalism:

> For between the said Fore-land of *Kent* and *Calais* in *France*, [Britain] so advanceth it selfe, and the sea is so streited, that some thinke the land there was pierced thorow, and received the seas into it, which before-time had been excluded. For the maintenance of which their conceit, they allege both Virgil in that verse of his
> *Et penitus toto divisos orbe Britannos:*
> And Britans people quite disjoin'd from all the world besides.
> Because Britaine, saith Servius Honoratus, was in times past ioyned to the maine. And also Claudian, who in imitation of him wrote thus:
> *Nostra deducta Britannia mundo.*
> Britaine, a land, which severed is from this our [Roman] world.[8]

Whilst recognising the seductive mythologies which had grown up around these Fortunate Isles situated initially beyond the orbit of the *Pax romana*, Camden's scholarly endeavours, as was recognised in the previous chapter, concentrated upon recuperating a more substantial, heroic narrative for his nation with the resources of textual and artefactual memory: 'to restore antiquity to Britaine, and Britain to his antiquity'.[9]

Unsurprisingly, *Britannia* chose not to stress unduly indeterminacies in the fate of a weakling nation, frequently located down the centuries on the edge of continental theatres of power and subject to the predatory desires of foreign potentates. Instead, the invasion of the realm and its introduction into Roman *imperium* are endowed with a markedly salvific status:

> When Fortitude and Fortune were so agreed, or Gods appointment rather had thus decreed, that Rome should subdue all the earth, Caius Julius Caesar, having now by conquests over-run Gaule, to the end, that by a successive traine of victories atchieved both by land and sea, he might joyne those Lands together which nature had severed (as if the Roman world would not suffice) cast an eye unto the Ocean; and in the foure and fiftieth yeare before the incarnation of Christ, endeavoured to make a journey into Britaine.[10]

Even if, on occasions, the historian concedes that the Roman yoke were 'grievous', the reader is reassured that ultimately it proved a 'saving health' for the island: 'for that healthsome light of Iesus Christ shone withall upon the Britans ... and the brightnesse of that most glorious Empire, chased away all savage barbarisme from the Britans minds'.[11] Thus, rather than emphasising geographical or chronological disjunction, Camden's *Britannia* figured forth a developing narrative of political and spiritual election – and his scholarly undertaking was clearly speaking directly to ideas which had gained currency amongst at least some quarters of the population. When the parson George Owen, for example, reviewed the progress of his own Welsh nation in Tudor times, he confessed 'that if our ffathers weare nowe lyvinge they wowld thinke it som straunge countrey inhabited wth a forran nation, so altered is the cuntrey and cuntreymen ... from evill to good, and from good to better'.[12]

Camden's endeavours were profoundly humanist in tenor: he committed his scholarship to bridging the intervening centuries between his own time and that of the Romano-British period, and to responding to the voids in his countrymen's knowledge with the nourishing resources of textual and artefactual memory – which is to say, in this instance, with the resources of narrative plenitude: 'in the studies of Antiquity, (which is alwaies accompanied with dignity, and hath a certaine semblance with eternity) there is a sweet food of the minde well befiting such as are of honest and noble disposition'.[13] In the same period, Shakespeare's history plays similarly reserved particular attention for the rehearsal of the island kingdom's past. However, these plays unearth a specifically fifteenth-century, martial cycle of events for their 1590s audiences in order to disclose the painfully close proximity of its violence and the fragile, nay illusory, nature of lasting political settlement.

By the sixteenth century, generations of humanist scholars had already ensured that, apart from rhetorical performance, one of the most significant ways in which the intellect might fulfil its ethical potential was through the mediation of *historia*.[14] In a tome to which Shakespeare clearly had recourse, Jacques Amyot had advised in his prefatory discussion to the English edition of Plutarch's *Lives of the Noble Grecians and Romans* (1579) that history 'is a certaine rule or instruction, which by examples past, teacheth us to iudge of things present, & to foresee things to come: so as we may knowe what to like of, & what to follow, what to mislike, and what to eschew'.[15] Indeed, in post-Reformation England, the widespread commitment to the reading, writing, translation and commentary of historical texts might contribute all too significantly to addressing a keenly felt cultural void: such accounts might acknowledge a profound desire to venerate that which had hitherto been reserved for the ageless relics, sacred spaces and precious rituals of Catholic Christendom. Yet the indomitable fascination and awe shared by Shakespearean characters (*and* audiences) in the Histories for recessive narratives is inevitably accompanied by a keen and growing realisation on- and offstage of the penetrating experiences of lack, loss and absence in the present.

The *Henry VI* plays evoke with graphic assurance what Camden termed 'that wofull war betweene the houses of Lancaster and Yorke',[16] or, what Locke would coin over a century later as 'the wars of the roses'.[17] They portray King Harry's son as a figure bequeathed absolute political priority. However, the vexed dramatic function which reverts to him is ultimately to articulate his power to suffer and his most flawed humanity, unrelieved by even parental tenderness. His subjectivity is wholly communicated on stage in terms of his remorseless experiences of dispossession and his eagerness to bear witness from the margins of a world which should be shaped by his governance. As such, these plays may indeed be scrutinising a version of what, in more recent times, Giorgio Agamben has termed the cultural paradox of the *homo sacer* – 'who may be killed and yet not sacrificed'.[18] In this instance, Agamben focused upon a juridical conundrum taken from Roman law in *De verborum significatione* by Pompeius Festus: the *homo sacer* is recognised as an 'homo malus atque improbus' (a bad or impure man) who is both invested with a sacral character (thus becoming, 'incompatible with the human world') and yet one whose death will go unpunished. Equally strikingly, the extraordinary status of this figure in Agamben's thesis continues to define those who survive him: thus, perplexingly, in the *homo sacer* 'we are confronted with a residual and irreducible bare life, which must be excluded and exposed to a death that no rite and no sacrifice can redeem'.[19] While Henry VI may not be perceived as wholly *malus atque improbus*, this sovereign is condemned to the unstinting enactment of moral, political and affective failure as the plays unfold. Indeed, he repeatedly unveils for audiences on- and offstage a profound appreciation of his own insufficiency, a rich sensitivity to the staging of his own victimisation and a febrile expectation of his own imminent demise.

Lex Loquens – Speaking and Stifling Sovereignty

Mikhail Bakhtin argued that 'Greatness always makes itself known only to descendents, for whom such a quality is always located in the past (it turns into a distanced image); it has become an object of memory.'[20] The emotionally charged quest for heroic transcendence and the unslakeable appetite for violent political mobility remain key mechanisms for narrative progression throughout the *Henry VI* plays. Paradoxically, the very scaffolding of these plays is both built upon and dismantled by 'That ever living man of memory,/Henry the Fifth' (*VI*: IV.iii.51–2). Beaufort praises the late ruler in markedly extravagant terms as one who stood 'Unto the French, the dreadful judgement-day /... The battles of the Lord of Hosts he fought' (*VI*: I.i.29, 31). Ultimately, the shrouded body of Henry V comes increasingly to act onstage as a most eloquent, if forbidding magistrate for the decaying political fortunes of the Lancastrian dynasty.

For the English camp and, at one remove, for the audience, the spectre of the dead king continues to haunt his son's newly inherited kingdom with its newly empowered warlords: the ceaseless regimes of militarised attrition to which the realm is subjected inevitably engender their own coarsened strains of identity and history. Thus, the hyperbolised memory of Henry V (or Richard II in the second tetralogy) is not only repeatedly awarded cultural priority in the political discourse of subsequent generations, it also offers a key vantage point from which to observe the seemingly apocalyptic fracturing of the commonweal. In this context, Mary Warnock remains timely in her reminder that memory is not purely the retrieving of the past, it is also the knowledge brought about by the past.[21] In the disorderly world of Becoming to which the warring parties of the Yorkists and Lancastrians condemn the nation, memory and violence offer precious hermeneutic modes with which to resist the unremitting experience of marginality and trauma. The determination to think historically, to position (what Bakhtin termed in his account of epic narrative) a foundational or '"absolute past" of gods, demigods and heroes',[22] is in this way linked intimately to the desire not to have subjectivity and social discourse wholly defined by the chaos and carnage of the present. Beaufort affirms that the late Henry V 'was a king blest of the King of Kings' (I.i.28), and his determination to pay fulsome tribute to the dead king is shared by many of the peers who survive to frame – or, rather, unframe – the English court. At this point, dramatic attention is not monopolised by the unharnessed brutality which the state is enduring (both within and without), but concentrates rather on the painful labours of memory for, what Robert C. Jones wittily identified as, the Shakespearean phenomenon of the 'lost leader'.[23]

The corpse of the fallen ruler may represent political rupture and communicate to the selective meditations of those who remain a fanta-sied memory of plenitude. However, in a play such as *1 Henry VI*, it also speaks directly to the insatiable appetite within that society for stainless gods as military commanders – an appetite which exploits energetically the narratives of a radically edited past. When Richard Plantaganet strives to have his noble status restored in the wake of King Harry's death, he reminds his adversaries of the fragility, nay possible erasure, of their own, present political fortunes: 'I'll note you in my book of memory/. . . Look to it well and say you are well warned' (*VI*': II.iv.101, 103). At the opening of *2 Henry VI*, if the beguiled king believes that he has at least secured a strategic advantage in the recent French wars through his alliance with Margaret of Anjou, for his uncle Gloucester the union may be read under quite different terms: it violates England's abiding commitment to national renewal through foreign conquest and, equally disturbingly, indicates that the court is now governed by a particularly self-serving and most destructive political creed. In the event, few onstage are minded to give credit to the lacklustre renewal of King Harry's deeds by his son or to stifle their misgivings over the new king's policies of capitulation and withdrawal. The young Henry is greeted with a profoundly disaffected court on his return to England. Indeed, Gloucester, proposes that, rather than triumphalism, the nation would do well to have recourse to jeremiads.

Thus, if the arrival of this new queen, along with that of the returning native forces, signals a key moment in the dissolution of Henry V's political legacy, it also points to an equally painful realisation that the new king and his aristocratic company have sought refuge in the consolations of amnesia.

Given this state of affairs, Gloucester is unsurprisingly remorseless in his chastising of an already dejected English court:

> O peers of England, shameful is this league,
> Fatal this marriage, cancelling your fame,
> Blotting your names from books of memory, . . .
> Undoing all, as all had never been!   (*VI²*: I.i.95–7, 100)

Gloucester's interventions at this juncture serve to chart for audiences the grave shortcomings of the nation's elite and the most limited capacities of a naïve and unremarkable king who has sought to disguise his own failings with extravagant ceremony – a ploy exploited by a far from negligible number of Shakespearean monarchs. In response to the consequent political haemorrhaging, it takes just a short time for the realm to rupture into warring factions led by the ruthless magnates. Nonetheless, the vigorous recourse to civil violence and adversarial politics makes little difference to the collective investment in retrospection. As the realm begins to groan under the inordinate pressures of Yorkist and Lancastrian ambitions, the resources of memory are seen again and again to offer the promise of some kind of dignity of purpose for or verdict upon the commonplace butchery of the present. In such a dramatic world, the law may be spoken from the throne (*lex loquens*), but it is rarely prosecuted from this seat of power.

The acute sense of cultural strain and disorientation at the beginning of *1 Henry VI* can only be communicated, it seems, in terms of military inertia ('arms avail not now that Henry's dead') and linguistic collapse ('What should I say? His deeds exceed all speech'; *VI²*: I.i.47, 16). As a result, the young and most errant king is compelled to assume an ever expanding range of identities. On his return from the French wars, this beleaguered Lancastrian tries to affirm his sovereignty by unveiling what he believes to be a guarantor of peace and a valuable trophy: Margaret of Anjou. If, with this alliance, Henry seeks to foreclose contentious debate at his court, he is only exploiting a familiar paradigm inherited from his father who returned to the island kingdom with a new spouse, Catherine of Valois, drawn from the ranks of his French adversaries. Nonetheless, even in the later *Henry V*, audiences are not encouraged by any reassurance of lasting political settlement at the hands of a king who mistakes the exporting of war overseas for the exercise of government: 'Is it possible dat I sould love de *ennemi* of France?' (*V*: V.ii.163).

René Girard famously argued that 'le sacrifice est une violence sans risque de vengeance',[24a] and it appears that it is with such sentiments in

---

[a] 'sacrifice is a form of violence with no threat of revenge'.

mind that Henry VI repeatedly enacts the surrender of his royal privilege: 'O that my death would stay these ruthful deeds!' (*VI³*: II.v.95). His reiterated desires are all too often expressed in terms of *otium* or cultural withdrawal – in this instance, culminating in the death wish. More generally, the young king seeks to mediate between the angry heavens and the blood-lusts of his overmighty subjects by affirming the desire to lead 'a private life/... in devotion' (*VI³*: IV.vi.42–3). In *The Letter of Violence*, a wide-ranging enquiry into the nature of cultural trauma, Idelber Avelar stresses that 'The function of pain in the Bible is to provide the *link that ties the subject to belief*.'[25] Yet, in the context of Shakespeare's Histories, the *Henry VI* plays do not ask their audiences to attend to any agonised commitment of faith on Henry's part or to his deliverance from a fallen world. They depict a human environment (uncannily familiar to many subjects of late modernity) where there is diminishing traffic with the sacred and its claims to the authority of retributive violence have devolved to lesser agents.[26] Nevertheless, the narrative function of suffering in the relation of the human condition remains a compelling enquiry, then and now. As Terry Eagleton has underlined, 'suffering is a mightily powerful language to share in common, one in which many diverse life-forms can strike up a dialogue. It is a communality of meaning ... injury, division and antagonism are the currency you share in common ... Sorrow implies value.'[27]

In the case of Shakespeare's plays, the staging of such suffering and pain comes emblematically to represent the bitter experience of failed transcendence. *1 Henry VI* carefully contrasts the motions of cultural withdrawal on the part of the king with those of the champion of his French antagonists who is 'A holy maid .../Which by a vision sent to her from heaven/Ordained is to raise this tedious siege/And drive the English forth the bounds of France' (*VI¹*: I.ii.51–4). The Pucelle, who has been variously construed critically from 'a virtual parody of the Marlovian prototype' to a thinly disguised Morality devil,[28] becomes increasingly implicated in the age's appetite for butchery, even offering to dismember her own body before her English captors save her the trouble. She bargains with her fiends, 'I'll lop a member off and give it you' (*VI¹*: V.iii.14). However, her body is not within her gift: it is repeatedly claimed by others. Even her rejected father protests, 'God knows thou art a collop of my flesh' (*VI¹*: V.iv.18). More generally, these history plays repeatedly problematise the political status and dramatic implications of Henry VI's declared piety and its relations with his subsequent psychic unravelling. In *Richard II* the fallen protagonist histrionically declares he would exchange his 'gorgeous palace for a hermitage' (III.iii.147). In both dramatic environments audiences are urged to consider these desires to withdraw with the utmost seriousness, querying whether they constitute a flawed abdication of political office or a resisting reading of the society's belligerence. Henry VI declares to Warwick and Clarence, 'I make you both Protectors of this land/While I myself will lead a private life/And in devotion spend my latter days,/To sin's rebuke and my Creator's praise' (*VI³*: IV. vi.41–4). Whatever the status of this repeatedly voiced piety, we are left in no doubt that it remains wanting as a political endorsement of the Lancastrian cause or the responsible act of a *pater patriae* to a world grown increasingly expert in the art of killing.

Firmly inscribed within a discourse of reassuring polarities, a specially commissioned 'Psalm and Collect of Thanksgiving' in the year of the Armada thundered that the Spanish 'communed of peace, and prepared for most cruel war; for they think that no faith nor truth is to be kept with us, but that they may feign, dissemble, break promise, swear, and forswear, so they may deceive us and take us unawares, and oppress us suddenly'.[29] As pamphlet literature, chronicles, martyrologies, epic poems and dramas proliferated during the course of the sixteenth century and continued to recuperate tales of blood-letting for newly minted mythologies of the nation, such evocations of unceasing violence also excited new forms of epistemology. They trained attention upon, what Paul Ricoeur has identified more generally in an account of historiography as 'des possibilités oubliées, des potentialités avortées, des tentatives réprimées (une des fonctions de l'histoire à cet égard est de reconduire à ces moments du passé où l'avenir n'était pas encore décidé, où le passé était lui-même un espace d'expérience ouvert sur un horizon d'attente)'.[30a] Thus, in the *Henry VI* plays, the unwieldy energies of rebellion, political factionalism or the wavering rhythms of the king's political and mental collapse need not, as many critical studies infer, be driven by an emphasis upon narrative closure, upon political silencing or dynastic consolidation. Indeed, Shakespeare's renewal of fifteenth-century England for late Elizabethan audiences devotes considerably more stage time to the enactment of froward passions than to the stifling of Cade's insurrection in *2 Henry VI*, to the unruly dynamism of Hotspur than to his destruction in *1 Henry IV*. The repeating structures in the performative play of history may direct attention not to the quelling of sedition, but stimulate a reawakened

---

[a] 'forgotten possibilities, aborted potentialities, repressed endeavours in the supposedly closed past. One of the functions of history in this respect is to lead us back to those moments of the past where the future was not yet decided, where the past was itself a space of experience open to a horizon of expectation.' See Paul Ricoeur, *Time and Narrative*, vol. III, trans. Kathleen Blamey and David Pellauer (Chicago: University of Chicago Press, 1988), p. 227.

consciousness of the multiplying possibilities of access to a most slippery political power. Again and again we are urged to concentrate on how competing political bids may be variously justified and heroised – and how the ever-fragile body politic may envisage and negotiate renewal through the terrifying availability of violence. This certainly proves to be an unexpected and bitter lesson for Henry VI when he seeks to respond to the shrill voices of dissent from his peers: 'Henry the Fourth by conquest got the crown.' York barks back, ''Twas by rebellion against his king' (*VI³*: I.i.132–3). For this same generation of late Elizabethan audiences, Oxford's Professor of Roman Law, Alberico Gentili, had underlined vexingly in *De Iure Belli* (1589), 'if it is doubtful on which side justice is, and if each side aims at justice, neither can be called unjust'.[31]

After the rigours of parleys between Henry VI and York, royal authority cannot be expressed, only ventriloquised with the rhetorical expertise of a Margaret of Anjou or of a court henchman like Clifford. Yet, by the time these latter agents are called upon to promote the cause of the House of Lancaster in *3 Henry VI*, the governance of England has become little more than a spectator sport for the king himself. Terrifyingly, figures such as Margaret and Clifford are able to match their words with deeds, but Henry VI (prefiguring the later Lear) is reduced to mouthing, rather than imparting his sovereignty. In *1 Henry VI*, when he welcomes Richard Plantagenet back to the company of his lords as Duke of York, the fledgling king announces, 'my loving lords, our pleasure is/That Richard be restored to his blood'. However, the seemingly unbiddable court requires the force of Warwick's echoics ('Let Richard be restored to his blood') before the authority of the Crown may be confirmed (*VI¹*: III.i.158–60). By the close of *3 Henry VI* the polity of England is able to support no internal systems of deference or restraint and so Henry's own ill-fated son, Prince Edward, attempts in vain to have the newly instituted Edward IV '[s]peak like a subject': even this youth acknowledges 'I am now my father's mouth' (*VI³*: V.v.17–18). At such moments, audiences may conclude, as Ralegh had advised in the posthumous publication *Instructions to his Sonne and to Posterity* (1632), 'Speaking much, is . . . a kinde of vanitie; for hee that is lavish in words, is a niggard in deeds, and as SALOMON sayth, the heart of a Foole is in his mouth.'[32]

Inheriting the Past

H. M. Richmond contended that 'The very choice of the weak Henry VI rather than the dashing Talbot as the play's pivot is curious . . . it is not a piece of useful political propaganda for the Tudors, like the conventional treatment of Richard III.'[33] Indeed, it might be argued that Henry VI remains incapable of assuming this dramatic function – a function more persuasively performed by the potent memory of his father. When Salisbury is slain in action in France, he is remembered by Talbot not only as one who 'In thirteen battles … o'ercame', but as symbolising a precious link with the heroic legacies of a swiftly receding past: 'Henry the Fifth he first train'd to the wars' (*VI*: I.iv.78–9). Furthermore, it occurs to Henry VI, himself eclipsed in the presence of Talbot, 'I do remember how my father said/A stouter champion never handled sword' (*VI*: III.iv.18–19).

In *Temps et récit*, Paul Ricœur is at pains to stress the wonted motions of the human psyche and how, again and again in our collective dealings, 'Le temps devient temps humain dans la mesure où il est articulé de manière narrative.'[34a] In the *Henry VI* plays, the endlessly renewing *narratio* of an absent patriarch not only calibrates all subsequent forms of political agency in the kingdom, it also exposes how an enduring appetite for violence has come to fashion political discourse itself: 1st serving-man – 'Ay, and the very parings of our nails/Shall pitch a field when we are dead' (*VI*: III.i.102–3). If Paola Pugliatti argues convincingly that 'Among Shakespeare's war leaders, Talbot is the one who most nearly approaches the ideals of knighthood', Alexander Leggatt has concluded more grimly that Talbot is 'a hero in a practical world in which he is first destroyed and then forgotten'.[35] The memories of military commanders such as Henry V, Talbot, Julius Caesar, Old Hamlet and the younger Antony, amongst many others, are often found to haunt Shakespeare's theatrical worlds. Yet, as the historian Rory Rapple has persuasively underlined, encounters with the past might not be limited to the *wooden O*, or even to the leaves of Hall's or Holinshed's chronicles. As was witnessed in the previous chapter, in such publications as Ralegh's, cultural expectations of retrospection (if not regression) frequently characterised early modern productions of non-European worlds. Nonetheless, these were underpinned by deeply historicised expectations of a land much closer to home where English projects of plantation had been in progress since Anglo-Norman times. In *2 Henry VI* Beaufort cautions York that 'The uncivil kerns of Ireland are in arms/And temper clay with blood of Englishmen' (*VI*: III.i.310–11); and,

---

[a] 'time becomes human time to the extent that it is organised after the manner of a narrative'. See Paul Ricoeur, *Time and Narrative*, vol. 1, trans. Kathleen McLaughlin and David Pellauer (Chicago and London: University of Chicago Press, 1984), p. 3.

in turn, Rapple stressed that to the minds of many of the English 'seneschals, constables and captains' located in early modern Ireland, 'the way in which factionalism and theft stalked the land was obviously retrograde, a throwback to an English *status quo ante*, the horrors of the Wars of the Roses'.[36]

Scriptural study among an ever-growing community of readers in post-Reformation England might easily revive the knowledge that kingship had been accorded by Jehovah to nations tainted by spiritual failure:

> But the thing displeased Samuel, when they said, Giue vs a King to iudge vs: and Samuel prayed vnto the Lord. And the Lord said vnto Samuel, Hearken vnto the voyce of the people in all that they say vnto thee: for they haue not reiected thee, but they haue reiected mee, that I should not reigne ouer them. (1 Samuel 8.6–7)

Moreover, the sixteenth century did not lack voices to remind its readers of their moral and devotional shortcomings. The humanist scholar Juan Luis Vives had submitted in *De Tradendis Disciplinis* (1531) that 'it is not to be doubted that our minds are now less powerful than they were before that first transgression. Now, we are more crafty in our wickedness.'[37] A decade later in *The lamentacyon of a Christe[n] agai[n]st the citye of London* (1542), Henry Brinkelow unveiled the Tudor capital in the final years of 'oure most Soueraygne Lorde Kynge Henry the eight' as populated with 'inordinate riche styfnecked Cytezens, [who] will not haue in their howses that lyuely worde of our soules ... but abhorreth and disdayneth all those which wolde lyue according to the Gospell'.[38] Indeed, by the close of the century in John Rainolds' *The overthrow of stage-playes* (1599), the Oxford printer, John Lichfield, might be found complaining that 'th'usual flocking and gadding ... to these Play-Houses and idel places of entercourse ... doth sufficiently discry a farre off of what mettle we are made, and wherein the treasure of our hart consisteth'.[39] In the most fallen world of the *Henry VI* plays, audiences might be repeatedly given to speculate how a political system of monarchical sovereignty (founded scripturally on evidence of decaying faith and human sinfulness amongst God's chosen people) could not return to its flawed origins. These plays chronicle the plight of a realm imploding as human existence reverts to an orgy of blood-letting. Indeed, as Gregory M. Colon Semenza persuasively argues, 'Burgundy's warning that war will become indistinguishable from sport – through a process of emasculation – is merely the most explicit statement of a general concern that runs throughout the entire trilogy. In early modern England it was assumed that sport would turn, or be turned, into war.'[40]

As these plays unfold, solemn exhortations to remember and desperate bids for political ascendency are articulated repeatedly in terms of a blood-lust – the grossest expression of the drive for social mobility in times of political flux. In the closing scenes of *1 Henry VI*, York threatens to 'plague' the French with 'incessant wars' if they do not submit to the demands of the English Crown (*VI¹*: V.iv.154). When we are asked to recall the fields of confused slaughter against what Exeter terms 'the subtle-witted French' (*VI¹*: I.i.25), or those at a more familiar proximity for the London audiences, such as Towton, St. Albans or Tewkesbury, it comes as little surprise that these military crises are being communicated synecdochically onstage as key phases in the dissolution of a failing state. Moreover, at a time when English imperial achievements on the continent are being swiftly consigned to the fastness of memory, Gloucester intones at the heart of the nation's supposed centre of power, the court, 'Is Paris lost? Is Rouen yielded up?' (*VI¹*: I.i.65). As this study indicates, the armed conflicts conjured up in early modern drama repeatedly offer anatomies of the racially and geographically polarised (as well as psychically transformative) discourses of war circulating more widely at the time. Yet, if in *1 Henry VI*, Warwick prophesies that the 'brawl . . ./. . . in the Temple-garden' between Yorkists and Lancastrians 'Shall send, between the red rose and the white,/ A thousand souls to death and deadly night' (*VI¹*: II.iv.124–7), the history plays, more generally, often remain remarkably (and, for some critics, perplexingly) even-handed in their identification of cultural alterity.

In his *liues of the III. Norman Kings of England William the first. William the second. Henrie the first* (1613) Sir John Hayward protested, 'what heart should the Souldiers fight, when they haue not his presence for whom they fight? . . . The presence of the Prince is worth many thousands of ordinarie Souldiers: The ordinary Souldier wil vndertake both labour and danger for no other respects so much, as by the presence of the Prince.'[41] However, in the *Henry VI* plays, the erring king is repeatedly expelled from the proliferating fields of combat and abandoned as a paltry witness to the successive misfortunes of his realm. From this perspective, Henry VI's feverish observation of the battle of Towton ('Now sways it this way, like a mighty sea/. . . Now sways it that way, like the selfsame sea/Forced to retire by fury of the wind' (*VI³*: II.v.5, 7–8)) intimates a telling instance of our own diminishing abilities to ascribe moral probity or justness of cause to either warring party in this *terra nulla* of anarchic England.

More generally, Shakespeare's age, like our own, was thoroughly conversant with the regime of 'incessant wars', and deeply exercised by the triage of multiple conflicts which might warrant the nation's attention.

As was witnessed in the previous chapter, Ralegh warned in 1593 that 'Therbe also others in Irland that lye in waite not suspected, which I most feare ... Wee ar so busyed and dandled in thes French warrs, which ar endless, as wee forgett the defens next the hart.'[42] The staging of endlessly duplicating cycles of armed hostilities in *Henry VI* not only urges onlookers to remember what the nation has been, but also how that past bleeds through into the present human continuum of unremitting carnage.[43] The evocation throughout *Henry VI* Parts 1, 2 and 3 of political diminution and deterritorialisation inevitably leads to the erosion of the expectations and practices of lordship, service and protection, so central to the feudal functioning of the medievalised polity: 'Guyenne, Compiègne, Rheims, Orléans,/Paris, Gisors, Poitiers, are all quite lost' (*VI*: I.i.60–1). In receipt of such constantly updated communications, the English peers are left to contemplate their own incompleteness with a highly charged politicised language of vacating spaces. York laments 'Anjou and Maine are given to the French,/ . . . 'Tis thine they give away and not their own' (*VI²*: I.i.211, 218). Warwick finally perishes with his thoughts wholly devoted to his own dislocation: 'My parks, my walks, my manors that I had./Even now forsake me, and of all my lands/Is nothing left me but my body's length' (*VI³*: V.ii.24–6). At such moments, late Elizabethan audiences might all too easily recall the collective experiences of anxiety and paranoia of a realm which had faced the threat of one Armada and had good reason to suspect that others were in preparation. One John Bonde informed the authorities in London in June 1588 that 'The best gentlemen in Spain cast lots who shall have England.'[44]

Negotiating Violence and Difference

The brutal factionalisation of the commonweal in the *Henry VI* plays can, as we have seen, be expressed in terms of slippery fealties, changeful topographies and unharnessed violence on and off the field of conflict. Nonetheless, in contrast to the dramatic narratives of the second tetralogy, these earlier plays offer sustained analyses also of the adversarial politics surrounding gendered engagement in the *res publica*. In *1 Henry VI*, Suffolk declares in summary fashion of Margaret, 'She's beautiful, and therefore to be woo'd;/She is a woman, therefore to be won' (*VI¹*: V.iii.79–80). Away from the misrule of the battlefield in *2 Henry VI*, Eleanor, Duchess of Gloucester, acknowledges the normative gender codes operating within her society, remarking bitterly, 'Follow I must; I cannot go before' (*VI²*: I.ii.61).

Early modern print culture offered ample evidence of the gender-marked expectations which conventionally informed any discussion of military combat in this period. In *De Iure Belli*, Gentili stressed that 'women, because they cannot handle arms, are treated like the clergy and excluded from feudal relations'[45] – but those who could 'handle arms' inevitably became a source of enduring fascination. Ralegh confessed in the *Discouerie* that he arrived (like his Iberian predecessors) in the New World seeking to reproduce Old World knowledge and to query its myths: he was 'very desirous to vnderstand the trueth of those warlike [Amazons], bicause of some it is beleeued, of others not'.[46] Shakespeare's Talbot is bewildered by the cultural inversions in this new military world where 'A woman clad in armour chaseth men' (*VI*: I.v.3). Moreover, the Pucelle remains adamant that she will 'ne'er fly from a man' in the heat of battle and the Dauphin hails this 'Amazon ... [who fights] with the sword of Deborah' (*VI*: I.ii.103–5). Encounters with what was perceived as culturally deviant excited fierce speculation both on- and offstage in the early modern period, and this fascination is exploited in a systematic manner as the *Henry VI* plays unfold. Indeed, at points, Bedford is left to function onstage as a choric voice, articulating for audiences near and far the perplexing aporia surrounding the *Venus armata* – 'A maid! and be so martial!' (*VI*: II.i.21).

A Yorkist chronicle, published in 1485, but with prefatory material dating from the final months of the reign of Edward IV, perhaps unsurprisingly promoted Henry VI's alliance with Margaret of Anjou as 'a dere mariage for the realme of englond'. The latter had relinquished Anjou and Maine as 'the keye of Normandie for the frenshmen to entre':

> Lo what a mariage was this ... [for] brekyng of this promisse [to the Duke of Armagnac] and for mariage of quene margaret what losse hath the realme of englond had by losing of normandie and guyan by diuision in the realme ... the rebellyng of comunes ayenst ther prince & lordis, what diuision among the lordis, what murdre & sleyng of them.[47]

If the Lancastrian cause was to enjoy renewed impetus with the arrival of Henry Tudor at, what Shakespeare terms in *Cymbeline*, 'blessèd Milford' (III.ii.59) in 1485, the political legacy of the Lancastrian queen does not appear to have enjoyed any significant rehabilitation at the hands of the Tudor chroniclers. In the *last part of the Mirour for Magistrates* (1578), Edmund, Duke of Somerset, stands accused all too convincingly of conspiring upon the life of the regent, Henry VI's uncle, Gloucester, but he himself indicts, 'dame Margaret the Queene,/By whose malice this mischife first began,/Did she (trow yee) her selfe not ouerwene/Death to procure to that most worthy man?'[48] A few years later, John Foxe's *Acts and Monuments* (1583) bewailed 'the vnprofitable and vnhonourable mariage betweene the kyng & Lady Margaret daughter of yᵉ Duke of Angeow'. Here, Margaret was extravagantly demonised as a

> sore enemy and mortall plague ... Who being of haute stomack, and all set vpon glory of wit and wilynes lacking nothing, and perceiuing her husband to be simple of wit, and easy to be ruled, tooke vpon her to rule and gouerne both the king & kingdome ... this manly woman and couragious Queene ceased not by all imaginations and practises possible, to set forwarde [Gloucester's] destruction.[49]

Nina S. Levine's critical study *Women's Matters* (1998) analyses such early modern gender expectations with particular reference to these early 1590s history plays, stressing 'that representations of women in power – whether in the plays themselves, in their chronicle sources, or within Elizabethan society – are shaped not by cultural myths of gender alone but by the intersection of these myths with specific political situations'.[50] However, Levine's subsequent contention that 'In writing women onto history's stage, Shakespeare's plays invited a scepticism about representations of power, both past and present' engages strategically with the broader exposition in the *Henry VI* plays of the very provisional nature of any attempt at conflict resolution.[51]

Both at home and abroad in *1 Henry VI*, audiences (on- and offstage) are repeatedly invited to encounter the alien, the potent force of cultural alterity, in the shape of the symbolic challenges posed to English nationhood by foreign, female agency: the Pucelle of Orleans, the Countess of Auvergne, and England's newly adopted French queen, Margaret of Anjou. Nonetheless, unlike the Pucelle, Margaret maintains her own role of *Venus armata* for the length of Henry's reign and demonstrates that she can thrive when her adopted land begins to test the further limits of its appetite for butchery. Margaret is as profoundly stimulated as any of the male adult members of the political elite by the spectacle of savagery and acknowledges that arresting acts of violence may indeed serve to confirm group allegiances. In *De Ira* Seneca reasoned that his understanding of this most unmasterable humour differed little from that of Aristotle, 'iram esse cupiditatem doloris reponendi'.[a] Yet the Roman philosopher was also at pains to caution his reader that 'Among the various ills to which humanity is prone there is this besides – the darkness that fills the mind, and not so much the necessity of going astray, as the love of straying.'[52][b] The *Henry VI*

---

[a] 'for he says that anger is the desire to repay suffering'. [b] 'sed errorum amor'.

plays address most specifically this pleasure principle, and Margaret continues to stage-manage her entries into this ruthless world of armed combat (from which the distaff sex is more generally barred in the later, second tetralogy) with carefully rehearsed performances. These performances are clearly executed to tempt the palates of audiences (on- and offstage) and we are left querying our own complicity in these compelling narratives of horror – complicity in what the philosopher R. G. Collingwood later termed a particularly tempting strain of 'malice':

> the desire that others, especially those better than ourselves, should suffer, is a perpetual source of pleasure to man … In Shakespeare and his contemporaries, bullying in its most violent form is so common that we can only suppose the average playgoer to have conceived it as the salt of life.[53]

In a dramatic world where the profession of killing appears to be the only means by which political players may distinguish themselves, Henry's queen unsurprisingly refuses to confine blood sports to the battlefield. She reserves the exquisite pleasures of Senecan torment for more intimate encounters with her abject victims:

> … where is your darling, Rutland?
> Look, York: I stained this napkin with the blood
> That valiant Clifford with his rapier's point
> Made issue from the bosom of the boy:
> And if thine eyes can water for his death
> I give thee this to dry thy cheeks withal.   (*VI*[3]: I.iv.78–83)

Baited by his captors, York insists that even 'the hungry cannibals/Would not have touch'd' his boy Rutland (*VI*[3]: I.iv.152–3). Yet he has strategically forgotten that Margaret, like himself, exploits the spectacular power of violence to command attention when she finds herself unable to wield political *auctoritas*. In these dramatic worlds, the persecutor determines to deny victims any form of agency, insisting that they warrant no further response from the surrounding society than the discipline of brutality. Thus, in the context of early modern terrorism, Robert Appelbaum has underlined that 'violence operates not only by destroying or harming, but also by communicating'.[54] Equally solemnly, the jurist Alberico Gentili concluded for his own sixteenth-century readers that

> an expedient cause for making war will be the right of taking vengeance for a wrong which one has suffered. … Now this is a just cause, since our own rights have been interfered with, which we ought not to allow to be infringed. Every one is justified in maintaining his rights. There is

a natural impulse which prompts self-protection and the right to avenge oneself.[55]

As Gail Kern Paster has demonstrated, men's bodies opened and wounded were frequently gender-marked as feminine in the early modern period.[56] In direct comparison with the actions of many of her male counterparts in these plays, Margaret's interventions, here as York's tormentor, are not designed to produce legitimacy or truth. Her words are the verbal counterpart of Clifford's rapier, an instrument of pain, a closing down of York's subjectivity to that of superlative victim, robbed of human status. In her endeavour to divest her prey of any autonomy, she constructs him as culturally illegible in the power games of her caste – and, thus, as violable. Earlier, the bereaved York had argued that women should be 'soft, mild, pitiful and flexible' (*VI³*: I.iv.41), and in this way sought to contain his adversary within language, to reduce her to a controllable stereotype. Nevertheless, the inadequacy of these stratagems soon becomes evident. The beleaguered Duke has failed to recognise that the hitherto inviolable laws of cultural difference have collapsed in the radical disordering of the nation, and that those seeking the very highest social advancement have an irrepressible need to spawn impotent subordinates, to coerce others into being eligible victims. Gentili contended in *De Iure Belli* that 'we are treating the laws of men, and we here follow the ways of men', but vexingly begged the question 'If a woman fights, why should she not allow war to be made upon her?'[57] One of the final acts of revenge of the Yorkists in *3 Henry VI* is to visit epistemic violence upon Margaret of Anjou, to consign her to the past, to stunted forms of political intervention, indeed to the silent limits of language itself. Richard of Gloucester queries, 'Why should she live, to fill the world with words?' (*VI³*: V.v.44).

Maurice Charney argued persuasively that 'Violent scenes in Elizabethan drama have a shock effect that forces us to draw immediate conclusions. Murders on stage, for example, are often used to shift our sympathies toward the victim, even if he [sic] has consistently alienated our sympathies during the play.'[58] Yet, in the *Henry VI* plays, audiences may be swiftly drawn to question the very efficacy of human sympathy itself as a viable response to trauma in a world given over to the gruesome festivities of a moral holiday. With a tenacious investment in normative gender codes, the grieving York unleashes an arresting *vituperatio* directed at the murderous queen, 'How couldst thou drain the life-blood of the child [?]' (*VI³*: I.iv.138) – a *vituperatio* suggestive, perhaps, of the fact that even if the dramatic world has exhausted its capacity for *pathos*, this may not be the case beyond the stage. The father has been publicly unmanned by Margaret's ambition to sound the uttermost depths of his anguish, to annul his future, to stage his own particular Day of Judgement while still in the company of mortals. In these endeavours of the Lancastrians to secure a monopoly of violence, the Yorkists are compelled to reassume their status as irrational political subjects, as amateurs in slaughter, as indulging in specifically private grievances. For the entertainment of the general company, the Queen is now bent on affirming that York has been conclusively (and creatively) eclipsed in his own chosen vocation of killing. As Garrard affirmed in *The arte of warre*, 'Experience of late daies hath taught vs, that those Nations which follow the warres, inuent euerie way how they may endomage the enemie in all their enterprises.'[59]

Earlier, in *The Discourses*, Machiavelli had repeatedly invited his reader to meditate the instrumentality of violence, arguing that although

> many peradventure will think this a matter of evil example, that the ordainer of a civil Government, as was *Romulus,* should first have taken his brother's life from him ... It holds well together, though the act accuse him, that the effect excuse him; and when that is good, as it prov'd to *Romulus,* it will alwaies excuse him; for he that uses violence to waste, is blameable, not he that uses it for redress and order.[60]

Even more grimly in the *Henry VI* plays, the promise of redress and order ever exceeds the grasp. Thus, audiences may be less inclined to award any performance of violence a degree of legitimacy when neither party has earned ethical priority on stage. Both factions are passionately devoted to brutal, partisan courses. If Margaret's zealous attempts to whet the Duke's suffering clearly move some of her fellow combatants (Northumberland – 'hardly can I check my eyes from tears', *VI³*: I.iv.151), it seems that these peers were not alone amongst Elizabethan audiences. Famously, such was the arresting stature of Shakespeare's Margaret and the verbal pyrotechnics of his verse in the early 1590s that Robert Greene was able to parody York's outburst against his tormentor ('O tiger's heart wrapt in a woman's hide!', *VI³*: I.iv.137) in his own invective against the 'upstart' dramatist 'with *his Tygers hart wrapt in a Players hyde*'.[61]

As the *Henry VI* plays succeed one after the other, the war-seasoned, like Margaret of Anjou, York and Warwick, seek out conclusive statements of violence on and off the battlefield to communicate in metaphoric terms the unassailable nature of their grip on power. In the event, it soon becomes evident that their acts are partial, metonymic in nature, denoting episodic supplements in an unending narrative of retaliatory politics. In the brutish world of Shakespeare's Histories, Margaret can secure no more lasting advantage than any of the other players and her political fortunes are irrevocably crippled when her own son, Edward, endures the same fate as York's child, Rutland. The duke's sons stab Prince Edward to death, and so ensure that Margaret does not bring her career at court to a close without being held in subjection by this grisly entertainment.

War and its Mythologies in *Henry VI*

In the final years of the sixteenth century, Henri IV's envoy to Elizabeth's court, André Hurault de Maisse, duly noted in his more general observations of the English court that the queen

> scait toutes les histoires anciennes et ne luy peut on rien dire qu'elle n'en dise quelque mot à propos. Elle me dit que l'on disoit qu'elle n'avoit jamais rien sceu que les livres de Calvin, elle me jura n'en avoir veu aucun, mais qu'elle avoit veu les Pères anciens et y avoit pris grand plaisir d'autant que ces derniers sont pleins de disputes de contentions et les autres n'ont que bonne intention de servir à Dieu et de profficter.[62a]

Whatever the depth of knowledge that Elizabeth had gained of the Church Fathers, it was clear that they were continuing to hold a significant influence over many of the leading intellectuals amongst her subjects, such as Donne, Foxe, Hooker and Ralegh. In the *Confessions*, Augustine famously promoted memory as a key axis along which to plot the formation of subjectivity, declaring, 'It is I who remember, I who am mind . . . Indeed the power of memory is something I do not understand when without it I cannot speak about myself.'[63] Nonetheless, if the English court at the beginning of *1 Henry VI* is notable for its excessive investment in recalling the past to restore a fragile, if diminishing link with an age of human greatness (read, military triumph), audiences quickly become aware that this realm's irrepressible appetite to remember is accompanied by a corresponding loss in cultural momentum. The inability on the part of the English peers to forget, or innovate, can render them hostages to

---

[a] 'She knows all the ancient histories, and one can say nothing to her on which she will not make some apt comment. She told me that it was reported that she had never read anything but the works of Calvin. She swore to me that she had never seen one, but that she had seen the ancient Fathers, and had taken great pleasure in them; all the more because later writers are full of disputes and strivings, and the others have only the good intent of rendering service and profit to God.' See De Maisse, *A Journal of All that was accomplished by Monsieur de Maisse, Ambassador in England from King Henri IV to Queen Elizabeth Anno Domini 1597*, ed. G. B. Harrison and R. A. Jones (London: Nonesuch Press, 1931), p. 59.

outdated information and wholly limited by the contingencies of prior experience. In such a context, we may be reminded, as Jacques Le Goff has argued, that 'Trop privilégier la mémoire c'est s'immerger dans le flot indomptable du temps.'[64a] Indeed, Michel de Montaigne revisited this debate inherited from antiquity on numerous occasions in his *Essais*, and provocatively submitted in 'Des menteurs' that 'il se veoid par expérience ... que les memoires excellentes se joignent volontiers aux jugements debiles'.[65b]

As we have witnessed, recollections of King Harry's sovereignty dominate the beginning of *1 Henry VI*, but they are soon forced to compete for their place against earlier medieval precedents of the exercise of power. At Rouen, Talbot's thoughts are monopolised by the memory that 'in this late-betrayed town/Great Coeur-de-lion's heart was buried' (*VI¹*: III.ii.82–3), whereas in *3 Henry VI*, Oxford is prompted to remind his auditors of 'great John of Gaunt,/Which did subdue the greatest part of Spain' (*VI³*: III.iii.80–1). In Shakespeare's recoveries of a fifteenth-century England, the warlords may mourn the hero of Agincourt, yet they never fail to proffer their own accounts of a profoundly tractable medieval past. Moreover, in a further recessive plane in this intertextual *mise-en-abîme*, we are urged to invest in ever more distant mythologies of belonging. Warwick may become a Ulysses or a Hector (*VI³*: IV.ii.19, IV.viii.25), and Talbot, an 'Alcides', in the company of his son becomes Daedalus supported by his Icarus (*VI¹*: IV.vii.60, IV.vi.54–5). Fleeing the Lancastrian cause, Clarence declares that 'To keep that oath were more impiety/Than Jephthah's, when he sacrificed his daughter', while Richard of Gloucester acknowledges his role as Judas at the heart of Edward IV's court (*VI³*: V.i.93–4, V.vii.33). The very *varietas* of this collective, feverish exploitation of proliferating antiquities unmasks the pervasive cultural quest to secure inviolable political authority by rehearsing its hallowed origins from the earliest records.

Confronted with the triumphing English armies in *1 Henry VI*, Alençon acknowledges that 'Froissart, a countryman of ours, records,/England all Olivers and Rowlands bred', but now they appear on the battlefields as 'none but Samsons and Goliases' (*VI¹*: I.ii.20–30, 33). Elsewhere, the hounded players in the mêlée of England's politics take refuge in

---

[a] 'To privilege memory excessively is to sink into the unconquerable flow of time.' See Jacques Le Goff, *History and Memory* (New York: Columbia University Press, 1992), p. xii.

[b] 'it is commonly seene by experience, that excellent memories do rather accompanie weake judgements'. See 'Of Lyers', in Michel de Montaigne, *Essayes or Morall, Politike and Millitarie Discourses* (London: Melchior Bradwood for Edward Blount and William Barret, 1613), p. 15.

mythologies of heroic origins. In the company of Richard Plantagenet, the dying Mortimer confesses himself 'Nestor-like', held captive by a past of political failure (*VI*: II.v.6). York casts himself as 'Ajax Telamonius' (*VI*: V.i.26), and Suffolk emerges for his enemies as 'ambitious Sulla' (*VI*: III.ii.117, IV.i.84). Margaret heroises herself as Dido (*VI*: III.ii.117), and if the Pucelle's gifts of prophecy, we are told, excel those of 'the nine sibyls of old Rome', she reputedly drives back the English troops 'like Hannibal' (*VI*: I.ii.56, I.v.21) – yet for York this 'ugly wench' appears more like Circe (*VI*: V.iii.34–5). Henry bids farewell to Warwick, celebrating 'my Hector, and my Troy's true hope' (*VI*: IV.viii.25), and styles himself as Daedalus at the end of the play imprisoned by a Minos-like Richard of Gloucester (*VI*: V.vi.21–2).

Jean E. Howard and Phyllis Rackin argue that 'although the early plays tend to demonise female characters, they also record women's power as orators, as warriors, as custodians of dynastic legitimacy. Institutions often depend on the very elements they feel compelled to dismiss or derogate, such as women's labour.'[66] Like the Pucelle and Margaret of Anjou, the Countess of Auvergne seeks to enter the one significant field of cultural intervention for her nation: that of Mars. In this instance, she aims to capture the celebrated warrior Talbot by spectacularly violating her own sacred act of hospitality. In the attempted execution of this daring act, the Countess proclaims she 'shall as famous be by this exploit/As Scythian Tomyris by Cyrus' death' (*VI*: II.iii.5–6). The constant iteration of all these competing narratives of antique heroism bequeathed from the past not only demonstrates the multifarious *exempla* which this dramatic community may deploy in the assertion of its many and various political ambitions, but how remote these heroic agents now appear in the midst of the grubby realities of an ailing state. The extravagant and yet endlessly fracturing allusiveness of the *Henry VI* plays is in many ways symptomatic of the anxiety-ridden investment its subjects have in the past, but also of the desperate urgency with which they seek out some form of political justification for their sordid acts of slaughter and betrayal.

More generally, the most unheroic dramatic worlds of the *Henry VI* plays are obsessively interested in analysing how their communities of persecutors seek to stage-manage the deaths of others. If the dramatic emphasis frequently falls upon how warlords, such as Suffolk, Clifford, York and Warwick, are robbed of any semblance of *dignitas* at their own destruction, Henry VI is singular onstage in his potent desire, repeatedly articulated, to become a fugitive from a hostile reality – a reality which acknowledges both his exceptional office and his exceptional unworthiness to occupy that office. The distinctly materially minded York spurns Henry's commitment to piety as symptomatic of a flawed exercise of power, having earlier condemned his centripetal sovereignty in more profane terms as a 'bookish rule [which] hath pull'd fair England down' (*VI²*: I.i.256). Leggatt argues persuasively that 'the first half of *1 Henry VI*, like the Roman plays, is set in a kingless world'.[67] However, this state of affairs is never remedied. In fact, it is only further aggravated as the plays succeed one another. In the political vacuum generated by the waning authority of this 'easy-melting king' (*VI³*: II.i.171), each of the warring parties comes to express its ambitions through a discourse of *substitution*. In a world unable to nourish lasting hopes of political settlement, there is perhaps inevitably little attention reserved for a commitment to spiritual transcendence. Instead, desire is excited in its inhabitants by the rather more earth-bound, rhetorical possibilities of *ethopoeia* – the redemptive ideal of assuming (or, rather, of violently appropriating) the identity of another extends even to figures beyond the pale of the stage: Talbot declares of Falstolf that he 'Doth but usurp the sacred name of knight' (*VI²*: IV.i.40). Thus, if in *2 Henry VI* the reluctant monarch confesses 'I do long and wish to be a subject', his desires for transformation are widely confirmed by the unruly band of political players who surround him: 'Were I a man, a duke, and next of blood,/I would remove these tedious stumbling-blocks' protests Eleanor, Duchess of Gloucester (*VI²*: IV.ix.6, I.ii.63–4). Subsequently, the cornered Suffolk rails, 'O that I were a god, to shoot forth thunder/Upon these paltry, servile, abject drudges!' (*VI²*: IV.i.104–5). Such extravagant performances of self-drama are facilitated in the plundered realm of a king who eagerly seeks to have himself impersonated by others: 'My lords, what to your wisdoms seemeth best,/Do or undo, as if ourself were here' (*VI²*: III.i.195–6). Indeed, his own followers advise him to 'depart the field:/The queen hath best success when you are absent' (*VI³*: II.ii.73–4). By *3 Henry VI*, 'the easy-melting king like wax' is characterised all too plausibly by his detractors as one who 'slily stole away and left his men' (*VI³*: I.i.3).

After the fainthearted Henry has stripped his own son of his birthright in their favour, Warwick and Clarence unite (albeit provisionally) in defence of the Lancastrian cause and rejoice in their new-found roles as 'Protectors' of the realm. Prefiguring the dramatic crisis occurring in the later *King Lear*, Warwick resolves with Clarence to

> . . . yoke together, like a double shadow
> To Henry's body, and supply his place –

I mean in bearing weight of government,
While he enjoys the honour and his ease   (*VI*³: IV.vi.49–52)

In both of these plays from very different phases of Shakespeare's career, we are asked to ponder the efflorescence of violence in a realm where a king seeks a 'kind nursery' away from the duties of governance and leadership – 'while we/Unburdened crawl toward death' (*King Lear* I.i.122, 38–9). Moreover, in direct comparison with other Shakespearean creations such as Richard II and Hamlet, Henry VI may be seen to warrant our attention most of all for the manner in which he remains acutely receptive to his own supersession. Thus, in many ways, his greatest dramatic achievement becomes the forensic interrogation of his own political displacement and of his impermanent status in the affections of others: 'I know not what to say, my title's weak' (*VI*³: I.i.134).

The Sons and Daughters of Mars

At the dawn of the modern period, Marx evoked the cumulative pressure of historical precedent in *The Eighteenth Brumaire of Louis Bonaparte* (1852) as 'The tradition of all the dead generations weighing like a nightmare upon the brain of the living.'[68] This sense of the foundational weight of the past pressing down upon those who survive is remorselessly figured forth in the *Henry VI* plays. In direct comparison with Old Hamlet, King Harry's principal legacy to surviving generations is that the efficient art of govern-ance is inextricably linked to the profession of violence and that the proliferation of conflict zones abroad may be usefully sought out to exhaust the blood-lust of companies at home.[69] While, in the theatre, audiences are transported back to the deadly contests of the Wars of the Roses, those onstage find themselves compulsively resurrecting the knowledge of earlier medieval divisions to understand the trajectory of their own lives. The English peers constantly urge audiences to look beyond the living memory of Henry V to stress their own superior bloodlines and claims to cultural priority. Somerset, for example, is hastily reminded by Warwick that Plantagenet's 'grandfather was Lionel Duke of Clarence,/Third son to the third Edward King of England' (*VI*¹: II.iv.83–4). Serving a similar cause (read, the legitimation of future violence), Mortimer reminds audi-tors on- and offstage that 'Henry the Fourth, grandfather to this king,/ Deposed his nephew Richard, Edward's son,/The first-begotten and the lawful heir' (*VI*¹: II.v.63). In short, the English camp is deeply exercised by the attempts of its own warring elites to lay claim to the future of the nation through editorial violence enacted on the past. Warlords, like York, Somerset, Clifford and Warwick, remain eager to attend to the exemplars lifted from clan memory and to police rigorously any attempts by rival factions to appropriate national histories for present emergencies.

If Shakespearean history returns attention again and again to the stress-ridden politics of a kingdom wracked by remorseless violence (both epistemic and material), it concentrates equally vigorously upon the exchanges of meaning which may be enacted across wonted principles of cultural difference. Initially, it may seem that the habitual codes of social priority and power transferral are radically scrambled in *1 Henry VI*. Sir William Lucy disdains the terms advanced by the enemy commander: 'Submission, Dauphin! 'tis a mere French word;/We English warriors wot not what it means' (*VI¹*: IV.vii.54–5). The desperation of Lucy's embassy to maintain linguistic distinction feeds into a much larger, feverish dramatic debate concerning what English political subjectivity might be: 'my lords, remember where we are', cautions the Lancastrian monarch: 'In France, amongst a fickle wavering nation' (*VI¹*: IV.i.138–9). Such experiences of hostility and estrangement were certainly uppermost in the mind of Robert, Lord Rich, when he wrote to the Earl of Essex from Rouen in 1596 during the English campaign to assist Henri IV in the French Wars of Religion:

> We are here come into a pestilent country both for soul and body, and full of excellent words and accomplements of courtsey which, together with chopt and larded meat, we are fed withal, reported to be of the King's charge, but the burghers of the town wish all our throats cut and gone, because they fear it must fall to their share to pay for it: and we that are but bad travellers can be content to hasten our retreat as soon as the King's patience will us.[70]

Yet, in the dramatic worlds of *Henry VI*, as we travel through foreign lands and uncharted political crises, the conditions of human existence remain eerily comparable.

The bitter reality occasioned by Henry V's death, that of England's collapsed *imperium* abroad and political insufficiency at home, can only be masked provisionally with fugitive memories of heroic authority – memories such as those revived on the battlefield by Talbot. His very name ('*"A Talbot! a Talbot!" They fly*', VI¹: II.i.78) appears to have a talismanic, apotropaic quality which seeks to keep destruction at bay for the nation. The iteration of the warrior's name not only transforms the signified, but also the signifier, and each political faction competes for a stake in his warrior mythology. Such is the lavish cultural capital associated with Talbot that it may even be renewed, nay ventriloquised, on the lips of a common soldier: 'The cry of "Talbot" serves me for a sword' (*VI¹*: II.i.79). However, as one cycle of the nation's tribulations succeeds the next, the moral or political distinctions that the characters wish to affirm evaporate in this vision of universal carnage. The profoundly changeful environment inhabited by 'Pucelle or puzzel, dolphin or dogfish' (*VI¹*: I.iv.105) is rendered all the more unmasterable in the misrule of battle when the invading forces meet with 'A woman clad in armour [who] chaseth men' – a woman who has herself already claimed 'I exceed my sex' (*VI¹*: I.v.3, I.ii.89).

Crucial to narratives of cultural indiscipline (then and now) is the frightening inability to locate or predict violence – most especially at a time when the relatively formalised arena of the battlefield was (and is) no longer monopolising the wider theatre of conflict. This question of the defendability, or porosity, of any community haunts the first tetralogy as much as it characterises the condition of late modernity. At the opening of *1 Henry VI*, a play which Maurice Morgann dismissed in the eighteenth century as 'that Drum-and-trumpet thing',[71] the ultimately hopeless endeavour to establish some fixity of purpose (and allegiance) at the heart of the English court swiftly buckles as the besiegers are besieged at Orleans, and back across the Channel we move from the vicissitudes of *imperium* to those of most ungoverned *urbs*. Thus, at a moment of acute political crisis for the English nation across the Channel, at the Tower of London the armed companies of Winchester and Gloucester are discovered in violent disorders. Gloucester's retainers thunder, 'Open the gates unto the Lord Protector,/Or we'll burst them open if that you come not quickly' (*VI¹*: I.iii.27–8). At such points, we are urged to question the status and function of these privileged sites of supposed cultural opposition (sieges at Orleans or the city of London) – to question the precise *locus* of the adversarial threat, the very identity of a barbaric Other and, for that matter, the validity of any form of violent intervention.

On Shakespeare's many and various stages, at the Tower of London, in the *mise-en-abîme* of the besiegers besieged at Orleans, beneath the walls of Ang[i]ers in *King John*, or in the initial blood-letting at Corioli in the company of Caius Martius, the hitherto reassuring oppositionality between native/foreign, allegiance/ambition, Self/Other becomes vexed, perplexingly imbricated. We are compelled to engage in interpretative strategies of analogy, rather than difference. In being asked to recall erstwhile enemies in the shape of French forces in *1 Henry VI*, *King John* or *Henry V*, London playhouse audiences were not plunged into the

oppositional politics of war with its familiar discourses of cultural belated-
ness and demonic agency. Instead, in the frenzied exchanges of invective,
the various strains of enmity are evenly weighted and only serve to indicate
that in this dramatic world we are navigating a complex cultural environment subject to terms of troubling similitude. The Bastard of Orleans
thinks Talbot 'a fiend of hell', whereas Talbot himself dismisses the Pucelle
as 'that railing Hecate' (*VI*: II.i.46, III.ii.66).

When, in *2 Henry VI*, York intones for audiences on- and offstage the
meandering genealogies of the royal line of kings with a litany of Edwards,
Richards and Henrys (*VI*: II.ii.), or when in *1 Henry IV* the battlefield of
Shrewsbury spawns seemingly endless versions of the usurper Bolingbroke/
Henry IV with which to bewilder enemy forces, audiences are alerted
forcefully to the very aleatory nature, the sobering reversibility with
which the narrative of history may be configured: 'Another king! They
grow like Hydra's heads', protests Douglas in *1 Henry IV* (*IV*: V.iv.24).
After the slaughter of Clifford in *3 Henry VI*, Warwick instructs Richard of
Gloucester 'From off the gates of York fetch down the head,/Your father's
head, which Clifford placed there;/Instead whereof let this supply the
room' (*VI*: II.vi.52–4). Indeed, similarly trapped within duplicating conditions of existence, Shakespeare's Richard rails at the close of his own
reign: 'I think there be six Richmonds in the field:/Five have I slain today
instead of him' (*Richard III*: V.iv.11–12).

In the English camp, the loss of Henry V is followed by the brutal
sacrifice of Talbot, whose ideals of service no longer bear relevance or
meaning in a world where the resources of government (indeed, self-
government) have been squandered. In the French camp, the Bastard of
Orleans seeks to remedy the 'cheer appalled' of his dispirited confederates
by producing a rival form of legitimacy, one worthy of devotion: 'A holy
maid' who 'by a vision sent to her from heaven,/Ordainèd is to raise this
tedious siege/And drive the English forth the bounds of France' (*VI*:
I.ii.51–4). As we have seen, this desperate (and, clearly, universal) search
for a military saviour excites the meditations and imaginative life of the
combatants much more powerfully than any profession of religious faith or
commitment to the ever-dwindling territory of the realm. Excited by the
spirit of victory which appears to attend on the Pucelle, Charles exclaims,
'Was Mahomet inspirèd with a dove?/Thou with an eagle art inspirèd then'
(I.ii.140–1). However, such references prepare Elizabethan audiences for
the seemingly irrevocable alien-ness, the perceivedly unnatural presence of
this woman who will ultimately be discovered communing with fiends.
France is limned in terms of a growing integrity as it builds allegiances with

such diverse, fickle figures as the Pucelle, the Countess of Auvergne and, eventually, Burgundy. However, the island kingdom, abandoned to a youth, is characterised by a beleaguered hero such as Talbot or, conversely, corrosive forces of self-interest expressed by its warlords. Thus, the dramatic world tilts back and forth precariously in cycles of violence: Dauphin – 'Late did [Mars] shine upon the English side;/Now we are victors; upon us he smiles' (*VI*: I.ii.3–4).

In their vigorous evocation of conflicted nation-building, the *Henry VI* plays constantly remind us that the early modern battlefield remained an arena in which religious professions, territorial acquisitiveness, trading ambitions as well as the defence (and the coveting) of regal power might be regularly set in play. For Elizabeth's own Accession Day festivities of 1595 an oracle was erected and, amongst the verses with which it was inscribed, the onlooker was informed: 'No nation breeds a warmer bloud for warre.' However, directly after, s/he was promptly reassured, 'And yet She calmes them with her Majesty.'[72] The presence of the spirit of Mars amongst England's political elite warranted, it seems, regular comment. Thomas Churchyard looked forward to Essex's arrival in Ireland, 'When MARS shal march, with shining sword in hand.'[73] However, such guardian spirits of war might be fickle, as Essex learned in 1599, and as Shakespeare's Antony discovers when the 'music i'th'air', or the passing of 'the god Hercules', signals the waning of his authority in the Eastern empire (*Antony and Cleopatra*: IV.iii.10, 14).

In *1 Henry VI* the Dauphin proclaims by way of tribute to the victorious Pucelle, 'A statelier pyramid to her I'll rear/Than Rhodope's or Memphis' ever was' (*VI*: I.vi.21–2). Equally anxiously, Walter Benjamin contended four centuries later that 'every image of the past that is not recognised by the present as one of its own concerns threatens to disappear irretrievably'.[74] As this discussion has sought to indicate, the *Henry VI* plays recreate, rather than recount, a highly selective account of the nation's narrative in order to engage specifically with representations of cultural experience which had currency with late-sixteenth-century audiences. If M. M. Reese insisted that the *Henry VI* plays were 'essentially didactic', offering 'a straightforward moralising of the Tudor pattern of history, with only an occasional glimpse of real people and recognisable human predicaments', Robert Ornstein reprised the discussion, insisting more persuasively that the plays' 'concern with the flesh and blood reality of politics and history is contrary to the conceptualistic and allegorical impulse of the Moralities'.[75] On further examination, it may prove that more urgent cultural pressures are shaping these dramatic narratives for a nation which Sidney allegedly believed was 'apt ... to corrupt with peace'.[76]

The longevity of Talbot, his son and Margaret of Anjou on Shakespeare's stage far exceeds that of their historical lives. Talbot never met the Countess of Auvergne, and the siege of Orleans did not coincide historically with the demise of Henry V. Acknowledging the tensions released when we excavate the past, Pierre Nora has identified an attritional relationship between Memory and History in which 'L'histoire est la délégitimation du passé vécu':

> Car notre rapport au passé, tel du moins qu'il se déchiffre à travers les productions historiques les plus significatives, est tout autre que celui qu'on attend d'une mémoire. Non plus une continuité rétrospective, mais la mise en lumière de la discontinuité.[77a]

Nonetheless, it might be argued that such a 'continuité rétrospective' always exceeds our grasp, whether we deal with the grand narratives of revolution and empire or the memorial distillations of our daily lives. Surely, nowhere is this more apparent than in the textual recuperation of the intensely volatile, partisan and fragmented environments of human warfare evoked in the first tetralogy. Henry VI himself declares, 'my state, 'twixt Cade and York distressed,/Like to a ship that, having scaped a tempest,/Is straightway calmed and boarded with a pirate' (*VI*: IV.ix.31–3).

The fine operations of selection, ellipsis, erasure and supplement, to which Shakespearean history is subject, may be found to shadow the arresting practices of acceleration, imposition, enhancement, excision, fragmentation and disjunction all too frequently evident in the narrativisation of the nation. The artfulness, or creative forgetfulness, invested in the narrative editing of Henry VI's reign for the Elizabethan stage allows for a questioning and insistent re-questioning of the political values of *natio, patria, pater* and *gens* which chronicles espoused with such regularity. Shakespeare's Histories exercise a power of intervention in late Elizabethan cultural debates in a highly strategic manner by invoking the civil disorders of the earlier century. Concertina-ing in inventive and provocative ways the narratives inherited from earlier sources, these plays stretch and compress the lives and ambitions of the political players who shape these dramatisations of the national life.

---

[a] 'History is the delegitimation of past experience'; 'Because our relationship with the past, at least such as it is represented in the most important historical narratives, is quite different from that which one expects from a memory. No longer a continuum receding back, but the revelation of discontinuity.'

In his own introductory discussion to Shakespeare's 'play of History', John Turner argued tellingly that 'in all the plays, whatever their genre, the imperfect cadences of their endings serve to create the imperfection of the world that has survived, and help us to articulate the sense of loss by which it may be judged'.[78] It is this relentless narrativisation of cultural dissonance which continues to speak so urgently to twenty-first century audiences. At the heart of the dramatic experience of the *Henry VI* plays lies the interpellation, the problematisation of the spectator: *we* are called into question. Addressing precisely these moral protocols of human exchange, Emmanuel Lévinas contended that 'Le spectateur est acteur. La vision ne se réduit pas à l'accueil du spectacle; simultanément, elle opère au sein du spectacle qu'elle accueille.'[79][a] Such contentions lead irrevocably in his philosophical discourse to an ethical undertaking: 'Je suis en principe responsable ... Autrui nous engage dans une situation où vous êtes obligé sans culpabilité mais votre obligation n'en est pas moindre. C'est en même temps une charge.'[80][b] The crises of interpretation in the *Henry VI* plays are excited by the very congested nature of the vicious acts depicted. Then as now, the harried onlooker all too often finds precious little time or opportunity to articulate resisting readings of what human life might constitute. Instead, in the theatre and beyond, we are condemned to bear witness to conditions of existence which sustain only radically imbalanced power relations and the terrifying availability of violence.

> Yea and it is better to have a tyraunte vnto thy kinge then a shadow, a passive kinge y^t doth nought hiselfe but sofre other to doo with him what they will and to leade him whither they lyst. (William Tyndale, *The Obedience of a Christen Man* (1528))[81]

---

[a] 'The spectator is actor. This vision is not confined to engagement with performance; simultaneously, [the spectator] operates at the heart of the performance with which s/he engages.'
[b] 'I am in principle responsable ... The Other engages us in a situation where you are implicated without any mark of blame, but your implication is no less for that. At the same time it is a commitment.'

CHAPTER 3

In the Realm of the 'unthankful King': Violent Subjects and Subjectivities in the Henry IV Plays

I know the inconstancy of the people of England, how they ever mislike the present government and have their eyes fixed upon that person that is next to succeed; and naturally men be so disposed: *Plures adorant solem orientem quam occidentem.*[1]

Drawing upon a sentiment expressed in Plutarch's *Life of Pompey* that 'more worshipped [is] the Rising, than the Setting Sun', Elizabeth I remained richly sensitive to the changeful allegiances of subjects and the improbable longevity of royal fortunes, as she demonstrated here in 1561 in conversation with the Scottish ambassador, William Maitland, Laird of Letherington.[2] By the final decade of her reign, a similarly minded Archbishop of York railed in *2 Henry IV*, 'O thou fond Many, with what loud applause/Didst thou beat heaven with blessing Bullingbrook,/Before he was what thou wouldst have him be!' (*IV²*: II.iv.295–7). In both instances, auditors were called upon to bear witness not only to a national politics shaped by the flawed exercise of memory, but to the potential for violent sedition among 'the wavering commons' (*Richard II*: II.ii.129) when the organising principles of the polity are affirmed in terms of analogy, rather than those of inviolable cultural privilege.

Elizabeth most famously claimed the identity of the doomed Richard II for herself ('I am Richard II. Know ye not that?'[3]) in 1601 in the aftermath of the Essex Rebellion, recognising that a company of the conspirators had attended a theatrical performance staging the regicide prior to attempting a coup d'état. However, this was only perhaps the most famous in a sequence of pointed comparisons that circulated throughout her reign, focusing upon an ill-fated monarch given to vacillation, vanity and favouritism. As early as 1578 Sir William Knollys had declared himself unwilling to fawn and 'play the partes of King Richard the Second's men'.[4] Keenly attentive to the reversals encountered by claimants to the throne, Shakespeare's irate Henry IV remonstrates with his errant son, 'For all the world/As thou art to this hour was Richard then/When I from France set foot at Ravenspurgh,/And even as I was then is Percy now' (*IV¹*: III. i.93–6). Signalling the anxiety which the counterfeiting of authority continues to generate in this society, Mistress Quickly forcefully reminds Falstaff of the occasion 'when the prince broke thy head for liking his father to a singing-man of Windsor', referring to the historical figure of a cleric from Richard II's chapel who, according to anti-Lancastrian opinion, was reputed to bear a striking resemblance to Bolingbroke himself. 'Canst thou deny it?' exclaims the hostess defiantly (*IV²*: II.i.69–70).

The discussion that follows of Shakespeare's *Henry IV* plays concentrates upon this question of duplicating and duplicitous strategies of sovereignty. We are presented with a monarch who scorns the accounts of the past served up for public consumption by his adversaries, but who is condemned nevertheless to rehearse mentally his implication in the crimes they describe: 'How I came by the crown, O God forgive' (*IV²*: IV.ii.346). Developing the analyses of the *Henry VI* plays pursued in Chapter 2, this discussion also reflects upon the ways in which violence may not only signal cultural decay and ethical failure at a personal and collective level.[5] The practice may offer the disturbing possibility of fostering a community of interest (strategic forms of cooperation, individual empowerment and/ or the maintenance of group identities) in Shakespeare's stage worlds and emerge as a tactical instrument of political authority. In the earlier discussion of the *Henry VI* plays, the dominant trope of their dramatic discourses was identified as *ethopoeia* – impersonation of another – as one character after another vies to assume the guise of the king. Conversely, in the *Henry IV* plays, in the company of yet another politically beleaguered, physically ailing and theatrically marginalised sovereign, we might turn to a related trope to illuminate the dark corners of their intrigues: *idolopoeia*, the impersonation of the dead.

Birthing the Political State

In a characteristic performance of feigned outrage, Falstaff berates the Justice's servant in *2 Henry IV* with the complaint, 'Is there not wars? Is there not employment? Doth not the king lack subjects?' (*IV²*: I.ii.58–9). Less familiar with the arts of skirmish and blockade than he would have his intimates believe, this 'fat-kidneyed rascal' nonetheless points up the constant, indeed commonplace, pressure of 'new broils' on Shakespeare's fifteenth-century England (*IV¹*: II.ii.5, I.i.3). Samuel Johnson found the intervention of Rumour at the beginning of *2 Henry IV* neither 'inelegant' nor 'unpoetical', but despaired that from a dramatic point of view it proved 'wholly useless, since we are told nothing which the first scene does not clearly and naturally discover'.[6] In the event, it might be argued that rather than being insufficiently motivated or dramatically underpowered, Rumour's intervention assists remarkably in the sustained commitment of both *Henry IV* plays to problematise and pluralise the possibilities of access to power and knowledge in this brutal environment. Speculating correctly at the beginning of *2 Henry IV* that 'the big year, swoll'n with some other grief,/Is thought with child by the stern tyrant War', Rumour's role is to unsettle yet further the state's ambition to monopolise violence by scrambling the codes of political expectation in the aftermath of the battle of Shrewsbury: 'To noise abroad' not that a Percy, but 'that Harry Monmouth fell' (*IV²*: Ind. 13–14, 30). In this way, rumour is seen to have the potential to divest speculative knowledge of its provisional status and to endow unwarranted ownership with a recognition of legitimacy.

As an experienced diplomat, the Reformist Hubert Languet remained acutely alert to the appetite of malcontents to invest in misinformation in order to blur the distinctions between knowledge and desire in the minds of the larger populace. He wrote anxiously to Philip Sidney from Vienna on Christmas Eve 1573 that

> At the beginning of the month letters arrived here from Lower Germany, stating that your Queen was dead . . . I hear since from Heidelberg that it is a false report . . . We hear now that the King of Scotland has been poisoned. I should be sorry if it were so, and I hope this too is a fiction.[7]

In the event, the latter would prove to be a genuine account of political change north of the border. However, with the establishment of the Tudor ascendancy and, indeed, subsequently of the Reformation during the reign of Henry VIII, English authorities were determined to suppress, violently if necessary, unwanted memories or desires for political change and to engage energetically in their own tactical versions of political myth-making. Indeed, one of the queen's adopted mottoes was *video et taceo* (I see and I remain silent); and, by the final decades of the sixteenth century, her regime regarded with intense suspicion those who were minded to think historically – and to give voice to their thoughts.[8] As we have seen, Holinshed's *Chronicles* notably fell foul of her censors. The *Second volume* (1586), focusing upon the prickly subject of the 'troblesome estate of Ireland', was at great pains to stress that 'I, as an historian vndertaking in this treatise, rather plainelie to declare what was doone, than rashlie to inquire why it should be doone: purpose, by God his assistance, to accomplish, as neere as I can, my dutie in the one, leauing the other to the friuolous deciding of busie heads.'[9] The bolder Ralegh would submit in his later *History* that 'if there be any, that finding themselves spotted like the Tigers of old time, shal find fault with mee for painting them over anew, they shall therein accuse themselves justly, and me falsly'.[10]

Strategic manoeuvres to deflect attention from thorny questions of analogy and reversibility in the accounts of kingdoms are equally expertly figured forth in the transactions executed by the Lancastrian regime in the *Henry IV* plays. Here, rebels may promote themselves as legitimate leaders, service and defence of customary right may be rendered treasonous, and the claims of Richard II's acknowledged heir, Mortimer, are consistently elided by the newly minted *powers that be*. As Yves-Alain Michaud persuasively underlined, whether it be in somatic or epistemic terms, 'toute violence a un effet de contrôle'.[11a] While initially producing a theatrical language of febrile oppositionality, the cultural divisions insisted upon in the *Henry IV* plays may ultimately exceed our grasp in a manner not experienced in other Shakespearean history plays, such as *Richard III* or *Henry V*. The repeated and vigorous recourse to contest and arms in the realm of one whom Hotspur terms 'this ingrate and canker'd Bullingbrook' (*IV*[1]: I.iii.135) clearly offers a broad textual canvas for scrutinising the nature of moral and social dysfunction within the kingdom. Nonetheless, if the insatiable commitment to violence serves to rupture the organisation and ambitions of the fledgling nation, it also progressively subverts the persuasiveness of any claim to authority made onstage.

Shakespeare's *Henry IV* plays interrogate the state's accounts of a founding violence, but they equally deftly query the Benjaminian distinction between 'law-making or law-preserving' hostilities – in this instance, in the development of the polity of a prematurely ageing and morally unremarkable monarch. The condemned rebel Worcester complains bitterly of the overweening Bolingbroke as 'that ungentle gull, the cuckoo's bird,/ [who] ... Grew by our feeding to so great a bulk/That even our love durst not come near your sight/For fear of swallowing' (*IV*[1]: V.i.60, 62–4). Indeed, in such a world, as Arendt later went on to explain for twentieth-century audiences, the disempowered may resort to a stunted lexicon of violence as a desperate remedy for their own blighted hopes.[12] In the precarious environment of *2 Henry IV*, armed force is deployed to respond to a palpable failure of patronage and of government (personal and political) as perceived by those subjects, like the Archbishop of York, who 'are

---

[a] 'all violence results in a form of control'.

denied access unto [the] person' of the king – and, thus, his privileged resources of lordship (*IV²*: IV.i.78).

'O, I do not like that paying back, 'tis a double labour'

In 1884, the critic Albert S. G. Canning affirmed that 'the chief hero' of *1 Henry IV* was Hotspur.[13] If, in the preceding centuries, audiences seem to have embraced Falstaff more robustly as the focus of theatrical attention, more recent scholars and theatre directors tend to concentrate with greater frequency on the disquieting ambiguities in Shakespeare's portrayal of Hal whose promise 'hereafter . . . [to]/Be more' himself is constantly called into question (*IV¹*: III.ii.92–3). Few critics or productions have been willing to accord theatrical or narrative precedence to Bolingbroke himself.[14] In the anonymous play *The Famous Victories of Henry the fifth* (1586–7? pub. 1598) Henry IV enjoys at times a good measure of royal vigour ('Ah Harry Harry, now thrice accursed Harry' – B2ʳ), even if he is never afforded sustained dramatic interest in the rather truncated playtext which has survived. However, Shakespeare's Henry is perceived from the very outset in terms of insufficiency – 'So shaken as we are, so wan with care' (*IV¹*: I.i.1). This newly instituted king becomes significant throughout both *Henry IV* plays mostly for his reactive policies of governance and his growing dependency on others. Unlike the irresistible *forza del destino* which he embodied in *Richard II* ('In God's name, I'll ascend the regal throne' – *Richard II* IV.i.114), in these later dramatic narratives Bolingbroke is not notably impressive for either the exercise of his leadership or his military prowess. Equally perplexingly, his affective life, when in evidence, has collapsed into public demonstrations of wrath or belated torments of guilt. Rather than having redeemed the nation from the turmoils endured under Richard II, Bolingbroke is placed repeatedly at the very heart of a manifestly unruly realm once again convulsed by power struggles – struggles which, in part at least, he has clearly engendered: 'I hate the murderer, love him murdered./ . . . my soul is full of woe/That blood should sprinkle me to make me grow' (*Richard II*: V.vi.40, 45–6).

In justly celebrated studies of early modern power relations, Alan Bray highlighted that 'The household was the classic form of patriarchy' and, nearly two decades earlier, the cultural historian Lawrence Stone specified that the 'sixteenth-century aristocratic family was patrilinear, primogenitural, and patriarchal'.[15] Yet the dramatic narrative of *1 Henry IV* is particularly exercised not only by egregious examples of familial misgovernment, but by the perceived need for the counterfeiting of kinship/

kingship and the uncomfortable pressing of urgent questions concerning personal obligation and premature inheritance. Offering key insights into the political scaffolding of the nation groaning under the immense pressure of contrary forces, Bolingbroke, Northumberland and Falstaff all fail to operate as effective *patres familias*, as instruments of restraint upon others or themselves. Furthermore, their families (adoptive in the case of Falstaff) invariably prove to be dynamic arenas of resistance and subterfuge, rather than potent sites of social conditioning. The court, the Percy household and the tavern are shaped by competing statements of cultural affiliation (in terms of rank, inheritance and/or locale), and so little, if any, time is dedicated to a mythology of belonging which might ordinarily be associated with the family nexus. Harry Berger Jr. has highlighted that 'The paternal project entails the reduction of the son's difference, his otherness, to assure . . . the genealogical continuity of the paternal archetype.'[16] In the *Henry IV* plays, the king's relations with his offspring are unsurprisingly afforded most dramatic attention, and yet are frequently communicated onstage in terms of anxious surveillance and painful regret: 'O that it could be proved/That some night-tripping fairy had exchanged/In cradle-clothes our children where they lay,/And called mine Percy, his Plantagenet!' (*IV¹*: I.i.85–8). If, in other Shakespearean plays, individuals may be publicly adopted as children and/or heirs, as is the case for Julius Caesar and Octavius, Duncan and Cumberland, or Claudius and a most unwilling Hamlet, in the history plays such crisis-ridden decisions or aspirations are most commonly effected in relation to the theatre of war.

In *The Famous Victories*, Henry acknowledges, 'I see it bootes me not to take/any phisick, for all the Phisitians in the world cannot cure/me, no not one' (C3ᵛ). However, more generally, throughout the history plays, the remorseless emphasis upon national and individual subjection and/or violation is limned symbolically in terms of the wasting of bodies, both on and off the battlefield. Indeed, in both of the *Henry IV* plays, the incremental account of figures such as Northumberland, Falstaff and Henry succumbing to the onset of physical and political debilitation operates synecdochically to communicate the miscarrying of the nation. The Duke feigns an illness that masks a failure of humanity. Hal recognises Falstaff's craven nature most often in terms of unfitness to inhabit his rank or profession. In *2 Henry IV*, the ailing sovereign submits in mind and flesh to a destiny marred by faltering ambitions and flawed oaths: 'you perceive the body of our kingdom/How foul it is, what rank diseases grow' (*IV²*: III. i.37–8). Freud argued in *Civilization and its Discontents* that 'We are threatened with suffering from three directions: from our own body, which is doomed to decay and dissolution and which cannot even do without pain and anxiety as warning signals; from the external world, which may rage against us with overwhelming and merciless forces of destruction; and finally from our relations to other men.'[17] In Shakespeare's history plays, the failure of the body to resist the corrosive forces of time is carefully dissected as audiences are asked to ponder human decay in terms of political dissolution.

At the beginning of *1 Henry IV*, we are introduced to a king beset ('shaken ... so wan with care' (*IV*[1]: I.i.1)) and, in this way, he joins the ranks of a host of ailing Shakespearean patriarchs presiding over the vicissitudes of their social orders, such as Edward IV in *Richard III*, the French King in *All's Well That Ends Well* and, of course, Lear. If Henry IV (like his adversaries) avails himself of the physic of armed hostilities, Shakespeare ensures we remain mindful that he cannot ultimately impose a moral discipline upon others which he has failed to observe in his own transactions with the Crown. John F. Danby concluded grimly that 'Every good in *Henry IV* is a damaged good.'[18] If Paul Ricoeur has proposed that 'The relation of historians to the past is first of all that of an unpaid debt in which they represent us all, we the readers of their works',[19] the *Henry IV* plays construct a narrative in which the newly instituted Lancastrian ascendancy is resolutely committed to evading these very questions of historical indebtedness, to masking its own origins of power, to editing the passage of time and, ultimately, to affirming legitimacy through the spectacle of military might. Moreover, painful memories of the changeful ownership of the Crown did not fail to exercise the subjects of Elizabeth herself – and from the very beginning of her reign, as was witnessed in Chapter 2. In a petition of 28th January 1563, the Commons reminded Elizabeth, 'In what miserable case . . . was this your realm itself when the title of the crown was tossed in question between two royal houses of Lancaster and York.'[20] Evidence of the mounting disaffection amongst some of the Crown's servants might easily be identified as Elizabeth's reign progressed. The Sidneys, for example, had distinguished themselves in royal service to successive sixteenth-century monarchs, both in the discharge of offices of political governance in Wales and in Ireland and in more personal court duties undertaken by Lady Sidney for the young Elizabeth. However, as Blair Worden highlights, such was the parlous financial state of the family under the final Tudor monarch that Henry Sidney 'was obliged to decline a peerage, "in consideration", his wife said, of the family's "inability to maintain a higher title than they now possess"'.[21] In the next generation, an exasperated Philip Sidney wrote to his father-in-law Sir Francis Walsingham in the year of his death, 1586, acknowledging 'how apt the Queen is to interpret every thing to my disadvantage'.[22] The Sidneys were not alone in feeling ill served and ill rewarded by their sovereign. The wonted parsimony of Elizabeth's patronage inevitably did little to endear her to a growing community of petitioners, high- and low-ranking. The dramatist John Lyly wrote to his 'most gratious and dread Soveraigne' in 1598 complaining, 'Thirteen yeares, yor: Highnes Servant; Butt; yett nothinge, Twenty ffrindes, that though they say, they wilbee sure, I ffinde them, sure to slowe, A thowsand hopes, butt all, noethinge; A hundred promises, butt yett noethinge.'[23]

Unwilling to widen access to elevated rank or, particularly in the 1590s, to have the charismatic Essex strengthen yet further his relations of lordship with her gentry, Elizabeth expressly forbade him to knight followers for their military prowess in the field in either the French or Irish campaigns of the 1590s when he was appointed to positions of command. As usual, Essex appears to have paid little heed. However, Burghley remained at great pains to remind him of the gravity of his misdemeanours during the campaign to assist Henri IV's cause in France, writing 'Your Lordship so liberal bestowing of knighthoods is here commonly evil censured, and when Her Ma^{ty} shall know it, which yet she doth not, I fear she will be highly offended.'[24] Years later, Elizabeth's godson, Sir John Harington, came to court and found the queen quite able to give vent to her wrath, berating him as one who had accepted honours at the earl's hand during the Irish campaign. He subsequently related in his correspondence that 'it is an ill hour for seeing the Queen ... In good soothe I feard her Majestie more than the Rebel Tyrone and wishd I had never received my Lorde of Essex's honor of knighthood.'[25] As the reign had worn on, cultural discontent and factional strife meant that expectations of patronage and obligation were increasingly articulated and frequently thwarted. Thus, the dissenting voices of malcontents were heard from one disaffected generation to the next. Philip Sidney's brother, Robert, wrote despairingly to Essex in a letter of 1591, 'When my brother and my uncles died, all their offices great and small were given away from me. Since that time I have not left to continue doing her Majesty service, and if nothing will light upon me, I must think either I deserve very ill or have very ill luck.'[26] In the same year Essex himself was unsuccessful in his ambition to be appointed as Chancellor to Oxford University, and did not fail once again to assume the familiar role of a most choleric peer, complaining 'comfort me nott for the Queens wrong and her unkindness is too great'.[27]

Equally importantly, early modern print culture not only invested in spectacular accounts of royal ingratitude in genres such as historiography and prose romance, it also gave voice to more specific instances of the strategic royal exercise of an *ars oblivionis*. In the preamble to *A breefe discourse, concerning the force and effect of all manuall weapons of fire* (1592), Humfrey Barwick attested that he

> was promised by the King of Spaine to haue a pencion of 200 crownes by yeere to be paide vnto me in England for my seruice doone vnto him at St. Quintins, but before I could come from whence I was prisoner, his Queen was dead, and hee againe married to the French Kinges Daughter, and at my return from my troubles in Fraunce, I was answered that the King was gone who did promise the said pencion, and the Queene was dead, wherefore the promise was not to be perfourmed.[28]

Thus, in the final decade of Elizabeth's reign the *Henry IV* plays might be seen to engage most eloquently with the vicissitudes accompanying the rule of one, whom Hotspur terms strategically 'forgetful' (*IV*¹: I.iii.159).

'May this be wash'd in Lethe, and forgotten?'

Lest there be any doubt in the minds of the audience, half-way through 2 *Henry IV* the anxiety-ridden monarch reminds us in a now celebrated manner that 'Uneasy lies the head that wears a crown' (*IV*²: III.i.31). Indeed, repeatedly throughout both of Shakespeare's *Henry IV* plays, audiences are urged to respond to the newly invested king by mirroring his own sense of suspicion and unease. Henry's crisis-ridden rise to power and subsequent flawed governance have insufficiently claimed the loyalties of his newly acquired realm, and this was a state of affairs with which English subjects in the later sixteenth century might find themselves intimately acquainted. The antagonism provoked in certain quarters by: the compromises of Elizabeth's religious settlement; a proposed marriage with a Catholic nobleman of the French royal house; her excommunication by the Pope; the subsequent intrigues among her Catholic subjects; the surreptitious arrival of priests on her shores; the execution of Mary, Queen of Scots; the threatened invasions by the Spanish Empire; and her childlessness and unceasing equivocations concerning the succession – all might, and often *did*, constitute ongoing sources of public anxiety, disenchantment and foreboding across the length and breadth of her realm. If the *Henry IV* plays never underestimate the violation which an assault upon the Crown represented or the profound disquiet generated by the threat of 'broils' in the state, it is perhaps often neglected that they never question the veracity of the rebels' claims that the king has been most 'forgetful' in his favour and patronage. Conversely, these texts also repeatedly query the rebels' own motivations and modi operandi.

The early modern historian Michael J. Braddick has justly highlighted that 'political power is distinctive in being territorially based, functionally limited and backed by the threat of legitimate physical force'.[29] The new king Henry IV seeks to enforce this very power with a good measure of artful amnesia, violating obligations rooted in the past and responding to present emergencies by claiming the trophies of the Scottish campaign led by the Percies. Yet, as E. A. Rauchut, amongst others, forcefully stressed, 'According to the law of arms, Henry IV can order Hotspur to turn over only those prisoners of noble blood, which in this case includes Mordake, Earl of Fife. The rest belong to Hotspur, who has the right to refuse even the king's demand for them.'[30] Shakespeare's regicide king distinguishes himself at the beginning of *1 Henry IV* by occluding, rather than promoting, the customary law of arms and, in the process, triggers a vigorous dramatic enquiry into the functions of and liaisons between violence and royal authority in the political life of the nation. Later, at the opening of *2 Henry IV*, Henry is discovered still complaining, 'were these inward wars once out of hand,/We would, dear lords, unto the Holy Land' (*IV²*: III.i.106–7). Nonetheless, the Lancastrian court (like that presided over by Richard II) is dramatised principally in reactive terms, mostly called upon to bear witness to the dynamic military achievements of elite subjects elsewhere. Unable to transport the hostilities of war away from native shores and handicapped by an heir who continues to privilege his own personal ambitions, Henry becomes dramatically significant for his political and dramatic dependency. The cherished desire on the part of the king to empty the nation of the competing ambitions of its men-at-arms by shunting them overseas will unexpectedly come to be his chief legacy to the dynasty he has founded – 'my Harry,/Be it thy course to busy giddy minds/ With foreign quarrels' (*IV²*: III.ii.340–2). In *The Prince*, Machiavelli advocated that 'a prince should have no other object, nor any other thought, nor take anything else as his art but that of war and its orders and discipline; for that is the only art which is of concern to one who commands'.[31] The Lancastrian successors to Richard II remain keenly alert to this political directive – indeed, so alert that they can conceive of no other mode with which to communicate their sovereignty. Given that the nation's government is thus reduced to crisis management and military hostilities, it remains unremarkable that rebellious spirits, such as Hotspur, do violence to their oaths of allegiance and become inveigled in the prevailing courtly discourse of equivocation: 'My liege, I did deny no prisoners./ . . . Answered neglectingly I know not what' (*IV*: I.iii.28, 52). Vacillation and mendacity become the only means to express political agency away from the battle-field in the newly instituted state of an 'unthankful King' (*IV*: I.iii.134).

The 'gallant Hotspur' is determined to privilege a prior, warrior iden-tity, quite independent of the Lancastrian court world, by exploiting his widely reported and triumphant encounter with 'brave Archibald,/That ever-valiant and approvèd Scot' and the Scottish forces at Holmedon (*IV*: I.i.52–4). In the opening scene of *1 Henry IV*, Henry, like the later Lear, rehearses a superlative test of the allegiances of those upon whom he clearly depends: in this earlier play, the king seeks to eclipse the grand narrative of royal service promulgated by his most choleric subject with an equally spectacular demand for definitive submission – the yielding of hostages. The ensuing dramatic struggle inevitably fixes our attention as the extrava-gantly irascible Hotspur competes in the court and on the battlefield for favoured status with a beleaguered king who has hitherto failed to temper his own kin, let alone the larger realm under his protection. Drawn in potentially contrary motions by responses of sympathy and judgement, audiences may ironically take counsel from a king who remains acutely responsive to the martial exemplarity of others. Henry is compelled to acknowledge the arresting truth of Westmoreland's claim that the victory at Holmedon is 'In faith . . . a conquest for a prince to boast of' (*IV*: i.I.76). As a consequence, the harried monarch must deflect attention from both Mortimer, Richard's acknowledged heir, and Hotspur by demonising them as traitors. Nonetheless, these manoeuvres still leave ample time for audiences on- and offstage to contemplate the inferior nature of Henry's bloodline and his own unlooked-for accession to the throne.

In opposition to his father, Falstaff and Hotspur, Hal is notable in the opening phases of *1 Henry IV* in seeking to establish the parameters of his own cultural intervention – by aping delinquency (rather than madness, as in the case of Hamlet), and by keeping his own counsel. Yet, ultimately, even the prince must submit to the judgement of arms and participate in the unwarranted forms of social exchange that the theatre of war has engendered in the nation. The remorseless accounts of civil disorders that both of Shakespeare's plays chronicle lead to a sustained dramatic investigation into the ways and means by which political hegemony may express itself. The *Henry IV* plays transport us into feudalised societies in which service, most particularly military service, would operate customar-ily as a guarantor of social mobility, civil protection and economic privil-ege. Furthermore, as Cynthia Marshall has persuasively argued, such strains of subjectivity, communicated in terms of suit and service, continued to shape the construction of public selves throughout the early modern period: 'acts of submission to one's social superiors, to political authorities, and ultimately to God'.[32] The *Henry IV* plays describe a collapse in these normative systems of cultural service designed to lead to public recognition. However, they also interrogate in a thoroughgoing manner the customary status, functions and responsibilities of the sovereign in these social relationships of fealty and patronage, together with those of his heir, whom Hotspur terms 'that same sword-and-buckler Prince of Wales' (*IV*: I.iii.227).

Richard II had opened with an acrimonious contest between Bolingbroke and Mowbray that concluded theatrically with a royal judgement involving dispossession and exile: 'Draw near,/And list what with our council we have done' (*Richard II*: I.iii.123–4). At Gaultree Forest in *2 Henry IV*, the Lancastrians are reminded that the lately instituted king had promised and failed to repeal Mowbray's banishment – and so all has 'since miscarried under Bullingbrook' (*IV²*: IV.i.129). Sigurd Burkhardt argued importantly that 'we always misread Shakespeare if our reading compels us to make light of cruelty and treachery – especially where these are not condemned and in some manner disowned in the play itself. More shocking even than Gaultree itself is the fact that it is accepted almost without comment.'[33] At the lists in Coventry in *Richard II*, the ever histrionic Plantagenet king had moved to support the Lancastrian peer: 'We will descend and fold him in our arms./Cousin of Hereford ... Farewell, my blood' (*Richard II*: I.iii.54–5, 57). Later in the play, Richard will be made to descend much further as he abandons his crown in the 'base court' at Flint Castle to his 'Cousin of Hereford': 'Down, down, I come, like glist'ring Phaëton' (*Richard II*: III.iii.178). As the ageing Henry IV becomes increasingly politically and morally tormented by his identity as regicide, audiences are reminded that he is not distinguished for his memorial prowess at court or on the battlefield. Despite the repeated attempts of the disaffected to tutor their political masters (Worcester: 'And yet I must remember you, my lord' – *IV²*: V.i.32), the king remains a notable exemplar in his realm for the dishonouring oaths and deeds: as Hotspur eloquently submits, 'well we know the King/Knows at what time to promise, when to pay' (*IV²*: IV.iii.52–3). A few years earlier, marshalling together instances of social and moral malpractice in his review of the profession of arms in *De Iure Belli* (1589), Alberico Gentili had promoted the conventional wisdom that 'everyone is obliged to defend his country and not to injure his sovereign'. However, he offered the timely reminder for those of all ranks that 'the vice of ingratitude includes every evil'.[34]

In a manner most influential for millenia to come, Aristotle specified in *The Nichomachean Ethics* that magnanimity (*megalopsuchia*, greatness of mind or soul) might be seen as the touchstone of the just ruler: he should possess a *magnus animus* as well as being capable of *magnum facere*. In the sixteenth century, Spenser was notably mindful of this intellectual legacy, as he stressed to Ralegh in a letter concerning the artistic undertaking of *The Faerie Queene*: 'So in the person of Prince Arthure I sette forth magnificence in particular, which vertue, for that (according to Aristotle and the rest) it is the perfection of all the rest, and conteineth in it them all.'[35] Elsewhere, arguing for a renewal of this concept under specifically martial terms, the Captain in Robert Barret's *The theorike and practike of moderne warres* (1598) insists that 'Military valour, is to be vnderstood with vs, as true Magnanimitie with the Latinists.'[36] In Shakespeare's *Henry V*, Fluellen endorses this sentiment with his wonted catachretical excesses. He praises Exeter as one who is as 'magnanimous as Agamemnon' in that, as prescribed by ancient writers, he 'keeps the pridge most valiantly with excellent discipline' (*V*: III.vii.5–10). Nevertheless, in the *Henry IV* plays, there is a remarkable dearth of Aristotelian eulogies of the liberality, wisdom or fair dealing conventionally associated with magnanimity where the new dynasty is considered. Instead of a king uniting his nation, fostering its well-being and dispensing judicious governance, we discover a painfully restive figure who is spawning resisting agents the length and breadth of his land – a figure who has more in common than he cares to admit publicly with his rebellious antagonists.

In *The mansion of magnanimitie* (1599), Richard Crompton reminded his readers in a timely manner that 'we must chiefly beware, namely of sedition, rebellion, and diuision amongst our selues, for out of doubt there is no greater mischief or inconuenience that can happen to a kingdome, then ciuill discord'.[37] Despite his intermittent evocations of future, alternative identities to be secured in heroic, reassuringly distant battlefields in the Holy Lands, Shakespeare's Henry IV is unable to free himself mentally or discursively from the thrall of 'short-winded accents of new broils' (*IV*: I.i.3). Similarly, the Tudor nation had to endure a succession of monarchs exercised by the prospect or threat of combat. James Raymond underlines that 'Following his accession to the throne, Henry [VIII] quickly established his desire to . . . re-open the Hundred Years War.'[38] Indeed, even in his twilight years the ageing, but tenacious king had commissioned the battle-seasoned Sir Thomas Audley to compose the *Booke of Orders for the Warre both by Sea and Land* for his heir, Prince Edward.[39] Other Tudor monarchs tended to be much more chary in giving support to military campaigns. Paul E. J. Hammer stresses that 'The bitter experiences of the 1540s and 1550s help to explain why Elizabeth saw foreign wars so differently from her father. . . . Where Henry sought "glory" to augment power, she therefore focused upon the "cost" of war and feared its potential to undermine her power.'[40] In the later, Jacobean period, Francis Bacon summoned up the image of the queen's grandfather, Henry VII, as a monarch strangely reminiscent of Shakespeare's own Henry IV, wasted by a remorseless attritional regime of armed hostilities and the consequent descent into profound morbidity:

> This excess of his had at that time many glosses & Interpretations. Some thought the continuall Rebellions wherewith he had been vexed, had made him grow to hate his People: . . . some suspected he had some high designe vpon forein Partes. . . . his Liberalitie, was rather vpon his owne state and memory, then vpon the deserts of others. . . . He was a Prince, sad, serious, and full of thoughtes, and secret obseruations: . . . *For his* Pleasures*, there is no Newes of them.* . . . *Certaine it is, that the perpetuall* Troubles *of his* Fortunes . . . *could not haue beene without some greate* Defects*, and mayne* Errours *in his* Nature, Customes, *and* Proceedings.[41]

As we have seen, early modern England might claim some acquaintance with political disaffection and failing royal patronage. However, in contrast to the customary practices of the Tudor sovereigns and to the many and varied dramatic evocations of conflict-ridden societies in the Shakespeare canon, the *Henry IV* plays offer no more varied strain of government from the king's lips than that of armed conflict – both present and future. From this perspective, rather than subverting his father's regime, the erring Hal, as we shall explore in Chapter 4, remains most instrumental in reaffirming its defining characteristic. In spite of his deeply flawed exercise of power, Richard II's legitimate claim to the throne, his fondness for ceremony and his exquisitely nuanced responses to his own victimisation all served to distinguish him in Shakespeare's narrative as a most singular dramatic and political entity: 'We were not born to sue, but to command' (*Richard II*: I.i.196). In the *Henry IV* plays, if we are left in no doubt of the self-interest of the elite malcontents who populate this fifteenth-century realm – subjects who always show themselves most willing to promote, nay to fetishise, their noble status and political service through performances of retrospection and armed combat – we are never presented with a convincing political hierarchy in which Bolingbroke *inevitably* assumes command. Henry participates fully and fluently in this dysfunctional society wholly animated by cycles of violent recrimination and unending militarisation. Indeed, the king's mind is powerfully stimulated by the prospect of violence: 'No more the thirsty entrance of this soil/Shall daub her lips with her own children's blood' (*IV*: I.i.5–6). Whether it be at court, in the elite household, on the Welsh marches or in the tavern, we are transported to loci where male dominion is held up for fierce scrutiny and, in each case, the commitment to war is portrayed as a questionable apprenticeship for service to the *res publica*.

In *De Iure Belli*, Gentili postulated for his late Elizabethan readers that 'We often read of counterfeit arms, counterfeit dress, and false standards'[42] – and such concerns are amply realised in the *Henry IV* plays. Indeed, in the *ballo in maschera* of the battle of Shrewsbury, it is not only Sir Walter Blunt who assumes a royal disguise. Hotspur exclaims that 'The king hath many marching in his coats' (*IV*: V.iii.25). Douglas threatens to 'murder all his wardrobe', but is quickly exasperated by the conjurings being practised in the clash of arms where he discovers yet 'Another king! they grow like Hydra's heads' (*IV*: V.iii.27; V.iv.24). In the context of this discussion, Huston Diehl remains illuminating in her emphasis that individuated acts of stage violence in the early modern playhouse promote 'the Renaissance aesthetic aim of expressing "much in little" – *multo in parvum*'.[43] Bolingbroke seeks to pass himself off militarily and politically as a substitute for the cousin he has had murdered; and the *Henry IV* plays are brought to a close with Hal anticipating (a little too vividly) the demise of his father and an opportunity to pilfer a crown – an act which he had formerly declined in the Gad's Hill robbery. Indeed, the marked facility with which Hal participates in this thieving fraternity at Eastcheap and its trafficking of crowns and bands of gold ('a seal-ring of my grandfather's', *IV*: III.iii.83) places audiences in increasing difficulties as we attempt to identify the precise nature of the prince's ethical constitution. Suddenly resuming acquaintance with a kindred spirit, the testy Falstaff exclaims, 'You confess then, you picked my pocket?' Unfalteringly, Hal replies, 'It appears so by the story' (*IV*: III.iii.139–40).

In the final phases of *1 Henry IV*, Henry disregards the rebels' complaints, declaring that 'never yet did insurrection want/Such water-colours to impaint his cause' (*IV*: V.i.79–80). In this way, the king seeks to disrupt the legitimacy of the parley by subjugating – indeed, alienating – the rebels through language. However, if Henry trivialises, or transforms, through ridicule the particular political *Other* symbolised by the Percies and their allies, the larger dramatic narrative continues more generally to interrogate the feasibility of such principles of difference in this playworld. It has become a truism of scholarship concerning the early modern history play that one of the dominant undertakings of the genre is to scrutinise the passage of human time, but not necessarily the triumphal progress of human time. Nonetheless, of interest here with reference to the exigencies of political performance in the life of the kingdom is a broader contention made by the sociologist Jean Piaget that 'the reconstruction of an irreversible succession of events presupposes a reversibility of thought'.[44] More recently, working a similar vein, Berber Bevernage has queried the notion that 'History . . . works with what has happened and now is irretrievably gone', stressing that such a 'discourse of jurisdiction assumes a *reversible* time in which the crime is, as it were, still wholly present and able to be reversed, annulled, or compensated by the correct sentence and punishment'.[45] I would argue that Shakespeare's *Henry IV* plays anticipate and invest in expectations and judgements, implicating audiences fully in their dramatic struggles and exciting speculation upon questions of reversibility and erasure. These plays insist upon such mental agility on the part of the audience. They do this by enabling the audience to disengage easily from the discursive control of the stage's ruling elite and to assent to the narrative's repeated invitations to keep company with the very agents that the Lancastrian powers wish to suppress from public record.

'We must all to the wars'

As we have seen, throughout the 1590s Shakespeare committed his history plays to a carefully orchestrated examination of the motivations, desires and performances surrounding misgovernment and the waging of war. These plays operate as a broad narrative lens through which to analyse social transactions of power, individual relations of force and tactics deployed to secure political hegemony. The *Henry IV* plays mark a movement from a finely nuanced dissection of 'inward wars' (*IV²*: II. i.106), of 'the intestine shock/And furious close of civil butchery' (*IV¹*: I. i.12–13), to the proposed relocation of military hostilities beyond the nation's shores. This movement from centripetal to centrifugal theatres of war not only accentuates the Lancastrian need for diversionary tactics to safeguard its sovereignty, the dream to redeem Jerusalem from Saracen hands also points to Henry's desperation to forge a legitimacy for his regime. He does this by bearing Christian witness in accordance with the desires of a Church Militant ('under whose blessèd cross/We are impressed and engaged to fight' – *IV¹*: I.i.20–1) and by drawing upon the symbolic authority and integrity of the medieval community of Christendom ('We would, dear lords, unto the Holy Land' – *IV²*: II.i.107). From the new king's perspective, such exploits far from English shores might indeed go a good way to expiate the sin of regicide that lies so heavily upon his soul. However, the heir apparent, Hal, appears in no mood for the moment to staunch the flow of blood in his native land. Indeed, the continuing slaughter assists the prince's own ambitions to stage his political and moral reformation 'on Percy's head': 'I will wear a garment all of blood,/ And stain my favours in a bloody mask,/Which, washed away, shall scour my shame with it' (*IV¹*: III.ii.132, 135–7).

In this context, we might be reminded of Michel de Certeau's more general contention that 'Il y a une *inquiétante familiarité* de ce passé qu'un occupant a chassé (ou crû chasser) pour s'approprier sa place. La mort hante le vif. Il re-mord (morsure secrète et répétée)'.[46a] Similarly, in the *Henry IV* plays, audiences can only anticipate with great difficulty narratives of political regrowth owing to the nation's unending regimes of violence. Instead, anxieties persist that the hitherto spectral past will definitively re-establish its conditions of existence:

> HENRY IV   God knows, my son,
> By what by-paths and indirect crooked ways
> I met this crown, and I myself know well
> How troublesome it sat upon my head.   (*IV²*: IV.ii.311–14)

The prospect and waging of war are carefully shown to construct the everyday selves of both the high- and low-born in many of Shakespeare's dramatic worlds. In the later Shakespearean collaboration *Pericles, Prince of Tyre*, for example, Bolt the Brothel servant enquires 'What would you have me do? Go to the wars, would you, where a man may serve seven years for the loss of a leg and have not money enough in the end to buy him a wooden one?' (*Pericles*: IV.v.173–6). In the *Henry IV* plays, Falstaff's own departure for the wars is preceded by a stint as recruiting officer in the shires. This was a profession (unlike that of being called to the Church or the Bar) for which society offered no sustained formal training, save on the battlefield itself – a locale to which Falstaff is repeatedly shown to give a wide berth. Mark Fissel points out that the Elizabethan military campaigns in Ireland were often conducted with '[u]ntrained and ill-equipped men, disembarked in a hostile environment that claimed more casualties than the locals' hit-and-run tactics, were rendered unserviceable rapidly, necessitating another hasty press'.[47] As we have seen, early modern print

---

[a] 'There is an "uncanniness" about this past that a present occupant has expelled (or thinks it has) in an effort to take its place. The dead haunt the living. The past: it "re-bites" (it is a secret and repeated biting).' See Michel de Certeau, *Heterologies: Discourse on the Other*, trans. Brian Massumi (Minneapolis: University of Minnesota Press, 1986), p. 3.

culture in many ways sought to respond to this marked absence of a formative environment for men-at-arms by issuing an impressive array of essays, chronicles, manuals and translations devoted to the business of soldiery. In the banned *Certain Discourses* (1590), Sir John Smythe reaffirmed the familiar knowledge '[that it was] verie well knowne in all shires by experience' that the preparations and execution of wars drew into their ranks 'malefactors and base minded people, [who] neuer had any desire, nor will to go into anie warres and actions Militarie, but haue hidden and absented themselues away during the times of musters and leuies, and when the same haue been past, they haue againe followed their vile occupations of robbing, pilfering and stealing'.[48]

Given this truth *universally acknowledged*, early modern writers remained eager to stress the discipline of body and mind and the precise exploitation of spaces of conflict required for securing military success. In *The arte of warre* (1591), William Garrard insisted that the true captain 'should possesse and bée indued with a noble mind'.[49] Earlier, in *The defence of militarie profession* (1579), Geffrey Gates had similarly reviewed all the ranks of those in military service, and concluded that he who 'hateth couetousnes, robbery, theft, extortion, brawlinges, striffe, murther, fornication, idlenesse and dronkenesse, that man is worthie and fit to be a Soldier'.[50] Yet Shakespeare's history plays showcase volatile political cultures in which even the military commanders themselves might have some considerable ground to make up in the estimation of Garrard and Gates. In *Richard II* Mowbray (like Cassius in *Julius Caesar*) is accused of pocketing funds earmarked for the levying of military forces: 'Mowbray hath received eight thousand nobles/In name of lendings for your highness' soldiers,/The which he hath detained for lewd employments' (I.i.88–90). In the later *Henry IV* plays, Falstaff remains a notable, but by no means solitary, example of delinquency.

In 1600, Thomas Wilson concluded that those who 'went to the warres' might be summed up as 'the common people ... of the basest and most unexperienced sort'.[51] However, he was only echoing the judgement of his sovereign who had protested in the early 1590s to Henri IV's emissary, André Hurault de Maisse, that the unbiddable English soldiers in France (notably, those under the command of Essex) 'were but thieves and ought to hang'.[52] It was perhaps unsurprising in certain instances that some of those bearing arms were indeed thieves, given that the Crown was not averse to recruiting from their number. The authorities had given orders regarding the siege of Le Havre in 1562, for example, for Newgate prison to be emptied to replenish the ranks of the nation's forces; and new troops were drubbed up in the same way in 1585 for military campaigns in the Low

Countries.[53] Such imaginative practices of recruitment were not halted even on the Sabbath. John Hale highlighted that in 1596 the 'aldermen of London posted guards on church doors during the Easter communion ... until they had persuaded enough men in the congregation to make up a force of 1000' for service in France.[54] Moreover, by the twilight of Elizabeth's reign in May 1602, Philip Gawdy, the younger son of Norfolk gentry, wrote home from London that 'All the playe howses wer besett in one daye and very many pressed from thence, so that in all ther ar pressed ffowre thowsand besydes fyve hundred voluntaryes, and all for flaunders.'[55]

Some two decades later, Thomas Barnes in his *Vox Belli, or, An Alarvm to Warre* (1626) decided to approve what had been viewed under Elizabeth as measures of military expediency, arguing with moral solemnity that

> it is as lawfull a thing to presse the bad, for Military service in times of warre, as to employ the good; yea, in the ordinary service of common souldiers, I doubt not it may stand as well with true piety, as State-policy, to spend the worst first ... Warre in itself is a punishment for sinne. As it comes from our lusts, so it comes for our lusts.[56]

Elsewhere, in *The arte of warre* (1591), Garrard was eager to stress the necessary rigour of the military life, insisting that 'a souldier must presume and perswade himselfe, that whatsoeuer he doth in secrete, that it shall come to the knowledge of the Captaine, whether it be good or euill'.[57] Nonetheless, only the year before, a royal proclamation from Richmond Palace had acknowledged that

> there have been of long time many gross and manifest frauds and deceits daily practiced and committed by captains and officers in the ordinary views and musters of their bands in service under her majesty's pay, who, led with an inordinate desire for gain and preferring their profit before their honest reputation and duties toward her majesty's services, have and do often present at the musters many persons borrowed and hired for one day's pay to serve for the time ... and thereby likewise their several companies are continued weak and defective, not only to the prejudice of her majesty's service but to their own particular shame and discredit.[58]

In *1 Henry IV*, as the Lancastrian forces prepare to do battle with the Percies and their allies, Hal resolves, while his tavern father slumbers, 'I'll procure this fat rogue a charge of foot' (*IV*: II.iv.457). At such junctures we may be alert to the fact that Falstaff more than matches his social superiors in their fondness for equivocating responses and their prosecution of self-interest: 'I would it had been of horse. Where shall I find one that can steal well? O for a fine thief, of the age of two-and-twenty or thereabouts!' (*IV¹*: III.iii.155–7). In this context, Derek Cohen is timely in his reminder that 'We need to remain aware . . . that Falstaff's world is a product, perhaps a deliberate product, of the culture and politics of the Henrys; their lawlessness, violence, and killing are roughly crammed into the confines of the legitimacy which they determine.'[59]

The subsequent business in *2 Henry IV* of pressing for the Crown's armies, Falstaff's recruiting strategies in the company of Mouldy, Shadow, Wart, Feeble and Bullcalf, have been afforded much critical attention down the centuries. This dramatic evocation of non-courtly, non-metropolitan life supplements strategically our existing acquaintance with Henry's subjects and clearly constitutes yet another valuable line of vision with which to scrutinise the power mechanisms of a decayed state. Bardolph confides to the recruiting officer that 'I have three pound to free Mouldy and Bullcalf' from this new levy of manpower. In the event, Falstaff is only too willing to accept the bribes available and to challenge any dissenting voices with an effortless display of histrionics: 'Will you tell me, Master Shallow, how to choose a man? Care I for the limb, the thews, the stature, bulk, and big assemblance of a man! Give me the spirit, Master Shallow' (*IV²*: III.ii.200-1, 211–13). The new conscripts thus promptly become 'good enough to toss, food for powder, food for Powder, they'll fill a pit as well as better. Tush, man, mortal men, mortal men' (*IV²*: IV.ii.54–6). However, locked increasingly within a comic subplot and bereft of the company of Hal in *2 Henry IV*, the tavern father recognises (like a number of other fathers in Shakespeare's dramatic narrative) that he has peddled some markedly extravagant fictions in the desire to wipe his misdemeanours from the record. Like the *malade imaginaire* Northumberland (who certainly contributes to the loss of his son) and the more convincing invalid Bolingbroke, Falstaff comes to acknowledge and be haunted by his own subterfuges. Already in *1 Henry IV* the knight is finding it increasingly difficult to conceal the nature of his errant ways, even from his own rather stunted conscience: 'If I be not ashamed of my soldiers, I am a soused gurnet. I have misused the King's press damnably. . . . And now my whole charge consists of . . . slaves as ragged as Lazarus in the painted cloth, where the glutton's dogs licked his sores' (*HIV¹*: IV.ii.11–23). The petty brigandry for which Falstaff has such a taste turns out to be in many ways little more than the staging of political life in Henry's realm writ small. Most arrestingly, at Shrewsbury, 'this huge hill of flesh' (*IV¹*: II.iv.202) tenders a convincing demonstration of *idolopoeia* as he loses himself provisionally amongst the fields of the dead.

Sovereignty and Its Pleasure Principles

In a momentous reversal of its opening scene, *1 Henry IV* concludes with Hal empowering his brother, John of Lancaster, to deliver the rebel hostage Douglas, 'Up to his pleasure, ransomless and free' (*IV^1*: V.v.28). The royal party which had coveted the Percies' prisoners of war now seeks to liberate them in a most public performance of magnanimous *sprezzatura*: 'His valours shown upon our crests today/Hath taught us how to cherish such high deeds,/Even in the bosom of our adversaries' (*IV^1*: V.v.29–31). Nonetheless, it should be underlined that this theatrical process of diastole and systole, of political *agon* and release, has been in operation throughout Shakespeare's dramatic narrative from the beginning. It has frequently governed the formation of everyday selves both at court and beyond, and excites thorny questions of whether agents, such as Falstaff, who have refused in the past to participate in the Lancastrian project, should be demonised – politically or dramatically.

In his discussion of the *Henry IV* plays, Samuel Johnson affirmed that 'Men only become friends by community of pleasures', and, developing this idea at the beginning of the modern period, Freud offered the influential postulate in *Civilization and its Discontents* of an attritional relationship between the pleasure principle and 'a threatening "outside", not-self'.[60] However, it is widely evident from early modern print culture that such concerns were not alien to the sixteenth century. Like many of his fellow writers of military publications, Garrard was remorseless in his insistence that 'Souldiers should be prohibited from ouermuch libertie, neither to vse whoorehunting, drunkennes, common swearing, quarelling, feighting, cosining, or such like, but that spéedie correction is to be vsed.'[61] Falstaff, as knight *most errant*, recruiting officer and Father of the (Ale-) House, would appear to pay little heed to such directives. The Eastcheap patriarch, as Hal recognises, is a most resisting reader of time and its discipline: 'What a devil hast thou to do with the time of the day? Unless hours were cups of sack, and minutes capons' (*IV^1*: I.ii.5–6). In the tavern world there is time enough to encounter and indulge in any number of pleasures and imaginative lives: 'thou didst swear to me then, as I was washing thy wound, to marry me and make me my lady thy wife' (*IV^2*: II. i.70–2). Nonetheless, Falstaff constitutes one of Shakespeare's most important dramatic devices for interrogating the cultural implications of ethical deviance and political dissent – that is to say, the implications of how we may anticipate and negotiate violence and subversion. For Jean E. Howard and Phyllis Rackin, such subversion is specifically gendered, and the Boar's Head emerges as 'a feminized theatrical space' dominated by a womaniser who is 'characterized in feminine terms'.[62] More generally, however, the tavern reveals itself as a *locus* governed, like the court that it apes, by personal and political introspection. If, from a dramatic perspective, its adoptive patriarch Falstaff may be seen to function primarily as a subject in dereliction of his manifold duties, he also provides traction (as he himself acknowledges) for movement in others' journeys towards self-knowledge: 'I am not only witty in myself, but the cause that wit is in other men' (*IV*: I.ii.6–7).

In this complex counterpointing of *urbs* and *suburbs*, Derek Cohen poses a timely challenge that 'Every critic accepts that the king is as corrupt at least as Falstaff, yet it is habitual to praise Hal for choosing the King's power over Falstaff's because, presumably, critics like most people prefer what they call "responsible government".'[63] Given the remarkable lapses in self-restraint and accountability on the part of Bolingbroke and his heir, audiences may indeed savour the irony that Falstaff, presiding over the tavern counter-culture, appeals to Hal 'let men say we be men of good government, being governed as the sea is, by our noble and chaste mistress the moon, under whose countenance we steal' (*IV*: I.ii.22–4). Both Bolingbroke and Falstaff are increasingly held in check by the knowledge of their own mortality and (like Elizabeth I at the beginning of this discussion) the provisionality of their claims upon the affections and loyalties of others. Indeed, such meditations are in evidence from the very earliest scenes of *1 Henry IV*:

> FALSTAFF   An old lord
> of the Council rated me the other day in the street about you, sir, but
> I marked him not, and yet he talked very wisely, but I regarded him not,
> and yet he talked wisely – and in the street too. (*IV*: I.ii.66–9)

More generally, 'Sir John Paunch' may wish to sentimentalise the operations of the tavern society, to mask its unheroic doings with appeals to idealised versions of what the tavern-dwellers might be: 'for we that take purses go by the moon and the seven stars . . . [we] are squires of the night's body be called thieves of the day's beauty. Let us be Diana's foresters, gentlemen of the shade, minions of the moon' (*IV*: I.ii.10-1, 19–22). Nonetheless, this highly protean, endlessly mulitiplying patriarch ('Monsieur Remorse', 'Sir John Sack, and Sugar Jack', 'sanguine coward', 'bed-presser', 'horseback-breaker', 'gross fat man', 'the hulk Sir John' – *IV*: I.ii.91–2, II.iv.201-2, 426, I.i.19[64]) is as haunted as many of the grandees at the Lancastrian court by the prospect of his own demise: 'but, I prithee,

sweet wag, shall there be gallows standing in England when thou art king?'
(I.ii.46–7).

In this context, we might be reminded of Richard Knolles' 1606 English
translation *The six bookes of a common-weale* (after Jean Bodin's *Les Six
Livres de la République* written in 1576) where Bodin was given to contem-
plating all kinds of radical, but strangely familiar forms of social mobility
and professions of violence:

> Not for that it is impossible to make a good Prince of a robber, or a good
> King of a rouer: yea, such a pirat there hath beene, who hath better deserued
> to be called a King, than many of them which haue carried the regall scepters
> and diadems, who haue no true or probable excuse of the robberies and
> cruelties which they cause their subiects to endure.[65]

The markedly friable nature of human relations described by Bodin feeds
an equally compelling enquiry in Shakespeare's *Henry IV* plays into how to
negotiate cultural discontinuity, the scrambling of the social hierarchy,
occasioned at all levels from the throne to the barstool, it seems, by an
acquiring taste. Samuel Johnson remained convinced that 'with all his
power of exciting mirth [Falstaff] has nothing in him that can be
esteemed'.[66] It might be added that modern theatre productions of these
plays have often pressed their audiences with increasing urgency to query
whether any object of esteem may be identified from amongst the number
dramatised onstage. Equally interestingly, in considering the expectations
of hedonistic riot surrounding *1 Henry IV*, W. H. Auden was given to
speculate 'what Falstaff is doing in this play at all':

> At the end of *Richard II*, we were told that the Heir Apparent has taken up
> with a dissolute crew . . . Surely, one would expect to see [Hal] surrounded
> by daring, rather sinister, juvenile delinquents and beautiful gold-digging
> whores. But whom do we meet in the Boar's Head? A fat, cowardly tosspot,
> old enough to be his father, two down-at-heel hangers-on, a slatternly
> Hostess and one whore, who is not in her earliest youth either; all of them
> seedy, and, by any worldly standards, including those of the criminal classes,
> all of them failures. Surely, one thinks, an Heir Apparent, sowing his wild
> oats, could have picked himself a more exciting crew than that.[67]

Auden is certainly persuasive in his contention that rather than being
thrust into a Jonsonian or Middletonian lair of vice, we are greeted by
a rather sorry vision of wayward ambitions and ill-completed selves: 'Now,
Hal, what time of day is it, lad?' (*IV^x*: I.ii.1). We are in the company of the
'fat-witted' who live 'out of all order, out of all compass', rather than
witnessing the sharp practices of expert criminals (*IV^x*: I.i.2, III.iii.15).

Nonetheless, as C. L. Barber famously argued, Shakespeare 'dramatizes not only holiday but also the need for holiday and the need to limit holiday',[68] and all the history plays scrutinise how the pursuit and conflict-ridden regulation of pleasure and self-interest invariably have nefarious effects upon the potential for human achievement and self-governance.

Indeed, we might be given to question the possibility of Hal's immaculate passage through this environment. R. J. Dorius, for example, argued that the prince 'is one of the few protagonists in Shakespeare outside the comedies who succeeds without much suffering';[69] and *1 Henry IV* is clearly at some pains to offer Hal opportunities to give evidence of his moral probity: 'Who, I? Rob? I, a thief? Not I, by my faith' (*IV*: I.ii.112). In stark contrast to the prince in *The Famous Victories* who requests 'But tell me sirs, thinke you not that it was a villainous part of me to rob my fathers Receiuers?' (A2^r), Hal takes counsel from no one – yet he remains most thoroughly acquainted with the grubbier needs and desires of others. The prince's exploits in *The Famous Victories* are dismissed out of hand by his auditor, Ned, as 'but a tricke of youth', yet the prince in that play does find himself in prison because of his antics with 'a very disordred companie'. The latter play includes 'a bloodie fray' in the streets of London, and the forces of the Sheriff and the Mayor are needed to restore order. Even in Shakespeare's *1 Henry IV*, there are some awkward questions to field. Admittedly, Hal confirms, by way of conclusion to the Gadshill escapade, that 'The money shall be paid back again/with advantage' (*IV*: II.iv.458–9). However, he asks Poins in the later *2 Henry IV*, when in receipt of the news of his ailing father, 'What wouldst thou think of me, if I should weep?' The reply is 'I would think thee a most princely hypocrite', because the prince has 'been so lewd and so much engraffed to Falstaff' (*IV*: II. ii.40–1, 46–7). In the posthumous publication *Instructions to his Sonne and to Posterity* (1632), Ralegh advised that 'There is nothing more becoming a wise man then to make choice of Friends; for by them thou shalt bee judged what thou art.'[70] Hal remains keenly aware of the incompatibility of his tavern and court selves, audiences perhaps less so.

In order to transition from one locale to another the prince believes that he must distance himself from what Johnson would later describe as the 'community of pleasures'. Yet it becomes increasingly evident in both *Henry IV* plays that the tavern and the court are thoroughly acquainted with each other's survivalist values and share many of the same ambitions for self-aggrandisement and deceit. Thus, Hal's apprenticeship in Eastcheap offers a valuable education in the requisite strategies for the domination of others. Barnabe Rich affirmed that 'generally it is seene, where pleasure is preferred so excessively, and the people followe it so inordinately, that they lye and wallowe in it so carelessly, they commonlie end with it most miserablyʼ.[71] No stranger to the pleasures of temptation and attention-seeking, Hal may be found indulging himself as trickster, clown, recalcitrant subject and belated warrior in the fulfilment of his ambitions. From this perspective, Falstaff constitutes an extension *ad absurdum* of his young confederateʼs idle delights. Both men exploit others for their own needs on more than one occasion. Indeed, when Mistress Quickly witnesses the departure of her principal debtor to the wars, she recognises that Falstaff remains ʻan infinitive thingʼ in her accounts. Both prince and knight are determined, to varying degrees, to mend their fortunes with soldier identities, and both are fully aware that they injure others in bringing their own objectives to fruition: ʻhe hath eaten me out of house and home, he hath put all my substance into that fat belly of his; but I will have some of it out again, or I will ride thee a-nights like the mareʼ (*IV2*: II.i.56–8). In addition, both men are quickly shamed by any memorial account that those close to them choose to prosecute. Henry protests ʻWhy, Harry, do I tell thee of my foes,/Which art my nearʼst and dearest enemy?ʼ (*IV¹*: III.ii.122–3). The counter-culture which they have hitherto embraced means, as Herbert and Judith Weil point out, that ʻFalstaff joyfully plays the Morality role of the Vice or "Iniquity", but other functions of the Vice, tempting, mocking, and entertaining, seem to be shared out more equally between Falstaff and the Prince himself.ʼ[72] The ambitions of each man complement those of the other. Falstaff seeks a patron for his tavern of misrule; Hal seeks camouflage and, finally, a scapegoat for his tactically errant selves. Thus, the prince provisionally indulges his corpulent tavern father (ʻO, my sweet beef, I must still be good angel to thee – the money is paid back againʼ – *IV¹*: III.iii.147–8), and the Lord Chief Justice confirms to the wayward knight ʻYou follow the young prince up and down, like his ill angelʼ (*IV²*: I.ii.130).

The transformative potential of the battlefield empowers Hotspur to challenge in a most public manner the flawed mores of a neglectful royal family. As was discussed in the Introduction, Hannah Arendt pointed out that violence ʻcan serve to dramatize grievances and bring them to public attentionʼ at a time when other forms of political expression may appear unavailable.[73] In asserting his determination to wage war, Hotspur reminds his audiences of the political possibilities of retaliation, the volatile status of the present ascendancy and the mortality of the nationʼs political masters. Indeed, even before rebellion has taken any palpable form, Hotspur is noticeably eager to heroise those, like ʻrevolted Mortimerʼ, who exist beyond Henryʼs affinity and distinguish themselves in military prowess against the nation's foes: the 'swift Severn's flood,/Who then, affrighted with their bloody looks,/... hid his crisp head in the hollow bank,/ Bloodstained with these valiant combatants' (*IV*: I.iii.102–3, 105–6). The young Percy thus challenges the court's claim to a monopoly of violence. The newly formed rebel party is in this way able to compose a dynamic counter-narrative of the nation's past and institute new collective rituals of contest and community in Glendower's household. However, the irascible Hotspur cannot forge an unwavering bond of allegiance amongst his fellow conspirators with the unruly resources of warfare. Despite his hope that violence may intensify group allegiances, may mask the reservations operating amongst its membership and unite these very disparate individuals, Hotspur is no more able to command the service of his kin than his adversary, the Lancastrian sovereign.

As Shakespeare's history plays unfold, the unending production of human strife appears inextricably linked to Georg Simmel's contention that 'Our opposition makes us feel that we are not completely victims of our circumstances.'[74] However, Hotspur's oppositionality is not limited to the battlefield: it dominates his waking and sleeping hours. Indeed, without encountering contradiction from her husband, the anxiety-ridden Lady Percy assumes the gendered prerogatives of a conventionally male *raisonneur* and reminds him of his fantasies of control: 'In thy faint slumbers I by thee have watched/And heard thee murmur tales of iron wars,/Speak terms of manage to thy bounding steed,/Cry "Courage! to the field!"' (*IV*: II.iii.41–4). Moreover, in an extravagant parody of the grieving farewells of Lady Percy to her kin in both *Henry IV* plays, Mistress Quickly consoles Doll Tearsheet with the sentiment that 'One must bear, and that must be you, you are the weaker vessel, as they say, the emptier vessel' (*IV*: II.iv.48–9). Nevertheless, despite the departure of Falstaff, Doll remains in no mind to dismiss the enormity of her loss: 'Can a weak empty vessel bear such a huge full hogshead? There's a whole merchant's venture of Bordeaux stuff in him' (*IV*: II.iv.51–2). In essence, all these female agents are discovered trapped within a narrative determined to chronicle the hazards of patrilinearity as a social principle. Equally importantly, as perceived non-producers of history, they are prevented from overcoming their cultural marginality: it is only their menfolk who are accorded the privilege of intervention when aggrieved by the knowledge of their own ailing or displaced status. In this context, Christopher Highley attends to the radical rescripting of normative gender codes enacted in the accounts of Welshwomen's mutilation of English corpses at the opening of *1 Henry IV*. From this perspective, these narratives indicate not only the attempt to destroy 'the soldiers' last vestigial claims to manhood', but also 'can be taken as symptomatic of the period's drive to criminalize women, a process that was most marked on the fringes of the nation-state'.[75]

Like most other inhabitants of this dramatic world, Lady Percy cannot frame thought to flesh out her ideas without recourse to the all too pervasive lexis of the battlefield, 'Of sallies and retires, of trenches, tents/ Of palisadoes, frontiers, parapets' (*IV*: II.iii.45–6). If only a relatively small number of the English nobility participated in military campaigns of the 1590s, the political threat of overmighty subjects remained current throughout the Tudor century. During Elizabeth's reign, as Richard C. McCoy underlines, despite the Act against Retainers, members of the nobility and elite courtiers, such as Norfolk, Leicester, Cecil and Shrewsbury, were permitted to retain some 100 men in their service.[76] Since the middle of the 1580s, when Elizabeth had sent military companies to assist England's co-religionists in the Dutch Revolt, the waging of war had come increasingly to preoccupy cultural debate in the realm. It was in this very period that Essex submitted in his *Apology* (1600), 'the greatnesse of her Majestie's favor must grow out of the greatnesse of her servants' merits: & I saw no way of merit lye so open as by service in her wars'.[77] If Shakespeare's plays regularly invite us to reflect upon the diversity and changing meanings of the pasts that his characters inherit, in the history plays this concern is articulated under specifically martial terms.

Fractured Lands, Fractured Tongues

Peacetime in plays such as *Richard III* and *Troilus and Cressida* comes to signify a condition of cultural disorientation and/or moral vacancy rather than a return to the eirenic pleasures of life in civil society. Conversely, Stuart Henry has argued that 'acts of violence . . . are acts that make others powerless to maintain or express their humanity, that is, that deny their ability to make a difference'.[78] In this conflicted debate, Hotspur's coercive attempts to introduce radical political change remain deeply problematic because they reaffirm the validity of rebellion. The anonymous publication *A Myrrour for English Souldiers* (1595) remained adamant in its advice that readers should 'Neuer giue charge in daungerous times, to a rash hare-braine, nor to a coward . . . He that will be a commander in armies, first let him be commanded in the same: for an ambitious souldier shall neuer be a temperate conducter.'[79] If Hotspur is not suspected of cowardice, his choleric disposition is never in question. The *Myrrour* cunningly advised 'Dissemble an iniurie, till you haue found time and occasion to reuenge it.

To dissemble an iniurie is signe of great wisedome.'[80] Indeed, the failure of the rebellion resides in great part in Hotspur's inability to reflect or to strategise adequately. Instead, he insists vehemently that, 'We must have bloody noses and cracked crowns' (*IV*: II.iii.87). Northumberland remonstrates with his 'wasp-stung and impatient fool' of a son ('Drunk with choler? Stay, and pause awhile', *IV*: I.iii.233, 127), yet the ireful nobleman, whose rash conduct invariably risks losing 'men's hearts and leaves behind a stain/Upon the beauty of all parts besides', never sheds his emblematic function of communicating excess – and he is not alone in the play in assuming this function. Indeed, such is this Percy's excessiveness that, in his hasty desires for political transformation, he imperils the very gendered identity upon which his warrior ideals are founded: 'this woman's mood,/ Tying thine ear to no tongue but thine own!' (*IV*: I.iii.234–5).

In the wider consideration of the soundscapes of Shakespeare's *Henry IV* plays, Lady Percy's interventions as eloquent, if unsuccessful counsellor may be located dramatically mid-way between the irrepressible loquacity of her husband and the guarded silences of Hal. They also link closely with debate in early modern publications devoted to military affairs: the discipline of mind, body and tongue. Like many pamphlets on soldiery, the *Henry IV* plays consider how military prowess may indeed be married to a *norma loquendi*, when to deviate from either might render the agent suspect in moral and cultural terms. While Gentili acknowledged in his *De Iure Belli* that 'Military life is freer from care, blunter, and far removed from the subtlety of the Forum', he nevertheless asserted elsewhere in his treatise that 'there is nothing that shows so servile a spirit as not to be able to abstain from foul language and insulting remarks in the presence of one's bitterest enemy. . . . It is particularly unbecoming a brave soldier to appear to be readier with his tongue than with his weapons.'[81] Considering more broadly a quite different strain of brutal interventionism, Jean-Marie Domenach concentrates on 'la violence sournoise, celle qui se dissimule derrière l'habitude, l'ordre'.[82a] The presence of such *violence sournoise* is widely in evidence in the *Henry IV* plays where sleights of hand and tongue are regularly encountered in the intrigues surrounding the attempted redemption of promises and enforcement of obligations – at court, in the rebel camps, in the tavern, at Gaultree and in the levying of troops. Domenach insisted that 'Il y a la violence qui menace et celle qui séduit',[83b] and in such practices Hal is a master tactician who tries to reassure his father that 'Percy is but my

[a] 'the underhand violence, that which hides itself behind routine, order'.
[b] 'There is the violence which threatens and that which seduces.'

factor, good my lord,/To engross up glorious deeds on my behalf' (*IV*: III. ii.147–8). In this context, Stephen Greenblatt highlighted a paradox that lies at the heart of *1 Henry IV*: 'We are continually reminded that Hal is a "juggler", a conniving hypocrite, and that the power he both serves and comes to embody is glorified usurpation and theft; yet at the same time, we are drawn to the celebration of both the prince and his power.'[84] At such points we may wonder how to evaluate the practice of *self-fashioning*, ethically or dramaturgically. Freud argued persuasively that 'the man of action will never abandon the external world in which he can essay his power'.[85] We are left in no doubt that Hal, as heir apparent, is determined to forsake the tavern world in order to stage a most spectacular triumphal entry into the theatres of war and power: 'I know you all, and will awhile uphold/ The unyoked humour of your idleness' (*IV*: I.ii.155–6). In an equally telling manner for his Elizabethan readers, Thomas Churchyard argued in *A generall rehearsall of warres* (1579) that

> now is he accompted no bodie, that can not deceiue a multitude. And the more finelier he can behaue hym self, the more affection is borne hym … For with artificiall courtezie, and double dessembled countenaunce, plaine people are carried from them selues, and made the bonde slaues of those wolues, that priuelie deuoures them.[86]

The perceived tensions and contrary motions at work in Shakespeare's dramatic narratives vary enormously as the cycles of the history plays unfold, but down the centuries audiences have remained captivated by the disturbingly creative ways in which Shakespearean cultures of war disclose hitherto occluded conditions of being and knowing, telling and withholding. Indeed, in the *Henry IV* plays, the battlefield constitutes but one arena where subterfuge and defeat are linked with arresting forms of violence. Hotspur may seek out armed hostilities with which to stage-manage his appetites for social advancement and adulation in this feudal-ised world, but others seek alternative modes of self-affirmation away from the levying of troops or the killing fields. In *De Iure Belli*, Gentili questioned 'whether it is lawful to deceive an enemy with any kind of falsehood'.[87] It soon becomes apparent in the Gaultree encounter that Lancaster, like Hal, does not scruple to assert his own party's interest to the detriment of others:

> YORK   Will you thus break your faith?
> LANCASTER   I pawn'd thee none.
>   I promised you redress of these same grievances
>   Whereof you did complain …

> Most shallowly did you these arms commence,
> Fondly brought here, and foolishly sent hence.
>
> (*IV²*: IV.i.430–2, 436–7)

If the new Lancastrian king claimed the right to challenge the arbitrary government and gross favouritism of Richard II, the dramatic world of *1 Henry IV* establishes a similarly riven state. Thus, 'those Welshwomen' who perform such acts of emasculation upon the corpses of the English troops 'as may not be/Without much shame retold or spoken of' (*IV²*: I. i.41, 45–6) expertly introduce us into a landscape wholly dominated by an interrogation of human and political violation.

In the decade following the union of Wales with England, Roger Ascham conjured up an image of Wales in his *Toxophilus the schole of shootinge contayned in two bookes* (1545) as 'being headye'. This was a land which

> rebelling many yeares agaynst vs, laye wylde, vntylled, vnhabited, without lawe, iustice, ciuilitie and ordre: and then was amonges them more stealing that true dealing, more suretie for them that studyed to be noughte, then quyetnesse for them that laboured to be good.[88]

Hotspur more than matches the 'headiness' of his Welsh ally, but the Lancastrian ascendancy has done little to heal the splintering of the kingdom. Indeed, if anything, Bolingbroke's rise to power has further exacerbated it through his misgovernance of feudal obligations and customary laws of arms. Henry's, like the later Lear's, attempts to assert his sovereignty merely engender a morbid fascination amongst political malcontents with division and appropriation. The rebel faction (nominally under the command of the Percies) is only the most potent expression of political disaffection in the realm. The widespread hunger for territorial spoils communicates in miniature the already profoundly divided state of the nation:

> The archdeacon hath divided it
> Into three limits very equally:
> England, from Trent and Severn hitherto,
> By south and east is to my part assigned.
> All westward, Wales beyond the Severn shore,
> And all the fertile land within that bound,
> To Owen Glendower. And, dear coz, to you
> The remnant northward, lying off from Trent.
>
> (*IV²*: III.i.68–75)

It takes little time for the audience to realise that the overweening Hotspur will not be content with this 'remnant northward'. More generally, concentrating on the ways in which Tyrone's Ireland is imaged for a 1590s audience through the narrative prism of an unruly Wales, Christopher Highley has argued persuasively that 'In the deterioration of Glendower from a principal scourge of the English to charlatan and palpable absence – and in the parallel fate of the alliance generally – the play can be seen as disempowering the figure of the Celtic chieftain by literally wishing him away.'[89]

Trying to unite against the Lancastrians, the rebel factions seek to formulate alternative narratives of national belonging, to stress the authority of their own superlative bloodlines. The conspiracy counts members from across the British Isles and thus summons up a remarkably diverse account of the realm's political and linguistic mosaic. Nonetheless, the *Henry IV* plays never underestimate how difficult it will be to harness these unruly bodies, forces, tongues.

'I would 'twere bed-time, Hal, and all well'

Briefly reviewing the reading practices of earlier generations in *Toxophilus*, the reformist Ascham contended that

> In our fathers tyme nothing was red, but bookes of fayned cheualrie, wherin a man by redinge, shuld be led to none other ende, but onely to manslaughter and baudrye. Y^f any man suppose they were good ynough to passe the time with al, he is deceyued . . . These bokes (as I haue heard say) were made the moste parte in Abbayes, and Monasteries, a very lickely and fit fruite of suche an ydle and blynde kinde of lyuynge.[90]

Generations of Shakespearean critics have elected to unpack the early narrativisation of war in his oeuvre in terms of chivalric and feudal practices and expectations. On occasions, as we have witnessed, one-to-one combat in the lists or on the battlefield is clearly treated as a theatrical synecdoche for the communication of large-scale warfare onstage. However, equally frequently, dramatic interest in the mores of military conduct inherited from the medieval centuries is seen to offer valuable insights into the ways in which a society might wish to reproduce itself in political and ideological terms. Theodor Meron remains a notable voice in this debate, affirming that 'Writing in the post-chivalric era marred by the savagery of religious wars, Shakespeare recognizes the continuing pertinence of ethical and protective values of chivalry.'[91] However, if Henry IV himself is frequently, like the theatre-goer, spectator to the military prowess of others, those in this playworld who exist on the margins or beyond his court culture altogether remind us repeatedly of the widely felt hunger for martial performances. In the shires, presiding over yet another instance of questionable procedure in this flawed Lancastrian state, Justice Shallow recalls fondly a particular foolery: 'I remember at Mile End Green, when I lay at Clement's Inn – I was then Sir Dagonet in Arthur's show' (*IV²*: III. ii.227). Indeed, this is a kind of foolery with which Shakespeare's world is perfectly conversant:

> FALSTAFF I am a rogue, if I were not at half-sword with a dozen of them two hours together. I have scaped by miracle. I am eight times thrust through the doublet, four through the hose, my buckler cut through and through, my sword hacked like a hand-saw – ecce signum! (*IV¹*: II.iv.141–5)

The final resting place of the knight is not discovered in *Henry V* in the company of Abraham, but 'in Arthur's bosom, if ever man went to Arthur's bosom' like any good 'christom child' (II.iii.8–11). At an earlier juncture, Falstaff had accompanied the emptying of his 'jordan' with a spritely song: 'When Arthur first in court ... And was a worthy king' (*IV²*: II.iv.26–8).

Ultimately, all the various human companies of the *Henry IV* plays review the esteem in which the performance of violence is held. However, Shakespeare's dramatic world unsettles such enquiries by offering us insights into the alternative to, the evasion of, the non-performance of, violence. We might recall Northumberland's early equivocations, Lady Percy's protestations, Falstaff's blusterings and plaintive requests, and how they invite audiences to query participation in any political project committed to the loss of human life:

> Counterfeit? I lie, I am no counterfeit. To die is to be a counterfeit; for he is but the counterfeit of a man who hath not the life of a man. But to counterfeit dying, when a man thereby liveth, is to be no counterfeit, but the true and perfect image of life indeed. The better part of valour is discretion, in the which better part I have saved my life. (*IV¹*: V.iv.113–18)

Falstaff's claims to Hotspur's corpse are met with derision by Hal: 'Why, Percy I killed myself and saw thee dead' (*IV¹*: V.iv.137). However, there appears little honour in laying claim to this quarry for either party: the older man can only reply 'Didst thou? Lord, Lord, how this world is given to lying!' (*IV¹*: V.iv.138). In this context, the linguistician Sergei Karcevskij is perhaps most timely in his contention that 'the simultaneous presence of ... two possibilities is indispensable for any act of comprehension'.[92] Counterpointed in narrative terms with the phoney demise of Falstaff, the dying Hotspur exclaims 'O, Harry, thou hast robb'd me of my youth!'

Nevertheless, David P. Young responds persuasively that 'Hotspur is robbed . . . of his youth, but not of his gallantry or any of the other qualities that have made him so attractive to us.'[93] Moreover, if Hotspur, on Hal's lips, becomes food 'For worms' (*IV*ˣ: V.iv.86), this is but one in a sequence of actions in which he purposely seeks to deprive others of dignity with verbal and physical violence. His energetic attempts to foster political consensus must await his own ascent to the throne.

Meanwhile, all the players (even Henry) contemplate the consequences of a morally and politically flawed monarchy. Falstaff informs the prince, 'Worcester is stolen away tonight. Thy father's beard is turned white with the news. You may buy land now as cheap as stinking mackerel' (*IV*ˣ: II. iv.295–7). In *2 Henry IV* Bolingbroke's dramatic and political decline is accelerated markedly as he retreats into a *vita contemplativa* which Shakespeare had reserved in his earlier tetralogy for the leader of another failed state, Henry VI: 'every thing lies level to our wish;/Only, we want a little personal strength' (*IV*²: IV.ii.7–8). In Aristotle's *Politiques* (1598) the late Elizabethan reader was invited to reflect that

> whosoeuer taketh vpon him to found a new State . . . if he be a politicke fellow by nature, and moreouer well instructed and experienced . . . hee shall fare much the better by being so schooled and prepared aforehand. Nay (which more is) I say that otherwise he shall . . . go groping like a blind man, and commit many worse errors than the ignorant phisitian and pilot, because the case which he vndertaketh is of farre greater importance and concerneth moe folke, as namely the tranquilitie, welfare, and honour of a whole countrey or Nation, or of a State sore attainted with the diseases of excesse and couetousnesse.[94]

In the *Henry IV* plays, we are profoundly exercised by this very narrative of one who sought to 'found a new State' and chose not to invest adequately in it. In *The Famous Victories*, the future Henry V pronounces that 'when I am King, we will haue no such things, but my lads, if the old king my father were dead, we would be all kings' and scampers off to court to update his knowledge on his father's failing health: 'for the breath shal be no sooner out of his mouth, but I wil clap the Crowne on my head' (C1ʳ– C1ᵛ). The prince is, however, not allowed to remain onstage in this morally unreconstructed state: 'My conscience accuseth me, most soueraign Lord,/ and welbeloued father.' Having undergone ethical reformation, he receives a royal pardon and strives to redeem those about him, such as Ned: 'thou saist I am changed,/So I am indeed, and so must thou be' (C2ᵛ, D2ʳ). As we have seen, Shakespeare never allows his Hal to be quite so explicitly sullied onstage, but at the close of *2 Henry IV* the dramatic emphasis nevertheless falls upon the theme of renewal. In this instance, it is the renewed integrity of hitherto discrete communities of the realm: 'Now call we our high court of parliament,/And let us choose such limbs of noble counsel,/That the great body of our state may go/In equal rank with the best govern'd nation' (*IV²*: V.ii.133–6).

As Shakespeare's *institutio principis* draws to a close, Jonas A. Barish remains illuminating in his contention that 'The rejection of Falstaff, like much else in Shakespeare, has tended to turn a searchlight on us, and make ourselves reveal ourselves either as moralists or as sentimentalists.'[95] Falstaff seeks a position of cultural privilege by the side of his future 'king, my Jove'. He is greeted with the rebuke 'I know thee not, old man'; and this 'tutor', this 'feeder of . . . riots' is reminded by his royal master to 'Presume not that I am the thing I was.' However, like the prince of *The Famous Victories*, Hal does offer former companions the possibility of a political future of sorts: 'And, as we hear you do reform yourselves,/We will, according to your strengths and qualities,/Give you advancement' (*IV²*: V.v.42–3, 58, 52, 64–6). Equally importantly, as Nigel Wood has argued most persuasively, 'Hal may banish Falstaff, but, as we have seen, the real test is whether he has banished the Falstaff within himself, and, perhaps more crucially, whether an audience can actually condone that action.'[96] Hal's undertaking in shedding former selves is to resolve the failings of the past onto the bodies (or corpses) of others. In such a discussion, Yves-Alain Michaud remains timely in his reminder that 'La vraie violence est toujours d'autrui, la mienne contre-violence ou libération.'[97][a] If, in the later *Henry V*, as we shall see in the next chapter, the discourse of nation becomes the medium through which the violence of warfare may be mediated and legitimised for future generations, reconciling subject populations to changing hierarchies of ownership and to the idealisation of suffering and service, it still requires notable and sustained reiteration in the later play that the new king has indeed undergone a veritable 'reformation' of manners and purpose.

Shakespeare's dramatisations of political regimes which seek closure to the divisions of the past (but maintain a vigorous investment in that same past's commitment to violence) must inevitably resonate powerfully with our own contemporary society – a society, which as Zygmunt Bauman has identified, is 'frankly admitting its own incompleteness and therefore anxious to attend to its own as yet un-intuited, let alone explored, possibilities; but in addition . . . a society impotent, as never before, to decide its own course

---

[a] 'Real violence is always committed by another, my own is [styled as] counter-violence or liberation.'

with any degree of certainty'.[98] Perhaps inevitably, Shakespeare's theatres of war return compulsively to this meditation on moral and political debilitation – the manner in which a victorious Hal, for example, may 'wear a garment all of blood' and render Hotspur 'dust' or food 'for worms' (*IV*: III.ii.135, V.iv.84–6). Auden convincingly nominated Falstaff as belonging to an '*opera buffa* world of play and mock-action'. However, as the *Henry IV* plays draw to a close, we must surely question whether indeed this is 'a world where no one can suffer', as Auden would have us believe.[99]

CHAPTER 4

'Now thrive the armourers':
Henry V *and the Promise of 'Hungry War'*

This prince was almost the Arabicall Phenix, and emongest his predecessors a very Paragon: For that he emongest all gouernors, chiefly did remember that a kyng ought to bee a ruler with wit, grauitie, circumspeccion, diligence and constancie ... he not to muche trustyng to the readinesse of his owne witte, nor iudgementes of his owne waueryng will, called to his counsaill sure prudent and politique personages ... that he might shewe hymself a synguler mirror and manifest example of moral vertues and good qualities ... For it is not so muche euill as Cicero saieth (although it bee euill in itself) a prince to do euill, as he by his euill doynges to corrupt others, because it is daily seen, that as princes change, the people altereth, and as kynges go, the subiectes folowe.[1]

As Edward Hall's *The vnion of the two noble and illustre famelies of Lancastre and Yorke* (1548) indicates, the sixteenth century remained as powerfully exercised by the substantial body of political mythology surrounding Henry V's reign (1413–22) as successive generations had been during the fifteenth century. Indeed, the Tudor century was heir to a singularly rich legacy of hagiography, legendry and chronicle panegyric (not afforded to any other medieval English king) which dated back even to the years of Henry's own reign, and included works such as the *Gesta Henrici Quinti* (1416–17) and Thomas Elmham's *Liber Metricus de Henrico Quinto* (c.1418).[2] In John Lydgate's *The hystorye, sege and dystruccyon of Troye* (c.1420), which had originally been commissioned by Henry himself before his accession, the king's subjects were greeted with a celebration of 'the most noble excellent Prynce kynge Henry the fyfthe ... Most worthy Prynce of knyghthode ... Whose highe renowne/through the worlde dothe shyne.'[3] Elsewhere, the late medieval Catholic narrative poem *ye batayll of Egyngecourte and the great sege of Rone* (pub. 1536?) moved swiftly from a prayer of Catholic devotion ('God that all this worlde dyde make/ And dyed for vs vpon a tree/Saue england for mary thy mothers/As y^u art stedfast god in trynyte') to hail the Lancastrian monarch as 'A courtyouse knyght and kynge ryall/. . . noble man of warre/. . . Of knyghthod . . . the very lodestarre.'[4]

In the opening years of his reign, in 1513, Henry VIII had commissioned an English translation of Tito Livio's *Vita Henrici Quinti* (1437), aiming strategically to revive for his own times a political model of successful kingship enhanced by military triumph on foreign soil. In the same years, Polydore Vergil's *Anglica Historia* (originally commissioned by Henry VII) was completed and dedicated to Henry VIII (though not published until 1534 in Basle). Here, readers were encouraged to greet the hero of Agincourt as

> the unique glory and light of his nation. No man was born more noble for the loftiness and greatness of mind, none more excellent for piety, and even today his lack is felt no less acutely than it first was among his contemporaries.[5]

Indeed, on into the succeeding reign of Edward VI, the humanist scholar Roger Ascham might be discovered in *Toxophilus* (1545) acclaiming the Lancastrian as 'a prince pereles and moste vyctoriouse conqueroure of all that euer dyed yet in this parte of the world'.[6] By the closing years of the sixteenth century, *A conference about the next succession to the crowne of Ingland* (1595) argued that the king was most remarkable in that 'for his exceding towardlynes, & for the great affection of the people towards him', he received the homage of his subjects even before his coronation.[7]

Despite the political project of the Stuart *rex pacificus*, in the Jacobean period such textual celebrations continued to have common currency. Hugh Holland's verse chronicle romance *Pancharis the first booke* (1603) recorded Henry as 'the first in fame, in name the fift';[8] and in *The nine English worthies* (1606), Robert Fletcher proclaimed 'This *Henry* was a king whose life was immaculate . . . he was the Myrror of al Christendome, and the glory of his Country, the flower of Kings passed, and the glasse of all succéeding Maiestie.'[9] Michael Drayton recalled in *Poly-Olbion* (1612) that Lydgate had saluted Henry as 'Protectour of Brutes Albion';[10] and indeed, some years earlier, in *A paean triumphall . . . congratulating his Highnes magnificent entring the citie* (1604), he had paid surprising tribute to James VI/I (or rather, perhaps, to the father of Prince Henry, given the dating of these publications) as one who encompassed 'Eu'ry rare vertue of each famous King/Since *Norman Williams* happie conquering.' Subsequently, his readers were asked to attend to the vision of '*Henry* the fifth leading his warlike troupes,/When the proud French fell on that conquered land,/As the full Corne before the labourers hand.'[11]

The present discussion considers the variety of ways in which Shakespeare's *Henry V* engages with a whole host of expectations surrounding this warrior king that had accumulated across the generations. In addition, building upon discussions in earlier chapters, the cultural undertaking of a society convulsed by violence is examined in the context of the declared ambition of Shakespeare's protagonist to forge a nation community through foreign wars.

'*Moy shall not serve*': Multiplying Nations and Selves

In Elizabeth's reign, quite apart from the extensive number of chronicles memorialising King Harry's celebrated triumphs, his presence might be identified in a range of more unexpected genres. In *The principal nauigations, voyages, traffiques and discoueries of the English nation* (1599–1600), for example, Richard Hakluyt hailed 'the marueilous werriour and victorious Prince, King *Henrie* the fifth'; and for those following the *Newes out of the coast of Spaine* (1587) in the tumultuous months preceding the Armada, there was the reminder, if reminder were needed, that the victorious Henry had been 'the furrower of *Gallia*'.[12] Given such widespread and unstinting interest in a king minded to 'rouse me in my throne of France' (*V*: I.ii.275), it was inevitable that the playhouses would turn their attention to this enduring cultural icon. *The famous victories of Henry the fifth containing the honourable Battell of Agincourt* (1586?) was published in 1598. There is evidence also of a lost play entitled *Henry V* (1595), and by the end of the century, in 1599, Shakespeare's own play was performed for London audiences. Such productions, like the chronicles and narrative poems before them, fixed Henry repeatedly as a model of sovereignty that warranted careful scrutiny, most especially for those negotiating the closing years of Elizabeth's reign. Late-sixteenth-century audiences and readers were thus repeatedly called upon to ponder an earlier ruler whose rise to the throne could not have been predicted, who swiftly earned the serious attention of his subjects and yet whose greatest achievement was the waging of victorious wars beyond England's shores which sought to 'make all Gallia shake' (*V*: I.ii.216).

Henry V thus offers a very particular dramatisation of a triumphantly belligerent (rather than rightful) governor of the nation who had 'no thought ... but France' (*V*: I.ii.302). Moreover, Shakespeare's play interrogates the manner in which spectacular performances of violence (or the failure to engage in such performances) might radically scramble expectations of political legitimacy and cultural priority.[13] Haunted by knowledge of the ways in which his own nation had been riven by successive wars, Jean Bodin concluded grimly in *Les Six Livres de la République* (1576, Eng. trans. 1606) that 'those which take small occasions to make warre, are like vnto flies, which cannot hold themselues vppon a smooth polished glasse, but vpon rough places. And those which seeke warre to inrich themselues with their neighbours spoyles, shall be in continuall torment, leading a miserable life.'[14] Nonetheless, like a host of characters in early modern comedies ending in a marriage, Shakespeare's Henry urgently questions the divisions of *meum* and *tuum*, and presses his neighbours to recognise those who have power in their grasp. In the event, the potentially eirenic vision of converging nations and a betrothal uniting two royal houses is deferred until the closing phases of this history play. The greater part of the dramatic narrative is locked within a quite different generic mode focusing upon the vicissitudes of the state. The new occupant of the English throne feels compelled to promote his royalty in bellicose terms and gives vent to bloodthirsty ambitions in France because he appears to have at his disposal no alternative scheme of governance with which to restrain his unruly realm. The prospect of military defeat can only be conceived of as an emblem of (political) death at a national and personal level. The new monarch's entire political project is thus committed unreservedly to the success of this foreign campaign – and one of his main dramatic functions remains to convince those around him of its (read, his own) legitimacy: 'There is some soul of goodness in things evil,/Would men observingly distil it out' (*V*: IV.i.4–5).

Happily discovering an audience serried within the confines of the playhouse, once again we encounter a Shakespearean Chorus demonstrating its capacity to invest in *dubia*. It summons us imaginatively into the presence of 'the warlike Harry' who will '[a]ssume the port of Mars; and at his heels,/Leash'd in like hounds, ... famine, sword and fire/Crouch for employment' (*V*: Prol.I.5–8). Yet Shakespeare had already shown himself attentive to this novice king's tastes for armed hostilities in distant lands. Even at the close of *2 Henry IV*, the young monarch's brother, John of Lancaster, had submitted 'I will lay odds that, ere this year expire,/We bear our civil swords and native fire/As far as France. I heard a bird so sing,/Whose music, to my thinking, pleased the king' (*IV²*: V.v.98–101). *Henry V* itself closes with a familiar refrain that the future Henry VI 'shall go to Constantinople and take the Turk by the beard' (*V*: V.ii.190–1). In so doing, the play recalls for Elizabethan audiences the parlous political conditions that had engendered this cycle in the nation's misfortunes: 'I'll make a voyage to the Holy Land/To wash this blood off from my guilty head' (*Richard II*: V.vi.49–50).

From the broader perspective of Shakespeare's Second Henriad, the centrifugal politics of Henry V's sovereignty represent just one in a marked succession of re-orientations signalling the transformation of wayward Hal to reigning monarch. Such an Augustinian template for the reinvention of selves circulated widely in early modern cultural discourse, but in Shakespeare's history play we are never allowed to forget that this narrative was a decidedly calculated production: 'the prince obscured his contemplation/Under the veil of wildness' (*V*: I.i.63–4).[15] Indeed, the Constable of France shrewdly confirms to his fellow peers that 'you shall find his vanities forespent/Were but the outside of the Roman Brutus' (*V*: II.iv.36). In *An arithmeticall militare treatise, named Stratioticos* (1579, repub. and enlarged 1590) Leonard and Thomas Digges insisted that 'A General ought first in his owne person so to reforme all disordered appetites, that his life maye serue as a mirrour to the whole Armie howe to reforme themselues.'[16] At the opening of *Henry V* we are informed that 'Never came reformation in a flood,/With such a heady currance' (*V*: I.i.32–3). The king's public determination to foreswear his tavern selves and to exhibit more conspicuously elite modes of subjectivity – those of sovereign and premier warrior – feeds an ongoing textual debate concerning the opportunities for social advancement made available throughout Shakespeare's historical worlds with the instrument of violence.

William Caxton's *cronicles of Englond* (1480) had celebrated Henry as 'a noble prynce after he was kyng', yet devoted some sustained attention to the fact that 'in his yougthe he had bene wylde recheles & spared no thyngs of his lustes ne desires, but accomplisshed them aftyr his likynge'.[17] More guardedly, Polydore Vergil had argued in his own account of the hero of Agincourt that 'this was the man who illustrated the truth of the proverb that honours change manners, since as soon as he became king he decided he must follow another way of life than he had previously led'.[18] The fascination with the unwieldy energies of this latter-day Proteus clearly persisted, for William Martyn's *Youths instruction* (1612) also remained eager to stress the presence of those 'vnthrifty companions of *Henry* the fift [who] made him a wild, and a swaggering Prince'.[19] Shakespeare's own Canterbury reiterates for auditors on- and offstage that the new king's 'addiction was to courses vain,/His companies unlettered, rude and shallow,/His hours filled up with riots, banquets, sports' (*V*: I.i.54–6). Furthermore, if there were any doubt still lingering in our minds, Henry himself acknowledges that his political capital continues to be challenged, and perhaps squandered, by mouthings at home and abroad that '[we] did give ourself/To barbarous licence' (*V:* I.ii.270–1). However, this recurring dramatic emphasis upon the exchanging or trafficking of selves, upon moral and psychic transfer ('The breath no sooner left his father's body,/ But that his wildness, mortified in him,/Seem'd to die too' – *V:* I.i.24–6), is maintained throughout the Second Henriad and undergirds the ongoing investigation into the nature of human (self-)government and a national politics of control. These are subjects which remained at the very heart of Shakespeare's conception of the history play.

Amongst a significant line of critics down the generations, Samuel Johnson proved to be a resisting reader of Hal's theatrical metamorphosis into royal Henry:

> I know not why Shakespeare now gives the King nearly such a character as he made him formerly ridicule in Percy. This military grossness and unskilfulness in all the softer arts does not suit very well with the gaieties of his youth, with the general knowledge ascribed to him at his accession or with the contemptuous message sent him by the Dauphin, who represents him as fitter for the ballroom than the field.[20]

Yet rather than understanding Henry as having masqueraded a carnival identity, or 'antic disposition', in the past so as to conceal some kind of core subjectivity, we might consider more assiduously the instructions of Shakespeare's hero himself to 'Presume not that I am the thing I was' (*IV²:* V.v.52). Indeed, from the very beginning of *Henry V*, the Chorus seeks to place such presumptions under exceeding pressure and, in the process, creates hermeneutic voids for audiences in the theatrical play between *diegesis* and *mimesis*. We move repeatedly from beguiling modes of heroic telling ('all the youth of England are on fire', *V:* Chorus II.1) which are then greeted by markedly contrary movements in the dramatic action: the squabbling Nym protests, 'If you grow foul with me, Pistol, I will scour you with my rapier' (*V:* II.i.47–8). The varied strains of human experience depicted in this playtext mean that the fledgling king might all too easily have determined, like Pistol, that 'Moy shall not serve; I will have forty moys' (*V:* IV.iv.11). Moreover, the play, or *pleye*, of Shakespeare's protagonist, his consuming, frequently aggressive interests in purloining and performing, remain firmly in place for this final element in the second tetralogy. Gower, for one, appears under no illusion about the continual maskings and masquings at work in his society: ''tis a gull, a fool, a rogue, that now and then goes to the wars, to grace himself at his return into London under the form of a soldier' (*V:* III.vii.57–9). As we have seen, of equal concern for the late sixteenth century were the doings of those pressed to fight abroad. In a public proclamation in November 1589 placing vagrant soldiers under martial law, Elizabeth's authorities signalled that they were abundantly aware of 'the great outrages that have been and are daily committed by soldiers, mariners, and others that pretend to have served as soldiers upon her highness' good and loving subjects'.[21]

Such mummery is widely in evidence throughout Shakespeare's play-world. Pistol resolves at the conclusion of the play, 'patches will I get unto these cudgelled scars,/And swear I got them in the Gallia wars' (*V*: V.i.77–8). Elsewhere, as we have seen, Gower appears fully conversant with the aping and posturing assumed by those styling themselves war veterans: 'such fellows are perfect in the great commanders' names, and they will learn you by rote where services were done . . . And this they con perfectly in the phrase of war, which they trick up with new-tuned oaths' (*V*: III. vii.59–65). Clearly, the figure of the *miles gloriosus* was commonplace both on- and offstage in the final years of the sixteenth century, and it remained a frequent challenge in late Elizabethan society to differentiate between competing narratives of the battlefield, peddled for public consumption on the streets, in the playhouses and at court. Indeed, a weary Gower concludes, 'you must learn to know such slanders of the age, or else you may be marvellously mistook' (*V*: III.vi.59–71).

'Mangling by starts': Doing Violence to Text and Nation

On the eve of the Second World War, Mark Van Doren expressed notably divided sympathies regarding *Henry V*, dismissing the Chorus's interventions as 'the first sign of Shakespeare's imperfect dramatic faith. Their verse is wonderful but it has to be, for it is doing the work which the play ought to be doing, it is a substitute for scene and action.'[22] However, some forty years later, Larry S. Champion deemed these same interventions to be a most necessary dramatic counterweight to 'the virtual absence of internalization in either the central or the surrounding figures'.[23] In keeping with many other chronicle plays of the period, *Henry V* may be seen to be shaped by episodic narrativisation, extravagant rhetoric and an appetite for spectacle. However, Shakespeare's play distinguishes itself for its thoroughgoing interest in sounding the furthermost limits of the audience's imaginative resources, imbricating the very business of history-making on page and stage with thorny concerns of metadramatic reflection, theatrical potentiality and the intelligibility of violence – 'Minding true things by what their mockeries be' (*V*: Chorus

IV. 53). Rather than imparting an 'imperfect dramatic faith', Shakespeare's play surely interrogates robustly the trust we may wish to place in stage representation ('ciphers to this great accompt' – *V*: Chorus I.17), testing our own craving for narrative continuity in a dramatic world where human desire – indeed, human life – meets frequently with arbitrary, nay bloody, response. Graham Holderness has identified persuasively in *Henry V* a kind of theatrical alchemy whereby 'a brutal, reckless and hypocritical warlord' is held in 'peculiar co-existence ... with the hero of a patriotic tradition'.[24] It might be added that the discursive frictions which subject Shakespeare's play to such stresses and strains are indeed thematic to this account of a novice king seeking to enforce national consensus with often arresting disjunctions of word and deed.

As we have seen, Johnson was one of the first voices in the critical tradition to betray unease with Shakespeare's theatrical purposes in *Henry V*. Indeed, he argued that 'The lines given to the Chorus have many admirers; but the truth is that in them a little may be praised and much must be forgiven; nor can it be easily discovered why the intelligence given by the Chorus is more necessary in this play than in many others where it is omitted.'[25] Whatever the textual imperatives of other Shakespearean plays, the choric interventions eliding great distances of time and space in *Henry V* function to accentuate the multifariousness of collective experience, to construct a broad panorama of trauma in human and narrative terms, and to challenge prevailing expectations of heroic and theatric possibility: 'Can this cockpit hold/The vasty fields of France? Or may we cram/Within this wooden O the very casques/That did affright the air at Agincourt?' (*V*: Chorus I. 11–14). In the play's final moments, the Chorus laments that 'mighty men' have been confined onstage in narrative terms '[i]n little room'. As has been witnessed in earlier discussions, contemporary cultural theorists, such as Willem Schinkel, have sought to define violence as the need to enact a 'reduction of being', a violation, a radical breach of sympathy with the human subject.[26] This ongoing critical concern with human abbreviation in manifestations of violence continues the length of *Henry V*. The Chorus fashions identities and experiences for the invading English forces that are never fully realised on stage. Its self-conscious figuration of Henry's reign ('Mangling by starts', *V*: V.iii.4) never fails to excite vexed enquiries for the audience. Its interventions describe a narrative arc extending from the assumption ('No king of England if not king of France!', *V*: II.ii.188) to the deferring of crowns ('rex Angliae et heres Franciae', *V*: V.ii.304–5) and political settlement: 'Henry the Sixth . . ./Whose state so many had the managing/ That they lost France and made his England bleed' (*V*: V.iii.9, 11–12).

Nicholas Grene stresses convincingly that 'For Shakespeare, and for most of the audiences of Shakespeare's time, the representation of war could only be the imagination of war.'[27] In this way, we are reminded that even in the company of 'four or five most ragged foils/Right ill disposed in brawl ridiculous', audiences maintain the unslakeable desire to penetrate the stirring world of armed conflict (*V*: Chorus IV.30–1). This indomitable fascination with the theatre of war is, of course, widely expressed on the stage itself. Fluellen confesses:

> It is the greatest admiration of the universal world when the true and ancient prerogatives and laws of the wars is not kept. If you would take the pains but to examine the wars of Pompey the Great you shall find, I warrant you, that there is no tiddle taddle nor pibble pabble in Pompey's camp. I warrant you, you shall find the ceremonies of the wars, and the cares of it, and the forms of it, and the sobriety of it, and the modesty of it, to be otherwise. (*V*: IV. i.64–71)

If Elizabethan and Jacobean print culture made an unstinting investment in vigorous contemporary debates surrounding the status and functions of militarised society, *Henry V* unveils a very avid reader of such literatures in the shape of this most voluble Welshman. The dramatist and prose writer George Whetstone asserted in *The honorable reputation of a souldier* (1585) that 'He that is studious, and occupieth his leasurable times, in working out of aduauntages, is likely to hurt ye enimie more by his deuises in y^e . . . campe, then by fighting in the field.'[28] Fluellen figures forth just such expectations. Indeed, he assumes in an extravagant manner the authoritative *persona* nurtured by successive generations of early modern pamphleteers on the subject – a *persona* that can only recognise the substance and distinction of those who most clearly mirror his own affect(at)ions: 'Gower is a good captain, and is good knowledge and literatured in the wars' (*V*: IV.vii.133–4). One of the functions of this seasoned combatant in Shakespeare's narrative is to bridge the yawning gaps between textbook and theatrical conditions of knowing, and Fluellen seeks to wield what authority he can muster through his acquaintance with Vegetius and Caesar, rather than that with the more changeful modes of human exchange on the battlefield.

If Fluellen shares his royal master's enduring appetite for contest, he is exposed on occasions as an almost clownish figure in a manner more familiar from Henri Bergson's theorisation of the comic in terms of 'du mécanique plaqué sur du vivant'.[29a] Primed with readings ancient and modern, Fluellen tirelessly fashions the butchery of his world according to textual directives: 'the mines is not according to the disciplines of the war: the concavities of it is not sufficient' (*V*: III.iii.4–6). The slippage which inevitably occurs between these two very different planes of understanding leaves the audience once again to cogitate competing and discrepant forms of human achievement. Appalled by the incompetent staging of hostilities he witnesses about him on the 'vasty fields of France', the increasingly exasperated Welshman protests that MacMorris 'has no more directions in the true disciplines of the wars, look you, of the Roman disciplines, than is a puppy-dog'. Such conduct is, it seems, in direct contrast to Captain Jamy, who cannot be bested in his knowledge of armed combat. The latter is hailed as 'a marvellous falorous gentleman ... of great expedition and knowledge in th'anchient wars ... he will maintain his argument as well as any military man in the world, in the disciplines of the pristine wars of the Romans' (*V*: III.iii.16–18, 21–4). Furthermore, there are those at hand, like Gower, who are willing to defend Fluellen's ability to straddle the realms of theory and practice in opposition to the 'gleeking and galling' of one such as Pistol. Gower contends 'You thought, because he could not speak English in the native garb, he could not therefore handle an English cudgel' (*V*: V.i.66–8). Yet the degree to which Fluellen is allowed to lay claim to dramatic or intellectual authority remains a constant source of negotiation onstage. His irrepressible desire to formalise – indeed, ritualise – his interventions and the petty squabbles (in camp and on the field of combat) by regaling audiences on- and offstage with a textbook wisdom of military protocols is carefully played off against the grubbier realities of looting, camp hangings and merciless slaughtering executed by both sides in this conflict.

'to busy giddy minds with foreign quarrels'

The anonymously published *A Myrrour for English Souldiers* (1595) affirmed that those entrusted with the keys of the temporal kingdom should 'Seeke all meanes possible to preuent war'.[30] Rather more pragmatically in the early Stuart period, in the midst of the endless blood-letting of the Thirty Years' War, James Achesone's *The military garden* (1629) recommended that 'Though Peace bee always to bee desired, yet Warre is to bee provided for.'[31] Shakespeare's Dauphin shows himself similarly minded and, like

---

[a] 'of the mechanical coated onto the living'.

a host of Elizabethan and Jacobean pamphleteers, argues that 'peace itself should not so dull a kingdom,/... defences, musters, preparations,/Should be maintained, assembled and collected,/As were a war in expectation' (*V:* II.iv.17–21).

Keenly aware of – and, indeed, having participated in – the civil 'broils' which characterised his own father's reign, Shakespeare's Henry V resolves upon a thorough rearticulation of political discourse for his English subjects, reserving spaces overseas where the insatiable appetites for violent engagement may be fully sated: 'Now beshrew my father's ambition! He was thinking of civil wars when he got me' (*V:* V.ii.205–6). Indeed, the fifteenth-century chronicler John Hardyng hailed the bellicose Lancastrian as one who, 'Above all thynge he kept the lawe and pese/Thrugh all Englonde, that none insurreccion/Ne no riotes than were withouten lese,/Ne neyghbours werre in fawte of his correccion.'[32] Nonetheless, by the closing years of a sixteenth century which unveiled a nation exhausted by successive campaigns and armed threats beyond its shores, it was inevitable that the successful leadership of a militarised state might remain a vexed source of enquiry. Across the Channel Jean Bodin had insisted that 'A good prince must trie all meanes, and dissemble many things, before he come to armes',[33] and Aumerle in *Richard II* concurs when he advises his sovereign 'let's fight with gentle words/Till time lend friends and friends their helpful swords' (II.iii.130–1). In *De Iure Belli*, Gentili argued more grimly that

> It is brutal to proceed to murder and devastation when one has suffered no injury ... It is fitting for fish and wild beasts and the birds of the air to devour one another, since they are entirely devoid of a sense of justice, as Hesiod sang ... we find that princes always allege some plausible reason for beginning their wars; although frequently they have not reason at all.[34]

Henry certainly commits himself to (or, more persuasively perhaps, rehearses) due process of solemn reflection in the opening scenes of Shakespeare's play when he warns his arch-prelate to take the utmost care in counselling the nation or, more particularly, his king: 'take heed how you impawn our person,/How you awake our sleeping sword of war:/... For never two such kingdoms did contend/Without much fall of blood' (*V:* I.ii.21–2, 24–5). The stage is thus set for an abbreviated court disputation upon the strictures of the *ius ad bello*.

Like a number of the members of Elizabeth's Council in the 1590s, Shakespeare's protagonist confidently asserts that if hostilities must be countenanced, they should be played out beyond native shores: he thus continues his father's consuming interests in extravagant political ambition and bloodshed, but transplants these pleasure principles to new climes. Expelling warfare from his realm in this manner, the new king asserts not only reformation for himself but for the whole realm. In swiftly identifying an alien foe, Henry ensures that the heroic identity of rebel (to which Hotspur so imperiously aspired) is no longer available to his countrymen, and so any resistance to Lancastrian sovereignty may now be aligned with the treasonous imperilling of the nation's security in time of crisis. Furthermore, this royal commitment to a grand narrative of international warfare expertly deflects attention away from the factional strife in which his own dynasty took shape. Through Exeter, his emissary to the French court, Henry promises 'hungry war' which 'Opens his vasty jaws' on the arrival of the English invaders (*V*: II.iv.105–6) and is unmoved initially by the French king's offer of 'Katherine his daughter, and with her, to dowry,/ Some petty and unprofitable dukedoms' (*V*: Chorus III.30–1). The insatiable appetite on the part of Shakespeare's protagonist to perform spectacular acts of control is repeatedly expressed onstage: the various executions of dissenting subjects and prisoners of war; the prising open of Harfleur ('Let it pry through the portage of the head', V: III.i.10); the marshalling of forces on the battlefield; the conquest of French territories; the submission of the French court (French Queen: 'So happy be the issue, brother England,/Of this day', *V*: V.ii.12–13) and his future consort. Indeed, even in the rival party, the Dauphin does not hesitate to recall his nation's defeats in specifically sexualised terms:

> Our madams mock at us, and plainly say
> Our mettle is bred out and they will give
> Their bodies to the lust of English youth
> To new-store France with bastard warriors.   (*V*: III.vi.28–31)

Initially (and inevitably) rebuffed by the French court in his attempts to secure the French crown, Henry determines to turn his own nation away from the internal politicking reprised by Cambridge, Gray and Scroop.[35] The Chorus reports that 'the nimble gunner/With linstock now the devilish cannon touches' (*V*: Prol.3.30–3) and, as his ailing father had advised, Henry gives himself full liberty 'to busy giddy minds/With foreign quarrels' (*IV²*: III.ii.340–2). In *The arte of warre* (1591) William Garrard urged that the military commander (or 'High Marshall of the Field') must 'call continually to memory, that the art of warre doth require a sharpe and exemplar manner and condition of chastisement, therby to remaine the better obeyed'.[36] Mindful of such imperatives, one of Henry's first public actions as king is staged at Southampton, where we discover him with his potential for mercy 'suppressed and killed' (*V*: II.ii.77).[37] Like a later Shakespearean sovereign lamenting the treachery of his cherished Macdonwald in whom he 'built an absolute trust' (*Macbeth*: I.iv.13–14), the now seemingly disabused Henry protests to Scroop 'Thou that didst bear the key of all my counsels,/That knew'st the very bottom of my soul' (*V*: II.ii.93–4). French gold was in part a motive for Cambridge (whose claim to the throne is carefully occluded in Shakespeare's dramatic narrative), but only 'The sooner to effect what I intended' (*V*: II.iii.152). As Garrard had advised, the royal response is swift ('Get you therefore hence,/Poor miserable wretches, to your death'), but, equally remarkably, this changeful monarch is identified moments later affirming the prospect of 'a fair and lucky war,/Since God so graciously hath brought to light/This dangerous treason' (*V*: II.iii.172–3, 179–81). Thus, as in *1 Henry IV*, this hero is once again seen to reassert his claim on lands and crowns by amassing corpses. Resisting readers of his sovereignty find themselves politically silenced and/or textually erased. However, it might be noted that the Folio *Henry V* has already asked us to attend to the death of another: Falstaff perishes with his heart apparently 'fracted and corroborate'. This also has been charged to the Lancastrian's account before any ship has hoisted sail from Southampton docks: 'The king has killed his heart' (*V*: II.i.100, 70).[38] Having shed the models of paternal (in)discipline proposed by the fathers he acknowledged in the *Henry IV* plays, the new king seeks no other tutelage than that of war itself. The case is altered for others. Rather than eagerly preparing to take French leave with his fellow men-at-arms, as the Chorus would have us believe, Pistol is most exercised in doling out equivocal words of comfort for his companions: 'Let us condole the knight; for, lambkins we will live' (*V*: II.i.103). Indeed, even before he bids farewell to his native soil, Bardolph is heard to submit in cheerless fashion, 'Would I were with [Falstaff], wheresome'er he is, either in heaven or in hell!' (*V*: II.iii.6–7).

As was witnessed in Chapter 2, Henry V is not the only sovereign in these 1590s history plays to risk his authority in a cross-Channel endeavour: Shakespeare's Henry VI advises caution to his unruly peers once they have crossed the seas to this 'fickle wavering nation' (*VI*: IV.i.139). Nonetheless, *The Myrrour for English Souldiers* exhorted its late Elizabethan readers, 'Neuer be cruell in a straunge countrey, especially being a conquerour.'[39] This sobering advice is far from uniformly heeded during the course of *Henry V*. John H. Walter stressed that 'Henry's threats to Harfleur sound horrible enough, but he was precisely and unswervingly following the rules of warfare as laid down by Vegetius, Aegidius Romanus and others. Harfleur he regards as his rightful inheritance.'[40] Rejoinder might be made that the whole of the second tetralogy is a problematisation of what constitutes the 'rightful inheritance' of the Lancastrians. These complex dramatic narratives remain acutely sensitive to York's urgent questioning of the last Plantagenet king: 'how art thou a king/But by fair sequence and succession?' (*Richard II*: II.i.199–200). More generally, Shakespeare's audience is compelled to attend to the new king's peerless resources of artful strategising and eloquence, rather than any persuasive claim he might make to political legitimacy through legal precedent or hereditary privilege. If, as we have seen, with a bloody battle in prospect, Henry reasons 'There is some soul of goodness in things evil,/Would men observingly distil it out' (*V*: IV.i.2), auditors on- and offstage are left to meditate the chopped logic alternating between rights and wrongs, goods and evils, that all the Lancastrian sovereigns deploy with unfailing ease in Shakespeare's plays to promote their own interests: 'I was banished Hereford;/But as I come, I come for Lancaster' (*Richard II*: II.iii.112–13).

As was witnessed in the Introduction, Lévinas argued that 'the justification of the neighbour's pain is certainly the source of all immorality'.[41] The rise to political power of both Henry IV and Henry V in the second tetralogy engages most explicitly with such propositions – and, it might be added, neither of Shakespeare's monarchs emerges unscathed under interrogation. If Richard II realised his theatrical identity most effectively on stage through the extended meditation and enactment of his victim status, Henry V is frequently accorded priority by dominating not the spaces, but the soundscapes of his dramatic world. Indeed, one of the most dynamic ways in which King Harry excites dramatic interest from audiences on- and off-stage is through his rhetorical mastery, and this mastery is typically in evidence when anticipating his auditors' horror of violence. His evocations of 'the flesh'd soldier, rough and hard of heart', 'The blind and bloody soldier with foul hand' (and, later, 'Herod's bloody-hunting slaughtermen') ranging 'In liberty of bloody hand' and violating 'fresh-fair virgins' and 'flowering infants', offer some of the most arresting, figuratively compelling examples of the young sovereign's verbal strategies (*V*: III.iv.9–12, 32, 39). Nevertheless, these extended evocations clearly fire the speaker's *own* imagination and yield unanticipated insights into his need to blur the distinctions between human dynamism and violent action, refusing to view the latter as a corrosive form of sociality. Moreover, instead of being a refuge from the narrative's remorseless drive towards the maiming and yielding of human lives, the company of the

French princess and her gentlewoman Alice may constitute yet another recessive space in a grim *mise-en-abîme* of brutality. This is a dramatic *locus* in which the human body may once again be summoned, emblazoned and dissected for the play's very own *School for War*: 'La main, de hand; les doigts, de fingres. Je pense que je suis le bon ecolier' (*V*: III.v.11–12).

At Harfleur, Henry thunders at deserting soldiers, 'when the blast of war blows in our ears,/Then imitate the action of the tiger;/Stiffen the sinews, summon up the blood' (*V*: III.i.5–7). However, this king's resolve not to 'leave the half-achieved Harfleur/Till in her ashes she lie buried' (*V*: III. iv.6–7) becomes a spectacular speech act matching his own urgent need for political completion through destruction. (It is only in the final act of the play that this need may be afforded expression under alternative, courtly terms.) In the event, Harfleur does not capitulate in anticipation of the English rage predicted by Henry's impassioned rhetoric, but it does respond keenly to the doleful tidings that the Dauphin's forces will not arrive in time to relieve the town. Thus, the French king is left to bemoan that, 'Harry England . . . sweeps through our land/With pennons painted in the blood of Harfleur' (*V*: III.vi.48–9). If the English king asserts that 'France being ours, we'll bend it to our awe,/Or break it all to pieces' (*V*: I. ii.224–5), more generally Shakespeare's play maintains a consuming inter-est in such scenes of contest and dismemberment in its accounts of the Lancastrian party's many and various endeavours to secure its grip on power:

> But if the cause be not good, the king himself hath a heavy reckoning to make, when all those legs and arms and heads, chopped off in battle, shall join together at the latter day and cry all 'We died at such a place' . . . I am afeard there are few die well that die in a battle, for how can they charitably dispose of anything when blood is their argument? (*V*: IV.i.123–6, 129–31)

Gentili did not shirk either from addressing such fields of enquiry, con-tending that 'It is not for a subject to inquire too curiously which side took up arms with the better right. And hence many soldiers do not know whether or not their wars are just. . . . [Yet] a subject is not justified in slaying an innocent person at the order of his commander.'[42] On the eve of battle, a beleaguered Henry submits that 'the king is not bound to answer the particular endings of his soldiers, the father of his son, nor the master of his servant' (*V*: IV.i.141–2). In such a context Cynthia Marshall remains timely in an illuminating study of early modern textual politics with her caution that 'What a culture in its official version of itself is suturing together and publicly solidifying – such as the outlines of the individual subject in early modern England – texts designed for entertainment or mediation might be busily undoing.'[43]

Shakespeare's *Henry V* has all too often down the centuries been exploited to reassure anglophone audiences of their nation's elect destiny. However, the persistent need to promote narrative closure in terms of French defeat has meant that the arresting eloquence of voices such as that of Williams above (who summons up an apocalyptic vision for his undercover prince) has often failed to be fully weighed in the balance against that of Henry himself. Such inadequate readings necessarily prioritise the return to the breach in Harfleur's walls, rather than the staunching of the flow with 'English dead'. Shakespeare's king commits himself from the outset of the play to beating the boundaries of his newly acquired realm through the staging of foreign wars. Such policies not only traumatise those lodged in the new field of vision over the Channel. Henry presses combatant identities strenuously upon his followers – and, in the process, he exposes the perilously intimate relationship that may exist between vigorous governance and commonplace practices of brutality: 'he to-day that sheds his blood with me/Shall be my brother' (*V*: IV.iii.62). The superlative iteration of this intensely politicised *amicitia* occurs in Exeter's elegiac account of the patriciate's assent to Henry's bellicose mythology of belonging:

> Suffolk first died: and York, all haggled over,
> Comes to him, where in gore he lay insteep'd,
> And takes him by the beard; kisses the gashes
> That bloodily did spawn upon his face;
> And cries aloud 'Tarry, dear cousin Suffolk!
> My soul shall thine keep company to heaven'.   (*V*: IV.vi.11–16)

The surprisingly lyrical evocation of a political ideal 'steeped' in gore does not go unquestioned. The vaulting ambitions of both Chorus and protagonist are textually placed in uncomfortably close quarters with the remorseless depiction of violation, theatrical or otherwise: '*O, prenez miséricorde! ayez pitié de moi!*' Whatever the grubby realities that surround such encounters on the field of combat, the 'swaggerer' Pistol has clearly been well-schooled by those who wish him to 'Be copy now to men of grosser blood,/And teach them how to war' (*V*: III.i.24–5). The attempt to forge a renewed citizen subjectivity through the spilling of blood is a strategic dramatic concern also in the later *Coriolanus*, yet in neither play is the proliferation of corpses seen to blur social divisions or resolve partisan loyalties. Indeed, in both plays sustained attention is devoted to the courting and carving up of bodies, to how the prevailing modes of sovereignty may be safeguarded (and ritualised) with scored limbs: 'And say "To-morrow is Saint Crispian."/Then will he strip his sleeve and show his scars,/And say "These wounds I had on Crispin's day"' (*V*: IV.iii.45–7).

Held fast within its own authoritative stage reality, the Chorus in *Henry V* may reassure us in seeming to harness the theatre of war within tales of finished actions in a distant past, in communicating our safe distance from the killing fields onstage. However, our seemingly irrepressible attraction down the centuries to engage with Shakespeare's characters in their bloody contests of Harfleur and Agincourt must inevitably excite interpretative labour on our own part as it speaks to the immense forces that spill into and warp our own everyday lives.

'To England will I steal'

In *A pensiue soules delight* (1615), John Norden urged his readership 'seeke you peace, and bee reconciled to God, before you vndertake warre with man'.[44] A generation later, Thomas Hobbes advised in his *Leviathan* (1651) that 'WARRE, consisteth not in Battell onely, or the act of fighting; but in a tract of time, wherein the Will to contend by Battell is sufficiently known.'[45] Shakespeare's audiences are similarly urged to attend to the feverish preparations for war.

As we have seen, *2 Henry IV* concludes with the young king's brother laying 'odds that, ere this year expire,/We bear our civil swords and native fire/As far as France' (*IV²*: V.v.98–100). *Henry V* duly opens with the newly crowned king orchestrating an extended meditation upon the justification of international theatres of war and the imperatives of his own political project. In this context, Paul Ricoeur remains illuminating in challenging expectations that intellectual disputation and the practice of violence might draw in contrary directions: 'La parole, la discussion, la rationalité ... elles sont une entreprise de réduction de la violence. La violence qui parle, c'est déjà une violence qui cherche à avoir raison; c'est une violence qui se place dans l'orbite de la raison et qui commence déjà de se nier comme violence.'[46][a] Hotspur resists his wife's pleas to tease out in language (and thus attenuate) his heady passions: 'hark you, Kate,/I must not have you henceforth question me' (*IV²*: II.iii.96–7). In the broader public sphere of the court, Henry ensures his resolve to wage war is

---

[a] 'Word, discussion, rationality ... they are an undertaking to diminish violence. Violence which speaks is already a violence which is seeking justification: it is a violence which locates itself within the domain of reason and which is already beginning to deny itself as being violence.'

successful because it is confirmed authoritatively by verbally sophisticated and eminently partisan speakers. Both king and prelates have a vested interest in arriving at the same conclusion. As Jean Bodin protested in *Les Six Livres de la République*, 'who is more enemie to a peaceable man, than a furious souldiour? to a mild countrey man, than a bloodie warrior? to a philosopher, than a captaine? to the wise, than fooles?'[47] However, on reflection, enemies may take on even more diverse shapes. The Church's expert disputants at the beginning of Shakespeare's play vividly recall an earlier 'scambling and unquiet time' when civil unrest deflected prying eyes from the wealth of the lords spiritual. In contrast, they must now bring to mind the present emergencies ('urged by the Commons') and, into the bargain, the loss of 'the better half of [their] possession' in the levying of funds for the Crown (*V*: I.i.4, 71, 8). At the dawn of the modern period, Georges Sorel insisted that 'To examine the effects of violence it is necessary to start from its distant consequences and not from its immediate results.'[48] Enlisted into the Lancastrian political project to perform selective acts of retrieval from the collective memory, the beleaguered Archbishop of Canterbury remains alert to his own interests. Nonetheless, in a play that trains audience attentions hard on the slippery, transformative potential of rhetoric, it might give the king further pause for thought that if 'fellows of infinite tongue can rhyme themselves into ... favours, they do always reason themselves out again' (*V*: V.ii.147–9).

Thomas Barnes argued vigorously in *Vox Belli, or, An Alarvm to Warre* (1626) that 'Our Lords counsell to love our enemies, doth no whit prejudice the just causes of warre',[49] and Shakespeare's prelates are similarly minded when the Church is being pressed to yield its bounty to the Crown. Thus spurred on, Canterbury questions the exercise – indeed, the very legitimacy – of Salic law, affirming English military intervention to be a rightful response to French resistance: 'There is no bar/To make against your highness' claim to France' (*V*: I.ii.35–6).[50] Here, Henry is not only empowered to redress a grievance with the instrument of violence, the play also thus initiates a thoroughgoing investigation into the privileges of history-making and political assertion.[51] In the course of this carefully managed debate, the audience must savour the referencing of 'pilfering borderers' amongst the king's British neighbours (*V*: I.ii.142) – a practice with which the English court itself appears thoroughly conversant, being prepared to raid the coffers of prelates and alien kings alike. Indeed, *Henry V* continues to probe this political discourse of larceny in all the dark corners of this dramatic world: ambitions of conquest across the Channel; Pistol's securing of Nell Quickly from Nym; and Bardolph's light-fingered antics, to name but a few. Emerging not for the first time as one of the playtext's many mock kings, Pistol urges his confederates 'let us to France, like horseleeches, my boys, to suck, to suck, the very blood to suck!' (*V*: II. iii.43–4).

While in *1 Henry IV* the heir apparent baulks at the nabbing of crowns at Gad's Hill, it appears that no such scruples hinder his actions in *Henry V*. In this arbitrary dramatic world, the 'Boy' takes the measure of members of the English forces like Pistol and concludes that 'Bardolph and Nym had ten times more valour than this roaring devil i'th'old play . . . and they are both hanged' (*V*: IV.iv.55–7). Unlike Bardolph, 'executed for robbing a church' (*V*: III.vii.86–7), Henry does not need to pilfer the wealth of his own lords spiritual. Their coffers have yielded abundant funds for his present needs to redeploy, nay like the French ladies to rename, the bodies and territories of others: 'in loving me you should love the friend of France, for I love France so well that I will not part with a village of it. I will have it all mine' (*V*: V.ii.160–2). The outraged Boy remarks that his masters 'will steal any thing, and call it purchase' and resolves 'I must leave them, and seek some better service: their villainy goes against my weak stomach, and therefore I must cast it up' (*V*: III.ii.36–7, 46–9). In the event, he tarries too long. Before Henry is able to unveil the nation's 'band of brothers', the audience has already been invited into the company of 'sworn brothers in filching' (*V*: IV.iii.60, III.ii.39–40). Indeed, by the close of the play, even Nell, like so many characters in this play, has fallen foul of the highly contagious 'malady of France', and so the newly widowed Pistol resolves 'To England will I steal, and there I'll steal' (*V*: V.i.75, 80).

In John Taylor's *A briefe remembrance of all the English monarchs* (1618), Henry is heard to utter 'Much bloud I shed, yet bloud-shed loued not.'[52] Such assertions are placed under severe scrutiny in Shakespeare's dramatic world, which is clearly dynamised by a blood-lust of various complexions – a blood-lust which, like all kinds of violence, seeks to close down the victims' potential for agency:

> ORLÉANS   The Duke of Bourbon longs for morning.
>
> RAMBURES   He longs to eat the English.
>
> CONSTABLE   I think he will eat all he kills.   (*V*: III.viii.82–4)

If French adversaries may, on occasions, be demonised for their illegitimate, nay inhuman, conduct, they are very far from being the only party to transgress in this manner. Strategies employed to render antagonists monstrous were widely in evidence in early modern print culture. However, more recently, the cultural theorist Idelber Avelar has enquired 'Can the very act of differentiating among various kinds of violence be accomplished without vindicating, justifying, or excusing any one kind of violence in particular?'[53] As we move frantically in *Henry V* from one enemy territory to another, audiences are prompted with increasing frequency to negotiate this thorny question. The invaders are vilified by Bourbon as nothing but 'Normans, but bastard Normans, Norman bastards!' belonging to 'that nook-shotten isle of Albion' (*V*: III.vi.10, 14). However, it remains a moot point how impressed we should be by Shakespeare's protagonist, who seeks to reconstitute regal subjectivity and to silence civil disorder with the massacring of foes abroad. The cumulative accounts of lost lives in Shakespeare's dramatic narrative are related in direct proportion to the king's commitment (like that of his father) to violate the prevailing political order and to plot alternative axes of governance.

'War is His beadle, war is His vengeance'

The brutal rescripting of cultural hierarchies occasioned by Henry's military ambitions had been promised even at the close of *2 Henry IV*. Here, the shedding of the affections (and indeed lives) of those formerly close to him are not seen to warrant distraction from his larger political ambitions. However, unlike his father or his son in Shakespeare's history plays, Henry V is found to inhabit (both verbally and politically) the savage spaces he creates with awe-inspiring vigour: 'What is it then to me, if impious war,/ Arrayed in flames like to the prince of fiends,/Do, with his smirched complexion all fell feats/Enlinked to waste and desolation?' (*V*: III.iv.15–18). In such contexts, we may be reminded of Judith Butler's formulation of 'ungrievable lives' – the lives of 'those that cannot be lost, and cannot be destroyed, because they already inhabit a lost and destroyed zone; they are, ontologically, and from the start, already lost and destroyed, which means that when they are destroyed in war, nothing is destroyed'.[54] Indeed, dispensing with the expendable has remained central to Henry's undertaking. On his accession, he forges a kingdom in which the valuable and transformative forces of deadly contest are no longer to be privatised and appropriated by factions. As a consequence, prompted by the interventions (and imperfect faiths) of clerics, kings, civilians and a time-defying Chorus, Shakespeare's audiences are urged to query the degree to which, in social, moral and political terms, violence may indeed be marked off as a deviant practice.

In his *Vox Belli, or, An Alarvm to Warre*, Barnes had pressed the question 'Is not the stretching out the sword to bloud sometimes *Gods* worke? Is it not a worke as *from* him, so *for* him? . . . To bee mercifull to him whom God would have destroyed by the sword, and to bee wise enough to provide for himselfe an escape from the curse, is very difficult.'[55] However, he was far from being the only voice in early modern print culture to marry God's work with that of the sword. In his sermon *Christiana-Polemica, or A preparatiue to warre* (1619), Abraham Gibson contended that 'King *Henry* the fifth of *England*, that good and valiant *Prince*, after his conquest in *France* . . . would haue all the glory ascribed to *God*.'[56] Furthermore, in accordance with the narrative emphases of earlier chronicles, Shakespeare's Henry is determined to affirm his own political authority by alluding repeatedly to his pious beliefs: 'some are yet ungotten and unborn/That shall have cause to curse the Dauphin's scorn./But this lies all within the will of God' (*V*: I.ii.287–9). In *Stratioticos* (1579), Leonard and Thomas Digges had insisted of the General that 'Aboue all things let him loue and feare God',[57] and Henry's prelates offer fulsome praise at the opening of the play that 'The king is full of grace and fair regard . . . a true lover of the holy church' (*V*: I.i.21–2).[58] Elsewhere, Geffrey Gates contended in *The defence of militarie profession* (1579) that 'He that is fitte for the Chappell, is meete for the fielde.'[59] Mindful of such expectations amongst contemporaries, Shakespeare returned with renewed energy to a dramatic technique he had employed earlier for the depiction of Richmond in *Richard III*. Here, the political saviour insists at several reprises in the company of his followers upon his right relationship with the highest authority. Thus, in his last history play of fifteenth-century England, Shakespeare's ambitious Lancastrian sovereign is heard to declare 'we have now no thought in us but France,/Save those to God' (*V*: I. ii.302–3).

In Leonard Wright's *The hunting of Antichrist* (1589), while Elizabeth is compared in a familiar manner to the Old Testament heroines Judith, Deborah and Esther, 'The triumphant victories of Machabeus' are equated with those of the 'inuincible Henrie the fift'.[60] If, in Shakespeare's play, an astonished Constable of France invokes the 'Dieu de batailles' (*V*: III.vi.15) in witnessing the unremitting victories of the British invaders, Henry is afforded an invocation onstage of much greater length to the 'God of battles' when he beseeches the avenging Lord to 'steel my soldiers' hearts' (*V*: IV.i.263). Nonetheless, it remains disputable whether piety, psychological crisis of purpose or political desperation (or a combination of all

three) prompt Shakespeare's king to perform the painful labours of memory and seek absolution from the sins of the fathers:

> Not to-day, O Lord,
> O, not to-day, think not upon the fault
> My father made in compassing the crown!
> I Richard's body have interred anew;
> And on it have bestow'd more contrite tears
> Than from it issued forced drops of blood:
> Five hundred poor I have in yearly pay,
> Who twice a-day their wither'd hands hold up
> Toward heaven, to pardon blood; and I have built
> Two chantries, where the sad and solemn priests
> Sing still for Richard's soul. More will I do;
> Though all that I can do is nothing worth,
> Since that my penitence comes after all,
> Imploring pardon.   (*V*: IV.i.266–79)

Here, momentarily, Shakespeare's play concerns itself with the cleans-
ing, rather than the spilling, of blood. Henry has actively sought to
militarise his world by assuming the 'port of Mars', and yet here he pleads
for protection from a greater wrath than his own. This turning to the Lord
on High assumes a number of guises in this play. Most cynically, in
a dramatic world convulsed by brutality and mired in bloodshed,
Bourbon has already had recourse to Scripture and concluded that '*Le
chien est retourné à son propre vomissement, et la truie lavée au bourbier*' (*V*:
III.viii. 59–60). A number of critical voices have remained markedly
unimpressed by the acts of spiritual and historical recollection performed
on the eve of battle by Shakespeare's hero himself. While A. C. Bradley was
able to identify 'many fine traits' in the hero of Agincourt, he could not
repress the conclusion that 'he is still his father's son, the son of the man
whom Hotspur called a "vile politician". Henry's religion, for example, is
genuine . . . but it is also superstitious – an attempt to buy off supernatural
vengeance for Richard's blood; and it is also in part political, like his
father's projected crusade.'[61] Significantly, Henry's pious interjections are
most often reserved for public performative spaces at court or the vicinity
of the battlefield. However, if, as in *Hamlet*, we are here unexpectedly
invited to an intimate encounter with a king in private meditation, it must
be conceded that every soliloquy that the protagonist has been afforded in
the Second Henriad has been focused in one way or another upon his
political survival. The early modern age, like our own, interrogated vigorously the status and function of the profession of faith on the field of

combat and frequently arrived at no more sanguine conclusions than many of those circulating in more contemporary cultural debates. Elizabeth's closest counsellor, Lord Burghley, soberly advised his own son not to 'train' his own offspring 'up to the wars, for he that sets up his rest only to live by that profession can hardly be an honest man or good Christian'.[62] In the rival political camp of Philip II's Spanish empire, Francisco de Valdés is discovered proffering similar advice in his *Espeio y deceplina militar* (1589) for his Spanish readers: 'The day a man picks up his pike to become a soldier is the day he ceases to be a Christian.'[63]

More generally, each of the dramatic episodes associated with the protagonist in Shakespeare's play returns to this concern with dynastic preservation at all costs. Nowhere, of course, is this more evident than at Agincourt itself. Some two years before the staging of *Henry V*, John Norden had argued in *The mirror of honor* (1597) that 'True glorie is neuer gotten in the warres without Religion and virtue.'[64] The magnitude of Henry's purpose is not in doubt at the French court when his emissary, Exeter, urges the French King 'in the bowels of the Lord,/[To] Deliver up the crown'. If he will not, he must confront the prospect that 'in fierce tempest is [Henry] coming,/In thunder and in earthquake, like a Jove,/That, if requiring fail, he will compel' (*V*: II.iv.100–4). Subsequently, on the battlefield of Agincourt, on hearing that 'The French have reinforced their scattered men', Henry rails 'Then every soldier kill his prisoners' (*V*: IV.vi.36–7). Shakespeare's king thus reserves the full performance of his Olympian ire for the moment he hears of the refusal of the French forces to submit to his invading troops.

Gentili argued authoritatively,

> Frequently ... a prisoner is slain through no fault of his own, but because of the ambition and avarice of his captors, each of whom wishes him for his own. That is altogether cruel and unjust. Unjust, too, is the act of the one who preferred to kill men when he might have captured them. Therefore prisoners are not to be slain.[65]

Somewhat earlier in the play, the Boy is discovered, reflecting ominously upon his vulnerable plight: 'I must stay with the lackeys, with the luggage of our camp: the French might have a good prey of us, if he knew of it; for there is none to guard it but boys' (*V*: IV.iv.58–61). Gentili added in his own treatise that 'Children should always be spared'; and, in response to the report of the subsequent slaughter, the outraged Fluellen protests, 'Kill the poys and the luggage! 'Tis expressly against the law of arms' (*V*: IV. vii.1–2).[66] Indeed, Gower attributes Henry's decree to slay French captives to be a direct response to the enemy's own inhumanity: 'There's not a boy left alive . . . wherefore the king, most worthily, hath caused every soldier to cut his prisoner's throat. O, 'tis a gallant king!' (*V*: IV.vii.4, 7–8). Interestingly, the Chorus makes no mention of this event, but Henry is swiftly heard to proclaim, 'I was not angry since I came to France/Until this instant' (*V*: IV.vii.45–6).[67]

John Masefield concluded that 'Henry V is the one commonplace man in the eight [history] plays.'[68] Might the order to slaughter French captives add to our disaffection with this 'commonplace' man who relies upon the blows of word and sword to realise fully his ambitions? At this point, it might be remembered that such a man had also instructed his 'uncle Exeter' earlier in the action to 'use mercy' to all the capitulating inhabitants of Harfleur (*V*: III.iv.51, 54). However, is Henry's decisive action at Agincourt an unyielding response of outrage at his antagonists' savagery, a telling example of battlefield tactics then current or, perhaps, yet another lucid insight into a disarming ruthlessness limned earlier in his progress through the Henriad? Shakespeare's protagonist himself queries, 'Art thou aught else but place, degree and form,/Creating awe and fear in other men?' (*V*: IV.i.211, 218–19). In these same years, Robert Barret's 'Captain' argued in *The Theorike and Practike of Moderne Warres* (1598) that 'the souldier is bound to serue his Prince, and to defend his desseignes; and it toucheth him not, much to examine whether the warre be iust or iniust, not being against Gods true religion: but in such a case, I would wish men to be well aduised'.[69] The proliferation of responses *and silences* which greets this enquiry on Shakespeare's stage has inevitably excited enduring debate amongst critics and audiences, feeding the ongoing interrogation of the political leadership of Shakespeare's most successful warlord.

> HENRY   I myself heard the king say he would not be ransomed.
> WILLIAMS Ay, he said so, to make us fight cheerfully: but when our throats
>   are cut, he may be ransomed, and we ne'er the wiser.
>
> (*V*: IV.i.171–3)

'And what have kings, that privates have not too'

Elaborating upon her critical thesis of 'ungrievable lives', Judith Butler argues gravely that 'we do not feel the same horror and outrage over the loss of their lives as we do over the loss of those lives that bear national or religious similarity to our own'.[70] Equally grimly, Shakespeare's *Henry V* repeatedly places principles of oppositionality and difference under severe pressure in a dramatic world where the only unassailable governing force is that of violence itself.

The Constable of France likens his English aggressor to 'the Roman Brutus' (*V*: II.iv.36). Among the community of his own British country-men, there is evidence that the Lancastrian sovereign may be celebrated in notably affectionate terms: 'The king's a bawcock, and a heart of gold, a lad of life, an imp of fame, of parents good, of fist most valiant' (*V*: IV.i.44–5). However, the play continues to engender varying, sometimes contradict-ory responses to the political project that Henry seeks to impose. The king imagines for his courtiers how the 'guiltless drops' of blood of the slaugh-tered might mouth 'every one a woe, a sore complaint' if the nation committed itself to an unjust war (*V*: I.ii.25–6). Nonetheless, this is also the commander who urges his deserting troops to 'close the wall up with our English dead' (*V*: III.i.2). In the chaotic landscape of strewn bodies in the aftermath of Agincourt, Montjoy laments that as princes 'Lie drowned and soaked in mercenary blood/So do our vulgar drench their peasant limbs/In blood of princes' (*V*: IV.vii.66–8). In this way, he summons up an apocalyptic vision in which principles of parentage, social privilege and nation have been found wanting in the face of indiscriminate violence and, as a consequence, have utterly collapsed on these killing fields.

In this respect, *Henry V* certainly shares a thematic kinship with *Hamlet*, a play staged just a year or so later, with its meditations upon the profession of violence and political command. Indeed, in the later tragedy, the protagonist also reminds us that 'Imperial Caesar, dead and turned to clay,/Might stop a hole to keep the wind away' (*V*.i.196–7). Nonetheless, in the same year that *Henry V* was being performed, Richard Crompton published *The mansion of magnanimitie* (1599). In its opening pages the reader was advised, 'There is no difference betwixt the greatest person & the meanest man, when they are both dead, if there be no vertues or deedes of fame done by them, whereby to commend their name to posteritie.'[71] All these texts point to a radical questioning of the laws of cultural priority that shaped the early modern commonwealth. Indeed, in direct comparison with dramaturgical modes exploited in the later *Hamlet*, in *Henry V* Shakespeare deploys a range of characters strategically around his protagonist who serve to place him in striking relief. All too often Henry is found to rub shoulders in the narrative with those like Fluellen who are 'touched with choler, hot as gunpowder,/And quickly will return an injury' (*V*: IV.vii.162–3), or those like Bardolph who are 'white-livered and red-faced, by the means whereof a faces it out but fights not' (*V*: III.ii.27–8). In the midst of this unruly crew, we may find ourselves captivated, like the Chorus, by the arresting performances of impassioned leadership which Henry exhibits as he threatens his adversaries: 'if we be hindered,/We shall your tawny ground with your red blood/Discolour' (*V*: III.vii.142–4). However, the Lancastrian, like the Danish prince, is distinguished dramatically by the multiple and strategic production of public selves. If, as was noted in Chapter 3, Thomas Churchyard railed that 'now is he accoumpted no bodie, that can not deceiue a multitude',[72] it might be recalled that princess Katherine confirms that '*les langues des hommes sont pleines de tromperies!*' (*V*: V.ii.112–13) – and indeed, there appears no reason for the audience to drop its own guard in such matters.

From the very beginning of *Henry V* (and indeed throughout the second Henriad), we are urged to take Hal-Henry-Harry seriously as a shrewd tactician and an expert rhetorician. Indeed, the unscrupulous Canterbury waxes lyrical in the celebration of his new sovereign: 'Hear him but reason in divinity,/. . . You would desire the king were made a prelate' (*V*: I.i.38, 40). Such praise of the protagonist's 'sweet and honeyed sentences' (*V*: I.i.50) resembles the tributes reserved for eirenic intercessors like Marina, Perdita and Katharine of Aragon in the later romances. However, before we invest too deeply in the young king's prowess in ethical matters and those of faith, Canterbury identifies a singular talent in which Shakespeare's hero appears to have garnered particular success: 'List his discourse of war, and you shall hear/A fearful battle rendered you in music' (*V*: I.i.43–4). While we are given ample opportunity to bear witness to Henry's rhetorical expertise on the battlefield, Shakespeare's narrative reserves his final triumph of oratory for the chambers of the French court. A testy Samuel Johnson protested that 'The character of the King is well supported except in his courtship, where he has neither the vivacity of Hal, nor the grandeur of Henry . . . The great defect of this play is the emptiness and narrowness of the last act, which a very little diligence might have easily avoided.'[73] It does indeed seem that Henry's desires have been wholly sated in combat and, in the company of the French princess, auditors on- and offstage discover him assuming an unexpected, less expansive persona of courtly lover: 'Is it possible dat I should love de *ennemi* of France?' (*V*: V.ii.158).

Norman Rabkin proposed that in order to 'complete' Shakespeare's portrayal of 'achieved manhood', Shakespeare was compelled to confirm his negotiation of 'mature sexuality'.[74] If this were the case, it remains interesting that all these acts of completion (justification of title, promotion of authority, and security of royal tenure) must be accomplished for the new king away from his realm of England. In a final display of tactical assertion, Henry decides to vest his final claim to lordship (surely the pleasure principle that has governed all his proceedings in the Henriad) in the body of Katherine: 'thou must therefore needs prove a good soldier-breeder. Shall not thou and I, between Saint Denis and Saint George, compound a boy [?] ... What sayest thou, my fair flower de luce?' (*V*: V. ii.188–9). In *The Famous Victories* this courtship is played out unequivocally in terms of irrepressible appetite (Henry – 'Nay I loue her and will haue her') or military exchange between unequal parties: 'I would to God, that I had your Maiestie,/As fast in loue, as you haue my father in warres' (F3ᵛ). The Elizabethan jurist Gentili concluded that 'it is the will of the victor which settles everything ... [and] it is the part of him who grants peace, not of him who sues for it, to lay down the conditions'.[75] In the event, the dramatic emphasis upon the commerce of bodies, dead and alive, in both *The Famous Victories* and *Henry V* continues until the very closing moments of each play.

'Oui, coupe la gorge, par ma foi'

The aim of this discussion has been to interrogate the motivations (early modern and modern) surrounding the appetite for violence in our recoveries of the distant, foreign territory of the past. From the study of *Henry V* it may indeed appear that in the desire to unpick our own politics of violence, we are locked into a beguiling *mise-en-abîme*. We look back to the productions of early modern playhouses, as their own audiences were invited to behold the figuration of their own riven society in the conflicts of previous centuries. Indeed, the plays' own characters, like Shakespeare's Henry V, are urged to 'unwind your bloody flag' whilst simultaneously instructed to recognise that their future is also embedded in the past:

> Look back into your mighty ancestors
> Go, my dread lord, to your great-grandsire's tomb,
> From whom you claim; invoke his warlike spirit ... (*V*: I.ii.101–4)

Following in the footsteps of Ciceronian, but most notably subsequent Augustinian reasoning, the medieval theologian Thomas Aquinas emphasised that 'The role of prudence is to direct the prudent man to do what ought to be done by considering not only the present but also the past.'[76] Ralegh was similarly disposed in the opening decades of the seventeenth century when he came to consider the purport of his own memorial ambitions in *The History of the World*: 'it [is] the end and scope of all

History, to teach by example of times past, such wisedome as may guide our desires and actions'.[77]

As we have seen, Shakespeare's novice king enlists the memories and suave intellects of his clerics at the beginning of *Henry V* to excavate the past so that he (or his nation) may secure a privileged and highly politicised mnemonic space – turning back to historical precedent in order to seek redress for present emergencies. Equally thought-provoking in the modern period, one of the most significant contributions that Michel Foucault offered contemporary cultural debate was his insistence that 'History', the selective discharge of collective memory, was 'the discourse of the obligations power uses to subjugate'.[78] In Shakespeare's dramatic narrative, the French (like their English adversaries) are minded to concentrate upon prior narratives of political defeat (to 'late examples/Left by the fatal and neglected English/Upon our fields' (*V*: II.iv.12–14)) in order to forge more cohesive (or effective) strategies for the governance of their nation. Indeed, the French king proves himself unable to shake off his age's fondness for exploiting the past, recalling 'our too much memorable shame/When Cressy battle fatally was struck,/And all our princes captiv'd by the hand/Of that black name, Edward, Black Prince of Wales' (*V*: II.iv.53–6).

More generally, as we have witnessed from discussions in this and earlier chapters, Shakespeare's history plays focus unwaveringly on the decline of human (self-)government, and on the manner in which acts of violence are intimately connected with the need to resist such decline. Henry does not initiate a radically innovative regime of government in 'the port of Mars', but revives the figure of 'the Black Prince, that young Mars of men' for a new generation. Drawing strategically upon the mythologies of the nation and supported vigorously by those who (need to) commit themselves to his political project, the young king affirms his legitimacy with an awe-inspiring violence of purpose. This is facilitated by the imaginative resurrection, the tactical recollection, of his 'great-grandsire' at Crécy on both sides of the Channel: 'Awake remembrance of these valiant dead,/ And with your puissant arm renew their feats' (*V*: I.ii.115–16).

In such contexts, Phyllis Rackin remains illuminating in her contention that 'It takes three plays for Henry to reconstruct the royal authority that was lost when [Bolingbroke] usurped the English throne ... [yet] the authority he reconstructs is deeply compromised by his recourse to Machiavellian strategies of political manipulation and theatrical display.'[79] It is unsurprising that a play such as Shakespeare's *Henry V*, which is so obsessively focused on the formation of group identities, maintains a thoroughgoing investigation into the means by which such processes operate. Moreover, it is evident from the writings of Shakespeare's contemporaries, such as Bacon, Hayward and Ralegh, discussed in Chapter 1, that the playwright was not alone in interrogating the moral and political efficacy of violence as an instrument of political government. Indeed, Henry himself re-examines ancient times in order to excite the spirits of the 'noble English' to match earlier paradigms of violent excess: 'Whose blood is fet from fathers of war-proof,/Fathers that, like so many Alexanders,/Have in these parts from morn till even fought' (*V*: III.i.17–20). Ultimately, as the Henriad unfolds, whether in combat against the forces of Hotspur, the Archbishop of York or the French king, Hal-Henry-Harry produces his own history as triumphant survivor without sustained – indeed, often negligible – concern for the casualties amassed. Shakespeare invites his audiences to remain richly sensitive to the very singular, nay single-minded, nature of his hero's vaulting ambition: 'when France is mine and I am yours, then yours is France and you are mine' (*V*: V.ii.162–3).

As was witnessed at the opening of this discussion, when Shakespeare turned his attentions to the figure of Henry V, he had an embarrassment of textual riches dating back some 200 years from which to draw his narrative. In his own time, Holinshed had proclaimed that 'This Henrie was ... a capteine against whome fortune never frowned, nor mischance once spurned', as well as rehearsing a strain of praise already in evidence in earlier sources: 'a paterne in princehood, a lode-starre in honour, and mirrour of magnificence'.[80] In the centuries which followed there were voices, like that of Thomas Carlyle, who affirmed an unbroken continuity between the chronicle celebrations and Shakespeare's dramatisation of the medieval monarch: 'That battle of Agincourt strikes me as one of the most perfect things, in its sort, we anywhere have of Shakespeare's.'[81] However, as has also been witnessed, Johnson was notable in the eighteenth century for striking some emphatic notes of dissent in the play's critical reception. Half a century later, an impassioned William Hazlitt confessed he felt 'little love or admiration' for Shakespeare's Henry: 'He was a hero, that is, he was ready to sacrifice his own life for the pleasure of destroying thousands of other lives ... How then do we like him? We like him in the play. There he is a very amiable monster.'[82] One hundred years later, A. C. Bradley submitted grudgingly that Henry V was 'perhaps, the most *efficient* character drawn by Shakespeare, unless Ulysses, in *Troilus and Cressida*, is his equal'.[83] In the twentieth century, theatre and cinema audiences on occasions found urgent reasons in their consumption of *Henry V* for the moralising and reaffirmation of violence, for the recovery of triumphant war heroes. However, there is less evidence in the critical history of that century of a warm reception for the military idealism inherited from earlier ages. J. C. Bromley remains broadly representative of a large and ever-growing corpus of Shakespearean criticism devoted to the history plays in submitting dolefully 'Much has been written, and more will be, about ideal kings and ideal relationships in Shakespeare. We have found no ideal kings.'[84]

In recent decades, Paul Ricoeur has continued to scrutinise for modern readers the complexities surrounding the human compulsion to remember, underlining the unequal, assymetrical relations that exist between recollection and forgetfulness:

> there cannot be a happy forgetting in the same way as one can dream of a happy memory. What would be the mark of forgiveness on this admission? Negatively, it would consist in inscribing the powerlessness of reflection and speculation at the head of the list of things to be renounced, ahead of the irreparable; and, positively, in incorporating this renouncement of knowledge into the small pleasures of happy memory when the barrier of forgetting is pushed back a few degrees. Could one then speak of an *ars oblivionis*, in the sense in which an *ars memoriae* has been discussed on several occasions?[85]

Shakespeare's *Henry V* urges us to address precisely such questions concerning our appetites to forget or renounce, our motivations to remember and to misremember. At the heart of this play is the questioning of the status and function of violence in the political life of the nation. In 1599, the preacher Lancelot Andrewes hailed the departure of Robert Devereux, Earl of Essex, on a military campaign against the Irish as 'a war sanctified'.[86] However, even the commander himself had conceded a few years earlier that such ventures might not be covered in glory: as bodies were dishonestly trafficked back and forth by recruiting officers, the Earl declared to the Star Chamber in 1596 that 'the liege and free people of this realm are sold like cattle in a market'.[87] *Henry V*, like all of Shakespeare's history plays, repeatedly returns attention to the disturbingly creative ways in which cultures of violence disclose the sobering realities of corruption and human failure. From the troubled vantage point of the twenty-first century, it can come as no surprise that we turn back to such four hundred year-old dramas to re-engage with these pressing and vexed enquiries.

CHAPTER 5

'the childe of his great Mistris favour, but the sonne of Bellona': The Conflict-Ridden Careers of Robert Devereux, 2nd Earl of Essex

The rumour is gaining ground here that your Queen has ordered troops to be sent to the help of the Belgians; and it is added that the most noble Earl of Leicester will command the forces that are to go. If this report be true you have obtained what you so greatly desired, for I doubt not you will have a share in the enterprise. I would not even if I could, weaken or blunt the edge of your spirit, still I must advise you now and then to reflect that young men who rush into danger incautiously almost always meet an inglorious end, and deprive themselves of the power of serving their country; for a man who falls at an early age cannot have done much for his country. Let not therefore an excessive desire of fame hurry you out of your course . . . It is the misfortune, or rather the folly of our age, that most men of high birth think it more honorable to do the work of a soldier than of a leader.[1]

It is in this manner that the ageing diplomat and counsellor Hubert Languet wrote to his much younger correspondent, Philip Sidney, in February 1578. As becomes apparent from the tenor of this cautionary advice, the reformist had assumed much of the role of mentor for the young Englishman and remained keenly alert to the nobleman's passionate investment in chivalric heroism and to its likely outcomes.[2] Such passions on the part of Sidney clearly permeated all aspects of his intellectual and political ambitions. Earlier in 1574, he had written from Padua to Languet, 'I long so greatly to be acquainted with [geometry], and the more so because I have always felt sure that it is of the greatest service in the art of war.'[3] Indeed, this frustrated warrior recruited those close to him to his ways of thinking. Sidney's brother, Robert, sent a letter from Prague to their father at the end of the decade, confessing 'My brother wrote if there were any good wars I should go to them, but as yet I have heard of none.'[4] By 1581, Languet would be dead, and his protégé would only survive him by five years: Philip was injured on the battlefield of Zutphen in 1586 and died of his wounds. In that same year, in *The Blazon of Gentrie* (1586), Sir John

Ferne submitted that 'To obtayne estate of gentlenes, through seruice done, in your soueraignes warres, to the defence of the Church, your kinge, or Countrie, is of all humaine actions, most excellent and worthy.' However, a more plangent note would be sounded by Barnabe Riche as the century drew to a close: 'Nothing waxeth young in this world but warre.'[5]

Focusing upon Robert Devereux, 2nd Earl of Essex, the present discussion explores the depictions witnessed in earlier chapters of the military commander hungering for a field of combat on which to found a new, international project for his nation. However, more than anywhere else in this study, we are compelled to attend to the perception of, and responses to, the earl's words and actions in a thoroughly European context as the continent progressively made acquaintance with this new player wishing to enter its many and various fields of conflicts.

Sidney Redivivus

The 2nd Earl of Essex aligned his cause explicitly with that of Philip Sidney and assumed publicly the mantle of his heir in the years after Sidney's death. This was a loss mourned widely abroad as well as in his native land. The French reformist scholar and diplomat Philippe du Plessis-Mornay wrote to Sidney's father-in-law, Sir Francis Walsingham, at the beginning of 1587 in response to 'la triste nouvelle de la mort de M. de Sidney':

> J'ai eu des travaulx et des traverses en ce miserable temps, mais rien qui m'ait tant pesé ni tant percé le coeur, rien qui m'ait plus vivement touché ni en particulier, ni en public; je l'ai ressentie en moi pour vous et pour moi mesmes; je le pleure encores et le regrette, non pour l'Angleterre seulement, mais pour la chrestienté. C'est ce qui me faict desesperer de mieulx quand le bon s'en va, et la lie nous demeure.[6a]

Essex had been knighted by Leicester on the field of conflict at Zutphen and he inherited Sidney's military ambition ('I give to my beloved and much honoured Lord, the Earl of Essex, my best Sword'[7]), married his widow Frances (née Walsingham) and, in time, drew Sidney's kin, such as his brother Robert, and the nobleman's close associates, such as Fulke Greville, into his ambit. Indeed, in the year following Sidney's death in

---

[a] 'The sad news of the death of Sir [Philip] Sidney'; 'I have had trials and tribulations in these wretched times, but nothing that has so weighed upon me or so riven my heart, nothing which has more keenly touched my heart either in my private or my public life; I have felt it on your account and on my own; I still weep for him and miss him, not only on England's account, but for the whole of Christendom. This is what renders me the most dejected, when the good pass away, and we are left with the dregs.'

1587, the earl offered the queen a jewel representing a rainbow uniting two pillars: one fractured, denoting Sidney, and the other intact, assuming the undertakings of both. Moreover, others were similarly mindful of the earl's self-proclaimed act of succession.[8] James VI of Scotland had contributed lyrics to the Cambridge collection *Lachrymae* recalling Sidney's passing, yet noted in a communication to Essex (via Anthony Bacon) that he was 'bien aise d'avoir recouvert en sa person Sire Philipe Sydnay'.[9a] Elsewhere, the English translation of Francesco Colonna's *Hypnerotomachia: The strife of loue in a dreame* (1592) had been initially dedicated to Sidney, but now Essex was asked graciously to accept the tribute as dedicatee in his stead: 'When I had determined (Right honorable) to dedicate this Booke, to the euerlyuing vertues of that matchlesse Knight Syr Phillip Sydney; me thought that I could not finde out a more Noble personage then your selfe, and more fit, to patronize, shield, and defende my dutie to the deade, then your Honour.'[10]

Nonetheless, Essex remained restive. In 1589 he was writing in his habitual state of impatience to the Huguenot military commander and theorist François de la Noue (or 'Bras de fer'). The latter had previously made the acquaintance of the Sidney brothers and now learned from the earl that he 'should be very happy to see some opportunity by which we could together win honour and serve the common weal. I am idle here, and have nothing to do but to hearken for such opportunities.'[11] In the same year, George Peele's panegyric *An Ecglogve Gratvlatorie* (1589) welcomed Essex back from military exploits in Portugal: if there was still time and space to mourn the loss three years earlier of 'that great *Shepherd* good *Philisides*', this was also the moment, Peele affirmed, to honour 'this louelie swaine' in '*Nue reared Troy*'.[12] Again, it seems, at the Accession Day Tilt (17th November) of 1590 there was still considerable cultural capital to be drawn from an association with the Sidneian legacy. Peele celebrated, amidst the procession of valiant knights, the arrival of 'Yoong Essex, that thrice honorable Earle,/Yclad in mightie Armes of mourners hue,/And plume as blacke, as is the Ravens wing,/ ... And all his companie in funerall blacke,/As if he mourn'd to thinke of him he mist,/Sweete Sydney.'[13] As Roger B. Manning has underlined, 'At first sight, the courtly ritual of jousting appears to be remote from the tactical needs of modern cavalry warfare with its emphasis upon group action and discipline, but it may have been closer to the reality of how noblemen fought, since they continued to show a fondness for individual displays of prowess.'[14]

---

[a] 'well pleased to have Sir Philip Sidney restored in him [i.e. Essex]'.

Strikingly, even after the earl's execution in 1601, Sir Thomas Smith demonstrated how the fallen courtier continued to be inscribed within markedly Sidneian narratives:

> that Noble but vnfortunate *E. of Essex,* of whom many through the world, do make in diuers kinds, but (as that learned and heroycall Poet *Sir Phil. Sidney* speaks of *Prince Plangus*) neuer any can make but honorable mention.[15]

Nor, during his career, did Devereux forsake Sidney's consuming preoccupation with military affairs. Henri IV's envoy to Elizabeth's court at the close of the 1590s reported that '[il] a très grande part au Conseil de la Reyne. Le Comte d'Essex n'en ose quasi parler pour conseiller la guerre, se rendant suspect comme celuy qui se veut agrandir par les armes'.[16a] Indeed, in the years after his execution, a former member of the earl's secretariat, Robert Naunton, concluded that 'this noble Lord' was caught in a highly volatile 'mixture between prosperity, and adversity, once the childe of his great Mistris favour, but the sonne of *Bellona*'.[17]

England, Essex and Bellona

As the French Wars of Religion continued to rage year after year (we have already seen that Ralegh thought them 'endless'), the envoys from the Venetian Republic remained eager to assess the radically changing political climate of Europe in their wake – and the political agency of Elizabeth's England never slipped from their sights. Already by 1569, the *Serenissima*'s ambassador at the French court, Giovanni Corero, was indicating in his *relazione*: 'Verso la regina d'Inghilterra non possono quelle maestà avere bona volontà, perchè, oltre l'odio che è fra quelle due nazioni come naturale, e fa che gl'Inglesi nei consigli cono da' Francesi chiamati *nostri nemici antichi*, si è anco veduto che quella regina . . . ha sempre accarezzati i ribelli di Francia.'[18b] As was discussed in Chapter 1, English gentlemen might view the French Wars of Religion as an apprenticeship in arms, and

---

[a] '[he] plays a very large part in the Queen's council. The Earl of Essex is scarce so bold as to speak out to counsel war, causing himself to be suspected as one who seeks advancement by arms.' See De Maisse, *A Journal of all that was Accomplished by Monsieur de Maisse, Ambassador in England from King Henri IV to Queen Elizabeth anno domini 1597,* trans. and intro. G. B. Harrison and R. A. Jones (London: Nonesuch Press, 1931), p. 17.

[b] 'There can be no accord between the Queen of England and His Majesty [in France], for, apart from the hatred which is a habit of thinking between the two nations, and which means that the English are referred to in the councils of the French as *our old enemies,* it is also known that that the queen . . . has always extended aid to the rebels in France.'

Elizabeth's administration (and Shakespeare's fifteenth-century kings) were not averse to exporting the warrior ambitions of headstrong subjects to foreign climes. Nevertheless, as her own reign wore on, more and more voices were given to discussing the great reluctance of the last Tudor sovereign to implicate herself in military affairs abroad. Apart from the bloody campaigns in Ireland, there were precious few opportunities on the battlefield before the mid-1580s for young noblemen (reared on Roman military histories and chivalric romances) to win the attentions of their sovereign. Manning has stressed that 'Elizabeth I and James VI and I neglected to foster martial values',[19] and the billowing rhetoric of empire circulating regularly at the English court did little to impress audiences further afield, as the Venetian envoy in Paris, Giroloamo Lippomano, demonstrated in his own *relazione* in 1577:

> non voglio restar di dire che ritrovandomi io un giorno sopra il fosso di Parigi per di fuora via, con un segretario dello ambasciatore d'Inghilterra, e passando per dinanzi la porta del Tempio, che sta per ordinario sempre fermata, egli mi disse: 'Per questa porta entraron gl'Inglesi quando presero questa città.' E io gli dissi: 'E per quale uscirono?' Al che egli non mi seppe che risponder mai, se non che la lor regina ancora s'intitola regina d'Inghilterra, d'Irlanda e di Francia. Ed io soggionsi che così avevo inteso; ma che li re di Francia erano padroni di Guascogna e di Normandia.[20a]

By the mid-1580s Elizabeth resolved at last to approve formally her government's military intervention to assist England's fellow Reformists in the Dutch Revolt. In Burghley's opinion, the Tudor state would have to 'sustayn a gretar war, than ever in any memory of man it hath done'.[21] Above all, Elizabeth's government sought strategically to prevent the consolidation of Spanish power in the Low Countries.[22] This significant reorientation in foreign policy finally offered some possibilities for experience in the field (and social mobility) amongst the realm's aspiring subjects.

Earlier in the century, Walter Devereux, 1st Earl of Essex in this latest creation and father to Robert, had sought advancement for himself and his family by assuming military command in the Elizabethan Plantation of Ulster. Beginning in 1573, Walter Devereux's campaigns involved

---

[a] 'I cannot refrain from mentioning that I was walking out one day beyond the Paris ditches with a secretary of the English ambassador and as we passed in front of the Temple Gate, which is nearly always closed, he said to me: "It is by this gate that the English entered when they took this city." And I said to him: "And by which did they exit?" To which he did not deign to make answer but added that their sovereign still holds the titles of Queen of England, Ireland and of France. And I added that I had heard that, but the Kings of France still ruled over Normandy and Gascony.'

numerous scenes of slaughter and blood-letting in Ireland (notably, at Rathlin Island[23]), and brought little apart from bankruptcy and illness to his personal fortunes. He was named Earl Marshal of Ireland in March 1576, but died of dysentery in the autumn of that year in Dublin Castle. His son was but ten years old at the time. Richard Davies gave the funeral sermon at Carmarthen in West Wales two months later, stressing presciently the fields of experience which would shape the newly orphaned Robert: 'The naturall and vnforced courtesie and affabiliy that was in your Father, and that excellent mixture of disposition and aptnesse, both for warre and peace, doth promise to the worlde a singular perfection in you hereafter.'[24]

In reality, Essex's inheritance was one riddled with debts, mostly owed to the Crown. In the spring of 1589 on the eve of departure for a raid on Portugal, the earl wrote to the Vice Chamberlain plaintively, 'my Debts at the least two or three and twenty Thousand Pounds. Her Majesty's Goodness hath been so great ... No Way left to repair myself but mine own Adventure ... If I speed well, I will adventure to be rich; if not, I will never live to see the End of my Poverty.'[25] Almost a decade later, as the sixteenth century (and Essex's fortunes) drew to a close, the earl penned and published an *Apologie* which again bore witness to this resolution to be a man-at-arms: 'I sawe no way of merite lie so open to me, as by seruice in her warres.'[26]

Shortly after the death of her husband, Essex's mother, Lettice Knollys, curtailed her widowhood and married Robert Dudley, Earl of Leicester, in 1578 – in fact, the couple had been suspected of a long-standing liaison for some time. In these years Essex entered Trinity College Cambridge (fondly termed 'Ithacam meam'[27]) and appears to have engaged in his studies with remarkable industry.[28] In his later *Apologie*, he would promote his intellectual interests as marked since his earliest years – 'my contemplatiue retirednesse in *Wales*, and my bookishnesse from my very childhoode'.[29] Nonetheless, even in his adolescence, Essex was also given to a showmanship that would characterise so much of his later adult life. The sixteen-year-old sent a request to his estate manager for 'one verie faire suite of apparel against St. George day; satten doublet, velvet hose, and jirkin of crimson laid on wth silver lace, wth my foote-cloth, my mens lyveries, etc.'.[30] Although he may have been received at court in the years after his father's death, Essex seems to have been more regularly in attendance from 1584 at the age of nineteen. Subsequently, he joined the military campaign led by his stepfather, Leicester, in the Low Countries. By 1586 he had clearly confirmed his entrée into the court under the auspices of Leicester: he made his first appearance in the

Accession Day Tilts in that year, and by May it was being reported that 'when [the queen] is abroade, noboddy [is] neere but my lord of Essex. At night my lord is at cardes or one game or an other with her.'[31] Indeed, by June 1587 he was named Master of the Horse (one of his stepfather's former offices).

More generally, audiences at home and abroad continued to receive updated information concerning the political changefulness of the Tudor court. Reports to Madrid by diplomats and agents in London gave clear and repeated indications of the choleric factionalism that lay at the heart of Elizabeth's entourage. In August 1587, the Spanish court learned that 'The earl of Essex, who is a very handsome youth, Master of the Horse to the Queen, and much favoured by her, has quarrelled with Ralegh the other favourite, and during the dispute Essex boxed Ralegh's ears.'[32] Steven May argues persuasively that some court lyrics penned during these years (in this case by Essex himself) might relate directly to animosities being played out within the nation's elite: 'But oh, no more, it is to much to thinke,/So pure a mouth should puddle water [or Walter] drinke.'[33] Once again, at the beginning of 1589, it was reported by one Marco Antonio Micea (or Messia) to his masters in Spain that 'Certain titles of Earl and Baron are to be granted in this Parliament. This is, however, in suspense at present as they are all falling out amongst themselves.'[34] If the fractious temperament of Elizabeth's court persisted until the end of her reign, Robert Naunton would much later claim that the faultlines in the heady relationship between the earl and his ageing patroness were in evidence from the very beginning:

> the first was a violent indulgency of the Queen, (which incident to old age, where it encounters with a pleasing and suitable object) towards this Lord ... the second was a fault in the object of her grace; my Lord himself, who drew in too fast, like a childe sucking on an over uberous Nurse, and had there been a more decent decorum observed in both, or either of those, without doubt, the unity of their affections, had been more permanent, and not so in and out as they were, like an instrument ill tuned, and lapsing to discord.[35]

Ultimately, Essex failed to be schooled in the manner that Elizabeth sought. Robert Sidney's agent wrote to his master on the occasion of yet another rupture in this key relationship at court: 'Full fourteen days His Lordship kept in; Her Majesty, as I heard, is resolved to break him of his will and to pull down his great heart, who found it a thing impossible and says he holds it from the mother's side, but all is well again and no doubt he will grow a mighty man in our state.'[36]

Foreign ambassadors, such as Henri IV's ambassador extraordinary from 1597–8, André Hurault, Sieur de Maisse, could not fail to be impressed by 'le principal homme du Royaume d'Angleterre pour le regard de la Cour … Il est entierement addonné aux armes et à la guerre et est seul en Angleterre qui ait acquis réputation.'[37a] Moreover, like his diplomatic counterparts, de Maisse was offered ample occasion to bear witness to the tumultuous life of Elizabeth's court, recounting that 'Cette Cour est ordinairement pleine de mescontentements et divisions et la Reyne mesme est bien aise de les y entretenir.'[38b] One of the ways in which Elizabeth maintained the allegiances of those around her was through the careful expression of royal munificence: this might take the form of an appointment to an office central to the operations of state power or at the very least lucrative to the officeholder in question. However, as Lawrence Stone recognised, such largesse might also be communicated more directly into the coffers of favoured elite figures: in the latter years of her reign 'nearly half of what little was given poured into the bottomless pockets of a single individual, Robert, Earl of Essex'.[39] Indeed, amongst the Earl of Derby's New Year correspondence for 1589 were the tidings that 'There is a newe Byshoppe of Oxeforde … The chieffe of the lands thereof are to be gyven unto the Erle of Essex; some parte lykewyse is solde: I suppose the Byshopricke of Bristoll is to goe in lyke sorte.'[40] More generally, the 1590s would bear witness to the young earl's spectacular ascent in the nation's political life as he rose progressively from being a leading royal favourite and courtier, to military command in Europe (admittedly, with varying success), to the Privy Council in 1593, Mastership of the Ordnance in 1596, Earl Marshall in 1597 and the Chancellorship of the Cambridge University in 1598.

In the ominously titled *Polimanteia, or, The meanes lawfull and vnlawfull, to iudge of the fall of a common-wealth* (1595), the cleric William Covell hailed 'Englands *Scipio*: of *France* his ayde: of *Fames* glorie: of the *Muses* eldest sonne: of *Arts* ornament: of vertues miracle: of Religions champion: of thrise honorable, & worthilie-worthie-honored-noble *Essex*.'[41] In his dedicatory address Covell reflected that it was 'easie to gesse (honourable Lorde) why Schollars flocke under the patronage of men in your place; their condition is so weake, that unless men truly honourable doe defend them, they are most of all in this age distressed'.[42] More grimly, Naunton argued later that 'those that stood Sentinels about him, who might have

---

[a] 'Amongst the courtiers the Earl of Essex is the chief person in the Realm of England … He is entirely given over to arms and warfare, and is the only man in England who has won any renown thereby.' See De Maisse, *A Journal*, p. 33.

[b] 'This court is ordinarily full of discontent and factions, and the Queen is well pleased to maintain it so.' See De Maisse, *A Journal*, p. 18.

advised him better, but that like men intoxicated with hopes, they likewise had suckt in with the most, and of their Lords receipt, and so like *Caesars* would have all or none'.[43] Towards the close of his term of office in London, de Maisse reported to Henri IV that the constant regime of attrition at court was taking its toll: '[Elizabeth] suppliait [Henri IV] de considérer en l'estat auquel elle estoit qu'elle estoit femme vieille et impuissante d'elle mesme, qu'elle avoit affaires à de grandes et diverses humeurs et à des peuples lesquels si bien faisoient grande démonstration de l'aymer que néantmoins ils estoient légers et inconstans et qu'elle debvoit craindre toutes chozes.'[44a] Equally revealingly, William Jones, translator of Pomponio Nenna's *Treatise of Nobility* (1595), declared that in the quest to 'behold a true Idea of right, & accomplished Nobility . . . your L[ordship] need but as in a glasse to view your selfe'. However, if the earl had deigned to peruse this tribute at greater length, he might later discover a cautionary tale, 'whereof the ancient noble men of Rome, did weare vppon their shooes little Moones, that they might alwaies beare in minde, the instabilitie of the honour of this world, which changeth like vnto the Moone'.[45]

Essex and the School of War

As we have witnessed, the (seemingly) unceasing good fortunes of the young earl in the final decades of Elizabeth's reign inevitably rendered him increasingly attractive to those seeking patronage. He found himself the dedicatee of a vast array of texts – indeed, it has been estimated that they exceeded those dedicated to Elizabeth herself in the final decade of her reign.[46] Essex agreed to be godfather to the son of Alberico Gentili, Regius Professor of Civil Law at Oxford. In the latter's dedications to his own multiple legal commentaries upon the practices of war, the earl was variously invoked as 'Comes Excellentissime', 'nobilissime Essexi' and 'Illustrissimo Comiti Essexio'[47] – as Alexandra Gajda has underlined, Essex digested Gentili's tracts on military practice to the degree that he was able to quote from them in his own writings.[48]

In *Henry V* Shakespeare could offer extravagantly comic portraits of those well versed in the bookish learning of warfare. However, more generally, the age was not uniformly given to mocking avid students of military science or

---

[a] '[Elizabeth] begged [Henri IV] to consider the position in which she was placed; that she was a woman, old and capable of nothing by herself; she had to deal with nobles of divers humours, and peoples, who, although they offered great shows of affection towards her, nevertheless were fickle and inconstant, and she had to fear for everything.' See De Maisse, *A Journal*, p. 110.

those who put such knowledge into practice in the field. In the case of Essex, dedications might be, and frequently were, couched in singularly heroic terms by those seeking his favour. Indeed, in the great number of dedications offered as tributes to the Earl, certain identities were repeatedly assigned to him – notably that of a certain rage-ridden warrior from antiquity. In reviewing the political stage of his nation, Gabriel Harvey proposed a timely parallel: 'Essexius, Achilles'.[49] If one of the earl's primary agents (Antonio Pérez) greeted him on at least one occasion as 'Achilles alter', perhaps the most influential dedication to '*most true* Achilles' was that of Chapman's *Seauen bookes of the Iliades of Homere* (1598).[50] Furthermore, the *Briefe discourse of warre* by the war-seasoned Sir Roger Williams was dedicated to 'my singular and best Lord, Robert Earle of Essex', who (like Williams) had been knighted by Leicester on the field of Zutphen.[51]

If, from the mid-1580s, the earl was exploring multiple routes by which to showcase his various talents in international conflicts, he could be found participating with a good measure of swagger in the theatrics which were often used to quell the appetite for military combat at Elizabeth's court. In 1586, at the age of twenty-one, he first participated in the Accession Day tilts and, in 1592, we learn that

> Uppon the coronation day at nyght ther cam two knightes armed vpp into the pryvy chamber videlicet my L. of Essex and my L. of Cumberland and ther made a challenge that vppon the xxvjth of ffebruary next that they will runn with all commers to mayntayn that there M[istress] is the most worthiest and most fayrest Amadis of Gaule.[52]

Later, in the Accession Day Tilt of 1595, the mighty earl was the queen's champion and wore her favours.

At the turn of the century, the essayist Sir William Cornwallis enquired, 'If in *Arthur* of *Britaine*, *Huon* of *Bordeaux*, and such supposed chiualrie, a man may better himselfe, shall hee not become excellent with conuersing with *Tacitus*, *Plutarch*, *Sallust*, and fellowes of that rank?'[53] During the 1590s it was precisely to such reading matter that Essex and his entourage were applying themselves. The earl's retinue during these years included such scholarly minds as Edward Reynoldes, Henry Wotton, William Temple, Richard Greneway, Henry Cuffe, Lionel Sharpe, John Hayward, Thomas Chaloner (later tutor to Prince Henry), Anthony and (more briefly) Francis Bacon, Essex's chaplain (and subsequent convert to Catholicism) William Alabaster and Giles Fletcher. When not actively employed in military campaigns, Essex's mind appears often to have been exercised by the ancient arts of war. Paul E. J. Hammer has drawn

attention importantly to the vigorous learning programme unfolding in
the Earl's household, whereby 'Lord Henry Howard, himself a former
Cambridge don, wrote advices for Essex on political conduct studded with
quotes and references from Thucydides and Livy. With Cuffe and Savile,
Essex scrutinised ancient history for insight into war and politics.'[54] Henry
Savile, tutor in Greek and warden of Merton College, Oxford, translated
and published editions of Tacitus's *Histories* and *Agricola* in addition to
a tract on fortifications: 'A View of Certain Military Matters, for the better
understanding of Ancient Roman Stories.' However, it is clear that Savile
had taken the measure of the changeful status of his patron, writing
shrewdly to Robert Cecil in 1595 that 'one commendation in cold blood,
and seeming to proceed in judgment [from your father, Lord Burghley],
shall more prevail with the Queen than all the affectionate speech that my
lord of Essex can use'.[55]

In differing capacities, all of these figures seem to have assisted the earl in his
reading programme of carefully selected texts from antiquity.[56] In
Obseruations vpon the fiue first bookes of Caesars commentaries (1600), Sir
Clement Edmondes remained committed to the notion that 'Reading and
Discovrse are requisite to make a Sovldier perfect in the Arte Militarie.'[57] One
'A. B.' wrote a prefatory address to Savile's translation *The ende of Nero and
beginning of Galba Fower bookes of the Histories of Cornelius Tacitus* (1591).
Here, the reader was duly informed that 'There is no treasure so much
enriches the minde of man as learning; there is no learning so proper for the
direction of the life of man as Historie; there is no historie (I speake onelie of
profane) so well worth the reading as Tacitus.'[58] The conviction of some early
modern voices, such as those of Ben Jonson and Edmund Bolton, that this 'A.
B.' was Devereux himself might certainly have given these prefatory thoughts
added piquancy for those Elizabethans who subscribed to such opinions.[59]

Antonio Pérez, ex-secretary to Philip II and fugitive from Spanish justice
since 1591, joined the earl's service in these years. In his former life in Spain,
he had been an acknowledged scholar of Tacitus. Moreover, as Lisa Jardine
and Anthony Grafton have demonstrated, reading in the early modern
period might all too often constitute a 'public performance, rather than
a private meditation, in its aims and character'.[60] In the context of Essex's
own career, they stress the protestations of innocence by Sir Thomas
Arundel in February 1601 to Robert Cecil:

> I can not but wrighte what I think may avayle you so dothe my love
> manyfest my follye. Theare is one Cuffe a certayne purytane skoller one of
> the hottest heades of my lo: of Essex his followers. This Cuffe was sente by

my lo: of Essex to reade to my lo: of Southampton in Paris where hee redd
Aristotle's polyticks to hym wth sutch exposytions as, I doubt, did hym but
lyttle good: afterwards hee redd to my lo: of Rutlande.[61]

Like many of the age, the earl and his entourage appear to have been
attracted to: Tacitus's incisive scrutiny of state decadence, corruption,
tyranny and the perils of permitting obligations to subjects to go
unrewarded; Cicero's unsentimental accounts of human motivation;
Seneca's espousal of Stoic doctrine (the latter had been renewed for
the attention of late-sixteenth-century Europe by publications from
Henri Estienne and Justus Lipsius); and to earlier philosophers, such
as Aristotle, in their aims to dissect and evaluate the nature of political
systems of governance.

For a New Year's gift of 1596–7, Francis Davison presented his
'Worthily famous lord' with copies of the Roman histories of Caesar
and Tacitus, contending that his 'Sword with enuy imitates/Great
Caesars Sword in all his deeds victorious,/So your learn'd Pen would
striue to be glorious.'[62] Elsewhere, in the publication of the *Annales of
Cornelius Tacitus: The Description of Germanie* (1598) the translator
Richard Grenewey submitted, 'I present [Tacitus] therfore to your
Honors fauourable protection ... no otherwise then as a glasse, representing in liuely colours of prowesse, magnanimitie and counsell, not
onely woorthie personages of ages past and gone, but also your L[ord-
ship's] owne honorable vertues, wherof the world is both wit[n]es &
iudge.'[63] Indeed, Essex's extensive library attracted the attentions of the
powerful. After his execution, it was noted that in 'his "Studdy" in ...
Essex House, [were] divers printed books of divers kinds and languages;
and our aforesaid Most Serene Lady Elizabeth was pleased to remove
these books for herself.'[64] Moreover, the earl's adversary, Lord Cobham,
sought to borrow 'a paper boke of my lord of Essex notations of Cornelius
Tacitus' two years after his demise.[65]

Essex, a Lord of War at Home and Abroad

Having served in the Normandy campaign, the cleric Matthew Sutcliffe
seems to have selected his dedicatee, Essex, with care for *The practice,
proceedings, and lawes of armes* (1593), insisting that although some 'mislike
nothing more, then to haue their eares grated with the sound of drummes,
& rumors of warres ... [others] foresee those stormes that hang ouer our
heads, and see that there is no other sheltre, but in the practise of armes'.[66]

Essex had been appointed colonel-general of the cavalry when Leicester's company left for the Low Countries in 1585, and commander of the horse in England's preparations against the Armada in 1588. In 1589, against the queen's wishes, he joined Drake and Sir John Norris in a revenge attack for the Armada in an attempt to capture Lisbon from Phillip II, who had assumed the Portuguese Crown in 1581. For audiences at home and abroad, the attention-seeking Essex certainly rendered himself conspicuous in this adventure. Indeed, his irrepressible penchant for histrionics was remarked upon, as John Speed later related in his account of the assault: 'the noble *Essex* . . . ranne his speare and brake it against the Gates of that City: demanding alowde, if any *Spaniard* mewed therein, durst aduenture forth in fauour of his Mistresse to break a staffe with him'.[67] Other theatres of war also beckoned for the young earl. If, by the middle of the 1590s, Essex believed that 'ffraunce is at thys daye the theater and stage wheron the greatest actions are acted', many aspiring combatants (as we saw in the case of Ralegh) had long been of the same mind.[68] As early as 1585, Henri de Navarre (later Henri IV) had written to his co-religionist, the English queen (in a missive penned by Philippe du Plessis-Mornay), 'Madame, je crois que vous aurés esté advertie des grands remuemens qui se sont faicts en ce royaume, depuis quelque temps, par ceulx de la maison de Guise et leurs adherens.'[a] However, the French Protestant leader suspected greater forces at work: the formation of 'la ligue generale que le pape a practiquee entre les princes et potentats qui lui adherent, de laquelle le roy d'Espaigne soit le chef'.[69b]

The Catholic monarch Henri III was assassinated in the summer of 1589 and the ensuing conflict saw the entry of Henri de Navarre into the mêlée of seemingly interminable wars. Elizabeth acknowledged support for the French Protestant cause, but her administration's resources were already stretched, shouldering military interventions in Ireland and elsewhere against Spanish interests. Nonetheless, by the beginning of the 1590s Essex was turning his attention across the Channel and, after much pleading at court, left for Normandy. The earl's company of some 4,000 men and 60 volunteer-gentry was financed by himself and arrived in Dieppe in the first week of August 1591. Robert Cecil wrote from Portsmouth, 'Nues here ar none, but all in expectation what will come of the French cawses. My lord of Essex shalbe joined with the Marishall Byron in the siedge of Roan [Rouen] . . . it is hoped that Roan wilbe the

---

[a] 'Madame, I believe that you will have been alerted to the great upheavals taking place for some time in this kingdom [stirred up] by the House of Guise and their retainers.'
[b] 'the broad league that the Pope has forged between monarchs and rulers under his power and of whom the King of Spain is the leader'.

easilier obtained.'[70] The earl's appetite for showmanship was once again indulged in spectacular fashion when he decided to cross the war-torn country to meet Henri IV near Compiègne soon after his arrival. It was reported of Essex and his entourage

> il ne pouvait rien voir de plus magnifique, car entrant dans Compiègne, il avait devant lui six pages, montés sur de grands chevaux, habillé en velours orangé tout en broderie d'or, et lui avait une casque de velours orangé toute couverte de pierreries ... son habit et la parure de son cheval valaient seuls plus de soixante mil escus.[71a]

Henri effused to Elizabeth that 'la journée de la premiere entreveue que j'ay eue de mon dict Cousin ... [fut] l'une des plus heureuses de ma vie', acknowledging everything 'qu'il m'a dict de vostre part, de vostre singuliere bien-veuillance en mon endroict: dont je vous remercie très humblement'. The Tudor queen replied presciently, 'Vous n'auray jamais cause de doubte de la hardiesse de son service; car il a faict que trop souvent preuve qu'il ne craint hazarde quelque qui soit.'[72b]

Richard Hillman argues intriguingly that the figuring of Rouen in the dramatic narrative of the *Henry VI* plays in these years would have been a telling reminder of England's hopes resting on the earl: 'from the ashes of the slain Talbots (father and son) "shall be rear'd/A phoenix that shall make all France afeard"'.[73] Nonetheless, within a short space of time, Elizabeth was regretting the absence (and performances) of her favourite, as well as her financial investment in the French campaign. On 20th September 1590 Burghley wrote to Sir Henry Unton, English ambassador in Paris, stressing that the earl's improvised visit to 'Mons[r] de Byron ... [was] by her Majestie greately disallowed ... I knowe no remedie but to have my Lord of Essex to retourne to make here satisfaction.' Four days later, Burghley added that despite communications received, 'her Majestie was noe waie moved to change her former purpose for revocation of the Earle and her forces ... her Majestie hath absolutely commanded the Earle to retourne, and likewise contineweth in mynde to have her forces retourne'.[74] However, Devereux was enjoying other entertainment. At

---

[a] 'nothing more magnificent could be imagined, for at his entry to Compiègne, he had before him six pages, mounted on great horses, dressed in orange velvet all with golden embroidery and [the earl himself] with a doublet of orange velvet all covered in precious stones ... his clothing and the livery of his horse alone were worth more than 60,000 ecus'.

[b] 'The day of my first meeting which I had with my Cousin ... [was] one of the most felicitous in my life'; 'the account he gave me of yourself, of how extremely well disposed you are towards me: for which I thank you most humbly'; 'You will never have reason to doubt his valour in his services [to you]; because he has too often given proof that he fears no danger whatsoever it may be.'

the siege of Rouen, the chivalrous nobleman threw down a challenge to the Governor, proclaiming 'Si vous voulez combattre vous-même à cheval ou à pied, je maintiendrai que la querelle du Roi est plus juste que celle de la Ligue, et que ma Maîtresse est plus belle que la vôtre.'[75a]

In the event, within three months the English contingent would be depleted by two thirds owing to the casualties of war and sickness. Meanwhile, the besieged Rouen with its beleaguered populace would endure hardship upon hardship. A member of Essex's company, Sir Thomas Coningsby, recorded in November 1591 that 'The contynewall burnynge of houses are verie greate and pytyfull to behold; how much bound are our people to God, that know not these myseries!'[76] Indeed, such an attritional regime of warfare could remain, on the field and behind the lines, unedifying for both sides to behold, as is so eloquently evoked in Shakespeare's histories. Essex would witness the loss of his own brother in the hostilities – a loss immortalised in verse by Geneviève Petau de Maulette's *Deuoreux Vertues* (English translation by Gervase Markham, 1597).[77] By October 1591, Christopher Hatton cautioned the earl 'that the late accident of your noble brother, who has so valiantly and honourably spent his life in his Prince's and country's service, draw you not through grief or passion to hazard yourself over venturously'.[78] However, rather stronger feelings, this time of resentment, seem to have been brewing at the English court in a queen who was not in the habit of finding herself eclipsed in the eyes of Europe by one of her subjects, and who wished no one from her realm to be beholden to any person but herself for their advancement.

Just before Christmas 1591, Burghley was writing both to Unton and to Sir Thomas Leighton that the earl might no longer ignore the royal demands for his return: 'And because it maie be, he will not of him selfe so readely followe our advice as were fitt, we require you bothe to take knowledge therof, and to desire of his Lordship the sight of our letter.'[79] As the new year opened, Elizabeth's temper had not subsided. Henri IV's envoy, Philippe du Plessis-Mornay, was informed bitterly by her majesty that the headstrong earl had left for France 'contre son gré, menacé de defaveur, & preferant sa reputation à ses commandemens', and that Henri IV 'ne devoit rien attendre d'elle pendant l'absence du Comte d'Essex'.[b] During this animated audience, du Plessis-Mornay reported that her speeches were

---

[a] 'If you seek combat on horseback or on foot, I will maintain that the King's cause is more just than that of the [Catholic] League, and that my Mistress is more beautiful than your own.'

[b] 'against her will, under threats of loss of favour, and privileging his [own] reputation over and above her orders'; 'should not expect anything from her as long as the Earl of Essex remained absent [from her kingdom]'.

tousiours entrecouppees de digressions de courroux, d'iniures & de menaces contre le Comte d'Essex, qu'elle le feroit le plus petit compagnon d'Angleterre, qu'il faisoit accroire au Roi qu'il gouvernoit tout, & qu'elle lui feroit bien voir que non: estant resoluë, non seulement de ne lui envoier point nouvelles forces, mais mesmes de rappeller tous ses Anglois.[80a]

Essex remained convinced that he was practised against by his enemies at court – and he was not alone in his suspicions. The Duc de Bouillon wrote to him in May 1596, protesting that all courts 'ont des humeurs sambables' and that the earl's 'ruine est desiree et finimant recherchee'.[81b] Others, like de Maisse, also clearly thought that this earl would be wise to be on his guard during his absences from court. Indeed, de Maisse reported to Henri IV in 1597 regarding the so-called Islands Voyage (see below) that 'Le Grand Trésorier, l'Admiral et Monsieur Cecille sont bien aises de voir le dict Comte d'Essex aller en un voyage loingtain et hazardeux ... s'il revient victorieux ils prennent occasion de là de le rendre suspect à la Reyne.'[82c] Later, Robert Naunton would judge from his own, partisan perspective that Burghley was 'a person of a most subtill and active spirit', while Robert Cecil, who succeeded him as a minister of state under Elizabeth and James, 'was a Courtier from his Cradle'.[83] Unsurprisingly, Naunton was not alone among the Essex society in expressing enmity towards these ministers. As Janet Dickinson has underlined, Francis Davison referred to the younger (hunch-backed) Cecil as the earl's 'arch-enemy (i.e. *made like an arch*)', Anthony Standen named him 'Monsieur *de Bossu*' and Pérez abused him as '*Roberto il diavolo*', 'Microgibbon' and 'gibbosum'.[84] Nonetheless, part of the complexity of Elizabeth's court was the very mobility with which political factionalism operated from one moment to the next. As was witnessed in Chapter 1, different interest groups might coalesce swiftly as the political situation changed. Rowland Whyte reported in coded communication from London to Robert Sidney in Flushing in March 1596: 'I heare of the secrets in Court. 24 [Ralegh] hath bene very often very privat with 1000 [Essex] and is the mediator of a peace between hym and 200 [Robert Cecil] who likewise hath bene privat with hym.'[85]

---

[a] 'punctuated by angry outbursts, insults and threats towards the Earl of Essex, that she would reduce him to the lowest rank in England, that he was making the [French] King believe that he managed everything, and that she would show him how wrong he was; being determined, not only to refuse him any further troops, but even to recall all her English forces'.

[b] 'exhibit similar displays of temper'; 'ruin is desired and being expertly sought out'.

[c] 'The Lord Treasurer [Burghley], the Admiral [Charles Howard] and Master [Robert] Cecil are well content to see the Earl of Essex go on a distant and hazardous voyage ... If he comes back victorious they take occasion thereby to render him suspect to the Queen.' See De Maisse, *A Journal*, pp. 6–7.

Essex returned to England after the siege of Rouen, to the great disappointment of Henri IV, who continued to insist that this man was 'plein de valleur et de courage'.[86a] By February 1592 Essex was acknowledging to du Plessis-Mornay that his further participation in the campaign was not to be hoped for because 'l'humeur de la Roine à esté si amere'.[87b] In the event, by 1593 the beleaguered Henri had made terms with the Catholic League and forsaken the Protestant faith. His coronation took place in February of the following year at Chartres cathedral. Nonetheless, the potential for glorifying Essex's exploits in the service of the House of Navarre was not lost on contemporary writers. It would not have taken a supersubtle reader at the time of the 1596 publication of *The Faerie Queene* to identify Essex as a possible reading for Sir Artegall in Book Five, who goes forward to rescue Burbon (or Henri IV), 'a Knight in daungerous distresse' (V.xi.44). Burbon had earlier been dubbed a knight for his valour by the Protestant warrior Redcrosse (V.xi.53), but thus far had been unable to win back his damsel, Flourdelis (or France), from the countless forces ('a swarme of flyes' V.xi.58) of the tyrant Grandtorto. Colin Burrow has stressed persuasively that '[Spenser's] knights often hover between pity and rage, before they act in anger',[88] and Artegall eventually succeeds in restoring a rather truculent Flourdelis to her swain and tempers the latter's taste for slaughter at the close of Book Five, canto eleven. Nonetheless, by 1597, de Maisse, the representative of 'Flourdelis' in London, might be discovered to be rather more uneven in his praise for England's *preux chevalier*: 'Il est tout son conseil luy mesmes. Il me fait beaucoup d'honneur et monstre estre très affectionné au Royaume. Je croy que c'est autant que peut estre un Anglois, il est désireux de gloire.'[89c]

After his military service in the Low Countries, against the Armada and in Normandy, Essex co-commanded with Lord Admiral Charles Howard a naval expedition in 1596 for the taking of Cadiz. Returning via Faro with booty and two Spanish warships, Howard wrote to Burghley, 'My lord I assure you there is not a braver man in the worlde then the Earle is.'[90] Nonetheless, the campaign itself was a disappointment for Devereux in its failure to secure in Cadiz a permanent foothold for England on the continent. In the second half of the decade, as English policy turned increasingly to naval ventures (and, as we shall see, to Ireland), Elizabeth eventually gave her consent in 1597 for an English-led attack upon the Spanish fleet at Ferrol. Hampered by adverse weather, the 'Islands Voyage' eventually set sail in August, but was ill-equipped

---

[a] 'full of valour and courage'.   [b] 'the mood of the Queen has been so embittered [towards him]'.
[c] 'He is entirely his own Councillor. He did me much honour, and showed himself very kindly disposed to our Realm. I believe that, so far as an Englishman can, he covets glory.' See de Maisse, *A Journal*, pp. 33–4.

for an assault on Ferrol and so (with royal permission) made for the Azores in the hope of surprising the Spanish treasure fleet. The English failed to engage with the Spanish fleet and arrived back to find Spanish ships from Ferrol now with their courses set on Falmouth. Interestingly, for this voyage, as for his other military ventures, accounts survive of the severity of the earl's command. Wotton, for example, later recalled 'the Island Voyage where [Essex] threw a Souldier with his owne hands out of a Ship; the other in *Ireland* where hee decimated certaine troops that ran away, renewing a peece of *Roman Discipline*'.[91] However, this master could also be given to clemency. In the dedicatory address to *A theologicall discourse of the Lamb of God and his enemies* (1590), Richard Harvey chose to recall when at the gates of Lisbon, the earl 'vnhorsing himself he mercifully saued a poore wounded souldier from the mouth of the sword'.[92] Whatever the accuracy of such accounts, these contrary testimonies bear telling witness once again to the widely differing appreciations of the earl in both life and death.

On the return from the Islands Voyage, Sir Francis Vere recalled discovering the queen once again 'seeming greatly incensed against my Lord of *Essex*, laying the whole blame of the evil success of the journey on his Lordship, both for the not burning and spoiling of the fleet at *Faroll*, and missing the Indian fleet'. Nevertheless, he continued that in due course,

> her Majesty well quieted and satisfied sate her down in the end of the walk, and calling me to her fell into more particular discourse of his Lordships humours and ambition; all which she pleased then to construe so graciously that before she left me she fell into much commendation of him, who very shortly after came to the Court.[93]

Essex, Spymaster

Richard Perceval dedicated his *Bibliotheca Hispanica* (1591) to the earl, 'vndertanding that your Honor bestoweth much time with happie successe, as well in the knowledge of the toongs; as of other commendable learnings beseeming your place and person'.[94] Indeed, the polyglot Essex could find himself drawn into state affairs that extended the length and breadth of the continent. When, during an audience, Elizabeth perused letters from Czar Ivan (the Terrible) of Muscovy, she proposed that her favourite 'could quicklie lern . . . the famousest and most copious language in the world'. The earl allegedly replied that he 'did much affect and delight it, if he might ateyn therunto without paienstakinge and spendinge more time then he had to spare'.[95]

If, as we have seen, Essex publicly assumed the role of successor to the fallen
Sidney, after the death of his father-in-law, Sir Francis Walsingham, in 1590,
he seems to have taken on the latter's mantle as spymaster. Indeed, from 1592
onwards, he oversaw an extensive network of agents and 'intelligencers' across
Europe which came to supersede that of Burghley himself. When not exercised by the prospect of military campaigns, the earl frequently sought to
influence political decision-making with information from agents relayed
through his secretariat. In July 1595, he complained to Unton in Paris, 'I am
so handled by this crew of sycophants, spies, and delators, as I have no quiet
myself nor much credit to help my friends.'[96] Notwithstanding, Essex certainly viewed these intelligence activities as highly instrumental in realising his
military ambitions and as a strategic resource with which to render more
secure his wavering fortunes at court. Such aims inevitably raised the suspicions of others. On one occasion, Unton clearly did not appreciate being
landed with one of Essex's men (in this case, Pérez), writing to Burghley that
'the Earle doth not deall so kyndlye with me as I expected ... [Pérez would]
imparte nothynge vnto me but such genneralytyes as the lackyes doe know; so
as I feare hee would bee a spy vppon me.'[97]

In 1595 the earl sent another member of his secretariat, Robert Naunton,
across the Channel, underlining that 'To attayne the Frenche quickly you
must converse with ffrenche.' However, he stressed equally characteristically (and with a solemnity worthy of Shakespeare's Fluellen) that the 'rules
and patternes of pollecy, are as well learned out of olde Greeke and
Romayne storyes, as out of states which are at thys daye'.[98] In this, he
was at one mind with the cleric Matthew Sutcliffe, who seems to have
witnessed Essex in military action, perhaps in the Low Countries campaign
(where he was a Judge Martial) or in France. Sutcliffe contended that 'men
imagine by reason of the vse of artillery lately inuented, that the reasons &
rules of armes are changed ... but they are much abused, for the generall
rules [of the Romans and the Greeks] are always the same'.[99]

Continental politics continued to attract the attentions of the earl.
Henri IV's envoy, de Maisse, esteemed that Essex was an 'homme d'en-
tendement, mais qui ne croit conseil que de luy mesme et est impossible de
luy oster de la teste ce qu'il a une fois entrepris. Il est bon Anglais et
Français l'autant qu'il estime que cela sert à ses desseins.'[100a] Cherishing
a strong bond of common interest with his former comrade-at-arms, in

---

[a] 'a man of judgement, but one who believes no counsel save his own; once he has undertaken a thing it
is impossible to get it out of his head. He is a good Englishman and Frenchman inasfar as he believes
that it accords with his aims.' See de Maisse, *A Journal*, p. 7.

October 1595 Henri IV reminded the earl (if reminder were necessary) that 'L'Espagnol est nostre ennemy commun, ses desseings sont contre l'Estat de la Royne ma bonne soeur et le mien'.[101a] In the event, Essex never doubted the truth of such matters, submitting to Elizabeth on one occasion, 'Yow two are like mightie champions entered into the lists to fight for the two generall quarrels of Christendome ... [Philip II] aspringe to an universall monarchie, your Majestie at relieving the oppressed.'[102] However, by the spring of 1598 the tables were turned once again. It became known that Henri IV was negotiating peace with Spain, and Francesco Contarini, the Venetian ambassador in France, reported in September of that year that

> The [Dutch] States make [Elizabeth] great offers if she will continue the war. ... But if the news that the Lord Treasurer is dead ... be true, that will cause more change than anything else. ... He was the chief advocate of peace, and now that he is gone the Earl of Essex may carry his way.[103]

In this atmosphere of violent antagonism between factions and nations in late-sixteenth-century Europe, ciphers continued to be resorted to in all manner of communications. In his correspondence with Pérez, Essex was repeatedly identified as Aeneas attempting to prepare the way for a new empire, but often thwarted by the contrary forces of the Queen of Olympus and the ministrations of her factotum, Aeolus or Cecil. In 1595, for example, Pérez wrote to his master, 'Sed, Mylorde, quid de isto tempestuoso mari? Quid de Junone, quae Æolum et ventos contra te convocat et commouet?'[104b] Later, a direct quotation from Virgil was integrated into a communication from Essex to Pérez, evoking the enraged Juno: 'Flectere si nequeo superos, Acheronta movebo.'[105c] In fact, it seems that in these years masses of coded messages proliferated concerning this seemingly all-powerful earl. One Thomas Fowler at the Edinburgh court wrote back to Burghley in October 1589 that letters were arriving there from Essex (Ernestus) and from his sister, Lady Penelope Rich (Ryalta) to James VI (Victor), noting that 'an alphabet of cipher [was required] to understand them by. I can tell few of their names, but the Queen's Majesty is Venus ("Pallas"), and the Earl the "wery" knight, as I remember, but

---

[a] 'The Spaniard is our common enemy, he plots against both the realm of the Queen, my dear sister, and my own.'
[b] 'But, my lord, why do you find yourself in this sea-tempest? What of Juno who summons Aeolus and the winds and stirs them against you?'
[c] 'If Heaven I cannot bend, then Hell I will arouse!' See Virgil, *Aeneid VII–XII*, trans. H. Rushton Fairclough (Cambridge MA/London: Harvard University Press – Loeb Classical Library, 2000), p. 25.

always he is exceeding weary, accounting it a thrall he lives now in, and wishes the change.'[106] By the mid-1590s, Essex's support seems to have strengthened significantly for the monarch north of the border – 'a king of so much worth, whose servant I am born by nature . . . such as I am, and all whatsoever I am (tho' perhaps a subject of small price) I consecrate unto your regal throne'.[107] Henri IV's envoy, de Maisse, was similarly convinced that preparations for change were afoot: '[should the queen die] il est certain que les Anglois ne se soubmettroient jamais plus à la domination d'une femme'.[108a]

Essex and Ireland

In August 1595 Thomas Lake – Walsingham's personal secretary and, later in the Elizabethan period, an MP – wrote anxiously to Robert Sidney in Flushing, 'I am wary in sending letters as the postes letters are often viewed.' He nonetheless confided that 'In Ireland we do little good, and consume much money on small hopes.'[109] By 1598, unrest and outright rebellion in that land warranted the most urgent attention of Elizabeth and her counsellors. De Maisse gave report of the desperate state of affairs whereby 'Les Anglois et la Reyne mesme désireroient que l'Irlande fust abismée en mer car elle n'en peut retirer aucun proffict et ce pendant la despence et le soin en est tres grand et ne se peut aucunement fier à ces peuples.'[110b] By the autumn Contarini was writing from Paris back to Venice that 'The Queen intended to send the Earl of Essex to Ireland to put down the rebellion. He refused on various pretexts. She became exceedingly angry and he retired from Court. He has been recalled.'[111] If, by the close of 1598, Henri IV was writing to his ambassador, Jean de Thumery, Sieur de Boissise, that 'c'est mon intention de le [Essex] favoriser en toutes choses',[112c] it was becoming clear that Essex's stock at home was in a depleted state and he could in no way count upon support at the court in London.

In a wide-ranging discussion of the cultural production of Ireland in the context of Shakespeare's *Henry V*, Micheal Neill has justly proposed that 'nationality can only be imagined as a dimension of difference'. He

---

[a] 'it is certain that the English would never again submit to the rule of a woman.' See de Maisse, *A Journal*, pp. 11–12.
[b] 'The English and the Queen herself would wish Ireland drowned in the sea, for she cannot get any profit from it; and meanwhile the expense and trouble is very great, and she cannot put any trust in that people.' See de Maisse, *A Journal*, p. 51.
[c] 'It is my desire to forward his interests in all things.'

goes onto argue that the colonised land of early modern Ireland functioned as 'the indispensable anvil upon which the notion of Englishness was violently hammered out ... Yet if the Irish were essential to the formation of English identity, they also threatened it.'[113] The anxieties throughout the realm concerning developments in what Robert Cecil called 'the land of ire'[114] were plain for everyone to witness. As John S. Nolan has stressed, 'Elizabeth's government sent somewhere near twenty thousand troops to France in the six years following the Armada. ... The largest armies fielded by Elizabethan England were deployed in the pacification of Ireland between 1599 and 1603, reaching a level of nineteen thousand in 1599.'[115] Given the growing successes of the insurgents led by Tyrone, no time remained for hesitation. William Camden would recall later in his *Britannia* (Eng. trans. 1610) that 'In this desperate estate stood Ireland when Queene Elizabeth chose *Robert* Earle of Essex ... Lievtenant and Governour generall of Ireland, to repaire the detriments and losses there sustained, with most large and ample authority added in his Commission, *To make an end of the war*.'[116] If the earl wrote to Fulke Greville that Elizabeth had 'destined me to the hardest task that ever gentleman was sent about', he might also at the same time write more triumphantly to the queen's godson, Sir John Harington, 'I have beaten Knollys and Montjoye in the Councele, and by G–d I will beate Tyr-Owen in the fielde; for nothynge worthye hir Majesties honor hathe yet been atchievede.'[117] Some, like one John Johnstone, greeted the news of Essex's appointment as Lord Lieutenant of Ireland with euphoria: 'It was thy destiny to overrun the shores of the Pillars of Hercules, brandishing with Herculean grasp dread engines of war. What though Gaul was thunderstruck at thy onset, let Hibernia tremble at thy stroke.'[118] More shrewdly, Naunton would later contend that the earl was determined 'to reap the honour of closing up that Warre' so that 'none durst appear to stand for the place' – and so 'with much ado, he obtained his own ends, and withall his fatall destruction'.[119] Others of the earl's affinity were similarly minded in later years. Barnabe Barnes cursed the 'pestilent and inauspicious expedition to Ireland', and Henry Wotton wrote that the Earl's 'blackest [employment] was that to *Ireland*, ordained to be the Sepulcher of his Father, and the Gulph of his owne Fortunes'.[120] Nonetheless, for those disposed to listen or even join in the rejoicing, *A ballade of the tryump[h]es kept in Ireland ... by the noble Earle of Essex* circulated in 1599 to rally support for the campaign: 'Therefore, let all true English men,/With every faythful subiect then,/Vnto my prayers say Amen!/Now God and Saint George for England!'[121]

In *2 Henry VI* we learn that 'Th'uncivil kerns of Ireland are in arms/And temper clay with blood of Englishmen' (VI²: III.i.310–1); and, mindful of similarly perceived unrest, the courtesies extended by Essex to his first audiences in Ireland were soon dispensed with. The earl wrote in May 1599

> this warre is like to exercise bothe our faculties that doe manage it, and Her Majesties patience that must maynteine it. For this people againste whome we fighte hathe able bodies, good use of the armes they carie, boldness enough to attempte, and quicknes in apprehending any advantage they see offred them. Whereas our newe and common sorte of men have neither bodies, spirits, nor practise of armes ... how unequall a wager it is to adventure the lives of noble men and gentlemen against rougues and naked beggars.[122]

Wotton wrote dejectedly to John Donne about their new-found environs: 'This town of Dublin is rather ill inhabited than seated; the people of good natural abilities, but corrupted, some with a wild, some with a loose life; and, indeed, there is almost nothing in this country but it is either savage or wanton.' Nonetheless, Wotton seems to have comforted himself with the sentiment that 'For our wars, I can only say we have a good cause, and the worthiest gentleman of the world to lead it.'[123] Others were less convinced. The Irishman, Sir John Dowdall, complained to Robert Cecil, 'Why are the forces so weak and poor? One cause is the electing of captains rather by favour than by desert, for many are inclined to dicing, wenching and the like, and do not regard the wants of the soldiers.'[124] Elizabeth herself soon began to be critical of the poor leadership of the campaign. John Chamberlain wrote to Dudley Carleton at the end of June 1599 that 'The Quene is nothing satisfied with the earle of Essex manner of proceeding, nor likes anything that is don, but sayes she allowes him 1000li a day to go in progresse.'[125] By August, Rowland Whyte was writing to Robert Sidney, 'The news of Ireland is desperate. The Irish run to Tyrone in great numbers.'[126]

Given this atmosphere of growing urgency, Elizabeth was unsurprisingly outraged to learn in September 1599 of the earl's parley with Tyrone at a ford in the River Lagan, near Drumconragh. Faced with the mounting tide of adverse accounts of his conduct, Essex travelled unexpectedly back to London and famously burst into the queen's bedchamber, as Robert Sidney learned from his correspondent in London:

> my Lord of Essex ... staied not till he came to the Queen's bed chamber, where he found the Queen newly vp, the heare about her face ... It is a very dangerous tyme here ... Burn my letters, else shall I be afraid to write. Be

careful what you write here, or what you say where you are. Now are letters intercepted and stayed.[127]

Essex was swiftly placed in custody. By the beginning of October, Rowland Whyte confirmed to Sidney 'All eyes and ears are open to what her Majesty will determine with the Earl of Essex. It is said her displeasure and indignation is great.'[128] Nonetheless, even with the disgraced earl under guard, there was no immediate resolution in sight to bring down the Irish rebels. Philip Gawdy wrote back to his family in Norfolk: 'The newes out of Irelande is that Teron [Tyrone] waxes greater and more rebell euery daye then other ... My L. of Essex is [not yet] at lyberty but remayneth still in the same place he was.'[129] Moreover, others were also coming under suspicion for their connections to the earl. The despairing Robert Sidney learned from his agent in London that, 'Though you have some friends here, I find none that you may rely upon in any matter of preferment. I was told that the hindrance is the doubt that you, who have been great for many years with the Earl of Essex, are not to be trusted.'[130]

Further afield, given the record hitherto of the queen's relations with her favourite, others in Europe thought this downward turn in the earl's fortunes to be merely a provisional state of affairs. Contarini wrote from Paris to the Council in Venice that 'There is a rumour that the Earl of Essex's arrest will soon be terminated to his complete satisfaction.'[131] Henri IV wrote to de Boissise in London that the services rendered by Essex 'meritoyent ung oeil plus favorable. La guerre d'Irlande a, jusques à present, plus incommodé et consommé l'Angleterre, qu'elle n'a apporté d'honneur et d'avantage à la Royne, ma bonne sœur.'[a] Nonetheless, the French king began increasingly to realise that he and his ambassadors must move cautiously to avoid suspicion: 'Vous ne luy ferez toutesfois aucune demonstration, si vous ne jugez que cela puisse servir au dit comte et estre pris en bonne part de la dite dame, avec laquelle il fault patienter et dissumuler.'[132b] Contarini continued in his communications to *la Serenissima*:

Vuole la Regina che rendi conto della sua partenza d'Irlanda senza alcuna commissione di lei ne del suo consiglio, et insieme che riferisca le trattationi secrete che ha passato col Conte di Tirone, ribello, senza sua permissione. ... oltra che è di molta gelosia alla Regina il parere, ch'esso ha sempre sostentato di non farsi la pace col Rè di Spagna con fine di tenersi

---

[a] 'deserved a more kindly reception. Thus far, the war in Ireland has distressed and drained the resources of England more than it has delivered renown and profit to my dear sister, the Queen.'

[b] 'You should only offer any gesture of support for him if you consider that it may benefit the said Earl and be taken in good part by the said lady, with whom you must be patient and feign appearances.'

del continuo armato et con gran seguito, come in effetto ha; spetialmente per l'amore che generalmente li viene portato da'popoli; essendo per le sue qualità stimato in quelle parti nel medesimo modo a punto che se facceva del già Duca di Guisa in questo regno.[133a]

Later at the earl's trial, Francis Bacon would be similarly given to compare 'this rebellion of my Lord of Essex to the Duke of Guise's'.[134]

'the hower-glasse of time hath altered here'

Philip Gawdy wrote once again to his brother in Norfolk in the final weeks of 1599 that 'my L. of Essex is very weak and ill at ease, and viij phisitians have sett it downe vnder their handes that vnles he wer removed he colde not escape . . . I haue brought downe my L. of Essex his booke whiche I will bring to Harling.'[135] Here, the reference is to *An Apologie of the Earle of Essex*, mostly written in the spring of 1598 and circulating in manuscript copies (ostensibly against the earl's wishes). The *Apologie* would be published in 1603 after the accession of James I, when the fortunes of his family were rehabilitated.

Henri IV wrote to de Boissise in February 1600, 'j'ay grande compassion de la fortune du dit comte et ay plus grand regret encores de ne luy pouvoir estre plus utille'.[136b] However, sensing the precariousness of the political situation, in the following month the foreign monarch urged caution once again to his representatives: 'je feray volontiers, si vous l'estimez necessaire, pour les affaires du comte d'Essex; car, je l'affectionne tant, que je n'espargneray rien pour le favoriser, mais aussy, prenez garde que je ne luy face plus de mal que de bien'.[137c] In April 1600 Matthew de Oviedo, Archbishop-elect of Dublin, wrote to Philip III, insisting: 'I may say that O'Neil had almost prevailed upon the Earl of Essex to desert the Queen's cause and join that of your Majesty, and surrender all the realm to you . . . O'Neil gave him his son as a hostage. What more could the most loyal Spaniard

---

[a] 'The Queen desires him to explain his departure from Ireland, without her leave or that of her Council, and also to communicate the secret negotiations with the rebel Tyrone, which were not authorised by her. . . . Besides, his determination not to make peace with Spain, which he has always maintained, with a view to be constantly at arms and followed by a large train (as indeed he has succeeded in doing) has caused great suspicions in the eyes of the Queen; all the more on account of the love the people bear to him; for his qualities have won for him in those parts [England] exactly the same esteem as the late Duke of Guise enjoyed in this kingdom [France].'

[b] 'I have great compassion for the fate of the said earl and have even greater regrets that I cannot be of more service to him.'

[c] 'If you think it necessary, I will willingly do anything to assist the situation of the Earl of Essex; for I hold him in such high affection that I will spare no efforts to support his case, but also, take care that [in doing so] I do not do him more ill than good.'

have done?'[138] How much credence can be given to de Oviedo's account remains open to debate: he may be basing his report on Tyrone's own testimonies. However, by May 1600, the earl himself wrote to the queen likening himself to a wretched creature, 'as if I were thrown into a corner like a dead carcase, I am gnawed on and torn by the vilest and basest creatures upon earth'.[139]

As the year wore into summer, Henri IV was still clearly attentive to the earl's fate, advising his ambassador 'Plus il le supportera avec patience, il augmentera sa reputation et asseurera sa fortune.'[a] Nonetheless, he confessed himself

> fort scandalizé de la perfidie de ce Bacon, qui a receu de luy tant de graces . . . j'ay ouy dire qu'il a esté autrefois accusé de sodomie. Mais, comme vous dictes, les Espaignolz ne seront marris de la cheute du dit comte d'Essex, pour estre la royne d'Angleterre privée, par icelle, de l'assistance d'ung si digne serviteur.[140b]

By Accession Day in November of that year, the 'humblest vassal, Essex' was writing to his sovereign that 'Only miserable Essex, full of pain, full of sickness, full of sorrow, languishing in repentance for his offences past, hateful to himself that he is yet alive and importunate on death if your favour be irrecoverable, he joys only your Majesty's great happiness and happy greatness.'[141] Meanwhile, although 'not wise enough to give you advice', in the same year Ralegh was underlining in his correspondence to Robert Cecil that 'if you take it for a good counsel to relent towards this tyrant [Essex], you will repent it when it shall be too late'.[142]

On Saturday 7th February 1601, the earl was summoned to present himself before the queen's Council, which he refused to do. Some of Essex's following went to see a commissioned performance at the Globe Theatre of 'Kyng henry the iiiith, and of the kyllyng of Kyng Richard the Second' before returning to Essex House.[143] Whether this was Shakespeare's play or not, it was all too probable that the spectators might be greeted with a tale of a 'King [who] is not himself, but basely led/By flatterers' (*Richard II*: II.i.242–3). Did those amongst his entourage (or indeed the earl himself) view the fallen court favourite as a latter-day Bolingbroke, living up to his Hereford title and marching through the streets of London? In the event, as

---

[a] 'the more he bears his situation with patience, [the more] he will enhance his reputation and render secure his future'.

[b] 'most shocked by the treachery of this Bacon, who received such favours from [the earl] [. . .] I have heard it said that he was formerly accused of sodomy. But, as you say, the Spanish will not be sorry at the fall of the said Earl of Essex, at having the Queen of England deprived, by the former [Bacon], of the services of such a worthy subject.'

Paul Hammer has pointed out, given the unforeseen events of the morrow, 'the play performed on Saturday, 7 February, had no direct connection with what happened the following day'.[144] More generally, it was apparent that there were those, like the former Jesuit, Thomas Wright, who set great store by the prospect of yet another rise in the earl's fortunes: 'if the Earle of Essex were kynge it would be a glorious kingedome, and that it would be better for us ['Catholiques' is crossed out] for he could not be so inhumane as but to free us all'.[145]

On 8th February it was reported that Essex and his followers were 'making towardes Ludgate cryeing out for the Queen, for the Queen my masters, giveing out besides that the Earle of Essex that nighte before shoulde have been murthered by the Lord Cobham, Sir Walter Rayleigh and others'.[146] Elizabeth's authorities issued a warrant to the city's constables and 'all other her Majesty's loyal and dutiful subjects . . . upon your allegiance, forthwith to arm yourselves . . . presently to repair hither and with us to march to the Court for the defence of her Majesty's person'.[147] William Reynolds wrote to Robert Cecil that as he traced his way through the capital, 'when I cried: "Down with Essex the traitor!" divers rebuked me, and had some of his followers seen me, I am sure they would have done their best to kill me'.[148] In Shakespeare's earlier *Henry V* audiences were asked to envisage a victorious Essex (or, alternatively, his successor in command of the Irish campaign, Lord Mountjoy) as one 'from Ireland coming' and greeted by London dignitaries: 'Like to the senators of th'antique Rome,/With the plebians swarming at their heels', they welcome 'their conqu'ring Caesar in' (*V*: V.Prol.26–8).[149] This was certainly not the reception that greeted Essex and his following on the streets of the capital on this later occasion. Within hours the leading figures were forced to beat a retreat back to Essex House, where they were besieged by the Queen's forces and cannon from the Tower of London. In reviewing the collapse of the revolt, Mervyn James argues persuasively that 'Essex lacked the landed resources from which to raise a levy of tenants considerable enough to form the basis of a regional revolt even if he had wished to do so.' However, he also underlines that the earl was capable of inspiring lasting affection in certain quarters: 'About a third of those who, on 8 February 1601, accompanied Essex on his foray into the City had served under him in military offices.'[150]

Amongst others, Robert Sidney was sent to parley with the rebel leaders holed up in Essex House. Meanwhile, Southampton was attributing the cause of the broils to 'Theis aethist caterpillers I meane, whoe have layde plottes to bereave us of our lives for safegarde whereof (as the law of nature willeth us) wee have taken up those armes, though wee both dooe and will acknowledge all dutie and obedience to her Majestie unto our lives end.'[151] The Venetian ambassador in Spain, Francesco Soranzo, wrote from Vallodolid to the Doge and the Senate that

> In England there have been great tumults; the Earl of Essex supported by a number of gentlemen, has risen against the Queen. He hoped to have met with more favour from the people than he actually received. He showed great rashness in rebelling with so small a following ... Here [in Spain], of course, these events give satisfaction; for they think that the Queen, under pressure of internal if not of external alarm, will hasten to make peace with this Crown.[152]

Indeed, visitors closer at hand were offering their services to the Crown in its hour of need. When the uprising took place, Elizabeth's court had been playing host to the Russian ambassador, Gregory Ivanovich Mikhulin, from the Czar Boris Godunov. The members of the embassy were invited by the Lord Mayor of London to dinner, where animated enquiries were made about the rebellion.[153] When he returned to his native land in May 1601, Mikhulin was the bearer of a letter from Elizabeth herself, declaring

> Uppon an occasion of some rebellious attempts againste the peace of our government [the czar's representative] was readye to haue come forth and to have put himself in danger against the undertakers therof ... [and that the queen could] not but take it in very kind and thankfull part of him and think it worthy of your majesties knowledg.[154]

In the immediate aftermath of the rebellion, preachers were instructed to inform their congregations that the treacherous nobleman wished to 'sette the crowne of England uppon his owne head'.[155] If the evidence is wanting that Essex sought the highest office in the realm, he continued throughout his career to lay claim to a growing array of privileges and to identify enemies at every turn. He wrote to Robert Sidney,

> judge yow, brother, whether it can bee grief or not to a man desscended as I am to have lived in action and ye estamacion as I have doone, to be penned up so long together as I was, to be trodden under foote by such base upstartes, yea and more then that, to have my lief nerely soughte by them.[156]

More generally, rumours continued to circulate wildly at this time. It was reported that 'the plot of the Earl of Essex was known in Radnorshire in Wales, above a month since ... And further ... that it was reported in Wales that the Kings of France and Scotland had knowledge of this business.'[157] Soranzo would similarly report in the spring of 1601 from Vallodolid to the Doge and the Council that he understood that there were suspicions in Elizabeth's realm 'that the King of Scotland may have had a finger in the plot, for he was in intimate relations with the Earl of Essex and aware of all these internal commotions'.[158]

At the beginning of the earl's trial on 19th February 1601, the Queen's Sergeant, Yelverton, affirmed to the assembled company that

> the sedition of Catiline was in the city of Rome, and consequently England is in no less danger; for as Catiline entertained the most seditious persons about all Rome to join with him in his conspiracy, so the Earl of Essex entertained none but Papists, Recusants, and Atheists for his abettors in this his capital rebellion against the whole estate of England.[159]

Similarly, acting for the prosecution, Francis Bacon likened his former patron to the contemptible conduct of 'one Pisistratus, in Athens, who, coming . . . with the purpose to procure the subversion of the Kingdom, . . . entered the city, having cut his body with a knife, to the end [the citizens] might conjecture he had been in danger of his life'.[160] Whatever the heroics or mock-heroics described for the courtroom, the outcome of the trial was a foregone conclusion and the earl was beheaded on the scaffold on Ash Wednesday, 25th February 1601. As Elizabeth's Captain of the Guard, Ralegh was called upon to bear witness to the execution – how visible he was or how close he was to the scene of execution remains unclear.

The earl was thirty-four years of age and may have suffered as many as three strikes of the axe before his head was severed from his body. Camden's *Annales* has him repeating the first verses of Psalm 51 before kneeling at the block 'in humilitie and obedience'. Others, like David Lindsay, concurred that the 'noble and valorous Earle, ROBERT DEVEREUX, Earle of ESSEX, who suffred in the yeare 1601 for his rebellion ... died verie Christianlie, as Historians report'.[161] Indeed, Camden's *Annales* remind the reader of the earl's father who had ominously all those years before sought 'to warne his sonne, being then scarce ten yeares old to set always before his eyes the six and thirtieth yeare of his age, as the uttermost scope of his life, which neither he nor his Father had passed, and his sonne never attained vnto it, as in proper place we will shew'.[162] Nevertheless, it appeared to many that there were other lessons to be drawn from this sequence of events. In Rome, the Venetian ambassador Giovanni Mocenigo reported that 'We are informed from a very sure quarter that all these recent tumults in England which have cost the Earl of Essex his head, are the result of Spanish intrigues.'[163] Closer to home, there was little room for consolation now that the *sonne of Bellona* had been executed, as Sir John Harington intimated later in the autumn of 1601 to his correspondent, Sir Hugh Portman:

> [The queen] is quite disfavourd, and unattird, and these troubles waste her muche. She disregardeth every costlie cover that comethe to the table … Every new message from the city doth disturb her, and she frowns on all the Ladies. I had a sharp message from her brought by my Lord Buckhurst, namely thus, 'Go tell that witty fellow, my godson, to get home; it is no season now to foole it here.' I liked this as little as she doth my knighthood, so took to my bootes and returnd to the plow in bad weather. … . She walks much in her privy chamber, and stamps with her feet at ill news, and thrusts her rusty sword at times into the arras in great rage. My Lord Buckhurst is much with her, and few else since the city business; but the dangers are over, and yet she always keeps a sword by her table.[164]

CHAPTER 6

European Afterlives 1600–1770

> All you that cry, O hone! O hone!
>   come now and sing O Lord with me.
> For why[?] our Jewell is from vs goone,
>   The valiant Knight of Chiualrie . . .
>
> . . . His deedes did nought auaile,
>   more was the pittie:
> He was condemn'd to die,
>
> For treason certainely,
>   But God that sits on hie
>   Knoweth all things.[1]

Following the execution of the Earl of Essex, ballads and broadsides began to circulate (from whose lyrics the extracts above are taken), celebrating, heroising and memorialising the condemned leader of an attempted coup d'état. This final discussion and, much more briefly, the Conclusion consider just some of the ways in which this process continued internationally for the figures of Elizabeth, Essex, Ralegh and, indeed, Shakespeare himself as one generation succeeded the next.

As we have seen, the question of Europe, most especially a Europe divided against itself by rival communities and violent blood-letting, loomed large in Shakespeare's evolving conception of the history play in the 1590s and in the lives of those drawn to the court in the closing decades of the Tudor century. Strikingly, the profiles of the queen and her favourites continued to fascinate audiences on both sides of the Channel and beyond – and each audience, governed by particular political dispensations, cultures of worship and changing taste cultures, sought to impose and reimpose identities upon them in a host of different genres during the centuries which followed.

Rapid Response in Early Modern Britain

As has been witnessed in earlier chapters, voices could be heard from a number of quarters in the final years of Elizabeth's reign, expressing disaffection with the political policies being adopted by the administration of an ageing queen. Indeed, even those being solicited by the regime to defend its decisions might acknowledge publicly the adverse currents of opinion in evidence in the wider society. By 1st March 1601 the preacher William Barlow had been commissioned by Elizabeth's ministers to deliver a sermon responding to the most recent political vicissitudes. Barlow took as his text 'Give unto Caesar the things of Caesar' (Matt. 21.22), yet remained at pains to observe that some

> ill affected, and foule mouthed haue giuen out, that because we, being commanded by authority, on the Saboth after the insurrection, in our seuerall cures, did describe the nature and uglinesse of the rebellion, are becom *time servers & men pleasers*, leauing the great man that is dead, and now cleaving to others and closing with them for preferments.[2]

Moreover, working a vein that may indeed have occurred to others writing for the playhouses in these years, Barlow concluded that 'great natures, men of great mindes & parts, prove either excellently good, or dangerously wicked: it is spoken by *Plato*, but applied by *Plutarch* unto *Coriolanus*, a gallant young, but a discontented Romane, who might make a fit paralell, for the late Earle'.[3] Play-making was an activity which continued to enjoy particular scrutiny from the authorities in the aftermath of the Essex revolt.[4] Samuel Daniel's *Philotas* was a text that had been in gestation for a number of years and was finally acted by the Children of the Queen's Revels in January 1605. At the centre of this intrigue (where 'states of grace are no sure holds in Court'[5]) stands 'great Philotas' – one 'whom we all beheld/In grace last night', but who finds himself 'arraign'd today' (IV. i.1149–53). More broadly, this dramatic world is one in which 'greate men [may] cloath their private hate/In those faire colours of the publike good' (II.Chorus.1110–1); and, at the play's close, we learn that 'you civill Greeks .../... are but the same/As are our Sovereigne tyrants of the East' (V.Persian Chorus.1768, 1772–3). In due course, Daniel was summoned before the Privy Council: 'when called in question for the tragedy of Philotas, [he admitted] that he had read part of it to the Earl; had no other friend in power to help him; knows he shall live "inter historiam temporis"[a]; and will vindicate his innocence'.[6] Clearly continuing to feel

---

[a] '[caught] in the history of the time'.

vulnerable to censure, at the close of the published text of the play Daniel recognised that he was 'perticularly beholding to [Essex's] bounty, [but] ... would to God his errors and disobedience to his Sovereigne, might be so deepe buried underneath the earth, and in so low a tombe from his other parts, that they might never be remembred'.[7]

Indeed, for some, the overweening ambition of Essex had never been in question. At the Earl's arraignment, the government's attorney, Sir Edward Coke, had argued in his customary impassioned manner that the Earl '*affected to be* Robert *the first of that name King of England*'.[8] Nonetheless, in the aftermath of the execution, it was clear that others might view events rather differently. Richard Williams, for example, described the condemned man at the block 'yet as a lambe hee quyett laye'.[9] The Earl of Northumberland referred to 'my Lo: of Essex marterdowm'; and there was a story circulating of 'a certayne man [who] weares a litell neck-bone of his, which the giddie executioner of the first unluckie stroake forcst from the rebound of his valiant and hardie neck'.[10]

In his final captivity, Essex had complained to his sovereign that 'The prating tavern haunter speaks of me what he lists; the frantic libeller writes of me what he lists; already they print me and make me speak to the world, and shortly they will play me in what forms they list upon the stage.'[11] The extent to which the figures of Essex (and Ralegh) were staged in the playhouses continues to be a source of critical debate. Was Essex being represented as the restive warrior-hero in Shakespeare's *Henry V* (1599), as a petulant Achilles in *Troilus and Cressida* (1601–2) or as the inexorable, war-crazed protagonist in *Coriolanus* (1608)? If Jonson's account of political conspiracy and rebellion in *Sejanus, His Fall* (1603) failed to earn him ovations from the galleries, it generated sufficient concern in 1603 for him, like Daniel, to be summoned before the Privy Council.[12] Elsewhere, enjoying rather less critical attention, Thomas Heywood's political romance *The royall king and loyall subject* (1606? pub. 1637)[13] has its hero, the Lord Martiall, feasting with foreign dignitaries, yet beset by court enemies: King – 'You are too neare us yet; what are we King./Or have we countermanders?' (II.ii.). The dramatic thrust of this tragicomedy, like many in the period, focuses upon the expectations of *magnanimitas* which attend political sovereignty. If the jealous monarch drives his eminent courtier from the royal presence ('Since he a Subject would precede his Prince' (III.i.)), the play ponders at length the precarious fate of those whose lives become too tightly enmeshed with that of their masters: Audley – 'I have not seene a man hath borne his disgrace with more patience' (II.ii).

John Fletcher's *The Loyal Subject* (1618) was staged in the year of Ralegh's execution.[14] Here, the dramatic intrigue undergoes a light russification and there are a number of plots involving assumed identities. Indeed, the protagonist Archas attempts to avert the wrath of the tyrannical Grand Duke of Moscovia towards himself and his loved ones with some remarkable arts of disguise. At the opening of the play, the audience learns that the hero, who 'was the Father of the War,/He that begot, and bred the Soldier,/Why he sits shaking of his Arms, like *Autumne*' (I.i.). Royal misgovernment and unwarranted persecution of the loyal subject remain again thematic to this dramatic narrative where Archas is baited by enemies at court: 'this wasted Body,/Beaten and bruis'd with Arms, dry'd up with troubles,/Is good for nothing else but quiet, now, Sir' (I.i). In due course, like Ralegh, Archas finds himself divested of his country estate by those close to the sovereign. The intrigue is excited later by the threat of a Tartar invasion with no one to save Moscovia apart, it seems, from the disgraced hero. Triumphing once again on the battlefield, Archas (and the nation) has nevertheless to face the military antagonism of his disaffected son, incensed by the unmerited misfortunes of his father. Ultimately, however, the audience is presented with another tragic-comic denouement in which the staging of clemency, rather than corpses, brings the action to a close: 'To Joys and Revels, Sports, and he that can/Most honour Archas, is the noblest Man' (V.vi).

As we have witnessed, Essex was much more strategically placed than Ralegh in late-Elizabethan England in terms of rank, financial rewards, political resources (notably, spying) and international renown. Thus, the earl remained the recipient of a growing number of eulogies and dedications from authors seeking patronage of one kind or another. Year on year, writers of all complexions were minded to draw parallels between the aspiring nobleman and the fortunes of leaders from antiquity. Remembering the storming of Cadiz in *Troia Britannica* (1609), Thomas Heywood proclaimed that the English commanders led their forces to victory on the Spanish port, 'As *Greece* did *Troy*, great *Essex* and bold *Drake*.'[15] Elsewhere in these years after the earl's execution, Barnabe Barnes contended in his *Foure Bookes of Offices* (1606) that the wavering fortunes of great men of state such as Essex might recall those of David, 'who (though protected by the great prouidence of God) … [was] in danger to lose his life, by many treacherous conspiracies'.[16] Indeed, recalling fleetingly a figure resembling Shakespeare's *Henry V*, Barnes had declared in the 1590s 'I my selfe a Boy, have seene him in the French warres to communicate in sports and sometimes in serious matters with men of meane condition and place, their fortunes and parentage valued.'[17]

Nonetheless, as her own life drew to its close, Elizabeth continued to give ample proof of the changeful nature of her sovereignty. Like Essex, Ralegh had some mastery of French, Italian, Spanish and Latin, and she employed both men strategically as guides when foreign dignitaries visited her realm. Ralegh accompanied Henri IV's emissary, the Duc de Biron, on a tour of London in September 1601. In an audience with Biron, the queen might be heard 'sharply accusing [Essex] of ingratitude, rash counsel and obstinately refusing to ask pardon'. Camden added in this narrative that 'Some also report that she showed the skull of the Earl to the Duke ... in her closet, or fastened upon a pole; which is a ridiculous vain story, for that was buried together with his body.'[18] On another occasion, Elizabeth was apparently reviewing the question of the Earl's actions in an audience with the antiquarian William Lambarde, declaring 'He that will forget God, will also forget his benefactors.'[19] In reality, she seems to have found little source of comfort in these final years of her reign. In the aftermath of the revolt, Robert Sidney submitted that 'I do see the Queen often; she doth wax weak since the late troubles.'[20] By spring 1602 she was reprimanding even the preacher Barlow for entering the royal presence against her wishes, 'because she would not have the memory of the late Earl of Essex renewed by him who had preached against him at Paul's'.[21]

Sir Thomas Smith, who would be appointed as James's ambassador in the early years of his reign to the court of Czar Boris Godunov, was briefly imprisoned at the close of Elizabeth's reign for alleged complicity in the Essex rebellion. He subsequently recalled in his *voiage and entertainment in Rushia* (1605) the figure of 'the vnfortunate (too sudden rysing) *Earle of Essex*; wherein most mens mindes: for as many dayes as weekes, weare bewondred'.[22] With more circumspection, Gervase Markham paid guarded homage later to 'Robert (surnamed the Great) Earle of *Essex*, a man of whom it behoueth euery man to be carefull how to write.'[23]

The European Nations Respond

Speculation and political reflection surrounding figures such as Essex did not end at the frontiers of the Tudor realm. In Paris, Henri IV wrote to his ambassador in Madrid of the earl's 'soubzlevation' in the same week as the latter's execution: he feared that the nobleman and his circle 'payeront de leurs testes la faulte qu'ilz y ont faicte'.[24a] This monarch of a nation that

---

[a] 'uprising'; 'will pay with their heads for the crime that they have committed'.

was just emerging from decades of civil war recognised all too well that when 'la semence de rebellion est jettée en un estat, elle prend aisement de grandes et fortes racynes, qu'il est bien mal aisé d'arracher'.[25a] In the weeks which followed, Henri also wrote to his envoy in London, Monsieur de Boissise, asking for a detailed account of the Earl's actions, his supporters and the nature of the execution: 'pour m'en donner ung advis le plus exact et particulier que vous pourrez'.[26b] Uppermost in the king's mind was the anxiety that he would be accused of complicity with his erstwhile comrade-at-arms. In Paris, the Venetian ambassador Marin Cavalli confirmed in August 1601 that

> The King of France is also accused of being mixed up with the [Essex] plot on account of some old quarrel over money which the Queen says he owes her. She is suspicious of him now that he has become a Catholic … Moreover just at the moment of Essex's rebellion there came the report that the King was going to Calais.[27]

Mindful of the precarious situation, Henri sent messages to Robert Cecil that 'je serois le premier à le [Essex] condamner, tant j'ay en horreur la faulte, si elle est telle que l'on la publie'.[28c]

Like many others, the Venetian reports from London at the time chose to view the demise of the Virgin Queen through the lens of the execution of her court favourite two years earlier. Giovanni Carlo Scaramelli informed the Doge and Senate in March 1603 that he was indeed accurate in his

> last despatch [when he] said that her Majesty's mind was overwhelmed by a grief greater than she could bear. It reached such a pitch that she passed three days and three nights without sleep and with scarcely any food. . . . She fell to considering that the Earl of Essex who used to be her dear intimate might have been quite innocent after all.[29]

Furthermore, if accounts were to be believed, Spain maintained its own operations of data collection in this regard. In October 1597, Ralegh wrote to Cecil that the captain of a Spanish vessel declared 'of his own voluntary' that 'the earle our generall hath as mich fame and reputation in Spayne and Italy as ever and more then any of our nation had, and that for an enemy hee is the most honoured man in Europe'.[30] In 1602 Cecil received information that seamen aboard '2 Spanish ships and a pinnace which lie

---

[a] 'when the seed of rebellion is sown in a state it puts down large and strong roots which it is very difficult to pull up'.

[b] 'so as to furnish me with the most precise and detailed information on them that you can'.

[c] 'I would be the first to condemn him, such is my horror of the grievous action, if it be such as is reported.'

thwart of Plymouth' had interrogated local fishermen on 'these points following:- First, how the rebellion of the Lord of Essex had proceeded, and to what head it had grown, and what noblemen were interested in that business, and how many of them had lost their lives with him, and to what head it had grown since his death'.[31]

More generally, from across Europe the reports of the Venetian emissaries continued to offer to the Doge and the Council updated accounts concerning developments in London.[32] The ambassador from 1597 to 1602 to the courts of Philip II and Philip III in Madrid stressed to the *Serenissima* that

> La regina d'Inghilterra è stata sempre il maggior inimico che abbia avuto il re di Spagna, e che lo ha tenuto più d'ogni altro inquieto e molestato, e sebbene fanno gli Spagnuoli professione di sprezzare le sue forze, e le sue offense, niente dimeno hanno ricevuto dalle sue armate molte volte grandissime ingiurie.[33a]

Even in 1607 the republic's ambassador to James's court might still be found drawing attention to 'il conte di Essex, il quale fu il più favorito che avesse giammai la regina Elisabetta ... con li suoi artifizj gli fece rompere il collo'.[34b]

On the Italian peninsula itself at this time was to be found Henry Wotton, a former member of Essex's secretariat. In September 1600, the earl had furnished him with a letter of recommendation for the Gran Duca di Toscana, Ferdinando I di Medicis – the latter at that time under house arrest, like Essex. By April 1601, following news of the rebellion, Wotton informed Ferdinando from Florence that his former master 'finiva li suoi giorni nella Torre di Londra, dove era imprigionato per oviare a magiori movimenti che potevan nascere se l'essecutione fusse stata più essempio'.[35c] Indeed, declaring himself to be in a state of some distress, Wotton submitted, 'Perdoni in me V.Sig: a la vanità e la passion ch'Io uso nel contare la perdita d'un Signore che m'amava, et mi fidava nelli suoi più intrinsechi affair.'[36d] Wotton added in his correspondence at this time to the Grand Duke that

---

[a] 'The Queen of England has always been the greatest enemy that the King of Spain has had, and, more than any other, one who has rendered him anxious and harassed, and although the Spaniards declare that they despise her forces, and her insults, nevertheless, they have received on many occasions from her armies the greatest injuries.'

[b] 'the Earl of Essex, who was the most important favourite of Queen Elizabeth ... got his neck broken on account of his machinations'.

[c] '[The earl] finished his days in the Tower of London where he was imprisoned so as to avoid any great disturbances that might take place if the execution had been more public.'

[d] 'Excuse me your lordship: for the vain and passionate manner in which I relate the loss of a Lord who loved me, and trusted me with his most personal affairs.'

Il Popol d'Inghilterra resta molto sodisfatto con le ultime parole del Conte intorno alli fini suoi che non erano di far male nissuno all persona Reale (il che sigilava con la morte) et io per l'intrinseca notitia ch'ho havuto di lui so bene ch'haveva il cuore et li pensieri molto leali: anchor anche tutti li predicatori di Londra dopo l'imprigionamento suo fossino commandati di dichiarare il contrario all plebe, per render il fatto tanto più odioso.[37a]

Yet consternation extended well beyond the circle of former members of the Essex's secretariat on the peninsula: it was reported that Pope Clement VIII himself was shocked by the imprudent conduct of the Earl.[38]

Perhaps unsurprisingly, Ralegh's cousin, Sir Arthur Gorges, adopted a rather different perspective on these events. He insisted that the Earl was 'a man that did affect nothing in the world so much as Fame, and to be reputed matchlesse for magnanimitie, and undertaking, and could hardly indure any that should obscure his glory in that kinde, though otherwise he favoured them never so muche'.[39] Much further north, in 1601 James VI of Scotland assured his 'Richt trustie and uellbelouit' Cecil in coded correspondence that he knew that Elizabeth's minister

> mistrusted the aspyring mynde of essex … [and that James] can not but comend, taking it for a sure signe that [Cecil's] uoulde neuer allow that a subiect should climbe to so hie a roume … and yett [James] doth protest, upon his concience and honoure, that essex had neuer any dealing with him quhiche uas not most honorable and auouable.[40]

However, by April the Scottish monarch wrote from Edinburgh to his emissaries at Elizabeth's court, the Earl of Mar and Edward Bruce, cautioning them that they all had to tread a fine line between 'these two precipices of the Queen and the people, who now appear to be in so contrary terms'. The envoys were instructed to acquaint themselves with the 'sorts of discontentment the people are presently possessed'. The Scottish king remained anxious that 'the discontentment be grown to that height that they are not able any longer to comport either with prince or state'.[41] Moreover, like Henri IV, James saw the pressing need 'to give out a plain declairaitoure … that I am untouched in any action of practice that ever hath been intended against [the queen]', adding that his emissaries should petition Elizabeth 'to renew her old promise that nothing shall

---

[a] 'The English people remains very satisfied with the last words of the Earl concerning his aims that were not to harm in any way the royal person (which meant death) and given the in-depth knowledge I had of him, I know well that he had a very loyal heart and mind: moreover, after the period of imprisonment all the preachers of London were ordered to pronounce the very opposite to the crowds so as to render his actions even more vile.'

be done by her in her time in prejudice of [his] future right'.[42] For his own part, Henry (the wizard), 9th Earl of Northumberland, wrote to James affirming that

> althought [Essex] was a man endeued wyth good gifts, yet was his losse the happiest chaunce for yowr maiestie and England that cowld befawle ws; for ether doe I feale in my iudgment, or he would hawe bene ane bloody scowrge to owr nation. ... Did he not decree it, that it was scandalus to owr nation that a stranger sould be owr king? ... I must needs affirme rawleighs ever allowance of yowr right, and althowghte I knowe hem insolent, extreamly heated ... there is excellent good parts of natur in hem.[43]

Whatever the truth of the matter, within a very short time, Essex not only constituted a focus of enduring fascination across the continent, but the scene of his passing had also become swiftly a venue for tourism. When Philip Julius, Duke of Stettin-Pomerania, visited the realm of the ageing queen in 1602, there were already unmissable locations for a visit to the Tower of London:

> Als wir hinunter auf den Platz kommen ward uns der Ort gezeiget, da der tapfere Held Graf von Essex enthauptet und in der nächst dabei leigenden Kapelle begraben worden. Wie lieb und werth dieser Graf in dem ganzen Reich gehalten, stehet genugsam daraus zu ersehen, dass sein Lied darinnen er der Königin und dem ganzen Lande valediciret, und auch die Ursache seines Unglücks anzeignet, hin und wieder im Reiche, ja in dem königl. Hoflager sebsten in unserer Gegenwart ist gesungen und auf Instrumenten gespielet worden, da doch seine Memoria als eines rei majestatis publico judico damniret.[44a]

A New King and New Afterlives for Fallen Courtiers

In the years between Essex's execution and Elizabeth's death, the only publications that officially addressed the Earl's passing were Barlow's *sermon preached at Paules Crosse* (1601) and Francis Bacon's *A declaration*

---

[a] 'On descending to the courtyard, the spot was shown to us where the brave hero the Earl of Essex was beheaded, and lay buried in the chapel close by. How beloved and admired this Earl was throughout the kingdom, may be judged from the circumstance that his song, in which he takes leave of the Queen and the whole country, and in which also he shows the reason of his unlucky fate, is sung and played on musical instruments all over the country, even in our presence at the royal court, though his memory is condemned as that of a man having committed high treason.' See Gottfried von Bülow (ed.), 'Diary of the Journey of Philip Julius, duke of Stettin-Pomerania, through England in the year 1602', *Transactions of Royal Historical Society*, 2nd series, 6, 1892, 1–67 (p. 15). I am indebted to John Lee for his suggestion that the 'song' in question here might indeed be 'Sweet England's pride is gone'.

of the practises & treasons attempted and committed by Robert late Earle of
Essex and his complices, against her Maiestie and her kingdoms (1601).
However, with the advent of the new reign and James VI/I's return of
the family estate to the fatherless twelve-year-old Robert, the 3rd Earl of
Essex, it was altogether safer to laud Elizabeth's fallen courtier and reprise
the wonted eulogies of the 1590s.

The accession year of 1603 would bring in a host of surprises, one of
which was the newly recognised status of the Earl of Tyrone at the court in
London. Philip Gawdy wrote home to his brother in Norfolk in May of
that year that 'My Lo. of Southampton is in great fauor with the King.
Teron dothe offer vppon his othe to cleere my Lo. of Essex touching all
matters [that] wer obiected agaynst him concerning him selfe.'[45] More
testily, the late queen's grandson John Harington informed the Bishop of
Bath and Wells that under the new, Stuart dispensation

> I have lived to see that damnable rebel Tir-Owen broughte to Englande,
> curteouslie savourede, honourede, and well likede . . . How did I labour after
> that knaves destruction! . . . Essex tooke me to Irelande, I had scante tyme to
> putte on my bootes, I followede withe good wyll, and did returne wyth the
> Lorde Leiutenante to meet ill wyll . . . I shall never put oute of remem-
> braunce hir Majesties displeasure:- I enterd her chamber, but she frownede
> and saiede, 'What, did the foole brynge *you* too? Go backe to your
> businesse.'[46]

Years later, in his collection *Poems* (1619), Michael Drayton would also
lament 'Lastly mine Eyes amazedly haue seene/ESSEX great fall,
TYRONE his Peace to gaine.'[47]

The cultural capital of both Essex and Ralegh enjoyed quite different
forms of recognition in early Stuart society. Gervase Markham noted of the
young, orphaned Essex that '[James] has received the twelve-year-old son
of the Earl of Essex and taken him in his arms and kissed him, openly and
loudly declaring him the son of the most noble knight that English land has
ever begotten.'[48] Conversely, as we have seen, the new reign marked
a period of unremitting enmity from the Stuart king towards Ralegh.
Nonetheless, in 1618, it was reported to Dudley Carleton that Ralegh's
execution 'will doe more harme to the faction that sought it, then ever his
life could haue done'.[49] One of the prisoner's final adversaries, Francis
Bacon, was clearly once again in receipt of a royal commission in 1618 to
write *A declaration of the demeanor and cariage of Sir Walter Ralegh, Knight.*
If the reader was reminded at the outset that 'KINGS be not bound to giue
Account of their Actions to any but GOD alone', nonetheless 'his Maiestie

hath thought fit to manifest vnto the world, how things appeared vnto himselfe, and vpon what Proofes and euident Matter, and the Examination of the Commaunders that were employed with him'.[50]

Conversely, in the years that followed, Degory Wheare, Camden Professor of History at Oxford, wrote authoritatively for contemporaries in his *Methodus Legendi Historias* (1623) in fulsome praise of '*Gualterus Raulaeus* nostras, Eques auratus, vir clari nominis, & ob singularem fortitudinem ac prudentiam meliori fato dignus.'[51a] A generation later, Joseph Hall's *The Balm of Gilead* (1646) argued that Ralegh's 'noble history of the World' enabled the author to attain intellectual maturity and moral wisdom: 'the Tower reformed the Court in him, and produced those worthy monuments of art and industry, which we should have in vain expected from his freedom and jollity'.[52] The publication entitled (by the printer?) *Sir Walter Raleighs instructions to his sonne and to posterity* (composed c. 1609? 1st pub. 1632) was so popular that it ran to five editions alone between 1632–5. In 1645 the royalist James Howell hailed Ralegh as 'That rare and renowned knight, whose fame shall contend in longevity with the island itself.'[53] Elsewhere, holding rather different political sympathies, John Milton felt compelled in 1658 to prepare (what he thought was) Ralegh's *The Cabinet-Council* for publication because it would prove 'a kinde of injury to withhold longer the work of so eminent an Author from the Publick'.[54]

In the opening decades of the seventeenth century, the reputations of former court favourites might also be played off against each other. At Ralegh's trial, Coke, the Attorney General, reported that the defendant had advised Cobham in a letter that he 'should not be overtaken by confessing to any preacher, as the Earl of Essex did', concluding to the court: 'O damnable Atheist! He counsels him not to confess to preachers, as the Earl of Essex did. That noble Earl died indeed for his offence; but he died the child of God.'[55] Later, Algernon Sidney was not alone in contending that 'tho [Ralegh] was a well qualified Gentleman, yet his Morals were no way exact, as appears by his dealings with the brave Earl of *Essex*'.[56] Nevertheless, there were continued attempts to appropriate Ralegh's name for different causes. Thomas Scott followed up his *Vox Populi or Newes from Spayne* (1620) with *Sir Walter Rawleighs Ghost, or Englands Forewarner* (1626): in such productions, the *vox populi* of the dead courtier

---

[a] 'Sir *Walter Rawleigh* . . . our Countrey-man deserves the first place, a man of great Fame, and for his great both Valour and prudence worthy of a better Fate.' See Diggory Wheare, *The method and order of reading both civil and ecclesiastical histories* . . . (London: M. Flesher for Charles Brome, 1685), p. 41.

was left to do battle with the *fox populi* of the Spanish ambassador at James's court, Count Gondomar. Later, in 1631, appeared Lessius' *Rawleigh his Ghost* and, in the mid-century, an anonymous pamphlet circulated invoking Ralegh's name, *All is not Gold that glisters: Or, a Warning-Piece to England* (1651).

Thus, the execution of Ralegh in 1618 only served to enhance his cultural authority – and this was exactly as his enemies had feared. A Spanish agent in London reported in code to Madrid that '[t]he death of this man has produced a great commotion and fear here, and it is looked upon as a matter of the highest importance, owing to his being a person of great parts and experience, subtle, crafty, ingenious, and brave enough for anything'.[57] As Agnes Latham pointed out, '[w]ithout the traditions of the great house behind him, [Ralegh] had to create his own legend and he did it magnificently.'[58] Right up to the night before his execution in the Tower, the condemned prisoner was allegedly extending his textual legacy by writing his own epitaph, the celebrated lyric 'Even such is Time who takes in trust/our youth, our Joyes and all we have.'[59] Subsequently, his brother-in-law, Sir Arthur Throckmorton, amongst many others, offered his own poetic tribute to his dead kinsman: 'Beholde Brave Raleigh here.'[60] One of Ralegh's former captains on the Guiana expedition, Samuel King, is thought to have penned the famous eulogy 'Greate heart, who taught the so to dye.'[61] In addition, Henry King was not untypical amongst later elegists in wishing to shine a light upon the favourite's 'most industrious and freindly foes' who

> thought by cutting off some wither'd dayes,
> (Which thou couldst spare them) to eclipse thy praise,
> Yet gave it brighter foile, made thy ag'd fame
> Appeare more white and faire, then foule their shame.[62]

Across the Channel

In the years that followed Elizabeth's passing, European presses continued to cater to the ongoing interest in events occurring at the court in London. France saw the publication of Pierre Victor Palma Cayet's *Chronologie septenaire de l'histoire de la paix entre les roys de France et d'Espagne* (1606). Here, the death of the last Tudor monarch is once again attributed in large measure to the grief occasioned by the earl's death. In addition, there was the appearance of the *Entreprise, jugement et mort du Comte d'Essex, Anglois* (1606). Barnabe Barnes had wished that 'it had so pleased God, that [Essex] might have died in the warres upon the enemies of his countrey, that I might heroically with good cheere have registred his death', and this sentiment was echoed in the *Histoire e la Vie et Mort dv Comte d'Essex avec vn Discours Grave et Eloquent de la Royne d'Angleterre au Duc de Biron sur ce subiect* (1607):

> il faut croir que la mort eust esté glorieusement douce si le Comte d'Essex fut mort, dans ce braue exploict de la prise de Cadix, & que les derniers iours de la vie n'eussent esteint la clarté des premiers.[63a]

For additional accounts of the misfortunes of the earl, French sources such as André du Chesne's *Histoire Générale d'Angleterre, d'Écosse, et d'Irlande* (1614) and Jacques-Auguste de Thou's *Historiae sui temporis* (complete edition pub. 1620) might be consulted, as well as Paul de Bellegent's 1627 translation of Camden's *Annals*.[64] In this growing mêlée of narratives for public consumption, Cayet's publication and Webster's *The Devil's Law Case* (1617–20) remained influential for subsequent generations. They both stressed the supposedly tardy delivery of messages and tokens at the close of the earl's life and the consequent despair of the queen: 'that worthy Princesse,/Who loathed food, and sleepe, and ceremony,/For thought of loosing that braue Gentleman,/She would faine haue saued.'[65] Similarly, Edward Grimeston's translation/extension of Jean de Serres' *Histoire des choses mémorables avenues en France* (1599), now entitled *A General Inventorie of the history of France* (1607), asserted that the order of execution upon the proud Essex might have been revoked if only he had humbled himself and asked his queen for a pardon. This point was also taken up in George Chapman's *Conspiracy and Tragedy of Charles, Duke of Byron* (1608): 'the Queene of England,/Told me that if the wilfull Earle of Essex,/Had vsd submission, and but askt her mercie,/She would haue giuen it, past resumption.'[66]

Furthermore, London was not the only performance venue in Europe given to recalling the supposed actions of Elizabeth and her favourites. From the fifteenth century in the Low Countries, chambers of Rhetoric (*rederikjerskamers*) had grown up initially in the provinces of Flanders and Brabant as well as those of Northern France. These chambers often participated in the municipal and religious cultures of their local communities. They became fora for political and intellectual debate as well as hosting and/or participating in festivals, celebrations and competitions

---

[a] 'One must imagine that the death would have been of a fitting glory if the Earl of Essex had died during this brave exploit of the taking of Cadiz, and that the last days of his life would not have tarnished the brilliance of earlier ones.'

between rival confraternities, often involving public addresses, recitals, dramatic productions and/or processions. Such gatherings constituted opportunities for showcasing the talents of writers, disputants, rhetoricians, educators, critics (social and literary), actors, poets and playwrights among the membership. Arjan van Dixhoorn confirms that 'between 1440 and 1740 over 400 Dutch-speaking chambers of rhetoric existed for a shorter or longer period'.[67] Some of these chambers had already been in existence for a century and a half by the time the earl's execution; and, by the second half of the sixteenth century, some of the fruits of their labours were finding their way into print.

Amongst the playtexts belonging to this culture of *rederijkerskamers*, there exists a script by one Michael Michaelis for the *'De Fiolieren'* (The Gillyflowers) chamber serving the community of the village of 's-Gravenpolder on the island of Zuid-Beveland in the province of Zeeland, not far from the English 'cautionary' town of Vlissingen, or Flushing.[68] His playtext, *Koningin Elysabeth*, survives in two scribal copies dated 1629 and 1694, but it may have been penned at a time (1605?) much closer to the events being described of Essex's rebellion and execution. If Michaelis probably drew selectively upon material from Camden's *Annals*, he chose to respond with much greater sympathy to the earl, who is the protagonist rather than Elizabeth.[69] Here, in keeping with the conventions of a large corpus of dramatic texts emanating from the Low Countries, the intrigue is linked with the mischief-making actions of the Sinnekens (in this instance, Jealous Practice (Jaloers Bedrijf) and Seeming Justice (Schijn van Recht)) who, in many ways, share characteristics with the Vice of late medieval English interludes.[70] These figures hold the stage for a good deal of Michaelis' narrative. As the action unfolds, we learn of the misfortunes of the Irish campaign and the earl's return to London. 'Den graaf Essex. Een Costelijck man'[71a] laments his fall from grace ('ick die eer geacht was en bent nu niet' – 105[b]), his isolation at the Tudor court ('de meeste heeren mij haten' – 133[c]) and the fact that his enemies have the ear of the ageing and beleaguered queen. However, such a situation is rendered more disquieting by the animated and trouble-making interventions of the Sinnekens onstage, who (as is customary for this kind of performance) are not above quarrelling with each other (indicating their fallen nature as well as their dramatic function as a comic resource).

---

[a] 'The Earl of Essex. A great [or perhaps "extravagant"] man.'
[b] 'I who was honoured and now am not.'   [c] 'most gentlemen hate me'.

In the opening phase of the action, the Sinnekins maliciously counsel the earl to act more decisively, while subsequently revelling in the prospect of wreaking further havoc if their words are heeded. Elsewhere, the earl's leadership in Ireland is judged harshly by the queen's advisers, a campaign which they view as mismanaged, both militarily and financially. Essex attempts strenuously to defend himself against these accusations, declaring that his senior commanders agreed on the course of the campaign and that all monies can be accounted for. Subsequently, in what may be dramatic asides, the Sinnekens voice conflicting estimates of the earl's actions to excite further strains in the intrigue. If the earl is not wholly condemned by the council, he is confined to his residence and forbidden from contacting the queen. It soon becomes apparent that Essex's principal antagonists, Cecil, 'Raeleijgh' and Cobham, had hoped for much worse. Indeed, stung by the apparent arrogance of the earl, Cobham suspects him of having ambitions on the Crown itself: 'Hij is mij te trots en groot van corage/ tschijnt tmoet hem al buijgen en eeren' (374–5[a]). Nonetheless, Raelijgh reminds Cobham that even those in the past who were 'in hoogen staat'[b], like Darius and Julius Caesar, were brought down by lesser mortals (431–6). More generally, throughout this highly rhetorical *de casibus* narrative, a good deal of classical allusiveness as well as homiletic wisdom characterises many of the major speeches.[72]

During his period of confinement, the earl is disoriented further by the duplicitous words and actions of the Sinnekens. When the queen herself later appears onstage *sola*, she laments the actions of the earl: a man who, she feels, has betrayed her trust and who has his sights on the Crown. In the ensuing action, the earl refuses a summons to court (declaring himself indisposed), and this is interpreted by his enemies as further evidence of his treasonous nature. Ultimately, the mighty queen resolves 'mijn monarchale regieringe seer groot/can de trotsheijt niet lijden van haar vassaal/tot verachtinge van mijn regieringe princepaal' (1622–4[c]). An account of the Essex revolt is given by the Sinnekens, and Cobham demands onstage that the earl must pay with his life for this act of sedition. Even as the protagonist is called for trial, the queen is asking her advisors, his judges, not to treat him harshly. In the courtroom, amongst the accusations made against the earl, it is claimed that he even sought to offer the crown to the Infanta of Spain. The judges condemn him to the scaffold, but the

---

[a] 'In my opinion he is too proud and full of bravado/It appears that everyone must bow to and honour him.'

[b] 'in high estate'.

[c] 'My peerless royalty will not suffer the pride of its vassal who holds my sovereign right in contempt.'

sentence has yet to be ratified by the anguish-ridden queen. Much soliloquising is afforded the hero during the course of the play and, at this point, Essex reveals his meditative nature: 'wat ist vanden mensche die hier op aarden leeft/hij leeft soot schijnt en tis gestadich sterven' (1794–5[a]). Elsewhere, the dilemma of tormented Elizabeth ('een bedaachde dochter'[73b]) is widely appreciated onstage ('hoe is de coninginne dus met pijn bedrouft' – 2074[c]) and further aggravated by the commentaries and machinations of the Sinnekens. Eventually, the queen signs the death warrant, but has Carew sleep at her chamber door overnight in case she changes her mind. Indeed, during the night she sends messages to revoke the death sentence and then another to overrule this decision. She then sends a third message for a stay of execution, but it arrives too late to save the earl, who continues to protest his innocence. The play closes signalling the enduring despair of the queen, the delight of the Sinnekens and the ills of overweening pride.[74]

Much further south, the Spanish play *Dar la Vida por su Dama. El Conde de Sex* (written 1633, pub. 1638 anonymously) has been variously attributed down the centuries to Antonio Coello, his brother Luis Coello, Calderón, Matos Fragoso, Pérez de Montalbán and even Philip IV himself.[75] A good measure of critical consensus now attributes the authorship to Antonio Coello (1611–52) – a dramatist who enjoyed recognition from audiences and fellow writers of the time.[76] If this 'Comedia Famosa … De un ingenio de esta corte'[d] was only the second play to be written by the twenty-two-year-old Coello, there is record of its performance by the company of Manuel Álvarez de Vallejo on 10 November 1633 at the royal palace in Madrid in the presence of Philip IV himself.[77e] This playtext concentrates principally upon the torments of love endured, in this case, by 'El Conde de Sex' and 'La Reyna Doña Isabel', and would prove so influential for a number of other European writers that it merits some detailed consideration. At the outset of this play, Essex is returning with his servant Cosme to London, covered in glory after the triumph over the Spanish Armada: 'Libre está el reino; dejamos/de los españoles leños/limpio nuestro mar britano' (I.xi.783–5).[f] If he is returning above all to see his beloved Blanca, on his arrival in the capital, the earl sees an unknown woman being confronted by an armed aggressor who cries 'Muere, tirana' – a shot misses its target, her attacker then tries to kill her with a sword, but

---

[a] 'what is a man who lives here on earth:/it appears that he lives, but it is a gradual dying'.
[b] 'an elderly woman'.   [c] 'how afflicted the queen is thus with her suffering'.
[d] 'celebrated drama … based on the account of a wit at this court'.   [e] 'poet of the court'.
[f] 'The realm is free from danger; we have cleansed our British seas of Spanish vessels'.

the Earl intervenes: 'Ah, villanos,/eso no. ¡Yo la defiendo!' (I.i.1, 6–7).[78a]
Wounded, Essex forces the assailant to flee and, as a mark of gratitude, he is
given a scarf by the unknown woman (the Queen). Essex is lovestruck. To
complicate matters further, Blanca is also loved by the Duque de Alansón,
or Alençon, who has arrived to ask for the Queen's hand in marriage:
'Blanca, que en mi pecho reina' (I.vi.289).[b] Alansón meets with Flora,
Blanca's maid, who refrains from informing him of her mistress's affections
for Essex, but draws him into another part of the house. Essex appears on
stage, informing Blanca that although their families have opposed their
marriage, now, as a war hero, he is determined to gain royal assent for their
union. To complete this complex web of relations, Blanca reveals that her
father and brother (amongst others) died in prison for supporting the cause
of Mary, Queen of Scots, and that she herself hatched the recent plot to kill
the Queen, employing her cousin Roberto to perform this (failed) mission.
Alansón remains in his role as eavesdropper while Blanca appeals for
Essex's assistance onstage. The latter pretends to agree, hoping to have
Roberto arrested and his mistress preserved from any accusation: 'Blanca,
sol humano,/que es blanco de mis finezas/y yo lo soy de sus rayos' (I.
v.90–2).[c]

In the next act, Essex confides the scarf to Cosme, but this is seen by
Blanca, who later obtains it. Learning the manner in which Essex was given
the scarf, the distressed Blanca determines to hasten their wedding plans
and a subsequent audience between the Queen and Essex is interrupted by
Blanca, who is wearing the scarf. In the ensuing action, the disappointed
Alansón agrees to act for Blanca and Essex in their quest for the queen's
consent, but without any positive outcome. Subsequently, the slumbering
queen is discovered by Blanca, who attempts to kill her with Essex's pistol:
'Ea, venganza, ¿qué temes?'[d] However, if the hero arrives once again to the
rescue, the waking queen initially does not know which of the intruders is
the would-be assassin: seeing the Earl holding the pistol, she has him
arrested. In the final Act, the queen learns from Alansón that Essex had
knowledge of a plot to kill her; and, in the face of growing evidence, the
love-torn monarch feels compelled to pass the death sentence: 'estoy sola
en mi pasión./¡Oh, si el Conde traidor fuera/para que a Blanca no amara!'[e]
In order not to incriminate Blanca, Essex contents himself with

---

[a] 'Die, tyrant'; 'Ah, villains, not that. I forbid it!'   [b] 'Blanca, who reigns in my heart.'
[c] 'Blanca, human sun, who is the focus of my affections and I am graced by her rays.'
[d] 'Now, vengeance, what are you afraid of?'
[e] 'I am alone in my passion. Oh, if only the Earl were treacherous, so that Blanca were not loved
by him!'

protestations of innocence. He writes a letter to Blanca declaring his allegiance to the Crown and urges her to abandon her conspiracies. This he confides to Cosme on the understanding that it should only be delivered after his death. The disguised queen once again enters the scene (the prison cell) and offers the hero a key to escape. The Earl refuses to have his honour besmirched by such an action: 'si es instrument/de mi libertad, también/lo habrá de ser de mi miedo' (III.vi.2473–5).[a] Meanwhile, Cosme has read the letter and gives it to the queen, hoping to save his master's life. Overjoyed at the news of his innocence, the queen is nonetheless too late to have the sentence revoked, because Essex has already been executed. The play closes with the vision of the beheaded Essex ('Descúbrese el CONDE degollado'[b]), an anguished queen and the decision that Blanca should suffer the death sentence.

Coello's Essex spends a good deal of the action adopting the roles of Petrarchan lover, protector of the Crown and defender of what he perceives as his own honour or that of loved ones: 'Viva Blanca aunque yo muera' (III. v.2294).[79c] Given the diffuse nature of such preoccupations in tragic drama of the Spanish *siglo de oro*, it may come as no surprise that a number of critics, such as Emilio Cotarelo y Mori, felt that Coello's Earl emerged as the 'carácter admirable y tipo ideal del cabballero español, tal como se concebía en aquel tiempo'.[80d] However, from the seventeenth century on, critics have also signalled the courage of a dramatist offering a sensitively nuanced depiction of an enemy monarch. Elizabeth had frequently been viewed in Spanish society of the time 'como un monstruo de lascivia y de crueldad, perseguidora inicua de católicos', and was vilified by Lope de Vega as 'incestuoso parto de la arpia Ana Bolena' and 'sangrienta Jezebel'.[81e] Indeed, in the closing decade of that century, Bances Candamo underlined that 'la comedia del Conde de Essex la pinta solo con el afecto, pero tan retirado en la majestad y tan oculto en la entereza que el conde muere sin saber el amor de la reina'.[82f]

If the details of the intrigue to *El conde de Sex* would go on to spawn many comic, tragic and operatic works, across the Pyrenees three seventeenth-century French dramatists focused upon the possibility of yoking together

---

[a] 'if it is an instrument of my freedom, it will also be my downfall'.
[b] 'the earl is revealed beheaded'.   [c] 'May Blanca live on even though I die.'
[d] '[the] admirable character and ideal type of the Spanish knight, as it was conceived in that time'.
[e] 'as a monster of lasciviousness and cruelty, a wicked persecutor of Catholics'; 'incestuous offspring of the harpy Ann Boleyn'; 'bloodthirsty Jezebel'.
[f] 'The drama of the Earl of Essex portrays her character only with affection, but so distant in her majesty and reserved in her integrity that the earl dies without knowing the love of the queen.'

a *tragédie d'amour* and a *tragédie d'état* with an Essex narrative. Recent British history had earlier been presented to French audiences in the shape of Antoine de Montchrestien's highly imaginative account of Mary Stuart in *L'Ecossaise* (1601), for example. However, Gaultier de Coste, Seigneur de la Calprenède (1609?–1663), had his tragedy *Le Comte DEssex* first performed probably in the years 1636–7 in Paris. He drew for his sources once again upon Camden's *Annals*, as well as Pierre Matthieu's *Histoire de France* (1631). H. Carrington Lancaster argued that 'In *Essex* the dramatic talent of La Calprenède reached its climax.'[83] Whatever the case, in his preface to *Le Comte DEssex*, La Calprenède made the rather surprising claim (at least to modern eyes) that

> Si vous trouvez quelque chose dans cette Tragedie que vous n'ayez point leu dans Historiens Anglois, croyez que ie ne l'ay point inuenté, & que ie n'ay rien escrit que sur de bonnes memoires que i'en auois receuës de personnes de condition, & qui ont peut estre part à l'Histoire.[84][a]

La Calprenède constructs a focused dramatic narrative observing the unities, unfolding in twenty-four hours in the environs of London and concentrating on a single intrigue. At its opening, the anguished 'reine Elisabeth', like so many later Racinian heroines, discovers that 'mon destin est le plus malheureux,/De nourrir dans mon ame vn feu si dangereux' (I. i).[b] To complicate matters even further, she is dismissed as a possible object of affection by the protagonist ('Qu'elle quitte l'amour, son âge l'en dispense' – II.v) and the play furnishes her with a rival in the shape of Madame Cecile![c] The proud Essex is charged with plotting with Tyrone to seize the crown. Now held in captivity, he continues to assert his innocence, despite being threatened with a death sentence by his irresolute sovereign: Elisabeth – 'Mon coeur est si pressé de rage & de douleur' (I.ii).[d] The earl has a royal pledge (the queen's ring) which can afford him a pardon, but he refuses to make use of it: 'vne confession si honteuse & si basse/Deshonore mon rang, mon courage & ma race' (II.iv).[e] Madame Cecile is sent to urge him to curb his pride and to petition for clemency. The hero is sent for trial and, in due course, the courtroom is treated to

---

[a] 'If you find something in this tragedy that you have not read at all in works of English history, be assured that I have not at all invented it, and that I have only written that which has been founded on accurate accounts received by myself from persons of quality and from those who may have had a role in the story.'

[b] 'I have the most unfortunate of destinies to nurture in my heart such a fearful desire.'

[c] 'Let her forsake matters of love, her age releases her from their cares.'

[d] 'my heart is so pained with anger and suffering'.

[e] 'such a low and shameful avowal is a dishonour to my rank, my courage and my family name'.

a full account of the defendant's most recent ambitions: 'Vous estes dans la ville entrez à main armée,/Croyant que par vos soins la reuolte allumée' (III.i). However, at the centre of this intrigue lies the angst-ridden queen: 'Quoy qu'il ayt entrepris & quoy qu'il m'en arriue,/Quoy qu'il ayt conspiré, ie veux, ie veux qu'il vive' (III.iv).[a] The bill of execution against Southampton is revoked, but that of Essex is not. Finally, Essex sends the queen's ring via Madame Cecile to petition for mercy from the Crown. However, Madame Cecile is now convinced by her husband to revenge herself as the spurned mistress and so retains the ring. Essex goes to the scaffold believing that the queen has failed to honour her promise. Overcome with remorse, the ailing Madame Cecile confesses everything to the queen, who faints, curses her minister's wife and bans Ralegh from her sight. Elizabeth, now wretched, foresees that she will soon follow the Earl to the grave: 'Ie perds le sentiment, & mon coeur s'affoiblit,/Pour la derniere fois, meine moy sur mon lict' (V.vi).[b]

Given their interests in cultural critique and historical/mythological play-making, the Jesuit community might be thought to be a fertile breeding ground in Catholic Europe for representing Elizabeth and her court onstage. Dramatic writing and training maintained an integral place in the curriculum of Jesuit schools and seminaries as a pedagogic resource, as a form of spiritual training and as an apprenticeship for the demands of subsequent ministry. Jesuit teachers might frequently be called upon to compose multi-medial dramatic texts and dialogues for their students.[85] Strikingly, however, as W. H. McCabe stresses, 'The English Colleges on the Continent, though they owed their exile precisely to the Reformation at home, seem not to have shown resentment to any notable extent on the stage.'[86] In terms of historical dramas at the College of St. Omer, McCabe points to the fact that no surviving texts treat subjects after the reign of Henry VIII.[87] Nonetheless, 'The New Moone' (1633?)[88], surviving from the collection of the English College at Rome, might initially appear to have potential in taking the moon goddess as its focus. Like Raleigh's extended poem 'The Ocean's Love to Scinthia', its heroine is 'Full of inconstancy without, neuer remayninge a day toge-/Ther in one shape' (I.iii) and impermanence is thematic to the whole text: 'for what/in this wide uniuers hath beeinge and is not subiect to mutability?' (I.i).[89] The

---

[a] 'You entered the town fully armed, believing by your action to spark a revolt'; 'Whatever he has undertaken, whatever happens to me, whatever he has plotted, my will, my will is that he should live.'
[b] 'My sense of feeling is fading, and my heart is giving way, for the final time, lead me to my bed.'

whole narrative is triggered by the refusal of Phebus 'to bestow his light/ Any more on his sister Cynthia' (I.i).[90]

Shaping influences upon such an example of Jesuit dramaturgy might be many and various, including Roman comedy, Erasmus' *Colloquies*, Lyly's dramatic intrigues and court entertainments in evidence across the continent. However, this English-language text would seem to have greater interest in engaging with mythological narrative in evidence in the baroque visual arts and elite masquing during the seventeenth century than in a specific referencing of political events unfolding at Elizabeth's court perhaps decades earlier. Nonetheless, this is not to say that Jesuit writing did not attend to the figure of Elizabeth at all. *La Cour sainte* by Nicolas Caussin (1583–1651), confessor to Louis XIII and later member of the regent's, Anne of Austria's, circle, was published for the first time in 1624. In a remarkably polarised account of Elizabeth and Mary Stuart (as a latter-day Catholic martyr), the former is described as the offspring 'd'un Roy desbordé, et d'une mere basse et honteuse'.[a] She grew to be a ruler whose mind was 'rusé, malin et funeste', with a heart which was 'malicieux, dissimulé et endurcy'.[b] Whereas the Scottish queen reared at the French court had the accomplishments 'necessaire à une honneste femme, qui ne doit pas paroistre trop sçavante', the vain Elizabeth was ridiculous in 'voulant faire la sçavante' and scandalous, living 'non mariée, et non vierge'.[c] Most importantly, for Caussin's hagiography of Mary, Elizabeth emerges as a butcher, driven by 'une furieuse et sanglante ambition qui n'espargnoit personne pour l'interest de sa grandeur'. While Mary ruled 'en colombe', Elizabeth comported herself 'en oyseau de carnage'.[91d]

This concern across the Channel to pass judgement upon the political and personal conduct of Elizabeth was also voiced in later decades in Fontenelle's *Nouveaux Dialogues des Morts* (1683). Here, in the Third Dialogue, we discover Elisabeth ('J'ay esté la Penélope de mon siècle') exchanging views with her erstwhile suitor, the Duc D'Alençon, who appears remarkably candid in his responses to the queen: 'Il y a icy de certain Morts, qui ne tomberoient pas d'accord que vous ressemblassiez tout-à-fait à Penélope; mais on ne trouve point de comparaison qui ne

---

[a] 'of a corrupt king and a lowly and shameful mother'.
[b] 'full of pretense, devious and deadly'; 'malicious, deceitful and hard-hearted'.
[c] 'requisite for an honest woman, who should not appear too learned'; 'wishing to play the intellectual'; 'unmarried and unchaste'.
[d] 'a passionate and bloodthirsty ambition which spared no one to achieve her aims for greatness'; 'as a dove'; 'as a deadly bird of prey'.

soient défectueuses en quelque point.'[92][a] During the second half of the seventeenth century, Fontenelle's *Nouveaux Dialogues* might find themselves competing with Louis Aubery du Maurier's *Mémoires pour servir à l'histoire de Hollande et des autres Provinces Unies* (1680, 1688) or, back in Britain, Francis Osborne's *Traditional Memoires on the Raigne of Queen Elizabeth* (1658) for an account of the queen's conduct.

In Paris, Thomas Corneille (1625–1709) composed his own, enormously popular tragedy *Le Comte d'Essex*, which premiered in January 1678. (Interestingly, it is this narrative that would become the basis of Cammarano's libretto for Donizetti's 1838 opera *Roberto Devereux*.) Initially with La Champmeslé in the role of Elizabeth and Michel Baron as hero for the 1678 production at the Hôtel de Bourgogne, this production went on to be performed on some 281 occasions at the Comédie Française in the period 1681–1812.[93] During the seventeenth century, audiences continued to prove highly responsive to these tales of thwarted love amongst elite characters. Madame de Lafayette's celebrated prose narrative *La Princesse de Clèves* (1678), for example, had even offered its own portrait in miniature of the Tudor queen: 'il y a apparence qu[' Élisabeth] voudra se rendre heureuse par l'amour'.[94][b] Corneille's drama drew upon the 1627 French translation of Camden's *Annals*, La Calprenède's tragedy and prose narratives, such as *Le Comte D'Essex: Histoire Angloise* (see below). In Corneille's play, Essex is accused by Cobham, Cecil and Raleigh of fomenting an insurrection against the Crown, while the former protests he was merely seeking to prevent his beloved mistress from marrying the Duc d'Irton. Thus, the queen is cast as spurned mistress rather than beleaguered monarch, railing at the Duchesse d'Irton

> Non, il faut qu'il périsse, et que je suis vangée,
> Je dois ce coup funeste à ma flamme outragée,
> Il a trop merité l'Arrest qui le punit,
> Innocent ou coupable, il vous aime, il suffit.[95][c]   (III.iv.1029–32)

The condemned Essex can only secure his freedom if he petitions the queen for a pardon, which the haughty earl (once again) refuses to do. The timing of the execution is hastened to prevent any intervention from the anguished

---

[a] 'I have been the Penelope of my century'; 'There are here some amongst the dead who would not agree that you resemble Penelope so very much; but no comparisons can ever be made which are not injurious in some respect.'
[b] 'It would appear that Elizabeth seeks her happiness in love.'
[c] 'No, he must die, and I must be avenged,/This deadly act is owed to my scorned passion,/He has only too well deserved the punishment of his sentence,/It matters not whether he is guilty or innocent, it is enough that he loves you.'

queen who, ultimately, foresees her own death in that of the earl. In the next century, Corneille's play was rendered into German by the Hamburg-based translator L. Peter Stüven and published in 1749 as *Der Graf von Essex: Ein Trauerspiel aus dem Französischen des Herrn Thomas Corneille.*[96]

In February 1678, Claude Boyer's (1618–98) own, less popular tragedy, *Le Comte d'Essex*, was premiered at the rival Théâtre de Guénégaud in Paris. He confessed in the prefatory discussion to the published text that 'Monsieur Corneille & moy nous avons puisé les idées d'un mesme sujet dans une mesme source: c'est-à-dire dans le Comte d'essex ... [de] Monsieur de la Calprenede.'[97a] Certain lines of verse and, elsewhere, plot details (which Corneille chose to discard) concerning the spurned mistress (Nottingham) and the thwarted attempt to convince the hero to petition for a pardon, were already present in La Calprenède's play – and this Boyer also acknowledges. Here, on the horns of a dilemma between love and duty, Boyer's Elisabeth ('Quelle indigne pitié s'eleve dans mon ame?' (I. viii)) suspects Essex (in love with the Duchesse de Clarence) of planning an insurrection. This suspicion is reinforced by accusations made by his enemies at court: Raleg – 'Ne perdons point de temps: tout conspire à sa perte' (I.i).[b] Moreover, it becomes apparent that Cobham, or Coban, aspires to be the queen's consort. Nonetheless, the centre-stage is dominated by the hero, the proud earl ('Je suis né, j'ay vécu, j'ay tout fait pour la gloire') who demands just treatment from his sovereign to quash the political accusations against him of conspiracy with Tyrone and treason to the Crown: Elisabeth – 'Tu t'es laissé tenter à ce grand nom de Roy'.[c] Driven to desperation, Clarence tries to deflect attention from Essex by claiming that Cobham is in love with her. Subsequently, she admits the real identity of her lover and asks the queen to save his life if she (Clarence) surrenders her hold on him: Elisabeth – 'Vous voulez que je sauve un sujet revolté,/Et que ce soit pour vous qui me l'avez osté.'[d] Unwilling to sue for pardon, the earl is tried by his peers. Despite an interruption in the trial's proceedings, Essex refuses to confess or to avail himself of the power vested in queen's ring. Elisabeth now threatens both the earl's and Clarence's lives. In order to save her, Essex confides the ring to his mistress to be

---

[a] 'Monsieur Corneille and I, we have drawn upon ideas on the same subject from the same source: that is to say *Le Comte d'Essex* ... [by] Monsieur de la Calprenede.'
[b] 'What shameful pity is growing in my heart'; 'Let us not lose any time: everything points to his destruction.'
[c] 'I was born, I have lived, I have done everything for glory'; 'You allowed yourself to be tempted by the great title of King.'
[d] 'You desire that I save a rebellious subject,/And that this should be for you who has taken him from me.'

delivered to the queen and insists that the revolt to be led by Clarence's brother be halted. In the event, Clarence is delayed and the message ordering a stay of execution arrives at the scaffold just as the earl's head is severed from his body. On interrogation, the captured Cobham admits that the hero was innocent of all accusations, and the play concludes with the tableau of an overwrought Elisabeth: 'O Heros trop aimé dont la perte m'accable!'[a] Boyer's tragedy was performed on eight occasions in 1678.

Moving away from the theatre, a novelised treatment of the narrative rolled from the presses in the same year (1678) in the shape of *Le Comte d'Essex. Histoire angloise*, subsequently appearing in English translation as *The Secret History of the Most Renowned Q. Elizabeth and the Earl of Essex* (1681). Here, Elisabeth has as her confidante the Comtesse de Nottingham, and is principally significant for her tormented attraction towards her unruly subject: 'il n'y a point de consolation pour moy, si le Comte d'Essex perit. Par l'état où sa prison me met, iugez de celuy où sa perte povrroit me reduire.'[98][b] In this prose romance, enjoying translation and republication, Essex is the focus of three women's attentions – the Countess of Nottingham, the Countess of Rutland (secret wife) and Elizabeth – but the denouement rehearses the same *tragédie d'amour* being played out on French stages at the time.

New Stages, New Genres for Elizabethan Favourites

Although Coello's *Dar la Vida* does not seem to have constituted a source text for French dramatists, its international influence is firmly attested in Italian productions later in the seventeenth century and into the next. The tragic opera *Il reo innocente* (1665), attributed to Pietro Piperno, declared on its publication that 'la presente Tragedia . . . con applause vniuersale fù rappresentata'.[99][c] Here, once again, we find ourselves in the company of 'Isabella, Reina d'Inghilterra' and the 'Conte Roberto', as well as the 'contessa d'Aisex'. The action begins with the declaration 'Mora, questa Tiranna',[d] and the subsequent intrigue follows closely Coello's dramatic narrative. Just a few years later, in 1668, another Coello-influenced production, Niccolò Biancolelli's *La Regina statista d'Inghiltera ed il Conte di Esex, Vita, Successi et Morte* (1668), made its appearance. This text would

---

[a] 'O hero too well-loved whose loss overwhelms me.'
[b] 'There is no consolation whatsoever for me if the Earl of Essex dies. Given the effect which his imprisonment has upon me, imagine in what state you would find me at the news of his death.'
[c] 'the present Tragedy . . . was staged to universal applause'.   [d] 'This tyrant must die.'

enjoy republication and, indeed, further additions in the final decades of the seventeenth century. Here, the earl and the queen are joined onstage by the queen's lover (Aldimiro) and the queen's cousin (Florisbe), who herself has two admirers apart from the hero. If *Il reo innocente* had a prologue involving such figures as 'Innocenza' and 'Amore', *La Regina statista* has a framing device involving 'Genio', 'Crudeltà' and 'Morte'. Interestingly, in Biancolelli's version, audiences were also treated to the figure of a love-torn hero unable to reconcile the contrary motions of his desires:

CONTE Amore mi combatte, Fede mi difende; Amore m'inalza, Fede mi sostiene; Amore, se non lo seguo, mi vuol morto, Fede, se l'abbraccio, me vuol vivo, che devo dunque fare, ò misero? la Regina senza dubbio mi ama, Florisbe senza pari m'adora; ò Amore, ò Fede, ò Fortuna, ò mia mente, ò miei confusi pensieri.

(I.x)[100a]

The details of Coello's earlier dramatic narrative remain firmly in evidence throughout Biancolelli's rendering of the action. When the disguised queen offers the imprisoned hero the possibility of escape with a key, he replies that if he accepted, it would constitute a 'grandissimo pregiudicio al mio honore'.[b] He then throws it away at the feet of the despairing heroine, who 'parte con un sospiro' (III.iv).[c] At its close, Biancolelli offers the now familiar final tableau of the dying queen tormented by the recent succession of events:

Scatenatevi dall'oscura caligine, e dal Regno di Flegetonte, ò Mostri d'inferno, e squarciandomi le viscere, fate a gara per più tormentarmi ... È morto il Conte, & è superfluo con il sangue, che stillò da gli occhi ritornarlo in vita? mà il dolere facendo l'officio di carnefice, già sento mi fà scorrere per l'ossa un gelato sudore, mi si adombra la vista, s'illanguidiscono i sensi, io manco, io moro. *E more.* (III.xiv)[101d]

An operatic production treating this same narrative is Francesco Rossi, Ludovico Busca and Pietro Simone Agostini's *La Floridea, Regina di Cipro* (1668–70?) with the libretto composed by Teodoro Barbò.[102] Once again,

---

[a] 'Love fights me, Faith defends me; Love exalts me, Faith sustains me; Love, if I do not follow him, wants me dead, Faith, if I embrace her, wants me alive, what must I do, O misery? the Queen without a doubt loves me, the matchless Florisbe adores me; O Love, O Faith, O Fortuna, O my spirit, O my confused thoughts.'

[b] 'greatest compromise of my honour'.   [c] 'departs with a sigh'.

[d] 'Be released from that fume-ridden darkness and from the realm of Phlegethon, O Monsters of hell, and tear open my bowels, see which of you can torment me most ... the Count is dead, and is it futile that the blood which dripped from his eyes will bring him back to life? But I know already that sorrow acting as executioner is bringing chill death to my bones, my vision is blurred, my senses are faint, I am fading, I die. *And dies.*'

there is an open acknowledgement of the Coello play as source text: '*[la] famosa Tragicommedia Spagnnola intitolata, La mas lachrymoia Tragedia del Conde di Sex*'.[103a] In this instance, the Cypriot queen Floridea engages in fraught relations with Ormondo and the intrigue is triggered (once again) with an attempt upon the queen's life: 'Mori, mori Tiranna' (I.iv).[b] Ormondo forces the would-be assassin to flee and the queen is left secretly smitten with her saviour: 'Piangi, piangi mio cor, piangi sì, sì' (II.xv).[c] The figure of the spurned woman (in this instance, Moralba) has a dominant role in the unfolding intrigue. Nonetheless, as in Coello's drama, she is prevented from shooting the queen by the felicitous arrival of Ormondo, who subsequently finds himself in prison. In the comic denouement, Ormondo is revealed to be of a princely bloodline and a faithful subject of the queen.[104]

In the eighteenth century, French drama depicting the torments of Elizabeth and Essex also remained of interest for new generations of writers. Antonio Salvi's libretto for the Italian opera *Amore e maestà* (1715, later entitled *Arsace*) is a direct response to Corneille's *Le Comte d'Essex*. The libretto was set to music by Giuseppe Orlandini, and the work was an inspiration for later works by Michel Angelo Gasparini and Baldassare Galuppi. Salvi acknowledged in his preface to the published text that he had drawn broad inspiration from 'le scene di Francia il famoso Tommaso Cornelio sotto il nome del Conte d'Essex'.[d] Even if the action in his own production was transposed to Persia, he underlined that 'i caratteri de'Personaggi principali' were those of the French original.[105e] This tragic opera, which continued to hold the stage throughout the eighteenth century, is dominated by the figures of Statira (Elizabeth) and Arsace (Essex). At every turn, Corneille's 'Essex and Elizabeth' narrative is faithfully reproduced: Arsace ('Supremo Generale del Regno',[f] and sung originally by a castrato) finds himself the principal concern of an all-too-passionate Persian queen Statira ('ecco l'ingrato; io gelo, ed ardo'[g] (I.x)), with the now seemingly inevitable consequences.

However, it was not only Italian dramatists who were intrigued by the potential of this narrative. Gregorio Leti's *Historia o vero Vita di Elisabetta, Regina d'Inghilterra: Detta per Sopranome la Comediante Politica* ('History or Life of Elizabeth, Queen of England, nicknamed the political play-actress')

---

[a] 'the famous Spanish tragicomedy entitled *The most sad tragedy of the Earl of Essex*'.
[b] 'Die, die, tyrant.'   [c] 'weep, weep my heart, weep, yes, yes'.
[d] 'the French play entitled *Le Comte d'Essex* by Thomas Corneille'.
[e] 'the profiles of the main characters'.   [f] 'supreme military commander of the realm'.
[g] 'Here is the ingrate; I am like ice and I burn with desire.'

was initially published in Amsterdam in 1693 and went onto enjoy multiple republications and translations into Italian, French, Dutch, Russian and German.[106] If, like a good number of his European counterparts, Leti drew upon Camden's *Annals* for many of the details of his own chronicle, as Giovanni Iamartino has underlined, the Italian chronicler had only 'limited proficiency in English'.[107] Nonetheless, lest there be any doubt, Leti was at pains to remind his reader that 'Li Catolici parlano della Regina Elisabetta come d'un monstro d'Inferno: come d'una Donna scelerata, e perversa, come d'un'ingorda di sangue humano, e come di una furia animata contro la Religione Catolica.'[108a] In addition, the reader is assured repeatedly that the queen was herself endowed with superlative acting talents: 'ch'Elisabetta, sapeva giocar la Farza dove bisognava, e la Comedia dove era necessario'.[109b] Most significantly for the purposes of this discussion, Leti makes mention that 'in Francia s'era fatta una Farza sopra alla sua Coronattione, trattando Anna sua madre da *Puttana*, e d'Adultera, e lei da Comediante, e Bastarda'.[110c]

The place of Elizabeth and her court in seventeenth- and eighteenth-century comedy and farce often relies upon such referencing because the scenarii themselves may not have survived, and, where they are available, they remain difficult to date in terms of initial composition or performance. The Italian artform of the *commedia dell'arte* drew some of its principal dramatic energies from the very plasticity of its *canovaccio* or scenario. These might include: improvised, as well as rehearsed, exchanges, setpieces and sketches, deploying familiar characters such as the *zanni* or quick-witted servants (e.g. Arlecchino, Colombina); pompous authority figures (e.g. Dottore, Pantalone); and the lovers (e.g. Orazio/Lelio and Isabella/Rosaura). It should be added that this was an artform with which certain early modern Britons might be acquainted, as Thomas Heywood's *An Apology for Actors Containing Three Brief Treatises* (1612) drew attention to French and Italian actors who interpret onstage 'the Doctors [dottori], Zawnyes [zanni], Pantaloones [Pantaloni], Harlakeenes [Arlecchini]'.[111] Within the corpus of the *commedia* form (which was not always wholly bound by comic expectations), there is the example of a canovaccio *Gli*

---

[a]   'The Catholics speak of Queen Elizabeth as a monster from hell, as a wicked and depraved woman, greedy for human blood, and as an unrestrained fury against the Catholic religion.' See Giovanni Iamartino, '"La Comediante Politica": On Gregorio Leti's 1693 Life of Queen Elizabeth I', in Donatella Montini and Iolanda Plescia (eds.), *Elizabeth I in Writing. Language, Power and Representation in Early Modern England* (Basingstoke: Palgrave Macmillan, 2018), pp. 145–70 (p. 154).

[b]   'that Elizabeth could play a farce when needed, and a comedy when it was necessary'. See Iamartino, 'La Comediante Politica', p. 160.

[c]   'in France they had staged a farce about her coronation, treating her mother Anne like a whore, and herself like a play-actress, and a bastard'. See Iamartino, 'La Comediante Politica', p. 159.

honesti amori della Regina d'Inghilterra con la morte del Conte di Sessa.[112]
This, once again, bears the mark of Coello's influence on its composition. However, apart from the 'Regina d'Inghilterra' and the 'Conte di
Sessa', the cast includes the Dottore, 'Bertolino Giardiniero' and
'Coviello servo'. In the first act, Coello's narrative is rehearsed (Essex
saving the queen from attackers) with the additions of *commedia* comic
play-making: 'Buffetto con lazzi si addormenta à poco à poco.'[113a] The
love-stricken Earl 'dice non poter piu'tener celato l'amore che porta
alla Regina'[b], and, advised by servants, hopes to gain access to the
queen through the leading courtier, Lucinda, who is a political enemy
of the monarch. By the second act, Lucinda has discovered the gift of
the scarf from the queen to the earl and wears it in the presence of her
now irate sovereign. Subsequently, in line with Coello's narrative,
Lucinda makes an attempt to shoot the queen and the attempt is
foiled by the arrival of the earl. The final act reveals the doomed
Essex once again in prison. The hero is executed despite the anguished
torments of the queen, who ultimately commits suicide.

There is also the *commedia* scenario entitled *Il Conte di Sex* (1700?).[114]
Like all *commedia* scenarii, the text is relatively brief, allowing for improvised performance (often, as we have seen, comic *lazzi*) on the part of
certain players. In this instance, the action is located in London, with
a conspiracy against the Crown brewing. To offer added colour to the
production, Queen Isabella finds herself not only among political enemies,
but sharing the stage with the dramatic company of Pollicinella and the
Dottore, amongst others, from the *commedia* repertoire. Here, the earl
returns to London at night, forsaking his military duties, to meet with the
queen's cousin, the Countess Aurinda. The intrigue, heavily influenced by
Dar la vida, is interestingly – and typically for the *commedia* – counterpointed with Coviello's attachment to Aurinda's maid, Rosetta. Elsewhere,
there is also the example of a commedia *canovaccio* in the shape of *La
Regina d'Inghilterra, Tragedia*, once again bearing the influence of Coello's
drama.[115] The principal players are the Regina, Conte di Sex, Principessa
Lucina and Cola, Essex's servant – the latter remaining a source of some
familiar comic *lazzi* in the company of 'Trappola, o vero Pulcinella' as the
narrative unfolds: 'in questo Trappola incontra Cola, fanno lazzi di notte'.[c]
In this version, Essex has turned his attentions to Lucina because his

---

[a] 'Buffetto with comic actions [*lazzi*] falls asleep little by little.'
[b] 'says that he can no longer conceal his love for the queen'.
[c] 'Trappola, alias Pulcinella'; 'into this scene arrives Trappola who meets Cola, they do night-time gags
[*lazzi*]'.

charms seem to have had no effect on his sovereign. Once again, the arrival of the earl, fresh from the triumph over the Spanish Armada, makes the queen's attackers flee. He is offered 'una banda'[a] as a mark of gratitude and discovers that Lucina is plotting with her brothers to have the queen killed (though in this instance, not to avenge Mary, Queen of Scots, but to restore the crown to her own royal house). In the Second Act, while the *lazzi* with Cola continue ('Cola vede Bagolino, li chiede la sua roba, lui vuol burlarlo con volerlo di nuovo bastonare, lui li volta una pistola alla vita, Bagolino paura, e via'[b]), the queen's gift of the 'banda' is discovered by Lucina, who wears it in the royal presence. Later, Lucina attempts to kill the sleeping queen, but the Earl (once again) intervenes and finds himself subsequently in prison. Act Three begins with the Earl in his cell ('si lamenta della fallacia della Corte'[c]), where he is visited by the disguised queen. After their meeting, he rejects any hope of escape from prison by throwing the proffered key away. In a now familiar denouement, the evidence of the Earl's innocence arrives too late, and in the final scene 'dopo viene fuora con la testa del Conte in bacile, Regina fa lamento, doppo si uccide, finisce la tragedia'.[d]

The Return to Native Shores

At the same time as Essex was winning favour with continental audiences, he was welcomed back to public attention on the London stage with John Banks' *The Unhappy Favourite, Or the Earl of Essex a Tragedy* (pub. 1682), which drew upon the translated prose fiction *The Secret History of the Most Renowned Queen Elizabeth, and Earl of Essex: By a Person of Quality* (1681) for much of its material. In direct comparison with the majority of the narratives being composed for the stage across Europe, this text concentrates upon the final years of the hero's life and exploits details selectively from Camden's *Annals*. However, in this instance, a spurned Countess of Nottingham persuades Burleigh to hatch a plot against Essex on the latter's return from Ireland. By Act II, as Essex's favour declines rapidly, Southampton recalls former times when the Earl was lavished with honours and 'the whole Court/Was so well pleas'd, and shew'd their wondrous

---

[a] 'a scarf'.
[b] 'Cola sees Bagolino, asks for his things, he wants to make fun of him by beating him again, he points a gun at him, Bagolino takes fright, and runs away.'
[c] 'complains about the deceptions of the Court'.
[d] 'after the Earl's head is presented in a basin, the queen makes lamentations and after kills herself, the tragedy ends'.

joy/In shouting louder than the *Roman* Bands/When *Iulius* and *Augustus* were made Consuls' (II.i).[116] In due course, the action moves to the mortal consequences of the rebellion for the earl, occasioned principally by the Countess of Nottingham's denial that she received the ring from him.

The production proved highly successful at the time, and a good deal of classicising allusion in Banks' text recalled the eulogies of Essex's contemporaries more than a century earlier. Nonetheless, if not every voice greeted with unalloyed joy this rising tide of popularity in 'Elizabeth and Essex' tales for the stage, the inanities of the verse did nothing to impair its rapturous reception among many London theatre-goers. *The Tatler* confirmed that '[Banks' tragedy] in which there is not one good Line … was never seen without drawing Tears from some part of the Audience.'[117] More generally, the next century witnessed no decline of interest in dramatised tales of the Elizabethan court, and George Sewell's *The Tragedy of Sir Walter Raleigh* (1719) struck a notably patriotic note for the new, Georgian age. In the published text's dedicatory address to a government minister, the author asserted grandiloquently:

> We have seen *Plots, Rebellions*, and *Gundamors* too, in our Days; but thank Heav'n we have a *Monarch* too *Wise*, and a *Ministry* too vigilant, to suffer them to succeed. No Man *Bleeds* in *England now* for asserting the Liberties of his *Country*; the Fate of Great *Raleigh* is only turn'd on a few *Parricides*, and *Traitors*.[118]

Indeed, the Prologue associates himself with such sentiments, declaring 'An ENGLISH MARTYR shall Ascend the Stage,/To Shame the Last, and Warn the Present Age' (Prol.). In the subsequent action, the demonised Spanish ambassador Gondomar (or Gundamor) bears a 'Face ne'er boded Good to *British* Hearts' (I.i). However, the faithful Raleigh remains steadfast in his Christian faith (despite being accused of atheism) and in his allegiance to the Crown (despite the conspiracies of Salisbury and Gundamor): Gundamor – 'And yet I'd give a Province for his Head' (III.ii). Refusing to be drawn into the conspiracy, Howard summons up for the audience the figure of the former favourite as one of Olympian fortitude: 'When from the Precipice of Mountain Waves/All Hearts have trembled at the Gulph below,/He, with a steddy, supplicating Look,/Display'd his Trust in that tremendous Pow'r,/Who curbs the Billows' (I.i). By Act III, the status of this meditative Ralegh is enhanced even further with some liberal additions of Shakespearianised tragic diction: 'To *Be*, is better far than Not to *Be*,/Else Nature cheated us in our Formation' (III.iv). Sewell's intrigue also includes a subplot in which Salisbury's daughter, Olympia, is in love with Raleigh's son and yet her attempts to have the hero's death sentence revoked come to nothing. Nonetheless, Raleigh is afforded a final aria before meeting his doom:

> If to have lov'd my Country, to have priz'd
> Her Fame and Safety above Gain and Life;
> If to have watch'd, travell'd, fought and bled for her,
> If these are Crimes[,] Posterity will judge,
> And Infamy pollute the Name of Raleigh.   (V.iii)

Still hungry, it seems, for further narratives celebrating Elizabethan luminaries, the capital's audiences were greeted with James Ralph's *The Fall of the Earl of Essex ... Alter'd from the Unhappy Favourite of Mr. Banks* (1731).[119] Here, we have a familiar format celebrating 'The darling Heroe of the British Stage' (Prol.). Like a good many history plays produced for the eighteenth-century stage, Ralph's determines to strike a patriotic note – in this instance, reaffirming the defeat of the Armada (Elizabeth – 'Heav'n declar'd for us, and valiant Drake/Dispers'd their broken Squadrons') and the unwarranted downfall of '*Essex* the foremost Hero of the Globe!' (Act I). Ralph's Earl stands accused of treatying with the Irish enemy and aiming to occupy the highest place in the land: Elizabeth – ''tis Time/T'assert the Throne, and crush him ere he soars/Beyond the Reach of Pow'r; double my Guards' (Act II). However, much more important for Ralph's intrigue is the fact that the spurned mistress (Lady Nottingham) seeks revenge on Essex with the assistance of Burleigh. By Act IV it is revealed that Lady Rutland is Essex's secret wife and, in due course, shadowing the denouements of earlier dramas, the queen learns of Essex's plea for mercy too late to bring about a stay of execution. The whole spectacle closes with the despairing queen submitting: 'Had my fond heart no soft Delusions known,/I'd still been happy tho' my Fav'rite's gone' (Act V).

Some two decades later, once again the stage was greeted with Henry Brookes' *The Earl of Essex* (staged 1749) – and, once again, a patriotic note was struck.[120] In the Prologue, read by 'Mrs. Sheridan', we learn that rather than the 'new Electras and new Phaedras' of Athens, or the 'Theban monarchs' of French tragedy, 'Much more a British story should impart/ The warmest feelings to each British heart.' The dramatic narrative begins with Essex in Ireland, and the occasions for celebrating a specifically British elect destiny appear to be manifold as the intrigue unfolds. In these mid-century years, Henry Jones' *The Earl of Essex: A Tragedy* (1753) also returned the familiar figures of the hero, accompanied by Elizabeth,

Burleigh, Ralegh and the Countesses of Nottingham and Rutland, to the stage, with a conspiracy being led by Burleigh on the earl's return from Ireland: "'Tis gone too far, he dies – proud Essex now,/Or Cecil falls. Now is th'important Crisis' (Act II).[121]

Given the proliferating number of such narratives across Europe, it comes as no surprise that Voltaire himself turned his attentions to this literary fascination with Elizabeth and her favourites. In his 'Remarques sur *Le Comte D'Essex:* Tragédie de Thomas Corneille, représentée en 1678', he confessed finding Boyer's a distinctly cold offering, and the idea in Corneille's (and others') plays of staging a love-torn Elizabeth is greeted with derision: 'Il est ridicule d'imaginer que l'amour pût avoir la moindre part dans cette aventure ... Une reine telle qu'Élisabeth presque décrépite, qui parle du poison qui dévore son coeur, et de ce que ses yeux et sa bouche ont dit à son ingrate, est un personage comique.'[122a] By way of conclusion to this discussion, it might be added that Voltaire has his own hero Candide attend a performance of an Essex play, probably that of Corneille: 'Vous avez grand tort de pleurer, cette Actrice est fort mauvaise, l'Acteur qui joue avec elle est plus mauvais acteur encor, la pièce est encor plus mauvaise que les Acteurs.'[b] As the episode draws to a close, the narrator confides 'Candide fut très content d'une Actrice qui faisait la reine Élisabeth dans une assez plate tragédie que l'on joüe quelquefois.'[123c]

---

[a] 'It is ridiculous to imagine that love could have played the smallest part in this tale ... A queen such as Elizabeth, almost decrepit, who speaks of poison consuming her heart, and of what her eyes and mouth have communicated to the ungrateful wretch, is a comic character.'

[b] 'You are wrong to weep, this actress is very bad, the actor playing onstage with her is an even worse actor, the play is still worse than the actors.'

[c] 'Candide was very happy with the actress who played the role of queen Elizabeth in a quite bland tragedy that is staged from time to time.'

Conclusion

> SEE, my lov'd *Britons*, see your *Shakespeare* rise,
> An awfull ghost confess'd to human eyes![1]

At the opening of John Dryden's *Troilus and Cressida, or, Truth found too late* (1679), the audience was greeted thus with a 'Prologue Spoken by Mr. Betterton, Representing the Ghost of Shakespear'. The introduction of this spectral figure, engaging variously in debates concerning aesthetic practice, theatrical taste cultures, political change and patriotic appeals, would recur periodically throughout the eighteenth century.[2] In Bevil Higgons' prologue to George Granville's *The Jew of Venice* (1701), for example, 'the ghosts of Shakespear and Dryden arise, crown'd with lawrel'.[3] Later, in the second act of Elizabeth Boyd's 'ballad-opera' *Don Sancho* (1739), the audience could look forward to an even more elaborate tableau: 'the Earth trembles, and the ghosts of Shakespear and Dryden rise as in Glory to a soft sweet Symphony'.[4] Strikingly, the eerie shadow of Shakespeare not only gained access to the playhouses in this period, but was also discovered in prose fiction and journalism. Garrick's entertainments, both within and without the theatre, in the mid-eighteenth century invited audiences to render homage to the late bard and his creations. Elsewhere, in Henry Fielding's prose narrative *A Journey from This World to the Next* (1749) a spectral Shakespeare, amongst other spirits, was once again encountered, but here as a rather abstracted resident of the Elysian Fields who seemed most concerned to deride one of the bard's editors (and a notably estranged acquaintance of Fielding), namely Theobald.[5]

The nineteenth century remained fascinated by the dramatic tensions engendered in the 'Elizabeth and Essex' narratives inherited from earlier centuries. Alexandre-Vincent Pineux Duval (1767–1842) composed the immensely popular and, from the perspective of this discussion, seminal work *Shakespeare Amoureux* (1804). Like many of his contemporaries, Duval had very little knowledge of Shakespeare's England or his writings,

213

but *Shakespeare Amoureux* was determined to have its hero domesticated in a dramatic narrative that strenuously obeys the unities of time, place and action. In Duval's rendering, the focus of all romantic interest is *la belle Clarence*, the leading actress in Shakespeare's company, under whose spell both the dramatist and milord Wilson have fallen. The intrigue of this short theatrical afterpiece is wholly occupied with Shakespeare's endeavours to gain access to his mistress in order to make an unequivocal declaration of love. The password into Clarence's chambers is 'Richard III', which chimes aptly with the play that the actress is known to be rehearsing for performance. In due course, Clarence yields to the romantic advances of the dramatist, and Duval's final *coup de théâtre* recalls the tale of Shakespeare's own alleged retort to a rival for the attentions of a mistress:

CLARENCE   C'est Wilson!
UNE VOIX   *Richard III.*
SHAKESPEARE   (s'avançant vivement à la croisée) *Richard III* est venu trop tard. Guillaume-le-Conquérant s'est emparé de la forteresse.[6a]

It soon became evident that the light comedy of Duval's playlet was very much to the taste of new audiences across the continent, being translated into all the major European languages as well as into several of the minor ones.[7]

In these opening decades of the nineteenth century, music audiences were greeted with Giovanni Schmidt's libretto *Elisabetta, regina d'Inghilterra* (1815), set to music by Rossini; Saverio Mercadante performed the same service for Felice Romani's libretto *Il conte di Essex* in 1833. In addition, Salvatore Cammarano's libretto was the basis for Donizetti's opera *Roberto Devereux* (1837), where we find once again an account of a familiar erotic triangle involving Elizabeth, Essex and the Duchess of Nottingham (Sara). Ralegh also figures in the cast, and the intrigue is set at the point of the earl's unexpected return from Ireland to court, where he finds himself surrounded by enemies and charged with treason. The queen is wracked with anguish for the beleaguered man she loves but who, she now discovers, does not return her affections: Elizabeth (to Sara) 'If I discover some other women,/Beware! The fury of my vengeance will shake/Hell's foundations' (Act I).[8] By Act II the now familiar scarf has been stolen and excites further erotic tensions. As the court intrigues unfold, the Earl of Nottingham appeals for Essex's execution and keeps his wife prisoner to stop her preventing it. By the end

---

[a] Clarence – 'It's Wilson'; A voice [offstage] – '*Richard III*'; Shakespeare (advancing in a spirited manner to the casement) '*Richard III* has come too late. William the Conqueror has already taken the fortress.'

of Act II, Sara has made her way to the court to reveal that she is the 'other woman'. In the doleful denouement of Act III, the news of Essex's execution leaves a bereft Elizabeth dominating the stage: 'Oh, leave me!/My crown I crave no longer' (Act III).[9] Also in 1837, the year of Victoria's accession to the throne, Hermann Müller's *Elisabeth, Koningin von England* (influenced by Schiller's rendering of historical narrative for stagings of Mary Queen of Scots and William Tell) was published in Berlin.[10] The latter once again concentrated upon a fictional relation of the final years of Essex's life and turned to the ring plot and the figure of the Countess of Nottingham to bring about its tragic denouement. In France, Jacques-Arsène-François-Polycarpe Ancelot's musical entertainment, *Elisabeth d'Angleterre*, was staged in 1829. The latter seems to have been influenced by La Calprenède and Corneille and would operate as another source for the libretto of Donizetti's opera.[11]

Following, consciously or otherwise, the precedent set by Duval, the figure of Shakespeare himself continued to be written onto the stage for nineteenth-century audiences. The first of these productions in Britain is thought to be Charles A. Somerset's *Shakespeare's Early Days* (1829), performed at Covent Garden with the Shakespearean actor Charles Kemble (1775–1854) in the title role.[12] In the first act of Somerset's brief text, young Shakespeare is discovered in rural Warwickshire, subject once again to all the passion, tenderness and magnanimity that Romantic writers had repeatedly attributed to him in the preceding decades. In due course, the good-hearted, but now slumbering wastrel succumbs to a vision whereby a succession of Shakespearean characters accesses the stage to celebrate the poet's great destiny: Titania – 'The son of Genius, who now slumbers there,/Hath from his youth been our especial care;/In him there dwells a great and mighty soul' (I.ii).[13] If the legend of Shakespeare as the poacher of Sir Thomas Lucy's deer is recalled by Somerset, we find in this instance that the poet's sole ambition was to supply nourishment for a destitute shepherd and his 'helpless babes' (I.ii).[14] Like George Sand decades later, Somerset briefly summons up the possibility of a bard with an acute sensitivity and social conscience in order to respond to the political turmoil and sedition in evidence in the world beyond the theatre – in this instance, the widespread economic distress of rural communities in early-nineteenth-century Britain.[15] By the second act, hounded by Lucy's men, Shakespeare flees to London, and swiftly enjoys the patronage of Southampton and the comradeship of Tarleton and Burbage. In the closing phases of the action, in the wake of the news of the defeat of Armada, a jubilant Elizabeth finds time to study his play script (and its author), remarking 'For in his eye there glows intelligence;/Which heaven alone, and not scholastic lore,/Could have inspired' (II.iii).[16] Here, as so often in such productions of the period, the principal woman focusing her attentions on Shakespeare is the queen herself and this motif would recur with great frequency in succeeding decades on both sides of the Channel.

In the following year, the prolific playwright William Thomas Moncrieff (1794–1857) produced *Shakespeare's Festival; or, A New Comedy of Errors!* (1830). The emphasis of the first half of this drama is upon the rather grubby dimensions of the Shakespeare industry, which was expanding rapidly in response to the growth of literary tourism and commercialism surrounding the national poet. Here, the chairman of the Shakespeare Club at Stratford-upon-Avon, one Mr. Arden Shakespeare, presides over a meeting of the august assembly at the Falcon Inn.[17] Subsequently, Moncrieff allows the broad humour deriding the Shakespeare Club and its associated agents to give way to more romantic intrigue. The entertainment comes to a spectacular resolution with a re-enactment of a Stratford civic ceremonial: 'The whole terminating with a grand allegorical natal tableau; homage of the drama; Coronation of Shakespeare by the Tragic and Comic muses. – Fall of the Curtain' (I.v).[18] Later in the decade, productions in 1838 such as *The Queen's Command* and *Shakespeare and Burbage* would be offered on the London stage, drawing some direct (if unacknowledged) inspiration from Duval's text. However, in the next decade, J. Stirling Coyne responded to the public outcry surrounding the proposed sale of Shakespeare's home with *This House to be Sold* (1847). Now familiar examples of satirical critique are in evidence throughout the play, as is the concern to provide the broadest possible entertainment to the paying audience. Shakespeare (appearing in 'William Shakespeare's dress') is included once again amongst the *dramatis personae* along with a substantial number of his characters (notably, Othello in 'Pink striped trousers, buff slippers, straw hat'), accompanied by the spirits of Tragedy, Comedy and Poetry. Coyne draws the theatrical extravagancies to a close with another visual feast of pageantry:

> The back flat of Chamber sinks and discovers a grand tableau, consisting of SHAKSPEARE's characters grouped round the poet, who occupies a pedestal in the centre. The GENII of TRAGEDY and COMEDY kneel at the foot of the pedestal on either side. The SPIRIT OF POETRY descends and places a crown of laurel on his brow. Music as the Curtain descends on the Tableau (sc.ii).[19]

Across the Channel, the celebrated novelist George Sand (1804–76) was also the author of a number of plays. In the revolutionary year of 1848, *Le roi attend* was an entertainment specifically commissioned for the opening of Paris's *Théâtre de la République* (formerly, the *Comédie Française*), marking a seemingly new, democratic dawning for the nation. Here, in Sand's short one-act play, we encounter a weary Molière confronted with the emergencies of an unfinished script and the imminent arrival of the king to view its performance.[20] Subsequently, a profound questioning wracks the court dramatist's mind that would have been very much to the taste of the revolutionary audience of 1848: 'Qu'est-ce qu'un roi? Un homme qui a puissance de faire le bien, et c'est seulement quand il le fait qu'il se distingue des autres hommes' (sc. ix).[21a] It is at this point that Sand looks back to a well-established tradition of welcoming the spirits of literary figures onto the stage. Indeed, as the exhausted dramatist sinks into his slumbers:

> un nuage l'enveloppe lentement; un choeur de musique chante derrière le nuage. Quand le nuage se dissipe, on voit debout, autour de Molière endormi, les ombres des poètes antiques et modernes: Plaute, Térence, Eschyle, Sophocle, Euripide, Shakspeare, Voltaire, Rousseau, Sedaine, Beaumarchais etc. La Muse du théâtre est au milieu d'eux, tout près de Molière (sc. ix).[22b]

Here, in *Le roi attend*, the bard is on hand to pin his colours to the new revolutionary age: 'Ces temps nouveaux sont remplis d'étranges événements … Quant à moi, je n'étais point de ceux qui supportent l'injustice avec un visage serein, et, si parfois j'ai ri comme Molière, j'avais l'âme et le visage sérieux' (sc. x).[23c] After the interventions of all the assembled spectral presences, Molière awakens from his highly charged slumbers with revolutionary sentiments coursing through his veins: 'Je vois bien un roi, mais il ne s'appelle plus Louis XIV; il s'appelle le peuple! Le peuple souverain!' (sc. xi).[24d] As the century wore on, drawing upon Coello, Corneille, La Calprenède and Banks, as well as Stüven's translation, Heinrich Laube would offer his own drama, *Graf Essex: Trauerspiel in*

[a] 'What is a king? A man who has the power to do good, and it is only when he does this that he rises above the level of other men.'
[b] 'a cloud slowly envelops him; a chorus sings from behind the cloud. When the cloud evaporates, around the sleeping Molière can be seen standing the spirits of ancient and modern writers: Plautus, Terence, Aeschylus, Sophocles, Euripides, Shakespeare, Voltaire, Rousseau, Sedaine, Beaumarchais etc. The Muse of the theatre is in the midst of them, very close to Molière.'
[c] 'A host of strange events is unfolding in this new age. … As far as I am concerned, I was never one of those who tolerated injustice with an easy expression and, if on occasions I was given to laughter like Molière, my spirit and my countenance remained serious.'
[d] 'I do indeed see a king, but that king is no longer called Louis XIV; he is called the people! The sovereign people!'

fünf Uften (1855). Some ten years later (1865), Ali Vial de Sabligny's one-act drama, *L'Anneau du Comte D'Essex*, was published in Paris. With a limited cast (Essex, Elisabeth, Lord Giffurk, Lady Wiffrid, Lord Sommerson), the text rehearses familiar intrigues, with Sommerson conspiring against the hero and Lady Wiffrid arriving too late with the ring to prevent the earl's execution.

For the operatic stage, in 1868 Charles Louis Ambroise Thomas (1811–96) composed *Le Songe d'une nuit d'été*, drawing upon a libretto by Joseph-Bernard Rosier and Adolphe de Leuven. This was performed at the Opéra-Comique in Paris on 20 April 1850. More than any other example of nineteenth-century dramatic narrative thus far discussed, this production invests unequivocally in the idea of an heroic, passionate identity for the Renaissance dramatist which Victor Hugo and his fellow Romantics had celebrated across Europe. By this mid-point in the century, it is clear that on both sides of the Channel, Shakespeare had become a known, commodifiable and potentially lucrative form of capital – and a capital which could be exploited internationally for a non-anglophone audience in the Opera house. Thomas' intrigue unfolds once again in Elizabethan England, where the queen *incognita* (soprano) and her maid Olivia seek shelter from a storm on the streets of London after having been to see one of Shakespeare's plays. In direct comparison to *Shakespeare Amoureux*, *Le Songe d'une nuit d'été* characterises Shakespeare as a rising and successful dramatist and a man wholly defined by his passionate nature. At the close of the opera we find the protagonists resigned to pursuing separately their respective paths to glory:

> ÉLISABETH (*à Shakespeare*) Non, vous n'avez pas rêvé, si vous vous êtes dit: La brillante couronne qu'avaient si noblement portée Dante et le Tasse, moi, William Shakespeare, je l'avais laissée tomber, et la main d'une femme s'est baissée pour la remettre sur mon front!
>
> (III.xii)[25a]

No examination of European representations of the Elizabethan court in the centuries which succeeded the passing of the major figures can ever be exhaustive, and a taste for such representations continued on into the twentieth century to cinematic as well as other textual retellings.[26] However, by way of conclusion to this account of a continent fascinated

---

[a] Elisabeth (*to Shakespeare*) – 'No, you have not dreamed, if you say to yourself: the sparkling coronet which Dante and Tasso wore with such nobility, I, William Shakespeare let it fall and the hand of a woman bent down and restored it to my brow!'

by the vicissitudes of the final years of the Tudor century, we might turn to a work that brings Elizabeth, Essex and Ralegh together with Shakespeare himself onstage: F. Couturier's *Le Comte D'Essex*, performed at Paris's Théâtre du Châtelet in 1868. Here, Shakespeare has a cameo role as a theatre impresario organising an entertainment at Essex House. Couturier's narrative remains highly coloured with extravagant emotions expressed by a love-torn queen and an Essex ('nouvel Achille') secretly wedded to Catherine Sidney. As antagonists, we have the 'maître fourbe' Ralegh, aided by Cecil. The latter have it broadcast abroad that Elizabeth's charms have palled for the hero and that he is secretly trying to usher in a new political order through his negotiations with the Irish leader, Tyrone. Meanwhile, far from guiltless, the Earl is engaged in plans whereby the queen will abdicate in favour of the Scottish monarch. In due course, the Earl receives the ring as a token of royal affection and, when threatened with a forced marriage, Ralegh confesses to the queen that Catherine is already the hero's wife. The latter is arrested and, in the final scenes of the drama, Lady Howard loses possession of the ring to her husband. Essex goes to the scaffold, Catherine takes poison and Howard stands accused by his agonising queen at the close of the proceedings.

.....

In examining the final decades of Elizabeth's reign and the opening ones of James VI/I in terms of theatrical and political spectacle, this study has sought to reflect upon the ways in which an appetite for violence was played out on the European stage. Repeatedly in these explorations of early (and, indeed, later) modernity, we discover subjects and communities situated in an international landscape shaped by the prospect, or the reality, of armed hostilities. In the accounts of the lives of Ralegh and Essex, the profession of violence has been seen to mould their identities for their contemporaries, both at home and abroad. Indeed, appreciations of these favourites frequently served as a searing critique of Crown policy and fixed the monarch for foreign eyes in charged narratives of political and personal disorientation.

Shakespeare's history plays intervened in this cultural debate concerning the militarisation of society, which had been unfolding in print culture and cultural exchange throughout Elizabeth's reign, and the plays studied here offer specifically cross-border contexts in which to judge the provocative proposal of violence as a remedy for national tribulations. After the passing of Elizabeth, Essex, Ralegh and, indeed, Shakespeare, European audiences and readers remained remarkably inquisitive about their (alleged) actions.

However, all too often in such productions, matters of state were exported to an offstage world and quite different accounts of violence held centre stage: it is arresting how frequently Essex, Ralegh and Elizabeth become locked for succeeding generations in Europe in narratives of erotic defeat, rather than those of overweening pride or political aspiration. In the twenty-first century, these intrigues from early modern England's court culture and playhouses continue to excite vigorous interest and urge us to question the ways in which violence, in all its forms, feeds the construction of our everyday lives and selves.

Notes

Introduction

1. Paul Hentzner, *A Journey into England by Paul Hentzner in the Year MDXCVIII*, ed. Horace Walpole, trans. R. Bentley (London: Strawberry Hill, 1757), pp. 41–3.
2. Samuel Daniel, *The ciuile wars* (London: Humphry Lownes for Simon Waterson, 1609), bk. IV, p. 99.
3. Frank Tallett, *War and Society in Early Modern Europe, 1495–1715* (London: Routledge, 1992), p. 13. In this context, see also Brian M. Downing, *The Military Revolution and Political Change* (Princeton: Princeton University Press, 1992), p. 65.
4. Qtd in Geoffrey Parker, *Empire, War and Faith in Early Modern Europe* (London: Allen Lane/Penguin Press, 2002), p. 33.
5. John Merriman, *A History of Modern Europe: Volume 1* (New York/London: W. W. Norton & Company, 1996), p. 5.
6. Lisa Hopkins, *Shakespeare on the Edge. Border-crossing in the Tragedies and the 'Henriad'* (Aldershot: Ashgate, 2005), p. 6. See also David Armitage, 'The Elizabethan Idea of Empire', *Transactions of the Royal Historical Society*, 6th series 14 (2004), 269–77.
7. See Zdeněk Stříbrný, *Shakespeare and Eastern Europe* (Oxford: Oxford University Press, 2000), p. 29ff.
8. See Fernand Braudel, *La Méditerranée et le monde méditerranéen à l'époque de Philippe II* (Paris: Librairie Armand Colin, 1949); Roland Mousnier, *Les XVIe et XVIIe siècles; les progrès de la civilisation européenne et le déclin de l'orient (1492–1715)* (Paris: Presses universitaires de France, 1954); Denys Hay, *Europe: The Emergence of an Idea* (Edinburgh: Edinburgh University Press, 1957); John Hale, *The Civilization of Europe in the Renaissance* (London: HarperCollins, 1993); Susan Doran, *England and Europe, 1485–1603* (London/New York: Longman, 1986).
9. See Gerard Delanty, *Inventing Europe: Idea, Identity, Reality* (Basingstoke: Macmillan, 1995), p. 3ff; Heikki Mikkeli, *Europe as an Idea and an Identity* (Basingstoke: Macmillan, 1998), p. 18ff.

10. Julius R. Ruff, *Violence in Early Modern Europe 1500–1800* (Cambridge: Cambridge University Press, 2001), p. 2. See also Malcolm Smuts, 'Organized Violence in the Elizabethan Monarchical Republic', *History* (2014), 418–43 (p. 443).

11. In this context, see, respectively: Hannah Arendt, *On Violence* (New York: Harcourt Brace, 1969), p. 35; Julien Freund, *L'essence du politique* (Paris: Sirey, 1965), p. 513; Wolfgang Sofsky, *Traité de la Violence*, trad. Bernard Lortholary (Paris: Gallimard, 2015), esp. p. 10; Slavoj Žižek, *Violence* (London: Profile, 2009), p. 2; Judith Butler, *Frames of War: When Is Life Grievable* (London/New York: Verso, 2010), p. xiii; Paul Virilio, *L'horizon négatif: Essai de dromoscopie* (Paris: Éditions Galilée, 1984), p. 275; Zygmunt Bauman, *Life in Fragments: Essays in Postmodern Morality* (Oxford: Blackwell, 1995), p. 139.

12. In this context, see N. Z. Davis, 'The Rites of Violence: Religious Riot in Sixteenth-Century France', in Alfred Soman (ed.), *The Massacre of St. Bartholomew* (The Hague: Martinus Nijhoff, 1974), pp. 203–42 (p. 241); Bernard Dagenais, *Éloge de la Violence* (Paris: Éditions de l'Aube, 2008), p. 205; Dominique Mondoloni, 'Comprendre...', *Notre Librairie. Revue des Littératures du Sud* 148.3 (July–September 2002: 'Penser la Violence'), p. 3; Emmanuel Bruno Jean-François, *Poétiques de la violence et récits francophones contemporains* (Leiden: Brill/Rodopi, 2017), p. 1.

13. See Véronique Le Goaziou, *La Violence* (Paris: Le Cavalier Bleu, 2004), pp. 5, 12. In this context, see also Francis C. Wade, 'On Violence: Comments and Criticism', *The Journal of Philosophy* 68.12 (17 June 1971), 369–77; Yves-Alain Michaud, *La Violence* (Paris: Presses Universitaires de France, 1973), p. 5.

14. Robert Paul Wolff, 'On Violence', *The Journal of Philosophy*, 19 (2 October 1969), 601–16 (p. 606). In this context, see also Dagenais, *Éloge de la Violence*, esp. pp. 11, 123, 189.

15. In this context, see Emmanuel Levinas, *Difficult Freedom: Essays on Judaism*, trans. Seán Hand (Baltimore: Johns Hopkins University Press, 1990), p. 6; Michel Wieviorka, *La Violence* (Paris: Librairie Arthème Fayard/Pluriel, 2005), p. 13; David Riches, 'The Phenomenon of Violence', in David Riches (ed.), *The Anthropology of Violence* (Oxford: Basil Blackwell, 1986), pp. 1–27.

16. Anthony Munday, *A second and third blast of retrait from plaies and theaters* (London: Henry Denham, 1580), pp. 3–4.

17. W. J. T. Mitchell, 'Foreword', in Allie Terry-Fritsch and Erin Felicia Labbie (eds.), *Beholding Violence in Medieval and Early Modern Europe* (Farnham: Ashgate, 2012), pp. xv–xxv (pp. xv–xvii).

18. For general discussion, see Wieviorka, *La Violence*, esp. pp. 51, 104; Georges Sorel, *Réflexions sur la Violence* (Paris: Marcel Rivière, 1910, 2nd ed.), p. 57.

19. Qtd in Joel Altman, '"Vile Participation": The Amplification of Violence in the Theater of *Henry V*', *Shakespeare Quarterly* (Spring 1991), 41.1, 1–32 (p. 9).
20. Qtd in Smuts, 'Organized Violence', p. 437.
21. Jean-François, *Poétiques de la violence*, esp. p. 102ff. See also Hélène Frappat, *La Violence* (Paris: GF Flammarion, 2000), p. 14.
22. Walter Benjamin, *Reflections: Essays, Aphorisms, Autobiographical Writings*, trans. Edmund Jephcott, ed. Peter Demetz (New York: Schocken, 1978), p. 287.
23. Arendt, *On Violence*, pp. 6, 56.
24. In this context, see Mary R. Jackman, 'Violence in Social Life', *Annual Review of Sociology*, 28 (2002), 387–415, anthologised in Peter Marsh, Elisabeth Rosser and Rom Harré, *The Rules of Disorder* (London: Routledge & Kegan Paul, 1980), pp. 387–415; Wieviorka, *La Violence*, p. 11.
25. See, for example: Étienne Balibar, *Violence et Civilité* (Paris: Galilée, 2010), p. 18; Bruce D. Bartholow, 'The Aggressive Brain', in Brad J. Bushman (ed.), *Aggression and Violence: A Social Psychological Perspective* (New York: Routledge, 2017), pp. 47–60 (esp. pp. 47–8).
26. Xavier Crettiez, *Les formes de la violence* (Paris: La Découverte, 2008), pp. 13, 34, 37. See also in this context: Mike Presdee, *Cultural Criminology and the Carnival of Crime* (London: Routledge, 2000), p. 63; Riches, 'The Phenomenon of Violence', pp. 4–5.
27. Jean Baudrillard, 'Le degré Xerox de la violence', *Libération*, 2nd Oct. 1995, p. 6.
28. Cynthia Marshall, *The Shattering of the Self: Violence, Subjectivity, and Early Modern Texts* (Baltimore: Johns Hopkins University Press, 2002), p. 5. For an alternatively framed enquiry, see Maurice Charney, 'The Persuasiveness of Violence in Elizabethan Plays', *Renaissance Drama*, II, 1969, 59–70 (p. 70).
29. Willem Schinkel, *Aspects of Violence: A Critical Theory* (Houndmills: Palgrave Macmillan, 2010), p. 128.
30. Thomas Lodge, *A Fig for Momus* (London: Thomas Orwin for Clement Knight, 1595), E1ʳ. In this context, see also, for example: Cicero, *The first book of Tullies Offices* (London: Henry Lownes, 1616), p. 79; William Garrard, *The arte of warre* (London: John Charlewood and William Howe? 1591), p. 64.
31. Niccolò Machiavelli, *The arte of warre* (London: John Kingston, 1562), A1ᵛ (2nd page sequence).
32. Robert Appelbaum, *Terrorism Before the Letter* (Oxford: Oxford University Press, 2015), pp. 61–2.
33. John Hooker, 'To the Right Worthie and Honorable gentleman sir Walter Raleigh', in Raphael Holinshed, *The Second volume of Chronicles* (London: Henry Denham, 1586), A2ᵛ. For further discussion, see Smuts, 'Organized Violence', esp. p. 422.

34. Rome, soon after 2 October 44 BC. See text and translation of Letter 345 (XII.3) to C. Cassius Longinus, in Cicero, *Letters to Friends*, 3 vols., ed. and trans. D. R. Shackleton Bailey (Cambridge, MA: Harvard University Press/ Loeb Classical Library, 2001): III.144–5.

35. René Girard, *La violence et le sacré* (Paris: Bernard Grasset, 1972), p. 45. See also Rafik Darragi, *La société de violence dans le théâtre élisabéthain* (Paris: L'Harmattan, 2012), p. 10.

36. For further discussion, see Kyle Pivetti, *Of Memory and Literary Form: Making the Early Modern Nation* (Newark: University of Delaware Press, 2015), p. 45. More generally in this context, see also Jean-Marie Maguin, *Shakespeare and the Rhetoric of Elocution* (New York: CreateSpace, 2017).

37. Carl von Clausewitz, *On War*, 3 vols., trans J. J. Graham, revised F. N. Maude (London: Routledge & Kegan Paul, 1968): I.2 (1.1).

38. Seneca, *Naturales Quaestiones*, vol. I, Eng. trans. Thomas H. Corcoran (London/Cambridge, MA: William Heinemann/Harvard University Press, 1971): I.205. See also *Controversiae* 2.1.10, in the Elder Seneca, *Declamations in Two Volumes*, trans. M. Winterbottom, vol. I: *Controversiae 1–6* (Cambridge MA/London: Harvard University Press/William Heinemann, 1974), p. 215; Seneca, *Ad Lucilium Epistulae Morales*, 3 vols., trans. Richard M. Gunmere (London/New York: William Heinemann/G. P. Putnam & Sons, 1925): I.77–9.

39. See, for example: Derek Cohen, *Shakespeare's Culture of Violence* (Basingstoke: Macmillan/St. Martin's Press, 1993), p. 55; Jonas Barish, 'Shakespearean Violence: A Preliminary Survey', *Shakespearean Criticism*, 43 (1999), 1–12 (p. 2).

40. Žižek, *Violence*, p. 52.

41. Dick Hebdige, 'Subculture', in Raiford Guins and Omayra Zaragoza Cruz (eds.), *Popular Culture: A Reader* (London/New Delhi: Thousand Oaks/Sage, 2005), pp. 355–71 (p. 355).

42. Girard, *La violence et le sacré*, p. 74.

43. Seneca, *Seneca: Moral Essays*, 3 vols., trans. John W. Basore (London/ New York: William Heinemann/G. P. Putnam, 1928): I.121.

44. Emmanuel Lévinas, *Humanisme de l'Autre Homme* (Paris: Fata Morgana, 1972), p. 49.

45. In this context, see Georg Simmel, '*Conflict*' and '*The Web of Group-Affiliations*', trans., respectively, Kurt H. Wolff and Reinhard Bendix (New York: Free Press of Glencoe, 1955), pp. 18–19; Wieviorka, *La Violence*, esp. p. 51.

46. See Schinkel, *Aspects of Violence*, p. 15.

47. In this context, see Sofsky, *Traité de la Violence*, esp. pp. 10, 11, 15, 24, 47.

48. For further discussion, see Françoise Héritier, *De La Violence* (Paris: Éditions Odile Jacob, 1996), pp. 31–2.
49. Presdee, *Cultural Criminology*, p. 11. For further discussion, see Thomas Elbert, James Moran and Maggie Schauer, 'Appetitive Aggression', in Bushman (ed.), *Aggression and Violence*, pp. 119–35.
50. Edgar Morin, *La Méthode*, I (Paris: Seuil/Points, 1977), p. 75.
51. Schinkel, *Aspects of Violence*, pp. 26, 80. See also in this context: Cohen, *Shakespeare's Culture of Violence*, p. 1; R. A. Foakes, *Shakespeare and Violence* (Cambridge: Cambridge University Press, 2003), pp. 16–17; Michaud, *La Violence*, p. 5; Presdee, *Cultural Criminology*, p. 4.
52. In this context, see Benjamin Griffin, *Playing the Past. Approaches to English Historical Drama 1385–1600* (Woodbridge: D. S. Brewer, 2001), p. 93; François Laroque, '"Bellona's bridegroom": la fête de la guerre dans le théâtre de Shakespeare', in M. T. Jones-Davies (ed.), *Shakespeare et la Guerre* (Paris: Les Belles Lettres/Société Française Shakespeare, 1990), pp. 25–46 (p. 26).
53. Alberico Gentili, *De Iure Belli Libri Tres*, trans. John C. Rolfe, vol. II (Oxford: Clarendon Press, 1933), p. 7(1.1).
54. See Seàn Hand (ed.), *The Levinas Reader* (Oxford: Blackwells, 2003), p. 33. See also Pierre Ferrari, 'Agressivité à l'Adolescence', in Pierre Benghozi et al. (eds.), *Violence, Passages à l'Acte et Situations de Crise* (Paris: Editions La Pensée Sauvage, 2000), pp. 7–14; Héritier, *De La Violence*, p. 15.
55. See Butler, *Frames of War*, p. 42.
56. Simone Weil, *The Iliad or the Poem of Force*, ed. James P. Holoka (New York: Peter Lang, 2008), p. 45.
57. Schinkel, *Aspects of Violence*, p. 45.
58. John Eliot, *Ortho-epia Gallica Eliots fruits for the French* (London: Richard Field for John Wolfe, 1593), A3^r.
59. See Jean Bodin, *Method for the Easy Comprehension of History*, trans. Beatrice Reynolds (New York: Columbia University Press, 1945), p. 95(ch. v).
60. Qtd in Sir John Smythe, *Certain Discourses Military*, ed. J. R. Hale (Ithaca, NY: Folger Shakespeare Library/Cornell University Press, 1964), p. xv.
61. Jean Bodin, *The Six Bookes of a Commonweale* (London: Adam Islip, 1606), ch. v. sect. v, pp. 598–9.
62. Qtd in Paul E. J. Hammer, *Elizabeth's Wars: War, Government and Society in Tudor England, 1544–1604* (Basingstoke: Palgrave Macmillan, 2003), p. 1 (see also p. 6). In this context, see also Roger B. Manning *The Apprenticeship of Arms: The Origins of the British Army 1585–1702* (Oxford: Oxford University Press, 2006), p. 5.
63. Accession speech to Parliament, 19 March 1603. See Arthur Wilson, *The history of Great Britain* ... (London: Richard Lownds, 1653), p. 14. For

further illuminating discussion of the difficulties encountered by early modern military-fiscal states, see Michael J. Braddick, *State Formation in Early Modern England c. 1550–1700* (Cambridge: Cambridge University Press, 2000), p. 181ff.

64. I. F., *King Iames his welcome to London* (London: R. Read? for Thomas Pauier, 1603), B3^r.

65. See David R. Lawrence, 'Reappraising the Elizabethan and Early Stuart Soldier: Recent Historiography on Early Modern English Military Culture', *History Compass* 9.1 (2011), 16–33 (pp. 17, 20).

66. John Norden, *A pensiue soules delight* (London: William Stansby for John Busby, 1615), p. 322. A shorter edition had been published in 1603.

67. 'To The Right Honorable, his singular good Mayster, Sir *Christopher Hatton*', in Appian, *An auncient historie and exquisite chronicle of the Romanes warres, both ciuile and foren* (London: Henry Bynneman, 1578), A2^r.

68. William Blandie, *The castle* (London: John Daye, 1581), 3^v.

69. Regarding Elizabethan military recruitment, see John S. Nolan, 'The Militarization of the Elizabethan State', *Journal of Military History* 58 (July 1994), 391–420(esp. p. 396). For further discussion of the presentation of the military identities in the playhouse, see Andrew Hiscock, '"Lay by thine Armes and take the Citie then": Soldiery and City in the Drama of Thomas Middleton', in Matthew Woodcock and Cian O'Mahony (eds.), *Early Modern Military Identities* (Woodbridge: Boydell & Brewer, 2018), pp. 235–55.

70. In this context, see Barbara Donagan, 'Halcyon Days and the Literature of War: England's Military Education before 1642', *Past and Present* 147 (1995), 65–100(esp. p. 68ff).

71. See Roger B. Manning, *Swordsmen: The Martial Ethos in the Three Kingdoms* (Oxford: Oxford University Press, 2003), p. 23.

72. Sir Humphrey Gilbert, *Queene Elizabethes Achademy . . .*, ed. F. J. Furnivall (London: Early English Text Society/N. Trübner, 1869), pp. 1–5.

73. For further discussion here, see Steven Gunn, David Grummitt and Hans Cools, *War, State, and Society in England and the Netherlands 1477–1559* (Oxford: Oxford University Press, 2007), pp. 177, 240–1.

74. Fissel records that 'A 1588 report from York confessed, "all men here have no liking to be inrolled in a muster book . . . They are unwilling to come into the muster book, lest they should be called upon for any service in Ireland".' See Mark Fissel, *English Warfare 1511–1642* (London: Routledge, 2016, 1st pub. 2001), p. 88. In this context, see also Hammer, *Elizabeth's Wars*, p. 98.

75. See Fissel, *English Warfare*, p. 87; Hammer, *Elizabeth's Wars*, p. 101. In this context, see also Nolan, 'The Militarization of the Elizabethan State', pp. 396–402; Neil Younger, *War and Politics in the Elizabethan Counties*

(Manchester: Manchester University Press, 2012), pp. 13, 104–7, 168–74; David R. Lawrence, *The Complete Soldier: Military Books and Military Culture in Early Stuart England, 1603–1645* (Leiden: Brill, 2009), pp. 32–3; Gunn et al., *War, State, and Society*, pp. 21, 45, 129.

76. Sir John Smythe, *Certain discourses* (London: Thomas Orwin for Richard Jones, 1590), A1^r.

77. For further discussion, see Nick de Somogyi, *Shakespeare's Theatre of War* (Aldershot: Ashgate, 1998), p. 110; Patricia A. Cahill, *Unto the Breach. Martial Formations, Historical Trauma, and the Early Modern Stage* (Oxford: Oxford University Press, 2008), p. 75.

78. Qtd in Altman, 'Vile Participation', p. 10. In this context, see also James R. Keller, *Princes, Soldiers and Rogues: The Political Malcontent of Renaissance Drama* (New York: Peter Lang, 1993), p. 73.

79. For Gervase Markham's disparagement of 'book soldiers', see Charles Carlton, *This Seat of Mars: War and the British Isles 1485–1746* (New Haven: Yale University Press, 2011), p. 59.

80. Arendt, *On Violence*, pp. 41–2.

81. More generally, the degree to which early modern states such as England experienced a 'military revolution' continues to be a vigorous source of debate amongst historians. See Downing, *The Military Revolution and Political Change*, esp. pp. 3, 10, 65. The term 'Military Revolution' was coined in 1955 by the historian Michael Roberts. Since then, some of the most important voices in this ongoing debate include (in alphabetical order): Jeremy Black, Brian M. Downing, Michael Duffy, David Eltis, Mark Charles Fissel, Geoffrey Parker, Michael Roberts, Clifford J. Rogers and R. B. Wernham. Central areas of discussion in this debate for the early modern period include: the increasing centralisation of European states and the growth in their schemes of military expenditure; changing practices of recruitment, organisation and training of large-scale armies; proliferation in publications and manuals devoted to military practice; and, especially importantly, technological advances in firearms and other weapons, fortifications and logistics in this period.

82. Smythe, *Certain discourses* (1590), A2^r. In this context, see Manning, *Swordsmen*, p. 6.

83. Humfrey Barwick, *A breefe discourse* (London: Edward Allde, 1592), A4^r.

84. George Peele, *The battell of Alcazar* (London: Edward Allde for Richard Bankworth, 1594), B1^r. In this context, see also Shakespeare, *Julius Caesar*, IV.iii.75–7.

85. Edmondes' need to promote greater logistical rigour in the organisation of military campaigns becomes clear on consulting the invaluable data collected by Ian Wallace Archer for his *Gazetteer of military levies from the City of*

London, 1509–1603. See, for example: (June 1600) 'Troops were to be at Chester by 25 July, and conduct money paid by crown at 8d per day per man. The captains were Edward Fisher and Thomas Mynn. 44 ran away'; (August 1600) 'In spite of council's express instructions for care to be taken in selection, 100 of the soldiers pressed ran away, and a further press was necessary.' Entries at 103 and 105, respectively, in https://ora.ox.ac.uk/objects/ uuid:adb577fc-6ffb-440b-9dd9-7c5c39a4a64c (accessed 3/7/20).

86. See, respectively: D. R. Woolf, 'Genre into Artefact: The Decline of the English Chronicle in the Sixteenth Century', *Sixteenth Century Journal* 19 (1988), 321–54 (p. 346); Patricia A. Cahill, *Unto the Breach*, p. 16. See also Lawrence, *The Complete Soldier*, p. 1.

87. Examples from the period include: Thomas Proctor's *Of the Knowledge and Conduct of Warres* (1578); William Blandie's *The Castle* (1581); Leonard and Thomas Digges's *An Arithmeticall Militare Treatise, Names Stratioticos* (1579); Geffrey Gates's *Defence of Militarie Profession* (1579); Paul Ive's translation of Raimond Fourquevaux's *The Practice of Fortification* (1589); John Smythe's *Certain Discourses* (1590); Gyles Clayton's *The approoued order of martiall discipline* (1591); Roger Williams's *A briefe discourse of warre* (1590); William Garrard's *The Arte of Warre* (1591); Matthew Sutcliffe's *The practice, proceedings and lawes of Armes* (1593); Anon., *A Myrrour for English Souldiers* (1595); Charles Gibbon's *Watch-word for War* (1596); John Norden's *The mirror of honor* (1597); Robert Barrett's *The Theorike and Practicke of Modern Warres* (1598). Nonetheless, J. R. Hale underlines that '[c]ompared with the continent, the production of books on warfare in England was meagre'. See J. R. Hale, *Renaissance War Studies* (London: Hambledon Press, 1983), p. 259. In this context, see also: Lawrence, *The Complete Soldier*, p. 17; Carlton, *This Seat of Mars*, p. 32.

88. Thomas Nashe, *Pierce Pennilesse* (London: Abel Jeffes, 1592), F3^r.

89. Indeed, Jeffrey S. Doty argues that 'Shakespeare turns the theatre into a space in which playgoers could practice thinking about how power works in the political domain. The theatre, in other words, was a training ground for citizenship.' See 'Shakespeare's *Richard II*, "Popularity", and the Early Modern Public Sphere', *Shakespeare Quarterly* 61.2 (2010), 183–205 (p. 185).

90. Philip Gawdy, *Letters of Philip Gawdy of West Harling, Norfolk, and of London to Various Members of his Family 1579–1616*, ed. Isaac Herbert Jeayes (London: Nichols & Sons, 1906), p. 18.

91. Michel Foucault, *'Society Must Be Defended': Lectures at the Collège de France 1975–1976*, ed. Mauro Bertani and Alessandro Fontana, trans. David Macey (New York: Picador, 1997), p. 15. In this context, see also Chris Hables Gray, *Peace, War, and Computers* (New York: Routledge, 2005), p. 23. In the first edition to *On War*, Clausewitz had affirmed that 'war is only a continuation

of state policy by other means'. See Carl von Clausewitz, *On War: The Complete Edition* (Rockville, MA: Wildside Press, 2009), p. 10.

92. See, respectively: 'Introduction', in Jeremy Black (ed.), *The Origins of War in Early Modern Europe* (Edinburgh: John Donald Publishers, 1987), 1–24 (p. 1); Susan Dwyer Amussen, 'Punishment, Discipline, and Power: The Social Meanings of Violence in Early Modern England', *The Journal of British Studies* 34 (1 January 1995), 1–34 (p. 10). In this context, see also Carlton, *This Seat of Mars*, p. 32.

93. Jan Glete, *War and the State in Early Modern Europe. Spain, the Dutch Republic and Sweden as Fiscal-military States, 1500–1600* (London/ New York: Routledge, 2002), p. 6. See also Max Weber, *Max Weber on Law in Economy and Society*, ed. Max Rheinstein, trans. *Wirtscharf and Gesellschaft* (1925) by Edward Shiels and Max Rheinstein (Cambridge, MA: Harvard University Press, 1954), p. 14ff.

94. Nicholas Grene, *Shakespeare's Serial History Plays* (Cambridge: Cambridge University Press, 2002), p. 83.

95. Susan Sontag, *Regarding the Pain of Others* (London: Penguin, 2004), p. 101.

96. Albert Camus, *L'Homme révolté* (Paris: Gallimard, 1985), p. 340.

97. Arendt, *On Violence*, p. 79.

98. Žižek, *Violence*, p. 63.

99. Sir William Cornwallis, *Discourses upon Seneca the Tragedian* (London: S. Stafford for Edmund Mattes, 1601), H1ʳ.

100. 'De la conscience', in Michel de Montaigne, *Essais*, ed. J.-V. Leclerc, vol. I (Paris: Garnier, 1878), p. 335 (II.v).

101. Qtd in Ronald G. Musto, 'Just Wars and Evil Empires: Erasmus and the Turks', in John Monfasani and Ronald G. Musto (eds.), *Renaissance Society and Culture: Essays in Honor of Eugene F. Rice, Jr.* (New York: Italica Press, 1991), pp. 197–216 (p. 201).

102. Qtd in Altman, 'Vile Participation', p. 12.

103. Virilio, *L'horizon négatif*, p. 274.

104. Emmanuel Levinas, 'Useless Suffering', trans. Richard Cohen, in Robert Bernesconi and David Wood (eds.), *Provocation of Levinas: Rethinking the Other* (London: Routledge, 1988), pp. 156–67 (p. 163).

105. 'To his father, 9th May 1588', in Gawdy, *Letters of Philip Gawdy*, ed. Jeayes, pp. 35–6.

1 'touching violence or punishments'

All references to Ralegh's *The History of the World* are taken from the 1617 edition (London: Walter Burre, 1617 [1614]) and are referenced: Book; Chapter; Section; Page as appropriate.

1. 'A Discovrse of . . . Warre', in Walter Ralegh, *Judicious and select essayes and observations* (London: T. W. for Humphrey Moseley, 1650), p. 3.

2. Ralegh, *Judicious and select essayes*, A4ʳ.

3. See *The Prerogative of Parliaments in England* ('Middleburg' [London]: s. p., 1628), n. p.

4. Sir Robert Naunton, *Fragmenta regalia* (London: s. p., 1641), p. 31. Steven May queries the sequencing and authenticity of some details of Naunton's accounts. See 'How Raleigh became a courtier', *John Donne Journal*, 27 (2008), 131–40 (p. 134).

5. *De jure belli ac pacis* (Paris: Nicolas Buon, 1625). Available for the early modern English-speaking reader, for example, in *The illustrious Hugo Grotius of the law of warre and peace* (London: T. Warren for William Lee, 1654).

6. Willem Schinkel, *Aspects of Violence. A Critical Theory* (Houndmills: Palgrave Macmillan, 2010), p. 45.

7. Regarding Ben Jonson's account of his role in the writing of the *History*, 'Conversations with Drummond', in Ben Jonson, *Ben Jonson*, eds. C. H. Herford and Percy Simpson (Oxford: Clarendon Press, 1925), vol. I: ll. 198–201, p. 138. However, while acknowledging the possibilities of Jonson's and others' input in Ralegh's *History*, Nicholas Popper argues that 'no evidence aside from Jonson's late complaint suggests that Ralegh was not, in fact, the final author of the *History*'. See *Walter Ralegh's 'History of the World' and the Historical Culture of the Late Renaissance* (Chicago: University of Chicago Press, 2012), p. 33. See also in this context: John Racin, *Sir Walter Ralegh as Historian: An Analysis of 'The History of the World'* (Salzburg: Institut für Englische Sprache und Literatur, 1974), p. 20.

8. *History*, 'Preface', D1ᵛ.

9. *History*: 1.2.3.28.

10. Francis Bacon, *The Works of Francis Bacon*, ed. J. Spedding, R. L. Ellis, and D. D. Heath, 14 vols. (London: Longman et al., 1857–74): VI.517.

11. *History*, 2.13.7.438.

12. *History*, 5.2.1.313.

13. Jean Bodin, *Method for the Easy Comprehension of History*, trans. Beatrice Reynolds (New York: Columbia University Press, 1945): ch. vi, p. 265.

14. Giving an alternative emphasis to Ralegh's project of the *History*, Popper proposes a chronicler who 'never ceased in his efforts to secure James's approval . . . A distinguished lineage of admiring royalist readers contradicts the claim that Ralegh's work was necessarily oppositional'. See *Walter Ralegh's 'History of the World'*, p. 34.

15. For full discussion here, see Racin, *Sir Walter Ralegh as Historian*, p. 7ff.

16. In this context, see Popper, *Walter Ralegh's 'History of the World'*, p. 18.

17. Entry 1184 – 18th December 1616. See CSP Col. East Indies, China and Japan, 1513–1616, p. 485.

18. *History*, 2.4.16.292. For further discussion of these principles in modern debate, see, for example, Jacques Derrida, *The Beast and Sovereign*, trans. Geoffrey Bennington, vol. I (Chicago: University of Chicago Press, 2009), p. 17.

19. See Oliver Cromwell, *The Letters and Speeches of Oliver Cromwell*, ed. S. C. Lomas (New York: Methuen & Co., 1904), 2 vols: II, p. 54.

20. Rowland Whyte to the Earl of Shrewsbury – 24th September 1606. See Edmund Lodge (ed.), *Illustrations of British History* …, vol. III (London: G. Nicol, 1741), p. 313.

21. See entry 375 – Antonio Foscarini, Venetian Ambassador in England, to the Doge and Senate – 22nd August 1614, in CSPM, relating to English Affairs, existing in the Archives and Collections of Venice, and in other Libraries of Northern Italy, vol. xiii. 1613–1615, ed. Allen B. Hinds (London: Eyre and Spottiswoode, 1907), p. 180.

22. See, respectively: Gervase Markham, *Honour in his Perfection* (London: B. Alsop for Benjamin Fisher, 1624), p. 24; Thomas Middleton, *The Peace-Maker* (London: Thomas Purfoot, 1618), A4^r.

23. [Thomas Scott?] Anon., *Robert Earle of Essex his Ghost; Sent from Elizian: To the Nobility, Gentry, and Communaltie of England* ('Paradise' [London]: J. Beale? 1624), p. 4.

24. This publication has been attributed to Robert Parsons (perhaps assisted by others) – see, for example, M. J. Rodriguez-Salgado, 'The Anglo-Spanish War: The Final Episode in "The Wars of the Roses"?', in M. J. Rodriguez-Salgado and Simon Adams (eds.), *England, Spain and the Gran Armada 1585–1604* (Edinburgh: John Donald Pubs., 1991), pp. 1–44 (p. 29). Albert J. Loomie also argued for the authorship of this tract being Richard Verstegan. See 'The Authorship of "An Advertisement written to a Secretarie of M. L. Treasurer of England…"', *Renaissance News* 15.3 (Autumn, 1962), 201–7.

25. Robert Parsons, *An aduertisement written to a secretarie of my L. Treasurers of Ingland, by an Inglishe intelligencer* (Antwerp: s.p., 1592), p. 18.

26. Anon., *Sir Walter Raleigh's Sceptick* (London: W. Bentley, 1651), B1^r.

27. *History*, 2.1.1.217.

28. 'Preface', *History*, B1^v.

29. 'The Author to the Reader'. Rendered here in the contemporaneous publication in English: *Britain*… (London: Eliot's Court Press, 1610), *4^r.

30. *History*: 5.2.4.385.

31. John Chamberlain, *The Letters of John Chamberlain*, vol. I, ed. Norman Egbert McClure (Philadelphia: American Philosophical Society, 1939), p. 568.

32. 'A Discovrse of Warre', D7^r.

33. 'A Discovrse of Warre', pp. 1, 3. In this context, see Robert Appelbaum, *Terrorism before the Letter* (Oxford: Oxford University Press, 2015), p. 46.
34. 'A Discovrse of Warre', p. 2.
35. 'A Discovrse of Warre', E4ᵛ–E5ʳ.
36. In this context of the bequeathing of violence to later generations, see Alberico Gentili, *De Iure Belli Libri Tres*, trans. John C. Rolfe, vol. II (Oxford: Clarendon Press, 1933), p. 83.
37. *History*, 5.3.1.426. For further contexts for these sentiments, see Lawrence Keymis, *A Relation of the Second Voyage to Guiana* (London: Thomas Dawson, 1596), F1ʳ.
38. *History*, 5.2.3.389.
39. 'last summer' here refers to August 1591.
40. Walter Ralegh, *A report of the truth of the fight about the Isles of Açores ...* (London: John Windet for William Ponsonby, 1591), B2ʳ, A3ʳ.
41. *Açores*, B3ᵛ.
42. *Açores*, B1ᵛ, C1ʳ.
43. *Açores*, C2ʳ.
44. *Açores*, C3ʳ, A4ʳ.
45. For critical accounts of this corpus of narratives of Spanish colonial brutality in the early modern period, see, for example: W. S. Maltby, *The Black Legend in England* (Duke University Press, 1971); Margaret R. Greer et al. (eds.), *Rereading the Black Legend* (Chicago: University of Chicago Press, 2007).
46. See *History*, 5.1.1.312.
47. *History*, 5.6.2.715.
48. Benjamin Schmidt, 'Reading Ralegh's America: Texts, Books and Readers in the Early Modern Atlantic World', in Peter C. Mancall (ed.), *The Atlantic World and Virginia 1550–1624* (Chapel Hill: University of North Carolina Press, 2007), pp. 454–88 (p. 458).
49. Naunton, *Fragmenta regalia*, p. 30.
50. William Cecil, Lord Burghley, 'Certain Precepts for the Well Ordering of a Man's Life' (ca. 1584), in Louis B. Wright (ed.), *Advice to a Son. Precepts of Lord Burghley, Sir Walter Raleigh, and Francis Osborne* (New York: Folger Shakespeare Library/Cornell University Press, 1962), p. 12.
51. Rory Rapple, *Martial Power and Elizabethan Political Culture* (Cambridge: Cambridge University Press, 2009), p. 48. See also Roger B. Manning, *Swordsmen: The Martial Ethos in the Three Kingdoms* (Oxford: Oxford University Press, 2003), p. 22.
52. Thomas Churchyard, *A generall rehearsall of warres ...* (London: Edward White, 1579), K2ᵛ. For further discussion of the Champernownes in the context, see David Trim, 'Calvinist Internationalism and the English

Officer Corps, 1562–1642', *History Compass* 4.6 (Nov 2006), 1024–48 (p. 1032).

53. Camden, *Annals*... (London: Thomas Harper for Benjamin Fisher, 1635), p. 117.
54. Rapple, *Martial Power*, p. 57.
55. Sir Thomas Smith, *De republica Anglorum*... (London: Henry Middleton for Gregory Seton, 1583), p. 95.
56. Churchyard, *A generall rehearsall of warres*, K2ᵛ.
57. J. H. Elliott, *Europe Divided 1559–1598* (London: Fontana/Collins, 1974), p. 108.
58. David J. B. Trim, 'Seeking a Protestant Alliance and Liberty of Conscience on the Continent, 1558–85', in Susan Doran and Glenn Richardson (eds.), *Tudor England and Its Neighbours* (Houndmills: Palgrave, 2005), pp. 139–77 (pp. 153–4).
59. *History*, 5.1.1.311.
60. *History*, 5.1.1.311.
61. John Foxe, *Actes and monuments*, vol. II (London: John Day, 1583), p. 2112.
62. For further discussion, see Charles R. Forker, *Skull Beneath the Skin: The Achievement of John Webster* (Carbondale: Southern Illinois University Press, 1986), p. 134ff.
63. *History*, 4.2.12.192, 4.3.7.250.
64. *History*, 4.2.16.197–8.
65. *History*, 4.2.16.198.
66. For a discussion of Ralegh's aunt, Kat Ashley (or Champernowne), and her importance for the young Elizabeth and her ability to offer an *entrée* into the young queen's retinue, see Mathew Lyons *The Favourite* (London: Constable, 2011), esp. pp. 23, 26–7.
67. Steven W. May, *Elizabethan Courtier Poets* (Asheville, NC: Pegasus Press, 1999), p. 361.
68. For further discussion, see May, 'How Raleigh Became a Courtier', p. 132.
69. Cited respectively in: May, *Elizabethan Courtier Poets*, p. 361; Mark Nicholls and Penry Williams, *Sir Walter Raleigh in Life and Legend* (London: Continuum, 2011), p. 26.
70. Naunton, *Fragmenta regalia*, p. 31.
71. And not only at court! See, for example, CSP Dom. reign of Elizabeth, 1591–1594, p. 19 (16th March 1591).
72. See Epigram 315 – 'Of Paulus, A Flatterer', ll. 5–6, in Sir John Harington, *The Epigrams of Sir John Harington*, ed. Norman Eybert Mclure (Philadelphia: University of Pennsylvania, 1930), p. 273.
73. Cited in Paul E. J. Hammer, *The Polarisation of Elizabethan Politics: The Political Career of Robert Devereux, 2nd Earl of Essex, 1585–1597* (Cambridge: Cambridge University Press, 1999), p. 85.

74. Cited in May, *Elizabethan Courtier Poets*, p. 122.

75. Cited in Nicholls and Williams, *Sir Walter Raleigh in Life and Legend*, p. 128.

76. Sir Francis Vere, *The commentaries of Sr. Francis Vere* (London: John Field, 1657), pp. 52, 53.

77. Sir Walter Ralegh, *The Letters of Sir Walter Ralegh*, ed. Agnes Latham and Joyce Youings (Exeter: University of Exeter Press, 1999), p. 186.

78. For further discussion here, see Robert Lacey, *Sir Walter Ralegh* (London: Phoenix Press, 1973), p. 167.

79. Cited in Rapple, *Martial Heroism*, p. 238. See also Roger B. Manning *The Apprenticeship of Arms: The Origins of the British Army 1585–1702* (Oxford: Oxford University Press, 2006), pp. 12–13.

80. Rapple, *Martial Heroism*, p. 88.

81. Cited in Vincent P. Carey, 'Grey, Spenser and the Slaughter at Smerwick', in Clodagh Tait, David Edwards and Pádraig Lenihan (eds.), *Age of Atrocity: Violence and Political Conflict in Early Modern Ireland* (Dublin: Four Courts Press, 2007), pp. 79–94 (p. 90). See also Charles Carlton, *This Seat of Mars: War and the British Isles 1485–1746* (New Haven: Yale University Press, 2011), p. 50.

82. John Hooker, 'The Svpplie of the Irish Chronicles …', in Raphael Holinshed, *The Second volume of Chronicles* (London: Henry Denham, 1586), p. 171. See also in this context, Edmund Spenser, *Selected Letters and Other Papers*, ed. Christopher Burlinson & Andrew Zurcher (Oxford: Oxford University Press, 2009), pp. 18–19; Andrew Hadfield, *Edmund Spenser: A Life* (Oxford: Oxford University Press, 2012), pp. 172, 232.

83. Languet to Sidney – Antwerp, 22nd October 1580. See Sir Philip Sidney/ Hubert Languet, *The Correspondence of Sir Philip Sidney and Hubert Languet*, ed. and trans. Steuart A. Pears (London: William Pickering, 1845), p. 189. For an account of English military atrocities in Ireland, see Charles Carlton, *This Seat of Mars: War and the British Isles 1485–1746* (New Haven: Yale University Press, 2011), p. 52.

84. Camden, *Annales*, p. 409.

85. Clodagh Tait, David Edwards and Pádraig Lenihan, 'Early Modern Ireland: A History of Violence', in Edwards et al. (eds.), *Age of Atrocity*, pp. 9–33 (p. 24). Also in this context, see David Edwards, 'The Escalation of Violence in Sixteenth-Century Ireland', in ibid., pp. 34–78 (esp. p. 43); Malcolm Smuts, 'Organized Violence in the Elizabethan Monarchical Republic', *History* 99.336 (2014), 418–43.

86. Malcolm Smuts, 'Organized Violence', pp. 419, 433.

87. Cited in Nicholls and Williams, *Sir Walter Raleigh in Life and Legend*, p. 20. In later years, regarding the 'variance between him, and my Lord *Grey*', see Naunton, *Fragmenta regalia*, p. 31.

88. Letter 60: 'To Sir Robert Cecil from Sherborne, 10 May 1595'. See Ralegh, *Letters*, ed. Latham and Youings, pp. 93–4.

89. For further discussion, see Andrew Hiscock, 'Barking Dogs and Christian Men: Ralegh and Barbarism', in Zsolt Almási and Michael Pincombe (eds.), *Writing the Other: Tudor Humanism/Barbarism* (Cambridge: Cambridge Scholars, 2008) pp. 168–82.

90. *History*, 2.4.15.291.

91. Cited in Nicholls and Williams, *Sir Walter Raleigh in Life and Legend*, p. 72.

92. Edward Thompson, Sir *Walter Ralegh. The Last of the Elizabethans* (London: Macmillan, 1935), p. 364.

93. Carey, 'Grey, Spenser and the Slaughter at Smerwick', p. 87.

94. Cited in Shannon Miller, *Invested with Meaning: The Raleigh Circle in the New World* (Philadelphia: University of Pennsylvania Press, 1998), p. 86.

95. Raphael Holinshed, *The Third volume of Chronicles...* (London: Henry Denham, 1586), p. 1369.

96. Richard Hakluyt, 'To the Right Worthie and Honorable Gentleman, Sir Walter...', in René Goulaine de Laudonnière, *A Notable Historie containing foure voyages made by certaine French captaynes vnto Florida*, trans. Richard Hakluyt (London: Thomas Dawson, 1587).

97. For further discussion, see David B. Quinn, *Raleigh and the British Empire* (London: Hodder & Stoughton, 1947), p. 142ff. For further examples of this discourse, see John Smith, *A Map of Virginia* (Oxford: Joseph Barnes, 1612), p. 20; William Morrell, *New-England...* (London: J. Dawson, 1625), p. 20; William Wood, *New Englands prospect* (London: John Coates for Thomas Bellamy, 1634), p. 93; Thomas Morton, *New English Canaan* (London: Charles Greene? 1637), p. 24.

98. Hakluyt, 'To the Right Worthie and Honorable Gentleman', n. p.

99. *History*, 4.2.4.178. See also in this context: *History*, 5.6.2.717; Sir Walter Ralegh, *The discouerie of the large, rich, and bewtiful empire of Guiana* (London: Robert Robinson, 1596), p. 52; 'A Relation of Cadiz Action in the Year 1596', in Ralegh, *An abridgment of Sir Walter Raleigh's History of the world in five books ... Publish'd by Phillip Raleigh ...* (London: Matthew Gelliflower, 1698), p. 24.

100. See the 1618 text 'Sir Walter Rawleigh His Apologie for His Voyage to Guiana', in *Judicious and select Essayes*, pp. 3–4.

101. John Everard, *The arriereban a sermon* (London: E. Griffin for Thomas Walkley, 1618), p. 17.

102. Gottfried von Bülow (ed.), 'Journey through England and Scotland made by Lupold von Wedel in the years 1584 and 1585', *Transactions of the RHS* 9 (1895), 223–70 (p. 251).

103. Cited in Thompson, *Sir Walter Ralegh*, p. 51. The memorial 'Of the Voyage for Guiana' has recently been republished in Sir Walter Ralegh, *Sir Walter Ralegh's Discoverie of Guiana*, ed. Joyce Lorimer (London: Ashgate/Hakluyt Society, 2006), pp. 253–63.

104. Languet to Sidney – Frankfort, 28th November 1577. See Sidney/Languet, *The Correspondence*, ed. Pears, pp. 124–5.

105. *Discouerie*, p. 96.

106. *Discouerie*, p. 39. In this context, see also Keymis, *Relation of the Second Voyage*, B4^v. Later in the narrative he renames the Orinoco 'Raleana' (E1^r).

107. Sir Walter Ralegh, *The Discoverie of the Large, Rich and Bewtiful Empyre of Guiana*, ed. Neil L. Whitehead (Manchester: Manchester University Press, 1997), p. 157, note 57. In this context, see *History* 2.1.10.230.

108. See *Discouerie*, A4^r.

109. Mary B. Campbell, *The Witness and the Other World: Exotic European Travel Writing, 400–1600* (Ithaca/London: Cornell University Press, 1988), p. 225.

110. *Discouerie*, pp. 6–7.

111. *Discouerie*, p. 40. See also *Discouerie*, pp. 46–7.

112. See Campbell, *The Witness*, pp. 240, 241.

113. However, as Rodriguez-Salgado points out, the perception and the reality of the riches destined for Spain's coffers from the 1580s onwards were different things: 'As for the Indies revenues, they amounted to a million or a million and half ducats annually, roughly an eighth of Philip's Spanish revenues, and about a tenth of the total cost of the [Armada] campaign.' See Rodriguez-Salgado, 'The Anglo-Spanish War', p. 8.

114. *Discouerie*, O2^r.

115. *Discouerie*, 3^v. In this context, see also: 'Sir Walter Rawleigh His Apologie', in Ralegh, *Judicious and select Essayes*, p. 51; Keymis, *Relation of the Second Voyage*, F2^v.

116. George Abbot, *An exposition vpon the prophet Ionah* (London: Richard Field, 1600), the III lecture, p. 46.

117. See Sir Philip Sidney, *A Defence of Poetry*, ed. J. A. Van Dorsten (Oxford: Oxford University Press, 1966), 'Narration', p. 20.

118. *History*, 4.2.3.173.

119. Francis Bacon, *A briefe discourse* … (London: R. Read for Felix Norton, 1603), A6^r.

120. Sir William Cornwallis, *The miraculous and happie vnion* … (London: Edward Blount, 1604), B4^v.

121. 'Preface', *History*, A1^v.

122. John Aubrey, *Aubrey's Brief Lives*, ed. Oliver Lawson Dick (Jaffrey, NH: David R. Godine Pubs., 1999), p. 257.

123. 'Preface', *History*, B2^v.

124. *CM Salisbury* (XV, 1930), p. 285.

125. Sir John Harington, *Nugae Antiquae* ..., 2 vols. (London: Archibald Hamilton, 1769): II.131.

126. In this context, see also entry 603 – Giovanni Battista Lionello, Venetian Secretary in England, to the Council of Ten, 19th January 1617, in CSPM, relating to English Affairs, existing in the Archives and Collections of Venice, and in other Libraries of Northern Italy, vol. xiv. 1615–1617, p. 413; Henri Lonchay and Joseph Cuvelier (eds.), *Correspondance de la Cour d'Espagne sur les Affaires des Pays-Bas au XVIIe siècle*, vol. I: Précis de la Correspondance de Philippe III (1598–1621) (Brussels: Librairie Kiessling, 1923), p. 166 (and also p. 173).

127. CM Salisbury (XV, 1930), p. 208.

128. Cited in Edward Edwards, *The Life of Sir Walter Raleigh* (London: Macmillan, 1868), vol. I., p. 375.

129. Philip Gawdy, *Letters of Philip Gawdy of West Harling, Norfolk, and of London to Various Members of his Family 1579–1616*, ed. Isaac Herbert Jeayes (London: Nichols & Sons, 1906), p. 137.

130. *History*, 2.8.2.363.

131. *History*, 4.3.6.221. In this context, see also *History*: 4.4.7.250; 5.6.12.773.

132. CM Bath (II, 1907), p. 51.

133. CM Salisbury (XV, 1930), p. 285.

134. David Jardine (ed.), *Criminal Trials*, 2 vols. (London: Charles Knight, 1832): I.404–7.

135. Cited in Nicholls and Williams, *Sir Walter Raleigh in Life and Legend*, p. 207. See also in this context, Edmund Lodge (ed.), *Illustrations of British History*, esp. pp. 172–3, 215.

136. Cited in Thomas Birch (compiler), *The Court and Times of James the First*, ed. Robert Folkestone Williams (London: Henry Colburn, 1849), vol. I, p. 20. In this context, see also CSP Col. East Indies, China and Japan, 1617–1621, p. 655 (7th July 1586?).

137. CM Salisbury (XVII, 1938), p. 502.

138. CM Salisbury (XVII, 1938), p. 548.

139. Cited in Sir Walter Ralegh, *The Poems of Sir Walter Ralegh*, ed. Agnes M. C. Latham (London: Routledge and Kegan Paul, 1951), p. xxi.

140. CM Salisbury (XX, 1968), p. 270.

141. In this context, CSPM, relating to English Affairs, existing in the Archives and Collections of Venice, and in other Libraries of Northern Italy, vol. xiv: pp. 444, 483–4.

142. Letter to Sir Ralph Winwood 21st March 1618 – unknown to Ralegh, Winwood had died on 27th October 1617. See Philip Edwards (ed.), *Last Voyages: Cavendish, Hudson, Ralegh: The Original Narratives* (Oxford: Clarendon

Press, 1988), pp. 219–20. See also entry 295 – Gregorio Barbarigo, Venetian Ambassador in England, to the Doge and Senate – 28th May 1616, in CSPM, relating to English Affairs, existing in the Archives and Collections of Venice, and in other Libraries of Northern Italy, vol. xiv, p. 210 (see also p. 416).

143. See Edwards, *Last Voyages*, pp. 200–3.

144. *Discouerie*, p. 51.

145. *Discoverie*, p. 51.

146. Letter to Lady Raleigh, 22nd March 1618. See Edwards, *Last Voyages*, p. 225.

147. Letter to Sir Ralph Winwood, 21st March 1618. See Edwards, *Last Voyages*, pp. 221–2.

148. Francis Bacon, *A declaration of the demeanor and cariage of Sir Walter Raleigh* . . . (London: Bonham Norton and John Bill, 1618), p. 48.

149. 'Sir Walter Rawleigh his *Apologie*' circulated in manuscript form and appeared in print for a sympathetic republican audience in such publications as *Judicious and select Essayes*.

150. Earl of Leicester to the Countess of Leicester, 10th September 1618. See RM Viscount L'Isle (V, 1962), p. 418.

151. Chamberlain, *Letters*, vol. II, pp. 177, 178, 185.

152. To Sir Dudley Carleton, London, 31st October 1618. See Chamberlain, *Letters*, vol. II, p. 176.

153. Cited in Anna Beer, *Sir Walter Ralegh and his Readers in the Seventeenth Century* (London: Macmillan, 1997), p. 96.

154. To Sir Dudley Carleton, London, 21st November 1618. See Chamberlain, *Letters*, vol. II, p. 185.

155. To Robert Cecil, 24th January 1597. See Ralegh, *The Letters of Sir Walter Ralegh*, p. 155.

156. *History*, 5.6.12.776.

2 'Undoing all, as all had never been'

1. Languet to Sidney – Frankfort, 28th November 1577. See Sir Philip Sidney/Hubert Languet, *The Correspondence of Sir Philip Sidney and Hubert Languet*, ed. and trans. Steuart A. Pears (London: William Pickering, 1845), p. 127.

2. All references to Ralegh's *The History of the World* are taken from the 1617 edition (London: Walter Burre, 1617 [1614]) and are referenced: Book; Chapter; Section; Page. Here, see Ralegh, *History of the World*: 5.3.8.455.

3. Thomas Nashe, *Pierce Pennilesse* (London: Abell Jeffes for J. Busby, 1592), F3^{r}.

4. Indeed, from the perspective of continental European politics, Rodriguez-Salgado argues that the ongoing political debate at the heart of the Spanish

government concerning the justness of an English invasion specifically involved Philip's 'Lancastrian' claims on the English throne. See M. J. Rodriguez-Salgado, 'The Anglo-Spanish War: The Final Episode in "The Wars of the Roses"?', in M. J. Rodriguez-Salgado and Simon Adams (eds.), *England, Spain and the Gran Armada 1585–1604* (Edinburgh: John Donald Pubs., 1991), pp. 1–44 (p. 12).

5. William Garrard, *The arte of warre ... Corrected and finished by Captaine Hichcock* (London: John Charlewood and William Howe? 1591), p. 2.
6. Letter 31st August 1599. Qtd in Paul A. Jorgensen, *Shakespeare's Military World* (Berkeley/Los Angeles: University of California Press, 1956), p. 157.
7. For a stimulating discussion considering the ways in which Shakespeare's characters exploit the resources of rhetoric in order to face the challenges of trauma, see Raphael Lyne, *Shakespeare, Rhetoric and Cognition* (Cambridge: Cambridge University Press, 2011), esp. pp. 2–3, 47ff.
8. William Camden, *Britain...* (London: Eliot's Court Press, 1610), p. 1.
9. Camden, *Britain*, *4. Such claims were widely in evidence in early modern historical publications. Indeed, Holinshed's *Chronicles*, with which Shakespeare had some detailed acquaintance, were still able to chart (sometimes with anxiety) heroic bloodlines for the Tudor realm, as Laura Ashe points out. See Ashe, 'Holinshed and Mythical History', in Paulina Kewes et al. (eds.), *The Oxford Handbook of Holinshed's Chronicles* (Oxford: Oxford University Press, 2013), pp. 155–69 (p. 169).
10. Camden, *Britain*, p. 34.
11. Camden, *Britain*, p. 63.
12. Qtd in Daniel Woolf, *The Social Circulation of the Past English Historical Culture 1500–1730* (Oxford: Oxford University Press, 2003), p. 23.
13. 'To the Reader', in Camden, *Britain*, *4ᵛ.
14. For further discussion, see Andrew Hiscock, *Reading Memory in Early Modern Literature* (Cambridge: Cambridge University Press, 2011) and 'Debating Early Modern and Modern Memory: Cultural Forms and Effects. A Critical Retrospective', *Memory Studies* 11.1 (2018), 69–84.
15. 'Amiot to the Readers', in Plutarch, *The Lives of the Noble Grecians and Romanes ... into English by Thomas North* (London: Thomas Vautroullier and John Wright, 1579), *3v.
16. Camden, *Britain*, p. 240.
17. Qtd in Keith Dockray, *William Shakespeare. The Wars of the Roses and the Historians* (Stroud: Tempus, 2002), p. 13.
18. Giorgio Agamben, *Homo Sacer. Sovereign Power and Bare Life*, trans. Daniel Heller-Roazen (Stanford, CA: Stanford University Press, 1998), p. 8. In this instance, we may be reminded of the claim in *Richard II*, 'Farewell, my blood;

which if today thou shed,/Lament we may, but not revenge thee dead' (I. iii.57–8).

19. Agamben, *Homo Sacer*, p. 100.

20. M. M. Bakhtin, *The Dialogic Imagination: Fours Essays*, ed. Michael Holquist, trans. Caryl Emerson/Michael Holquist (Austin: Texas University Press, 2001), p. 3.

21. See Mary Warnock, *Memory* (London: Faber and Faber, 1987), p. 27ff.

22. Bakhtin, *The Dialogic Imagination*, p. 21.

23. Robert C. Jones, *These Valiant Dead: Reviewing the Past in Shakespeare's Histories* (Iowa City: University of Iowa Press, 1991), p. ix.

24. René Girard, *La Violence et le sacré* (Paris: Bernard Grasset, 1972), p. 29.

25. Idelber Avelar, *The Letter of Violence. Essays on Narrative, Ethics, and Politics* (Houndmills: Palgrave Macmillan, 2004), p. 30.

26. For further discussion, see Robert Appelbaum, *Terrorism before the Letter* (Oxford: Oxford University Press, 2015), esp. p. 37.

27. Terry Eagleton, *Sweet Violence: The Idea of the Tragic* (Oxford: Blackwell, 2003), pp. xvi, 2.

28. See David Riggs, *Shakespeare's Heroical Histories. 'Henry VI' and its Literary Tradition* (Cambridge, MA: Harvard University Press, 1971), p. 22; Richard Courtney, *Shakespeare's World of War: The Early Histories* (Toronto: Simon & Pierre, 1994), p. 35.

29. Qtd in Jorgensen, *Shakespeare's Military World*, p. 175.

30. Paul Ricoeur, *Temps et récit*, vol. III : 'Le Temps Raconté' (Paris: Seuil, 1985), p. 329.

31. Alberico Gentili, *De Iure Belli Libri Tres*, vol. II: The Translation of the Edition of 1612, trans. John C. Rolfe (Oxford: Clarendon Press, 1933), bk. I, ch. VI, p. 32.

32. Sir Walter Ralegh, *Sir Walter Raleigh's Instructions to his Sonne and to Posterity* (London: Benjamin Fisher, 1632), p. 49.

33. H. M. Richmond, *Shakespeare's Political Plays* (Gloucester, MA: Peter Smith, 1977), p. 37.

34. Ricoeur, *Temps et récit*, vol. I (Paris, Le Seuil, 1983), p. 17.

35. See, respectively: Paola Pugliatti, *Shakespeare and the Just War Tradition* (Farnham: Ashgate, 2010), p. 162; Alexander Leggatt, *Shakespeare's Political Drama. The History Plays and the Roman Plays* (London/New York: Routledge, 1988), p. 5.

36. Rory Rapple, *Martial Power and Elizabethan Political Culture* (Cambridge: Cambridge University Press, 2009), p. 304.

37. Juan Luis Vives, *Vives: On Education. A Translation of 'De Tradendis Disciplinis' of Juan Luis Vives*, trans. and intro. by Foster Watson (Cambridge: Cambridge University Press, 1913), p. 74.

38. Henry Brinkelow, *The lamentacyon of a Christe[n]* ... (London: A. Scoloker/ W. Seres, 1548, 2nd ed.), A2^v.

39. 'The Printer to the Reader', in John Rainolds, *The overthrow of stage-playes* (Oxford: Richard Schilders, 1599), A2^r–A2^v.

40. Gregory M. Colon Semenza, 'Sport, War and Contest in Shakespeare's *Henry VI*', *Renaissance Quarterly*, LIV, 4.1 (Winter 2001), 1251–70 (p. 1251).

41. Sir John Hayward, *The liues of the III. Normans, Kings of England William the first. William the second. Henrie the first* (London: R. Barker, 1613), pp. 62, 63.

42. Letter 60: 'To Sir Robert Cecil from Sherborne, 10 May 1595'. See Sir Walter Ralegh, *The Letters of Sir Walter Ralegh*, eds. Agnes Latham and Joyce Youings (Exeter: University of Exeter Press, 1999), p. 93.

43. Indeed, Peter Lake invites us to see a play such as *1 Henry VI* as offering shrewd insights into the destructive factionalism and failing military campaigns witnessed in late Elizabethan England regarding Leicester divisions with Norris in the Low Countries' campaign in the 1580s, the rivalries between Drake and Norris in the Lisbon 1589 expedition and the 1591–2 siege of Rouen under the command of Essex. See *How Shakespeare Put Politics on the Stage* (New Haven: Yale University Press, 2016), pp. 138–48.

44. Qtd in Curtis C. Breight, *Surveillance, Militarism and Drama in the Elizabethan Era* (Basingstoke: Macmillan, 1996), p. 254. Breight argues at length how the 'Regnum Cecilianum' engineered paranoia in Elizabethan England with its policies of anti-Spanish militarism and its pervasive networks of surveillance at home.

45. Gentili, *De Iure Belli Libri Tres*, trans. Rolfe, vol. II: bk. II, ch. XXI, p. 251.

46. Sir Walter Ralegh, *The discouerie of the large, rich, and bewtiful empire of Guiana* (London: Robert Robinson, 1596), p. 23.

47. [William Caxton], *the cronicles of Englond* (Westminster: William Caxton, 1480), respectively V4^r, V3^r, V4^{r-v}.

48. William Baldwin and others, *The last part of the Mirour for magistrates* (London: Thomas Marsh, 1578), fol. 66r.

49. John Foxe, *Acts and Monuments* (London: John Daye, 1583), p. 729.

50. Nina S. Levine, *Women's Matters: Politics, Gender, and Nation in Shakespeare's Early History Plays* (Newark: University of Delaware Press, 1998), p. 14.

51. Levine, *Women's Matters*, p. 15.

52. Seneca, *Seneca: Moral Essays*, trad. John W. Basore, 3 vols. (London/ New York, William Heinemann/G. P. Putnam, 1928), I:113–15, 185.

53. R. G. Collingwood, *The Principles of Art* (Oxford: Clarendon, 1963. 1st pub. 1938), p. 87.

54. Appelbaum, *Terrorism Before the Letter*, p. 2.

55. Gentili, *De Iure Belli Libri Tres*, trans. Rolfe, vol. II: bk. 1, ch. 18, p. 83.

56. Gail Kern Paster, *The Body Embarrassed: Drama and the Disciplines of Shame in Early Modern England* (New York: Cornell University Press, 1993), pp. 64–112.

57. Gentili, *De Iure Belli Libri Tres*, trans. Rolfe, vol. II: bk. II, ch. XXI, pp. 255, 259.

58. Maurice Charney, 'The Persuasiveness of Violence in Elizabethan Plays', *Renaissance Drama*, II, 1969, 59–70 (p. 63).

59. Garrard, *The arte of warre*, p. 5.

60. Niccolò Machiavelli, *Machivael's discourses* (London: G. Bedell/T. Collins, 1663), pp. 40–1, 42.

61. Robert Greene, *A Groats-worth of Witte* (London: J. Wolfe/J. Danter for William Wright, 1592), F1^{v}.

62. PRO 31/3/29 fol. 220^{r}.

63. Augustine, *Confessions*, trans. Henry Chadwick (Oxford: Oxford University Press/World's Classics, 1998), p. 193 (X.xvi (25)).

64. 'Préface à l'édition française', in Jacques Le Goff, *Histoire et Mémoire* (Paris: Gallimard, 1998), p. 11. Mining a similar vein, Susan Sontag submitted that devotion to the past is 'one of the more disastrous forms of unrequited love'. See 'Unguided tour', in Susan Sontag, *The Susan Sontag Reader*, intro. Elizabeth Hardwick (Harmondsworth: Penguin, 1982 rep.), p. 372.

65. 'Des Menteurs', in Michel de Montaigne, *Essais*, ed. J.-V. Leclerc, vol. I (Paris: Garnier, 1878), I, IX, pp. 25–6.

66. Jean E. Howard and Phyllis Rackin, *Engendering a Nation. A Feminist Account of Shakespeare's English Histories* (London: Routledge, 1997), p. 26.

67. Leggatt, *Shakespeare's Political Drama*, p. 1.

68. See Karl Marx, *Selected Writings*, ed. David McLellan (Oxford: Oxford University Press, 1977), p. 300.

69. In this context, see also Andrew Hiscock, '"More warlike than politique": Shakespeare and the Theatre of War – A Critical Survey', *Shakespeare*, 7.2 (2011), 221–47.

70. Robert, Lord Rich to the Earl of Essex, 3rd October 1596, Rouen. See CSP Salisbury (VI, 1895), p. 415.

71. Maurice Morgann, *An Essay on the Dramatic Character of Sir John Falstaff* (London: for T. Davies, 1777), p. 49.

72. Anthologised in Steven W. May, *The Elizabethan Courtier Poets: The Poems and their Contexts* (Asheville, NC: University of North Carolina/Pegasus Press, 1999), p. 252.

73. Thomas Churchyard, *Fortunate Farewell to the most forward and noble Earle of Essex* (London: Edmund Bollifant for William Wood, 1599), A2^{r}.

74. Walter Benjamin, *Illuminations*, trans. Harry Zohn (New York: Schocken, 1969), p. 255.

75. See, respectively: M. M. Reese, *The Cease of Majesty. A Study of Shakespeare's History Plays* (London: Edward Arnold, 1961), p. 165; Robert Ornstein, *A Kingdom for a Stage. The Achievement of Shakespeare's History Plays* (Cambridge, MA: Harvard University Press, 1972), p. 6.
76. Fulke Greville, *The Prose Works of Fulke Greville, Lord Brooke* (Oxford: Clarendon Press, 1986), pp. 47–8.
77. 'Entre Mémoire et Histoire', in Pierre Nora, *Les Lieux de Mémoire*, vol. I (Paris: Editions Gallimard, 1984), pp. xx, xxi.
78. John Turner, 'Introduction', in Graham Holderness, Nick Potter and John Turner, *Shakespeare: The Play of History* (Basingstoke: Macmillan, 1987), p. 3.
79. Emmanuel Lévinas, *Humanisme de l'Autre Homme* (Paris: Fata Morgana, 1972), p. 26.
80. Emmanuel Lévinas, *Altérité et Transcendence* (Paris: Fata Morgana, 1995).
81. William Tyndale, *The Obedience of a Christen Man* (Antwerp: J. Hoochstraten, 1528), E1ᵛ.

3 In the Realm of the 'unthankful King': Violent Subjects and Subjectivities in the *Henry IV* Plays

1. September/October 1561: Elizabeth to William Maitland. See Elizabeth I, *Collected Works*, ed. Leah S. Marcus, Janel Mueller and Mary Beth Rose (Chicago/London: University of Chicago Press, 2000), p. 66.
2. Plutarch, *The fourth volume of Plutarch's Lives...* (London: Jacob Tonson, 1693), p. 100.
3. E. K. Chambers, *William Shakespeare* (Oxford: Clarendon Press, 1930), II.326. For further discussion, see Chapter 6, note 19.
4. Chambers, *William Shakespeare*, I.353.
5. For further discussion of the intimate relations between the expression of political authority and violence in the early modern period, see, for example: Carole Levin and Joseph P. Ward, 'Introduction', in Joseph P. Ward (ed.), *Violence, Politics, and Gender in Early Modern England* (Basingstoke: Palgrave Macmillan, 2008), pp. 1–13; Myron C. Noonkester, 'Power of the County: Sheriffs and Violence in Early Modern England', in Ward, *Violence, Politics, and Gender*, pp. 147–71.
6. See Samuel Johnson, *Samuel Johnson on Shakespeare*, ed. H. R. Woudhuysen (Harmondsworth: Penguin, 1989), p. 202.
7. Languet to Sidney, 24th December 1573. See Sir Philip Sidney/Hubert Languet, *The Correspondence of Sir Philip Sidney and Hubert Languet*, ed. and trans. Steuart A. Pears (London: William Pickering, 1845), p. 19. See also ibid., p. 10.

8. For further discussion, see Mary Thomas Crane, '"Video et Taceo": Elizabeth I and the Rhetoric of Counsel', *Studies in English Literature*, 28 (1988), 1–15.

9. *The Second volume of Chronicles* (London: Henry Denham, 1586), p. 26.

10. 'Preface', in Sir Walter Ralegh, *The History of the World* (London: Walter Burre, 1634 [1614]), C4ᵛ.

11. Yves-Alain Michaud, *La Violence* (Paris: Presses Universitaires de France, 1973), p. 7.

12. See Hannah Arendt, *On Violence* (Orlando, FL: Harvest/Harcourt, 1970), p. 53: 'Violence can always destroy power; out of the barrel of a gun grows the most effective command, resulting in the most instant and perfect obedience. What never can grow out of it is power.'

13. Albert. S. G. Canning, *Thoughts on Shakespeare's Historical Plays* (London: W. H. Allen, 1884), p. 127.

14. A notable example which contradicts this critical movement is Anne-Marie McNamara's article '*Henry IV*: The King as Protagonist', *Shakespeare Quarterly*, 10(Summer 1959), 3, 423–31.

15. See respectively: Alan Bray, *Homosexuality in Renaissance England* (London: Gay Man's Press, 1988 rep. 1982), p. 51 (Bray added importantly, 'it was not the only one'); Lawrence Stone, *The Crisis of the Aristocracy 1558–1641* (Oxford: Oxford University Press, 1967), p. 271.

16. See Harry Berger Jr., *Making Trifles of Terrors: Redistributing Complicities in Shakespeare* (Stanford: Stanford University Press, 1997), p. 151.

17. Sigmund Freud, *Civilization and Its Discontents*, trans. Joan Rivieres (London: Hogarth Press, 1973), p. 14.

18. John F. Danby, *Shakespeare's Doctrine of Nature: A Study of King Lear* (London: Faber & Faber, 1949), p. 86.

19. Paul Ricoeur, *The Reality of the Historical Past* (Milwaukee: Marquette University Press, 1984), p. 26.

20. The Petition continues, 'till your most noble progenitors King Henry VII and Lady Elizabeth his wife restored it to settled unity and left the crown in certain course of succession'. See Elizabeth I, *Collected Works*, p. 74.

21. Blair Worden, *The Sound of Virtue: Philip Sidney's 'Arcadia' and Elizabethan Politics* (New Haven/London: Yale University Press, 1996), p. 43.

22. Sir Philip Sidney, *The Prose Works of Sir Philip Sidney*, 4 vols., ed. Albert Feuillerat (Cambridge: Cambridge University Press, rep. 1968, 1st pub. 1912), vol. III: '*The Defence of Poesie*, Political Discourses, Correspondence, Translation', p. 167.

23. See John Lyly, *The Complete Works of John Lyly*, ed. R. Warwick Bond, 3 vols. (Oxford: Clarendon Press, 1902): I.70–1.

24. CM Salisbury (IV, 1892), p. 151.

25. Sir John Harington, *Nugae Antiquae*, 2 vols. (Bath: for W. Frederick, 1769): I.46.
26. CM Salisbury (VII, 1899), p. 108.
27. Qtd in Natalie Mears, 'Regnum Cecilianum? A Cecilian Perspective of the Court', in John Guy (ed.), *The Reign of Elizabeth I: Court and Culture in the Last Decade* (Cambridge: Cambridge University Press, 1995), pp. 46–64 (p. 50).
28. Humfrey Barwick, *A breefe discourse* (London: E. Allde for Richard Oliffe, 1592), B1^v–B2^r.
29. Braddick adds, 'Other kinds of power may have one or more of these qualities, but political power is unique in its combination of all three.' See Michael J. Braddick, *State Formation in Early Modern England c. 1550–1700* (Cambridge: Cambridge University Press, 2000), p. 9.
30. See E. A. Rauchut, 'Hotspur's Prisoners and the Laws of War in *1 Henry IV*', *Shakespeare Quarterly*, 45.1 (Spring 1994), 96–7 (p. 97).
31. Niccolò Machiavelli, *The Art of War*, trans. & ed. Christopher Lynch (Chicago: University of Chicago Press, 2003), p. 14.
32. Cynthia Marshall, *The Shattering of the Self: Violence, Subjectivity, and Early Modern Texts* (Baltimore: Johns Hopkins University Press, 2002), p. 21.
33. Sigurd Burkhardt, *Shakespearean Meanings* (Princeton, NJ: Princeton University Press, 1968), p. 150.
34. Alberico Gentili, *De Iure Belli Libri Tres*, trans. John C. Rolfe, vol. II (Oxford: Clarendon Press, 1933), p. 236.
35. Edmund Spenser, *The Faerie Queene*, ed. A. C. Hamilton et al. (London: Routledge, 2013), p. 716.
36. Robert Barret, *The theorike and practike of moderne warres* (London: Richard Field for William Ponsonby, 1598), p. 171.
37. Richard Crompton, *The mansion of magnanimitie* (London: Richard Field for William Ponsonby, 1599), F4^r.
38. See James Raymond, *Henry VIII's Military Revolution: The Armies of Sixteenth-Century Britain and Europe* (London: Tauris, 2007), p. 9. See also Steven Gunn, *The English People at War in the Age of Henry VIII* (Oxford: Oxford University Press, 2018), p. 5.
39. Raymond, *Henry VIII's Military Revolution*, p. 9.
40. Paul E. J. Hammer, *Elizabeth's Wars: War, Government and Society in Tudor England, 1544–1604* (Basingstoke: Palgrave, 2003), pp. 5–6.
41. *The Historie of the raigne of King Henry the seventh*, in Francis Bacon, *The Historie of the raigne of King Henry the seventh and other works of the 1620s*, The Oxford Francis Bacon, vol. VIII, ed. Michael Kiernan (Oxford: Clarendon Press, 2012), pp. 164, 167, 168.
42. Gentili, *De Iure Belli Libri Tres*, p. 165.

43. Huston Diehl, 'The Iconography of Violence in English Renaissance Tragedy', *Renaissance Drama*, XI, 1980, 27–44 (p. 35).

44. Jean Piaget, *The Child's Conception of Time* (New York: Basic Books, 1970), p. 6.

45. Berber Bevernage, *History, Memory, and State-Sponsored Violence: Time and Justice* (New York: Routledge/Taylor & Francis, 2012), p. 2.

46. Michel de Certeau, *Histoire et psychanalyse entre science et fiction* (Paris: Gallimard, 1987), p. 97.

47. Mark Fissel, *English Warfare 1511–1642* (London: Routledge, 2001), p. 96.

48. 'Sir John Smythe his Proëme Dedicatorie to the Nobilitie of the Realme of England', in Sir John Smythe, *Certain discourses* (London: Thomas Orwin for Richard Jones, 1590), A1^r.

49. William Garrard, *The arte of warre* (London: John Charlewood and Richard Howe? for Roger Warde, 1591), p. 145.

50. Geffrey Gates, *The defence of militarie profession* (London: Henry Middleton for John Harrison, 1579), p. 36.

51. F. J. Fisher (ed.), 'The State of England, Anno Domini 1600', *Camden Miscellany*, 3rd Series, III (1936), p. 36.

52. André Hurault de Maisse, *A Journal of All That Was Accomplished by Monsieur de Maisse, Ambassador in England*, ed. G. B. Harrison and R. A. Jones (London: Nonesuch Press, 1931), p. 109.

53. Hammer, *Elizabeth's Wars*, p. 66. See also David R. Lawrence, *The Complete Soldier: Military Books and Military Culture in Early Stuart England, 1603–1645* (Leiden: Brill, 2009), p. 31.

54. John R. Hale, *War and Society in Renaissance Europe 1450–1620* (Leicester: Leicester University Press/Fontana, 1985), p. 78.

55. Qtd in Nick de Somogyi, *Shakespeare's Theatre of War* (Aldershot: Ashgate, 1998), p. 108.

56. Thomas Barnes, *Vox Belli, or, An Alarvm to Warre* (London: H. Lownes for Nathanael Newbury, 1626), p. 14.

57. Garrard, *The arte of warre*, p. 32.

58. Ordering Musters – Richmond, 31st December 1590. See Paul L. Hughes and James F. Larkin (eds.), *Tudor Royal Proclamations. Volume III: The Later Tudors (1588–1603)* (New Haven/London: Yale University Press, 1969), p. 63.

59. Derek Cohen, *Shakespeare's Culture of Violence* (Basingstoke: Macmillan/St. Martin's Press, 1993), p. 7.

60. See, respectively: Johnson, *Samuel Johnson on Shakespeare*, p. 203; Freud, *Civilization and Its Discontents*, p. 12.

61. Garrard, *The arte of warre*, p. 149.

62. Jean E. Howard and Phyllis Rackin, *Engendering a Nation: A Feminist Account of Shakespeare's English Histories* (London: Routledge, 1997), p. 165.

63. Cohen, *Shakespeare's Culture of Violence*, p. 6.
64. Falstaff is naturally well able also to identify the protean qualities of others through equally eloquent invective. See, for example, IVᵗ: II.iv.203–6.
65. Jean Bodin, *The six bookes of a common-weale . . . done into English, by Richard Knolles* (London: Adam Islip, 1606), p. 2.
66. Johnson, *Samuel Johnson on Shakespeare*, p. 203.
67. W. H. Auden, 'The Fallen City: Some Reflections on Shakespeare's *Henry IV*', *Encounter* 13.5 (November 1959), 21–31 (p. 21).
68. C. L. Barber, *Shakespeare's Festive Comedy* (Princeton, NJ: Princeton University Press, 1959), p. 192.
69. 'Introduction', in R. J. Dorius (ed.), *Twentieth-Century Interpretations of Henry IV Part One* (Englewood Cliffs, NJ: Prentice-Hall Inc., 1970), 1–11 (p. 2).
70. Sir Walter Ralegh, *Sir Walter Raleigh's Instructions to his Sonne and to Posterity* (London: Benjamin Fisher, 1632), pp. 1–2.
71. Barnabe Rich, *Allarm to England* (London: Henry Middleton for C. Barker, 1578), F3ᵛ.
72. William Shakespeare, *The First Part of King Henry IV*, ed. Herbert Weil and Judith Weil (Cambridge: Cambridge University Press, 1997), p. 10.
73. Arendt, *On Violence*, p. 79.
74. Georg Simmel, *'Conflict'* and *'The Web of Group-Affiliations'*, trans. respectively Kurt H. Wolff and Reinhard Bendix (New York: Free Press of Glencoe, 1955), p. 19.
75. Christopher Highley, 'Defining the Nation', anthologised in William Shakespeare, *The First Part of Henry IV*, ed. Gordon McMullan (New York: W. W. Norton, 2003), pp. 433–52 (p. 445).
76. Richard C. McCoy, *The Rites of Knighthood: The Literature and Politics of Elizabethan Chivalry* (Berkeley: University of California Press, 1989), p. 19.
77. Robert Devereux, *An apologie of the Earle of Essex* (London: for J. Smethwick? 1600), A3ᵛ.
78. Stuart Henry, 'What Is School Violence? An Integrated Definition', *Annals of the American Academy of Political and Social Science*, 567 (2000), 16–30 (p. 20).
79. *A Myrrour for English Souldiers* (London: V. Sims for Nicholas Ling, 1595), B1ᵛ.
80. *A Myrrour for English Souldiers*, D2ʳ.
81. Gentili, *De Iure Belli Libri Tres*, pp. 145, 231.
82. Jean-Marie Domenach, 'Un monde de violence', *Recherches et Débats: La Violence*, 16.9 (1967), 30–7 (p. 31).
83. Domenach, 'Un monde de violence', p. 31.
84. Stephen Greenblatt, '"Invisible Bullets": Renaissance Authority and its Subversion, Henry IV and Henry V', in Jonathan Dollimore and

Alan Sinfield (eds.), *Political Shakespeare: Essays in Cultural Materialism* (Manchester: Manchester University Press, 2003), pp. 18–47 (p. 30).

85. Freud, *Civilization and Its Discontents*, p. 40.

86. Thomas Churchyard, *A generall rehearsall of warres* (London: John Kingston for Edward White, 1579), *3r.

87. Gentili, *De Iure Belli Libri Tres*, p. 149.

88. Roger Ascham, *Toxophilus* (London: Edward Whitchurch, 1545), 38ᵛ.

89. Highley, 'Defining the Nation', p. 443.

90. Ascham, *Toxophilus*, B1ʳ.

91. Theodor Meron, *Bloody Constraint: War and Chivalry in Shakespeare* (New York/Oxford: Oxford University Press, 1998), p. 8. See also Meron's *Henry's Wars and Shakespeare's Laws: Perspectives on the Law of War in the Later Middle Ages* (Oxford: Clarendon Press, 1993).

92. Sergei Karcevskij, 'The Asymmetric Dualism of the Linguistic Sign', in Peter Steiner (ed.), *The Prague School: Selected Writings 1929–1946*, trans. John Burbank et al. (Austin, TX: University of Texas Press, 1982), pp. 47–54 (p. 50).

93. 'Introduction', in David P. Young (ed.), *Twentieth-Century Interpretations of Henry IV Part Two* (Englewood Cliffs, NJ: Prentice-Hall Inc., 1968), p. 1.

94. Aristotle, *Aristotles politiques* (London: Adam Islip, 1598), C2ᵛ–C3ʳ.

95. Jonas A. Barish, 'The Turning Away of Prince Hal', in Dorius, *Twentieth-Century Interpretations of Henry IV Part One*, 83–8 (p. 83).

96. Nigel Wood (ed.), *Henry IV Parts One and Two* (Buckingham: Open University Press, 1995), p. 14. See also Howard and Rackin, *Engendering a Nation*, p. 166.

97. Michaud, *La Violence*, p. 5.

98. Zygmunt Bauman, *Liquid Times: Living in an Age of Uncertainty* (Cambridge: Polity Press, 2007), pp. 6–7.

99. Auden, 'The Fallen City', p. 22.

4 'Now thrive the armourers'

1. Edward Hall, *The vnion of the two noble and illustre famelies of Lancastre [and] Yorke* (London: Richard Grafton, 1548), F1ᵛ.

2. For a wide-ranging discussion of these texts, see Antonia Gransden, *Historical Writing in England c. 1307 to the Early Sixteenth Century* (London: Routledge, 1996), p. 194ff.

3. Here quoted from John Lydgate, *The auncient historie and onely trewe and syncere cronicle of the warres betwixte the Grecians and the* (London: Thomas Marshe, 1555), EE2ᵛ.

4. Anon., *Here after foloweth ye batayll of Egyngecourte [and] the great sege of Rone by kynge Henry of Monmouthe the fyfthe of the name that wan Gascoyne and Gyenne and Normandye* (London: John Skot, 1536?), A1[r].

5. Source text: 'unicum id temporis decus et lumen patriae, quo nemo vir animi celsitate et magnitudine ac virtute clarior natus, nemo pietate praestantior, cuius desiderium etiam nunc apud mortales pariter permanet atque a principio apud suos fuit'. For these parallel neo-Latin and English translation texts from the close of chapter XXII in Vergil's *Anglica Historia*, see www.philological.bham.ac.uk/polverg/ (accessed 28.8.2012).

6. Roger Ascham, *Toxophilus* (London: Edward Whytchurch, 1545), p. 40.

7. William Allen [R. Dol[e]man], *A conference about the next succession to the crowne of Ingland* (Antwerp: A. Conincx, 1595), p. 134. Allen insists that 'that this was neuer donne to any Prince before king Henry the fift' (p. 120). This statement is also taken up by Robert Fletcher in *The nine English worthies* (London: Humphrey Lownes for John Harrison, 1606), p. 13. However, such statements were refuted by others, such as the historian Sir John Hayward in *An answer to the first part of a certaine conference, concerning succession, published not long since vnder the name of R. Dolman* (London: Eliot's Court Press, 1603), O3[v]. Hayward goes onto cite instances concerning kings John, Henry III and Edward III.

8. Hugh Holland, *Pancharis the first booke* (London: V. Sims for Clement Knight, 1603), C1[v].

9. Fletcher, *The nine English worthies*, pp. 19, 21.

10. Michael Drayton, *Poly-Olbion* (London: Humphrey Lownes, 1612), p. 19.

11. Michael Drayton, *A paean triumphall* (London: Felix Kingston, 1604), A4[v].

12. See, respectively: Richard Hakluyt, *The principal nauigations* (London: George Bishop, Ralph Newberie and Robert Barker, 1599–1600), p. 203; Henry Haslop, *Newes out of the coast of Spaine* (London: W. How, 1587), B2[r].

13. For further discussion of Shakespeare's portrayal of the Lancastrians' need to affirm legitimate control of the throne and Henry's changing function in this narrative, see, for example: Sigurd Burckhardt, *Shakespearean Meanings* (Princeton, NJ: Princeton University Press, 1968), p. 161; Phyllis Rackin, *Stages of History. Shakespeare's English Chronicles* (London: Routledge, 1990), p. 78.

14. Quoted here and below from Richard Knolles's seventeenth-century translation, Jean Bodin, *The six bookes of a common-weale. Written by I. Bodin ... done into English, by Richard Knolles* (London: Adam Islip, 1606), p. 599.

15. For an example of this narrative as applied to Donne, for example, see Andrew Hiscock, *Reading Memory in Early Modern Literature* (Cambridge: Cambridge University Press, 2011), p. 165ff.

16. Leonard and Thomas Digges, *An arithmeticall militare treatise, named Stratioticos* (London: Henry Bynneman, 1579), p. 137.

17. William Caxton, *the cronicles of Englond* (London: William Caxton, 1480), ii5^r.

18. Source text: 'Hic vir, hic fuit, qui a primo docuit honores, ut est in proverbio, debere mutare mores, quippe qui statim est rex factus, statuens alio atque habebat vitae instituto sibi utendum.' For these parallel neo-Latin and English translation texts from the beginning of chapter XXII in Vergil's *Anglica Historia*, see www .philological.bham.ac.uk/polverg/ (accessed 28.8.2012).

19. William Martyn, *Youths Instruction* (London: John Beale, 1612), p. 38.

20. Samuel Johnson, *Samuel Johnson on Shakespeare*, ed. H. R. Woudhuysen (Harmondsworth: Penguin, 1989), p. 210.

21. See Paul L. Hughes and James F. Larkin (eds.), *Tudor Royal Proclamations. Volume III: the Later Tudors (1588–1603)* (New Haven/London: Yale University Press, 1969), p. 46.

22. Mark Van Doren, *Shakespeare* (London: George Allen & Unwin, 1941), p. 171. In this context of assessing choric interventions in early modern drama, see also Andrew Hiscock, '*Pericles, Prince of Tyre* and the Appetite for Narrative', in Andrew J. Power and Rory Loughnane (eds.), *Late Shakespeare, 1608–1613* (Cambridge: Cambridge University Press, 2012), pp. 16–35.

23. Larry S. Champion, *Perspective in Shakespeare's English Histories* (Athens, GA: University of Georgia Press, 1980), p. 153.

24. Graham Holderness, Nick Potter and John Turner, *Shakespeare: The Play of History* (Houndmills: Macmillan, 1987), p. 62. See also Norman Rabkin, 'Rabbits, Ducks, and *Henry V*', *Shakespeare Quarterly*, 28.3 (Summer 1977), 279–96 (p. 279).

25. Johnson, *Samuel Johnson on Shakespeare*, p. 211.

26. Willem Schinkel, *Aspects of Violence: A Critical Theory* (Houndmills: Palgrave Macmillan, 2010), p. 45.

27. Nicholas Grene, *Shakespeare's Serial History Plays* (Cambridge: Cambridge University Press, 2002), p. 65.

28. George Whetstone, *The honorable reputation of a souldier* (London: Richard Jones, 1585), F1^{r-v}.

29. Henri Bergson, *Le Rire, essai sur la signification du comique* (Paris: Félix Alcan, 1911), p. 39.

30. *A Myrrour for English Souldiers* (London: V. Sims for Nicholas Ling, 1595), B1^r.

31. James Achesone, *The military garden* (Edinburgh: John Wreittoun, 1629), *2^r.

32. C. L. Kingsford, 'The first version of Harding's Chronicle', *English Historical Review*, XXVII (1912), 462–82, 740–53 (p. 744).

33. Jean Bodin, *The Six Bookes of a Commonweale ... Out of the French and Latine Copies, done into English, by Richard Knolles* (London: Adam Islip, 1606), p. 636.

34. Alberico Gentili, *De Iure Belli Libri Tres*, trans. John C. Rolfe, v. II (Oxford: Clarendon Press, 1933): 1.7. (p. 34). See also *A Myrrour for English Souldiers*, B1^r.

35. Kristin M. S. Bezio notes that 'of the three kings in the Henriad, only Henry V does not face open rebellion'. See *Staging Power in Tudor and Stuart English History Plays* (Farnham: Ashgate, 2015), p. 119.

36. William Garrard, *The arte of warre...* (London: John Charlewood and William Howe [?], 1591), p. 240.

37. In this context, see Stephen Greenblatt, '"Invisible Bullets": Renaissance Authority and its Subversion, *Henry IV* and *Henry V*', in Jonathan Dollimore and Alan Sinfield (eds.), *Political Shakespeare: Essays in Cultural Materialism* (Manchester: Manchester University Press, 2003), pp. 18–47; David J. Baker, '"Wildehirissheman": Colonialist Representation in Shakespeare's *Henry V*', in R. J. C. Watt (ed.), *Shakespeare's History Plays* (London: Longman/Pearson Education, 2002), pp. 193–203.

38. Many critical studies point out that the first Quarto of *Henry V* is a substantially shorter text and fails to include, for example, any of the Chorus's speeches.

39. *A Myrrour for English Souldiers*, D1^v.

40. William Shakespeare, *King Henry V*, ed. John H. Walter (London: Methuen/ Arden, rep. 1979), p. xxv.

41. 'Useless Suffering', in *The Provocation of Levinas: Rethinking the Other*, ed. R. Bernesconi and David Wood (London: Routledge, 1988), p. 163.

42. Gentili, *De Iure Belli Libri Tres*, trans. Rolfe: 1.25. (p. 126).

43. Cynthia Marshall, *The Shattering of the Self: Violence, Subjectivity, and Early Modern Texts* (Baltimore: Johns Hopkins University Press, 2002), pp. 2–3.

44. John Norden, *A pensiue soules delight* (London: Will Stansby for John Busby, 1615), p. 324.

45. Thomas Hobbes, *Leviathan* (London: for Andrew Crooke, 1651): XIII.62.

46. Paul Ricoeur, 'Violence et Langage', *Recherches et Débats: La Violence*, 16.9 (1967), 86–94 (p. 87).

47. Jean Bodin, *The six bookes of a common-weale* (London: Adam Islip, 1606), p. 598.

48. Georges Sorel, *Reflections on Violence*, trans. T. E. Hulme and J. Roth, intro. Edward A. Shils (Glencoe, IL: The Free Press, 1950), p. 71.

49. Thomas Barnes, *Vox Belli, or, An Alarvm to Warre* (London: Humphrey Lownes, 1626), p. 29.

50. The point is made equally vigorously by the Archbishop in *The Famous Victories* (London: Thomas Creede, 1598), D2^r.

51. In this context, see Wolfgang Iser, *Staging Politic:. The Lasting Impact of Shakespeare's Histories*, trans. David Henry Wilson (New York: Columbia University Press, 1993), p. 138.

52. John Taylor, *A briefe remembrance of all the English monarchs, from the Normans conquest, vntill this present* (London: George Eld, 1618), s.p. See verse in section entitled 'Henry the Fift'.

53. Idelber Avelar, *The Letter of Violence: Essays on Narrative, Ethics, and Politics* (Houndmills: Palgrave Macmillan, 2004), p. 2.

54. Judith Butler, *Frames of War: When is Life Grievable* (London/New York: Verso, 2010), p. xix.

55. Barnes, *Vox Belli*, p. 27.

56. Abraham Gibson, *Christiana-Polemica, or A preparatiue to warre* (London: Edward Griffin, 1619), p. 26.

57. Leonard and Thomas Digges, *Stratioticos*, p. 137.

58. For an illuminating discussion of the medieval affirmation of military triumph as divine volition, see Christopher Allmand, 'The Reporting of War in the Middle Ages', in Diana Dunn (ed.), *War and Society in Medieval and Early Modern Britain* (Liverpool: Liverpool University Press, 2000), pp. 17–33.

59. Geffrey Gates, *The defence of militarie profession* (London: Henry Middleton, 1579), p. 37.

60. Leonard Wright, *The hunting of Antichrist* (London: John Wolfe, 1589), p. 14.

61. A. C. Bradley, *Oxford Lectures on Poetry* (London: Macmillan, 1909), p. 257.

62. Louis B. Wright (ed.), *Advice to a Son: Precepts of Lord Burghley, Sir Walter Raleigh, and Francis Osborne* (New York: Folger Shakespeare Library/Cornell University Press, 1962), p. 11.

63. Francisco de Valdés *Espeio y deceplina militar* (Brussels, 1589), fol. 40^{v}. Quoted in John A. Lynn II, *Women, Armies, and Warfare in Early Modern Europe* (Cambridge: Cambridge University Press, 2008), p. 41.

64. John Norden, *The mirror of honor* (London: widowe Orwin for Thomas Man, 1597), p. 12.

65. Gentili, *De Iure Belli Libri Tres*, trans. Rolfe: 2.16 (p. 210).

66. Gentili, *De Iure Belli Libri Tres*, trans. Rolfe: 2.21 (p. 251). See also ibid., 2.16 (pp. 211–12).

67. In this context, see the following illuminating discussions of early modern sources for this narrative which both did and did not come before Shakespeare's eyes: William Shakespeare, *King Henry V*, ed. Andrew Gurr (Cambridge: Cambridge University Press, 1992), p. 26ff; Matthew Woodcock, *Shakespeare*

Henry V: A Reader's Guide to Essential Criticism (Houndmills: Palgrave Macmillan, 2008), p. 14ff.

68. John Masefield, *William Shakespeare* (London: Holt & Co., 1911), p.121.

69. Robert Barret, *The Theorike and Practike of Moderne Warres* (London: Richard Field, 1598), p. 11.

70. Butler, *Frames of War*, p. 42.

71. Richard Crompton, *The mansion of magnanimitie* (London: Richard Field, 1599), A4^v.

72. Thomas Churchyard, *A generall rehearsall of warres* (London: John Kingston for Edward White, 1579), *2^v–*3^r.

73. Johnson, *Samuel Johnson on Shakespeare*, p. 210.

74. Rabkin, 'Rabbits, Ducks, and *Henry V*', p. 288.

75. Gentili, *De Iure Belli Libri Tres*, trans. Rolfe: 3.13 (p. 353).

76. Thomas Aquinas, 'Commentary on *On Memory and Recollection*', in *Commentaries on Aristotle's 'On Sense and What is Sensed' and 'On Memory and Recollection'*, trans. Kevin White and Edward M. Macierowski (Washington, DC: Catholic University of America Press, 2005), pp. 169–235 (p. 184).

77. Walter Ralegh, *The History of the World* (London: Walter Burre, 1634 [1614]): 2.21.6.458.

78. Michel Foucault, *'Society Must Be Defended': Lectures at the Collège de France 1975-1976*, ed. Mauro Bertani and Alessandro Fontana, trans. David Macey (New York: Picador, 1997), p. 68.

79. Rackin, *Stages of History*, p. 80.

80. Raphael Holinshed, *The Third volume of Chronicles* (London: Henry Denham, 1586), p. 583.

81. Thomas Carlyle, *On Heroes, Hero-Worship, and the Heroic in History* (London: James Fraser, 1841), p. 178.

82. William Hazlitt, *Characters of Shakespear's Plays & Lectures on the English Poets* (London: Macmillan & Co., 1903), p. 127.

83. A. C. Bradley, *Oxford Lectures on Poetry* (London: Macmillan, 1926), p. 256.

84. J. C. Bromley, *The Shakespearian Kings* (Boulder, CO: Colorado University Press, 1971), p. 123.

85. Paul Ricoeur, *Memory, History, Forgetting*, trans. Kathleen Blamey and David Pellauer (Chicago/London: University of Chicago Press, 2004), p. 503.

86. Lancelot Andrewes, *The Works of Lancelot Andrewes*, ed. J. P. Wilson and James Bliss (Oxford: J. H. Parker, 1841): 1.325.

87. Qtd in J. E. Neale, *Elizabeth I and Her Parliaments, 1584–1601* (London: Cape, 1957), pp. 309–10.

5 'the childe of his great Mistris favour, but the sonne of *Bellona*': The Conflict-Ridden Careers of Robert Devereux, 2nd Earl of Essex

1. Languet to Sidney, 15th February 1578. See Sir Philip Sidney/Hubert Languet, *The Correspondence of Sir Philip Sidney and Hubert Languet*, ed. and trans. Steuart A. Pears (London: William Pickering, 1845), p. 137.

2. On the enduring significance of chivalric ideals in modes of Elizabethan military command, see David J. B. Trim, 'The Context of War and Violence in Sixteenth-Century English Society', *Journal of Early Modern History* 3.3 (1999), 233–55 (p. 235); Steven Gunn, David Grummitt and Hans Cools, *War, State, and Society in England and the Netherlands 1477–1559* (Oxford: Oxford University Press, 2007), pp. 20, 127–8; Mark Fissel, *English Warfare 1511–1642* (London: Routledge, 2016, 1st pub. 2001), pp. 165–6.

3. Sidney to Languet, 4th February 1574. See Sidney/Languet, *Correspondence*, p. 28.

4. Robert Sidney to Sir Henry Sidney, 1st November 1580. See RM Lord L'Isle (II, 1934), p. 95.

5. See, respectively: Sir John Ferne, *The blazon of gentrie* (London: John Windet for Andrew Maunsell, 1586), p. 37; Barnabe Rich, *A souldiers wishe to Britons welfare* (London: T. Creed for Geoffrey Chorlton, 1604), p. 4.

6. Du Plessis-Mornay à Monsieur de Walsingham, January 1987. See Philippe du Plessis-Mornay, *Mémoires et Correspondance*, ed. A.–D. de La Fontenelle de Vaudoré and P.-R. Auguis, 12 vols. (Geneva: Slatkine, 1969): III.488, no. xcii.

7. Sidney bequeathed his other 'best' sword to Lord Willoughby. See Sir Philip Sidney, *The Prose Works of Sir Philip Sidney*, ed. Albert Feuillerat (Cambridge: Cambridge University Press, 1923): III.316.

8. For further discussion, see Paul E. J. Hammer, *The Polarisation of Elizabethan Politics. The Political Career of Robert Devereux, 2nd Earl of Essex, 1585–1597* (Cambridge: Cambridge University Press, 1999), pp. 53–4.

9. See, respectively: Anon., *Academiae Cantabrigiensis lachrymae tumulo nobilissimi equitis, D. Philippi Sidneij* (London: John Windet, 1587); British Library MS Additional 4125, 164^r, qtd in Maureen Claire King, '"Essex, that could vary himself into all shapes for a time": The Second Earl of Essex in Jacobean England', PhD thesis, University of Alberta, 2000, p. 17. King's discussion of James VI/I's responses to Essex (and of Carleton's *Devoraxeidos* in particular) is thorough and illuminating in this thesis.

10. See Francesco Colonna, *Hypnerotomachia: The strife of loue in a dreame* (London: Abell Jeffes, John Charlewood, and Eliot's Court Press, 1592), A2^r.

11. Essex to De La Noue, December 1589. See CM Salisbury (III, 1889), p. 445. Philip Sidney corresponded with De La Noue, and the Frenchman met Robert during his European tour in the late 1570s. See Philip Sidney, *The*

Correspondence of Sir Philip Sidney, ed. Roger Kuin (Oxford: Oxford University Press, 2012): I.892; David R. Lawrence, *The Complete Soldier: Military Books and Military Culture in Early Stuart England, 1603–1645* (Leiden: Brill, 2009), p. 60.

12. George Peele, *An Eglogve Gratvlatorie* (London: John Windet, 1589), A3^v, A4^r. In this context, see Hugh Gazzard, '"Many a Herdsman More Disposde to Mourn": Peele, Campion and the Portugal Expedition of 1589', *Review of English Studies*, 57 (2006), 16–42.

13. *Polyhymnia*, in George Peele, *The Life and Minor Works of George Peele*, 3 vols., ed. David H. Horne (New Haven: Yale University Press, 1952): I.235-236.

14. Roger B. Manning, *Swordsmen: The Martial Ethos in the Three Kingdoms* (Oxford: Oxford University Press, 2003), p. 7.

15. Sir Thomas Smith, *Sir Thomas Smithes voiage and entertainment in Rushia* (London: W. White & W. Jaggard, 1605), D3^v–D4^r. In this context, see also Gervase Markham, *Honour in his Perfection* (London: B. Alsop for Benjamin Fisher, 1624), p. 27.

16. PRO 31/3/29: André Hurault, Sieur de Maisse, *Journal de tout ce qu'a fact Monsr. de Maisse Ambassadeur du Roy en Angleterre vers la Reyne Elisabeth...*, 201^{r-v}.

17. Sir Robert Naunton, *Fragmenta regalia* (London: s. p., 1641), p. 35.

18. Jean Correro, *Relazione del clarissimo Signor Giovanni Corero, Ambasciator in Francia nell'anno 1569*, in M. N. Tommaseo (ed.), *Relations des Ambassadeurs Vénitiens sur les affaires de France au XVIe siècle*, vol.II (Paris: Imprimerie Royale, 1838), pp. 156, 175–6.

19. Manning, *Swordsmen*, p. 35.

20. Giroloamo Lippomano, *Viaggio del Signor Girolamo Lippomano, ambasciator in Francia nell'anno 1577, scritto dal suo segretario*, in Tommaseo, *Relations des Ambassadeurs Vénitiens*, II.514.

21. Qtd in Neil Younger, *War and Politics in the Elizabethan Counties* (Manchester: Manchester University Press, 2012), p. 4.

22. In this context, see Matthew Sutcliffe, *The practice, proceedings, and lawes of armes* (London: 'deputies of Christopher Barker', 1593), p. 8. In terms of Elizabethan foreign policy playing off France and Spain, see John S. Nolan, 'The Militarization of the Elizabethan State', *Journal of Military History* 58 (July 1994), 391–420 (pp. 392–3); Younger, *War and Politics in the Elizabethan Counties*, p. 2.

23. For further discussion of this massacre, see Paul E. J. Hammer, *Elizabeth's Wars: War, Government and Society in Tudor England, 1544–1604* (Basingstoke: Palgrave Macmillan, 2003), p. 77; Roger B. Manning *The Apprenticeship of Arms: The Origins of the British Army 1585–1702* (Oxford: Oxford University Press, 2006), p. 12.

24. Raphael Holinshed, *The Third volume of Chronicles* (London: Henry Denham, 1586), p. 1266.

25. 'The Earl of Essex, before his Departure to the Voyage of Portugal, to Mr. Vice Chamberlain, March/April? 1589', in William Murdin (ed.), *A Collection of State Papers relating to affairs in the reign of Elizabeth from 1571 to 1596...* (London: William Bowyer, 1759), pp. 634–5.

26. Robert Devereux, Earl of Essex, *An apologie of the Earle of Essex* (London: for J. Smethwick? 1600), A3ᵛ.

27. Qtd in Hammer, *The Polarisation of Elizabethan Politics*, p. 25.

28. See, for example, Markham, *Honour in his Perfection*, p. 27.

29. Devereux, *Apologie*, A1ᵛ. Devereux spent the winter of 1584–5 at his uncle's house in Lamphey in Pembrokeshire.

30. See Henry Elliot Malden (ed.), 'Devereux Papers, with Richard Broughton's *Memoranda* (1575–1601)', in *Camden Miscellany* xiii (1923), p. 22. William Vaughan contended that '*magnificence is a virtue, that consisteth in sumptuous & great expences* ... so [that it] ... is peculiar to Noblemen'. See *The Golden-grove, Moralized in Three Books* (London: Simon Stafford, 1600), H2ʳ⁻ᵛ.

31. Qtd in Hammer, *The Polarisation of Elizabethan Politics*, p. 56.

32. CLSP Relating to English Affairs preserved in, or originally belonging to, the Archives of Simancas, vol. IV: Elizabeth, 1587–1603, p. 127.

33. Steven W. May, 'The Poems of Edward De Vere, Seventeenth Earl of Oxford and of Robert Devereux, Second Earl of Essex', *Studies in Philology*, vol. 77, no. 5, 1980, pp. 1–132 (p. 43).

34. CLSP, the Archives of Simancas (IV, 1899), p. 513.

35. Naunton, *Fragmenta regalia*, p. 33.

36. Qtd in Wallace T. MacCaffrey, *Elizabeth I. War and Politics 1588–1603* (Princeton, NJ: Princeton University Press, 1992), p. 503.

37. PRO 31/3/29, 208ᵛ.

38. PRO 31/3/29, 202ʳ. See also Naunton, *Fragmenta regalia*, p. 6.

39. Lawrence Stone, *The Crisis of the Aristocracy: 1558–1641* (Oxford: Oxford University Press, 1965), p. 473.

40. William Fleetwood to the Earl of Derby, New Year's Day 1589, in Edmund Lodge (ed.), *Illustrations of British History...*, vol II. (London: G. Nicol, 1741), p. 383 (no. ccxxvi). Essex had been entangled romantically with Elizabeth Stanley, Countess of Derby, in the years 1596–7.

41. William Covell, *Polimanteia* (Cambridge/London: John Legate/J. Orwin, 1595), Q3ʳ.

42. Covell, *Polimanteia*, 2ʳ⁻ᵛ. For further discussion of the earl's patronage, see Hammer, *Elizabeth's Wars*, p. 209.

43. Naunton, *Fragmenta regalia*, p. 33.

44. 'Aucunes considérations' in PRO 31/3/29, 242^r.
45. 'To the Right Honorable *Robert Devereux*', in Pomponio Nenna, *Nennio, or A Treatise of Nobility . . . Done into English by William Jones Gent* (London: Peter Short, 1595), A2^{v,} A3^v.
46. For further discussion, see Andrew Hiscock, '*Achilles alter*: The Heroic Lives and Afterlives of Robert Devereux, 2nd Earl of Essex', in Annaliese Connolly and Lisa Hopkins (eds.), *Essex: The Cultural Impact of an Elizabethan Courtier* (Manchester: Manchester University Press, 2013), pp. 101–32.
47. Respectively in Gentili's works: 'most excellent Earl' – *De Iure Belli, Commentatio secunda* (London: John Wolfe, 1589), A2^r; 'most noble Essex' – *De Iure Belli, Commentatio tertia* (London: John Wolfe, 1589), A2^r; 'most illustrious Earl of Essex' – *De Iniustitia Bellica Romanorum Actio* (Oxford: Joseph Barnes, 1590), ¶3^r.
48. Alexandra Gajda, *The Earl of Essex and Late Elizabethan Political Culture* (Oxford: Oxford University Press, 2012), p. 76.
49. Qtd in Virginia F. Stern, *Gabriel Harvey: His Life, Marginalia and Library* (Oxford: Clarendon Press, 1979), p. 153. See also in this context: Sir Hugh Plat, *The Jewell House of Art and Nature* (London: Peter Short, 1594), A2^v; 'Epistle Dedicatorie', in Vincentio Saviolo, *His Practise in two Bookes. . .* (London: Thomas Scarlet for John Wolfe, 1595), n.p.; dedicatory text in George Silver, *Paradoxes of defence* (London: Richard Field for Edward Blount, 1599).
50. See, respectively: Letter from Pérez to Essex, 26th November 1595, in Gustav Ungerer (ed.), *A Spaniard in Elizabethan England: The Correspondence of Antonio Pérez's Exile* (London: Tamesis, 1974), vol. I, p. 368; George Chapman, *Seauen bookes of the Iliades of Homere* (London: John Windet, 1598), A4^r.
51. Sir Roger Williams, *A briefe discourse of warre* (London: Thomas Orwin, 1590), A2^r. John Dover Wilson would claim at the beginning of the twentieth century that Williams served as a source for Shakespeare's Fluellen. See *Martin Marprelate and Shakespeare's Fluellen: A New Theory of the Authorship of the Marprelate Tracts* (London: A. Moring, 1912), p. 35ff. This was vigorously challenged in John Evans (ed.), *The Works of Roger Williams* (Oxford: Clarendon Press, 1972), p. 155.
52. Philip Gawdy, *Letters of Philip Gawdy, 1579–1616*, ed. I. H. Jeayes (London, 1906), p. 67. For an account of Essex's profile at the Accession Day tilts, see Richard C. McCoy, '"A dangerous image": The Earl of Essex and Elizabethan Chivalry', *Journal of Medieval and Renaissance Studies*, 13 (1983), 313–29.
53. 'Of the obseruation & use of things', in Sir William Cornwallis, *Essayes* (London: S. Stafford and R. Read for Edmund Mattes, 1600–1), I8^v.

54. Hammer, *The Polarisation of Elizabethan Politics*, p. 307. See also Hammer, 'The Uses of Scholarship: The Secretariat of Robert Devereux, Second Earl of Essex, c.1585–1601', *English Historical Review*, 109 (February 1994), 430, 26–51.

55. Henry Savile to Sir Robert Cecil, 28th April 1595. See CM Salisbury (V, 1894), pp. 188–9.

56. For a full and illuminating discussion of Essex's secretariat, see Paul E. J. Hammer, 'The Earl of Essex, Fulke Greville, and the Employment of Scholars', *Studies in Philology*, 91.2 (Spring 1994), 167–80.

57. Sir Clement Edmondes, *Obseruations vpon the fiue first bookes of Caesars commentaries* (London: Peter Short, 1600), p. 1.

58. 'A. B. to the Reader', in Tacitus, *The ende of Nero and beginning of Galba Fower bookes of the Histories of Cornelius Tacitus: The life of Agricola*, trans. Henry Savile (Oxford: Joseph Barnes, 1591), ¶3ʳ.

59. See, respectively: 'Conversations with William Drummond', ll.372–3, in Ben Jonson, *The Complete Poems*, ed. George Parfitt (Harmondsworth: Penguin, 1975, 1996 rep.), p. 471; Ben Jonson, *Ben Jonson*, vol. I 'The Man and his Work', ed. C. H. Herford and Percy Simpson (Oxford: Clarendon Press, 1925), p. 167, note 368. Frances A. Yates also discussed the oblique referencing of A. B. as Essex from the *Worlde of Wordes* (1598) in *John Florio: The Life of an Italian in Shakespeare's England* (Cambridge: Cambridge University Press, 1934), p. 198.

60. Lisa Jardine and Anthony Grafton, 'Studied for Action', *Past and Present*, CXXIX (Nov 1990), 30–78 (p. 31).

61. Qtd in Jardine and Grafton, 'Studied for Action', p. 33. See also William Camden, *The historie of the life and reigne of the most renowmed and victorious Princesse Elizabeth, late Queene of England* (London: for Benjamin Fisher, 1630), p. 187.

62. Published after Essex's execution in Francis Davison, *A poeticall rapsodie* (London: V. Sims, 1611), pp. 94–5.

63. Richard Grenewey, 'To the Right Honorable Robert Earle of Essex and Ewe', in *Annales of Cornelius Tacitus: The Description of Germanie* (London: Arnold Hatfield, 1598), pp. 2–3.

64. Inventory of Essex House after execution excerpted in E. M. Tenison, *Elizabethan England...*, 13 vols. (Royal Leamington Spa, 1933–61): XI (1956), p. xl.

65. Qtd in Hammer, *The Polarisation of Elizabethan Politics*, p. 308, note 204.

66. Sutcliffe, *The practice, proceedings, and lawes of armes*, A2ʳ.

67. John Speed, *The theatre of the empire of Great Britaine* (London: William Hall, 1612), p. 865. For an account of the heavy costs of this expedition, see Hammer, *Elizabeth's Wars*, pp. 159–61, 187.

68. See Paul E. J. Hammer, 'Essex and Europe: Evidence From Confidential Instructions by the Earl of Essex, 1595–6', *English Historical Review*, III (April 1996), 441, 357–81 (p. 379).

69. 'Lettre du Roy de Navarre a la Royne d'Angleterre, faicte par M. Duplessis – Spring 1585' in Plessis-Mornay, *Mémoires et Correspondance*: III.18–19 (no. xiii).

70. Sir Robert Cecil to Michael Jicks, 25th August 1591, 'Stansteed near Portsmouth'. See CM Bath (II, 1907), p. 37.

71. Rachael Poole, 'A Journal of the Siege of Rouen in 1591', *The English Historical Review*, 17.67 (July 1902), 527–37 (p. 529). In this context, see also Sir Thomas Coningsby, 'Journal of the Siege of Rouen, 1591', ed. J. Gough Nichols, *Camden Miscellany* I (1847), 1–81 (p. 25).

72. See, respectively: M. Berger de Xivrey (ed.), *Lettres Missives de Henri IV*, vol. III: 1589–93 (Paris: Imprimerie Royale, 1846), p. 476; Tenison, *Elizabethan England*, vol. VIII (1947), p. 531.

73. Richard Hillman, *Shakespeare, Marlowe and the Politics of France* (Basingstoke: Palgrave, 2002), p. 114.

74. See Burghley to Unton, 20th September 1591, and Burghley to Unton, 24th September 1591, in Sir Henry Unton, *Correspondence of Sir Henry Unton, Knt. Ambassador from Queen Elizabeth to Henry IV, King of France in the Years MDXCI and MDXCII*, ed. Rev. Joseph Stevenson (London: William Nicol/ Shakespeare Press, 1847) – respectively pp. 85, 86.

75. See Walter Bourchier Devereux (ed.), *Lives and Letters of the Devereux, Earls of Essex in the Reigns of Elizabeth, James I and Charles I, 1540–1646* (London: John Murray, 1853): I.273.

76. Entry for 12th November 1591. See Coningsby, 'Journal of the Siege of Rouen, 1591', p. 39.

77. Geneviève Petau de Maulette, *Deuoreux Vertues teares … paraphrastically translated into English. Ieruis Markham* (London: J. Roberts, 1597), esp. 36$^{r–v}$.

78. Lord Chancellor, Christopher Hatton, 5th October 1591, London, to Earl of Essex. See CM Salisbury (IV, 1892), p. 146.

79. Burghley to Unton and Sir Thomas Leighton, 19th December 1591. See Unton, *Correspondence of Sir Henry Unton*, p. 211.

80. 'Negotiation de M. du Plessis en Angleterre en Ianvier 1592'. See Philippe de Mornay, *Memoires et Diverses Lettres de Messire Philippes de Mornay. . .* (Paris: Simeon Piget, 1647), pp. 90–2.

81. Duc de Bouillon at Gravesend to Essex, 30th May 1596. See CM Salisbury (XIII, 1915), p. 573.

82. PRO 31/3/29, fol. 196^{v}.

83. Naunton, *Fragmenta regalia*, pp. 16, 39.

84. Janet Dickinson, *Court Politics and the Earl of Essex, 1589–1601* (London: Chatto & Pickering, 2012), p. 103.

85. RM Lord L'Isle (II, 1934), p. 243.

86. 'Lettre du Roy à M. De Beauvoir, ambassadeur pour sa majesté en Angleterre, janvier 1592'. See Philippe de Mornay, *Mémoires et correspondance pour servir a l'histoire de la Reformation*, 12 vols. (Paris: Treuttel, 1824–5): V.148.

87. Essex to du Plessis-Mornay while the latter is at Dover preparing to return to France, February 1592. See Philippe de Mornay, *Memoires de Messire Philippes de Mornay*, 2 vols. (Paris: La Forest, 1625): II.181.

88. Colin Burrow, *Epic Romance* (Oxford: Oxford University Press, 1993), p. 101.

89. PRO 31/3/29, fol. 209^r.

90. CM Bath (II, 1907), p. 46.

91. Sir Henry Wotton, *A parallel betweene Robert late Earle of Essex, and George late Duke of Buckingham* (London: s. p., 1641), p. 12.

92. See Richard Harvey, *A theologicall discourse of the Lamb of God and his enemies* (London: John Windet, 1590), A3^r.

93. Sir Francis Vere, The commentaries of Sr. Francis Vere (London: John Field, 1657), pp. 66, 67.

94. Richard Perceval, *Bibliotheca Hispanica* (London: John Jackson for Richard Watkins, 1591), A2^v.

95. Qtd in Francesca Wilson, *Muscovy: Russia Through Foreign Eyes 1553–1900* (London: George Allen & Unwin: 1970), p. 48. For further discussion, see Edward A. Bond (ed.), *Russia at the Close of the Sixteenth Century. . .* (London: Hakluyt Society, 1856), pp. 232–3.

96. CM Salisbury (V, 1894), p. 280.

97. Ungerer, *A Spaniard*, II.77.

98. See Hammer, 'Essex and Europe', p. 378.

99. Sutcliffe, *The practice, proceedings, and lawes of armes*, B1^v. For Sutcliffe's possible connections to Essex, see Beatrice Heuser, *Strategy Before Clausewitz: Linking Warfare and Statecraft 1400–1830* (London: Routledge, 2018), esp. pp. 91–116; Manning, *The Apprenticeship of Arms*, p. 6.

100. PRO 31/3/29, fols. 196^v–197^r.

101. 'Lettre du Roy au Comte d'Essex', 5th October 1595. See PRO 31/3/29, 38. For further discussion, see MacCaffrey, *Elizabeth I: War and Politics*, p. 5ff. In this context of figuring forth a common enemy, see the account given by Lord Willoughby of Eresby, qtd in Gajda, *The Earl of Essex and Late Elizabethan Political Culture*, p. 72.

102. Qtd in Gajda, *The Earl of Essex and Late Elizabethan Political Culture*, p. 67.

103. See CSPM in the Archives and Collections of Venice, and in other Libraries of Northern Italy, vol. ix. 1592–1603, pp. 339–40.

104. Ungerer, *A Spaniard*, I.329. The association of Elizabeth with Juno is not without precedent in this period. In this context, see Fulke Greville, *The life of the renowned Sr Philip Sidney* (London: for Henry Seile, 1652), p. 181. See also Erasmus's examination of this passage from the *Aeneid* as the basis for an exercise in letters of request: *Collected Works of Erasmus*, ed. J. K. Sowards (Toronto/Buffalo/London: University of Toronto Press, 1985), XXV.172.

105. See Ungerer, *A Spaniard*, I.354. See also James VI/ I, *Letters of King James VI & I*, ed. G. P. V. Akrigg (Berkeley: University of California Press, 1984), pp. 131, 133.

106. CM Salisbury (III, 1889), p. 435. See also in this context Penelope Rich to James VI, qtd in Chris Laoutaris, '"Toucht with bolt of Treason": The Earl of Essex and Lady Penelope Rich', in Connolly and Hopkins, *Essex: The Cultural Impact of an Elizabethan Courtier*, pp. 201–36 (p. 206).

107. Letter dated 17th May (1597?) from London. See Thomas Birch, *Memoirs of the Reign of Queen Elizabeth from the Year 1581 till her Death* (London: A. Millar, 1754): I.176.

108. PRO 31/3/29, fol. 198ᵛ.

109. Thomas Lake from Nonsuch to Robert Sidney, 22nd August 1595. See RM Lord L'Isle (II, 1934), pp. 159–60.

110. PRO 31/3/29*l*, fol. 216ᵛ.

111. Francesco Contarini, Venetian Ambassador in France, to the Doge and Senate, 26th September 1598. See CSPM in the Archives and Collections of Venice, and in other Libraries of Northern Italy, vol. ix. 1592–1603, p. 346.

112. See, respectively: Henri IV to Jean de Thumery, Sieur de Boissise, 4th December 1598, in P. Laffleur de Kermaingant (ed.) *L'ambassade de France en Angleterre sous Henri IV: Mission de Jean de Thumery, Sieur de Boissise (1598–1602)* (Paris: Firmin-Diderot, 1886), p. 17; Henri IV to de Boissise, 29th December 1598, in P. Laffleur de Kermaingant, P. (ed.) *L'ambassade de France en Angleterre sous Henri IV: Mission de Jean de Thumery, Sieur de Boissise (1598–1602)* (Paris: Firmin-Diderot, 1886), p. 22.

113. Michael Neill, 'Broken England and Broken Irish: Nation, Language, and the Optic of Power in Shakespeare's Histories', *Shakespeare Quarterly*, 45 (Spring 1994), 1, 1–32 (p. 3). In this context, see also David J. Baker, '"Wildehirissheman": Colonialist Representation in Shakespeare's *Henry V*', in R. J. C. Watt (ed.), *Shakespeare's History Plays* (London: Longman/ Pearson Education, 2002), pp. 193–203 (p. 196).

114. Qtd in Hammer, *Elizabeth's Wars*, p. 218.

115. Nolan, 'The Militarization of the Elizabethan State', p. 407. Mark Fissel estimates that '[b]etween 30,000 and 40,000 troops left England and Wales

for Irish service between the years 1585 and 1602'. See *English Warfare 1511– 1642* (London: Routledge, 2016, 1st pub. 2001), p. 87.

116. William Camden, *Britain, or A chorographicall description...* (London: F. Kingston, R. Young and I. Legatt for George Latham, 1637), p. 117.

117. See, respectively: Essex writing to Fulke Greville in 1599, quoted in Tenison, *Elizabethan England*, vol. XI (1956), p. 1; Sir John Harington, *Nugae Antiquae*, 2 vols. (London: Archibald Hamilton, 1769): II.129.

118. Qtd in Tenison, *Elizabethan England*, vol. XI (1956), p. 2.

119. Naunton, *Fragmenta regalia*, pp. 34–5.

120. See, respectively: Barnabe Barnes, *Foure Bookes of Offices* (London: A. Islip, 1606), p. 180; Wotton, *A parallel*, p. 11. John S. Nolan adds that, 'While English soldiers from officer to private uniformly seem to have detested service in Ireland, it was an important part of many military careers.' See 'The Militarization of the Elizabethan State', p. 398.

121. See Andrew Clark (ed.), *The Shirburn Ballads 1585–1616* (Oxford: Clarendon, 1907), p. 326.

122. Qtd in Mark Fissel, *English Warfare 1511–1642* (London: Routledge, 2016, 1st pub. 2001), p. 101.

123. Sir Henry Wotton, *The Life and Letters of Sir Henry Wotton*, ed. Logan Pearsall Smith, 2 vols. (Oxford: Clarendon Press, 1907), pp. 309–10.

124. Qtd in Dickinson, *Court Politics*, p. 20.

125. John Chamberlain to Dudley Carleton, 28th June 1599. See John Chamberlain, *The Letters of John Chamberlain*, vol. I, ed. Norman Egbert McClure (Philadelphia: American Philosophical Society, 1939), p. 74. In this context, see also Camden, *Britain* (1637), p. 119.

126. Rowland Whyte to Robert Sidney, 29th August 1599. See RM Lord L'Isle (II, 1934), p. 386.

127. Rowland Whyte to Robert Sidney, 1599. RM of Lord L'Isle (II, 1934), pp. 395, 396, 397. In this context, see also Camden, *Britain* (1637), p. 120; L. W. Henry, 'The Earl of Essex and Ireland, 1599', *Bulletin of the Institute of Historical Research*, XXXII (1959), 1–23.

128. Rowland Whyte to Robert Sidney, 6th October 1599. See RM Lord L'Isle (II, 1934), p. 399. See also, in this context, Naunton, *Fragmenta regalia*, pp. 7–8.

129. Philip Gawdy to his brother, 23rd November 1599. See Gawdy, *Letters*, p. 97.

130. Rowland Whyte to Robert Sidney, 12th September 1599. See RM Lord L'Isle (II, 1934), p. 389.

131. See CSPM in the Archives and Collections of Venice, and in other Libraries of Northern Italy, vol. ix. 1592–1603, p. 386.

132. Henri IV to de Boissise. See, respectively, entries in correspondence for 26th October, 24th November and 3rd November 1599 in Kermaingant, *Mission de Jean de Thumery*, pp. 95, 101, 97.

133. See CSPM in the Archives and Collections of Venice, and in other Libraries of Northern Italy, vol. ix. 1592–1603, p. 384.
134. David Jardine (ed.), *Criminal Trials*, 2 vols. (London: Charles Knight, 1832): I.360.
135. Philip Gawdy to his brother, 19th December 1600, in Gawdy, *Letters*, p. 111.
136. Henri IV to de Boissise, 8th February 1600, in Kermaingant, *Mission de Jean de Thumery*, p. 114.
137. Henri IV to de Boissise, 30th March 1600, in Kermaingant, *Mission de Jean de Thumery*, p. 131.
138. See CLSP, the Archives of Simancas, vol. IV, pp. 655–6.
139. See Devereux, *Lives and Letters*: II.99. In this context, see also Sir Charles Davers to the Earl of Southampton, 5th May 1600. See CM Salisbury (X, 1904), p. 139.
140. Henri IV to de Boissise, 2nd July 1600, in Kermaingant, *Mission de Jean de Thumery*, p. 158.
141. See CM Salisbury (X, 1904), p. 385. In this context, see also Lena Cowen Orlin, *Private Matters and Public Cultures in Post-Reformation England* (Ithaca: Cornell University Press, 1994), p. 7ff.
142. See CM Salisbury (X, 1904), p. 439. See also William Camden, *Annals* (London: Thomas Harper for Benjamin Fisher, 1635), p. 536.
143. Qtd in Gajda, *The Earl of Essex and Late Elizabethan Political Culture*, p. 27.
144. Paul E. J. Hammer, 'Shakespeare's *Richard II*, the Play of 7 February 1601, and the Essex Rising', *Shakespeare Quarterly* 59.1. (Spring 2008), 1–35 (p. 18). In the context of the Hereford title, see also ibid., p. 28. For further critical discussion rejecting Shakespeare as the author of the play performed to the Essex followers, see Holger Schott Syme, '"But, what eur you do, Buy": *Richard II* as Popular Commodity', in Jeremy Lopez (ed.), *Richard II: New Critical Essays* (London: Routledge/Taylor & Francis, 2012), pp. 223–44 (p. 223); and Rebecca Lemon, 'Shakespeare's *Richard II* and Elizabethan Politics', in ibid., pp. 245–64 (p. 245).
145. Qtd in Gajda, *The Earl of Essex and Late Elizabethan Political Culture*, p. 56.
146. CM Bath (V, 1980), p. 278.
147. See CM Salisbury (XI, 1906), pp. 29–30.
148. See William Reynolds to Robert Cecil, 13th February 1601, in CM Salisbury (XI, 1906), pp. 46, 30. In this context, see also John Bargar to Lord Cobham, 8th February 1601 (ibid.).
149. Critical discussions have continued to debate the possibility of Mountjoy or Essex as the focus for this celebratory passage. See, for example: J. P. Bednarz, 'When did Shakespeare write the choruses of *Henry V*?', *Notes and Queries* 53.4 (2006), 486–9; J. P. Bednarz, 'Dekker's Response to the Chorus of *Henry V* in 1599', *Notes and Queries* 59.1 (2012), 63–8; Warren

D. Smith, 'The *Henry V* Choruses in the First Folio', *Journal of English and Germanic Philology*, 53 (1954), 38–57; David Bevington, *Tudor Drama and Politics: A Critical Approach to Topical Meaning* (Cambridge, MA: Harvard University Press, 1968), p. 290; Christopher Highley, 'Wales, Ireland, and *1 Henry IV*', *Renaissance Drama*, 21 (1990), 91–114 (pp.108–9); Richard Dutton, '"Methinks the Truth Should Live from Age to Age": The Dating and Contexts of *Henry V*', *Huntington Library Quarterly*, 68 (2005), nos. 1 & 2, 173–204.

150. Mervyn James, *Society, Politics and Culture: Studies in Early Modern England* (Cambridge: Cambridge University Press, 1988, 1st pub. 1986), pp. 424, 428.

151. CM Bath (V, 1980), p. 279.

152. See CSPM in the Archives and Collections of Venice, and in other Libraries of Northern Italy, vol. ix. 1592–1603, p. 448.

153. See Geraldine M. Phipps, *Sir John Merrick English Merchant-Diplomat in Seventeenth Century Russia* (Newtonville, MA: Oriental Research Partners, 1985), p. 30.

154. See Bond, *Russia at the Close of the Sixteenth Century*, pp. 232–3.

155. Qtd in Gajda, *The Earl of Essex and Late Elizabethan Political Culture*, p. 1.

156. See CM Bath (V, 1980), p. 280.

157. See CM Salisbury (XI, 1906), p. 43.

158. See CM Salisbury (XI, 1906), p. 450.

159. Jardine, Criminal Trials: I.315. See also Francis Bacon, *A declaration of the practises & treasons attempted and committed by Robert late Earle of Essex and his complices. . .* (London: Bonham Norton and John Bill, 1601), I4ᵛ.

160. Jardine, *Criminal Trials*: I. 351.

161. See, respectively: Camden, *Annales* (1635, 3rd ed.), p. 551; David Lindsay, *Funerals of a right reuerend father in God Patrick Forbes of Corse, Bishop of Aberdfne* (Aberdeen: Edward Raban, 1631), p. 57.

162. Camden, *Annales* (1635, 3rd ed.), p. 190.

163. See CSPM in the Archives and Collections of Venice, and in other Libraries of Northern Italy, vol. ix. 1592–1603, p. 457.

164. John Harington at Kelston Castle to Sir Hugh Portman, 9th October 1601, in Harington, *Nugae Antiquae*: I.46–7.

6 European Afterlives 1600–1770

1. See, respectively: Anon. , *A Lamentable new ballad vpon the Earle of Essex death. . .* (London: E[dward]. A[llde]., c. 1620); Anon., *A lamentable dittie composed vpon the death of Robert Lord Deuereux. . .* (London: [Edward Allde] for Margret Allde, 1603). In this context, see also W. H., *Englands sorrowe or, A farewell to Essex* (London: Valentine Sims for Henry Rocket, 1606).

2. William Barlow, *A sermon preached at Paules Crosse...* (London: R. Read, 1601), B7^v.
3. Barlow, *A sermon preached*, C3^v.
4. See, for example, Kristin M. S. Bezio, *Staging Power in Tudor and Stuart English History Plays* (Farnham: Ashgate, 2015), pp. 133–5.
5. All textual references to *Philotas* are taken from Samuel Daniel, *The Tragedy of Philotas by Samuel Daniel*, ed. and intro. Laurence Michel (New Haven: Yale University Press, 1949).
6. Qtd in Daniel, *Philotas*, ed. Michel, p. 37. For parallels between the language of Daniel's dramatic narrative and that of Essex's trial record, see also ibid., p. 50ff. For an account of the long gestation of Daniel's text, see Fritz Lang, 'The Theatre and the Court in the 1590s', in John Guy (ed.), *The Reign of Elizabeth I: Court and Culture in the Last Decade* (Cambridge: Cambridge University Press, 1995), pp. 274–300 (p. 299).
7. 'Finis The Apology', in Daniel, *Philotas*, ed. Michel, p. 157. For Fulke Greville's analogous fear of censure on account of his 'Antony and Cleopatra' narrative, see Greville, *The life of the renowned Sr Philip Sidney*, p. 179.
8. William Camden, *Annales...* (London: Thomas Harper for Benjamin Fisher, 1635), p. 544. For a more general discussion of contemporary appreciations of Essex's passing, see Andrew Hiscock, '"*Achilles alter*": The Heroic Lives and Afterlives of Robert Devereux, 2nd Earl of Essex', in Annaliese Connolly and Lisa Hopkins (eds.), *Essex The Life and Times of an Elizabethan Courtier* (Manchester: Manchester University Press, 2013), pp. 101–32.
9. Richard Williams, 'A Poore Man's Pittance': pt. II: 'The Life and Death of Essex', in *Ballads from Manuscripts*, vol. II, ed. F. J. Furnivall and W. R. Morfill (Hertford: Ballad Society/Stephen Austin & Sons, 1873), stanza xlvi (p. 33).
10. See, respectively: PRO SP 12/279 no. 59f. 98^r. Qtd in Maureen Claire King, '"Essex, that could vary himself into all shapes for a time": The Second Earl of Essex in Jacobean England', PhD thesis, University of Alberta, 2000, p. 35; from 'A Manuscript of the Time', in John Hutchins, *The History and Antiquities of the County of Dorset*, vol. IV (Dorchester: Dorset County Library, 1973, 1st pub. 1870) note a, p. 219. See also King, 'Essex, that could vary himself', p. 240.
11. Walter Bourchier Devereux (ed.), *Lives and Letters of the Devereux ... 1540–1646* (London: John Murray, 1853): II.99.
12. Ben Jonson, *Ben Jonson*, eds. C. H. Herford and Percy Simpson (Oxford: Clarendon Press, 1925): I.37.
13. All textual quotations from this play are taken from Thomas Heywood, *The royall king, and the loyall subject...* (London: Nicholas & John Okes for James Becket, 1637).

14. All textual quotations from this play are taken from Francis Beaumont and John Fletcher, *Comedies and tragedies written by Francis Beaumont and Iohn Fletcher* (London: Humphrey Robinson for Humphrey Moseley, 1647).
15. Thomas Heywood, *Troia Britanica* (London: William Jaggard, 1609), p. 163.
16. Barnabe Barnes, *Foure Bookes of Offices* (London: A. Islip, 1606), p. 179.
17. Barnes, *Foure Bookes*, pp. 181, 98, 180. However, Barnes does also voice politicly his reservations about this popular hero at these pages.
18. William Camden, *[Annals or] The historie of the most renowned and victorious princesse Elizabeth...* (London: Benjamin Fisher, 1630), p. 199.
19. Qtd in Mervyn James, *Society, Politics and Culture: Studies in Early Modern England* (Cambridge: Cambridge University Press, 1988, 1st pub. 1986), p. 417. Regarding the provenance of Lambarde's account see Jason Scott-Warren, 'Was Elizabeth I Richard II?: The Authenticity of Lambarde's "Conversation"', *The Review of English Studies* 64.264 (April 2013), 208–30.
20. Sir Robert Sidney to Sir John Harrington (1600), in Sir John Harington, *Nugae Antiquae*, 2 vols. (London: J. Wright, 1804): I. 318, 314
21. John Clapham, *Elizabeth of England...*, ed. Evelyn Plummer Read and Conyers Read (Philadelphia/Oxford: University of Pennsylvania Press/Oxford University Press, 1951), p. 272.
22. Sir Thomas Smith, *Sir Thomas Smithes voiage and entertainment in Rushia* (London: W. White & William Jaggard, 1605), I2^v.
23. See Gervase Markham, *Honour in his perfection* (London: B. Allsop for Benjamin Fisher, 1624), p. 26.
24. 'Henri IV to Monsieur de la Rochepot ... Mon Ambassadeur en Hespaigne (27 February 1601)'. See Henri IV, *Lettres de Henri IV au Comte de la Rochepot, Ambassadeur en Espagne (1600–1601)*, ed. P. Laffleur de Kermaingant (Paris: Georges Chamerot, 1889), p. 75.
25. 'Henri IV to Monsieur De La Rochepot (27 February 1601)'. See Henri IV, *Lettres de Henri IV au Comte de la Rochepot*, ed. de Kermaingant, p. 76.
26. Henri IV to M. de Boissise (7 March 1601). See P. Laffleur de Kermaingant (ed.), *L'ambassade de France en Angleterre sous Henri IV: Mission de Jean de Thumery, Sieur de Boissise (1598–1602)* (Paris: Firmin-Diderot, 1886), p. 198.
27. Marin Cavalli, Venetian Ambassador in France, to the Doge and Senate (20 August 1601). See CSPM, relating to English Affairs, existing in the Archives and Collections of Venice, and in other Libraries of Northern Italy, vol. ix. 1592–1603, p. 468.
28. Henri IV to M. de Boissise (7 March 1601). See de Kermaingant, *L'ambassade de France ... Sieur de Boissise*, p. 199.
29. Giovanni Carlo Scaramelli, Venetian Secretary in England, to the Doge and Senate (27 March 1603). See CSPM vol. ix. 1592–1603, pp. 557–8.

30. Ralegh to Robert Cecil, from Plymouth (30 October 1597). See Sir Walter Ralegh, *The Letters of Sir Walter Ralegh*, ed. Agnes Latham and Joyce Youings (Exeter: University of Exeter Press, 1999), p. 173.
31. Sir John Gilbert to Sir Robert Cecil (7 May 1601). See CM Salisbury (XI, 1906), p. 192.
32. For further discussion, see Filippo de Vivo, *Information and Communication in Venice: Rethinking Early Modern Politics* (Oxford: Oxford University Press, 2007), esp. pp. 2, 37, 57.
33. 'Relazione di Spagna di Francesco Soranzo Cav., Ambasciatore a Filippo II e Filippo III dall'anno 1597 al 1602', in Niccolò Barozzi and Guglielmo Berchet (eds.), *Relazioni degli Stati Europei: Lette al Senato dagli Ambasciatori Veneziani nel secolo decimosettimo*, serie I – Spagna, vol. I (Venice: Pietro Naratovich, 1856), p. 185.
34. 'Relazione d'Inghilterra de Nicoló Molin. Ambasciatore Ordinario appresso Giacomo I, 1607', in Niccolò Barozzi and Guglielmo Berchet (eds.), *Relazioni degli Stati Europei. Lette al Senato dagli Ambasciatori Veneziani nel secolo decimosettimo*, serie IV – Inghilterra, vol. I (Venice: Pietro Naratovich, 1863), p. 61.
35. Henry Wotton to Ferndinando I (12 April 1601). See A. M. Crinò, 'Trenta Lettere inediti di Sir Henry Wotton nell'Archivio di Stato di Firenze', *Rivista di Letterature Moderne e Comparate* 8 (1955), 105–26 (p.109).
36. Henry Wotton to Ferndinando I (12 April 1601). See Crinò, 'Trenta Lettere', p.109.
37. Henry Wotton to Ferndinando I (28 April 1601). See Crinò, 'Trenta Lettere', p.III.
38. See Henri Lonchay and Joseph Cuvelier (eds.), *Correspondance de la Cour d'Espagne sur les Affaires des Pays-Bas au XVIIe siècle*, vol. I (1598–1621) (Brussels: Librairie Kiessling, 1923), p. 67.
39. Qtd in Paul E. J. Hammer, *The Polarisation of Elizabethan Politics: The Political Career of Robert Devereux, 2nd Earl of Essex, 1585–1597* (Cambridge: Cambridge University Press, 1999), p. 232, n. 181.
40. See James VI of Scotland, *The Correspondence of King James VI and Sir Robert Cecil and Others in England*, ed. James Bruce (London: Camden Society, 1861), p. 2.
41. James VI/I, *Letters of King James VI & I*, ed. G. P. V. Akrigg (Berkeley: University of California Press, 1984), p. 173.
42. James VI/I, *Letters of King James VI & I*, ed. Akrigg, p. 174.
43. James VI, *The Correspondence of King James VI*, ed. Bruce, p. 65.
44. Gottfried von Bülow (ed.), 'Diary of the Journey of Philip Julius, duke of Stettin-Pomerania, through England in the year 1602', *Transactions of Royal Historical Society*, 2nd series, 6, 1892, 1–67 (p. 15).

45. Philip Gawdy, *Letters of Philip Gawdy*, ed. Isaac Herbert Jeayes (London: Nichols & Sons, 1906), p. 129.

46. Sir John Harington, *Nugae Antiquae* (London: J. Wright, 1804): I.340–1. For Elizabeth's responses at the end of her reign to Tyrone, see Paul E. J. Hammer, *Elizabeth's Wars: War, Government and Society in Tudor England, 1544–1604* (Basingstoke: Palgrave Macmillan, 2003), p. 234.

47. Sonnet 51 in the collection 'Idea'. See Michael Drayton, *Poems* (London: William Stansby for John Swethwicke, 1619), p. 270.

48. Markham, *Honour in his perfection*, p. 32.

49. Qtd in Anna Beer, *Sir Walter Ralegh and his Readers in the Seventeenth Century* (London: Macmillan, 1997), p. 96.

50. Sir Francis Bacon, *A declaration of the demeanor and cariage of Sir Walter Raleigh...* (London: Bonham Norton & John Bill, 1618), pp. 1–2.

51. Diggory Wheare, *Relectiones [sic] hyemales, de ratione & methodo legendi utrasq[ue] historias, civiles et ecclesiasticas* (Oxford: L. Lichfield, 1637), p. 45.

52. Joseph Hall, *The balm of Gilead...* (London: Thomas Newcomb, 1650), p. 217.

53. Qtd in Sir Edward Thompson, *Sir Walter Ralegh* (London: Macmillan, 1935), p. iii.

54. John Milton, 'To the Reader', in Sir Walter Ralegh, *The cabinet-council* (London: Thomas Newcomb, 1658), A2^r.

55. David Jardine (ed.), *Criminal Trials*, 2 vols. (London: Charles Knight, 1832), I.446.

56. See Algernon Sidney, *Discourses concerning government by Algernon Sidney* (London: n.p., 1698), p. 398.

57. Qtd in Beer, *Sir Walter Ralegh and his Readers*, p. 96.

58. Sir Walter Ralegh, *The Poems of Sir Walter Ralegh*, ed. Agnes M. C. Latham (London: Routledge and Kegan Paul, 1951), p. xvi.

59. 'Even such is Time who takes in trust', ll.1–2. See Sir Walter Ralegh, *The Poems of Sir Walter Ralegh*, ed. Michael Rudick (Tempe, Arizona: Arizona Center for Medieval and Renaissance Studies/Renaissance English Text Society, 1999), p. 80.

60. 'Beholde Brave Ralegh here interr'd', ll. 1–8. See Ralegh, *Poems*, ed. Rudick, p. 191.

61. 'Greate heart, who taught the so to dye', ll. 9–10. See Ralegh, *Poems*, ed. Rudick, p. 193.

62. 'I will not weep. For 'twere as great a Sinne', ll.16, 19–22. See Ralegh, *Poems*, ed. Rudick, p. 203.

63. See, respectively: Barnes, *Foure Bookes*, p. 181; Anon., *Histoire de la Vie et Mort dv Comte d'Essex ...* (Paris: n. p., 1607), p. 17.

64. William Camden, *Annales . . . Traduites en langue françoise par P. de Bellegent Poicteuin* (London: Richard Field, 1624).

65. John Webster, *The deuils law-case* (London: Augustine Matthewes, 1623), G1ᵛ. See also John Manningham, *The Diary of John Manningham of the Middle Temple 1602–1603. . .*, ed. and intro. by Robert Parker Sorlien (Hanover, NH: University of Rhode Island/University Press of New England, 1976), p. 222.

66. George Chapman, *The conspiracie, and tragedie of Charles Duke of Byron* (London: G. Eld, 1607), Q2ᵛ.

67. Arjan van Dixhoorn, 'Chambers of Rhetoric: Performative Culture and Literary Sociability in the Early Modern Northern Netherlands', in Arjan van Dixhoorn and Susie Speakman Sutch (eds.), *The Reach of the Republic of Letters. . .*, vol. I (Leiden: Brill, 2008), pp. 119–57 (p. 126). See also Charlotte Steenbrugge, *Staging Vice* (Amsterdam: Rodopi, 2014), esp. p. 18; Elsa Strietman and Peter Happé (eds.), *Urban Theatre in the Low Countries, 1400–1625* (Turnhout, Belgium: Brepols, 2006).

68. By the middle of the seventeenth century, the village of 's-Gravenpolder (of a marked Catholic character even into the opening decades of the seventeenth century) was still an agricultural village numbering 300–400 inhabitants. The membership of a Chamber of Rhetoric was uniformly male and in 's-Gravenpolder extended to some 31 people in the 1630s (numbers might vary widely according to the Chamber). I remain deeply indebted to Herbert Mouwen at the University of Groeningen/Middelburg for sharing some of the research findings of his doctoral research with me. Regarding the subject of 'cautionary' towns, see Hammer, *Elizabeth's Wars*, p. 120.

69. See Wim Hüsken, 'Queen Elizabeth and Essex: A Dutch Rhetoricians' play', *Leeds Studies in English*, vol. 32 (2001), 151–70 (p. 154); Paul Franssen, 'Gloriana's Allies: The Virgin Queen and the Low Countries', in Christa Jansohn (ed.), *Queen Elizabeth I: Past and Present*, vol. 19 (Münster: Verlag, 2004), pp 173–93. Apart from benefiting from Mouwen's research, I have relied upon the transcript of the older ms. transcribed by E. van Dijk, *Koningen Elysabeth: Spel van Sinnen van de Rederijkerskamer 'De Fiolieren' van 's-Gravenpolder* (1994; typewritten script in the collection of the Heinkenszand City Archives, Municipality of Borsele, the Netherlands). My sincere thanks to the archivists, Emiel Roodenburg and Leo de Visser, for making this text available to me. I am also deeply grateful to the following scholars: Wim Hüsken, Bart Ramakers, Charlotte Steenbrugge and Elsa Strietman, for their advice and guidance with this body of research.

70. In this context, see Steenbrugge, *Staging Vice*.

71. All line references for this playtext are taken from the later of the two manuscripts in van Dijk, *Koningen Elysabeth*. See p. 68. For a discussion of the suspicion with which of the *rederijkerskamers* plays often treat the military

leader, see Steven Gunn, David Grummitt and Hans Cools, *War, State, and Society in England and the Netherlands 1477–1559* (Oxford: Oxford University Press, 2007), p. 275.

72. Hüsken, *Queen Elizabeth and Essex*, p. 155.

73. See van Dijk, *Koningen Elysabeth*, p. 68.

74. A briefer synopsis in Dutch of this playtext may be found in Willem Marinus Hendrik Hummelen, *Repertorium van het rederijkersdrama 1500-ca. 1620* (Assen: Van Gorcum & Comp., 1968), pp. 378–80.

75. Coello's play was published along with works by Calderón and Lope de Vega in *Parte treynta y una de las mejores comedias que hasta oy han salido* (Barcelona: Emprenta de Jayme Romeu, A costa de Juan Sapera Mercader de libros, 1638). The earliest republications thereafter are 1651, 1653 and 1704. In this context, see Antonio Coello y Ochoa, '*El conde de Sex': A Critical Edition and Study*, ed. Donald E. Schmiedel (New York: Plaza Mayor, 1972); Raymond MacCurdy, 'The Earl of Essex: Antonio Coello, "El conde de Sex"', in *The Tragic Fall: Don Alvaro de Luna and other Favourites in Spanish Golden Age Drama* (Chapel Hill: North Carolina Studies in Romance Languages and Literatures, 1978), pp. 220–9; Anne McKenzie, 'Antonio Coello como discipulo de Calderón', in José Maria Diez Borque (ed.), *Calderon desde el 2000* (Madrid: Ollero & Ramos, 2001), pp. 37–59; Emilio Cotarelo y Mori, *Don Antonio Coello y Ochoa* (Madrid: Rev. de Arch. Bibl. y Museos, 1919); María Cristina Quintero, '"The Body of a Weak and Feeble Woman": Courting Elizabeth in Antonio Coello's *El conde de Sex*', in Anne J. Cruz (ed.), *Material and Symbolic Circulation between Spain and England 1554–1604* (Aldershot: Ashgate, 2008), pp. 71–87; Héctor Urzáiz Tortajada, 'Pérez de Montalbán y otros Autores de la primera Mitad del Siglo XVII', in Javier Huerta Calvo et al. (eds.), *Historia del Teatro Español*, vol. II (Madrid: Gredos, 2003), pp. 855–96; Marc Zuili, 'Une *comedia* espagnole du Siècle d'Or: *El conde de Sex* de Antonio Coello y Ochoa (éd. *princeps*: 1638)', *Études Epistémè* 16 (2009), https://journals.openedition.org/episteme/688#abstract-688-en.

76. For an account of appreciations of Coello's literary reputation, see Mori, *Don Antonio*, pp. 8–9; Antonio Coello, *El conde de Sex*, ed. Jesús Laiz (Madrid: Real Escuela Superior de Arte Dramático, 2006), p. 14.

77. Indeed, by the end of that decade, Jesús Laiz characterises Coello as the 'poeta de la corte'. See Coello, *El Conde de Sex*, ed. Laiz, p. 16.

78. All textual references are taken from Biblioteca Digital Artelope: Colección Emothe compiled at the University of Valencia and directed by Prof. Joan Oleza (http://artelope.uv.es). Coello's text may be found at http://emothe .uv.es/biblioteca/textosEMOTHE/EMOTHE0389_ElCondeDeSex.php.

Where possible, quotations located with act and scene references available in Coello, *El conde de Sex*, ed. Laiz.

79. For appreciations of the recurrence of these identities in evidence in Golden Age Spanish drama, see Domingo Ricart, 'El Concepto de la Honra de Juan de Valdes', *Revista de Filosofía de la Universidad de Costa Rica* IV.14 (1964 Jan–June), 147–64; Zuili, 'Une *comedia* espagnole du Siècle d'Or'.

80. Mori, *Don Antonio*, p. 51. See also Tortajada 'Pérez de Montalbán', p.884.

81. See, respectively: qtd in Juan Luis Alborg, *Historia de la Literatura Española*, vol. II (Madrid: Editorial Gredos, 1993), p. 815; Emilio Cotarelo y Mori, 'Dramáticos del siglo XVII. Don Antonio Coello y Ochoa', *Boletín de la Real Academia Española* V (1918), 550–600 (p. 583); qtd in Tortajada 'Pérez de Montalbán', p. 883. However, it was also possible for Elizabeth to have a more benign image in contemporaneous Spanish literature, as is evidenced in Cervantes' novella *La española inglesa* (1613), for example. See also in this context: Berta Cano-Echevarría, 'The Construction and Deconstruction of English Catholicism in Spain: Fake News or White Legend?', in Ana Sáez-Hidalgo and Berta Cano-Echevarría (eds.), *Exile, Diplomacy and Texts. Exchanges between Iberia and the British Isles, 1500–1767* (Leiden/Boston: Brill, 2021), pp. 77–102.

82. Qtd in John T. Cull, 'Dissembled Identities: Felipe II as a Possible Character in Antonio Coello y Ochoa's *Celos, Honor y Cordura*', *Romance Notes* 57.3 (2017), 415–26 (p. 416). In this context, see also Alborg, *Historia de la Literatura Española*, vol. II, p. 814.

83. See H. Carrington Lancaster : 'La Calprenède Dramatist', *Modern Philology*, 18.7 (November 1920), 345–60 (p. 347). See also Lancaster's *A History of French Dramatic Literature in the Seventeenth Century*, vol. I, pt. II (New York: Gordian Press, 1966), p. 179.

84. 'Au Lecteur', in Gautier de Costes de la Calprenède, *Le Comte DEssex* (Paris: Toussainct Quinet, 1650), n. p.

85. See Louis Oldani, 'Foreword', in W. H. McCabe, *An Introduction to Jesuit Theater* (Saint Louis: The Institute of Jesuit Sources, 1983), pp. v–x (p. vi).

86. McCabe, *An Introduction to Jesuit Theater*, p. 28

87. McCabe, *An Introduction to Jesuit Theater*, pp. 117–18.

88. Archivum Venerabilis Collegii Anglorum de Urbe, Scrittore 35/2 'The New Moone'. For further discussion, see Suzanne Gossett, 'Drama in the English College, Rome, 1591–1660', *English Literary Renaissance* 3.1. (Winter 1973), 60–93. I am indebted to Professor Maurice Whitehead for his assistance at the English College in Rome in preparing this research.

89. Archivum Venerabilis Collegii Anglorum de Urbe, Scrittore 35/2 'The New Moone', 5^v, 3^r.

90. Archivum Venerabilis Collegii Anglorum de Urbe, Scrittore 35/2 'The New Moone', 4^v.

91. See Nicolas Caussin, *La Cour sainte*, 2 vols. (Paris: Claude Sonnius & Denis Bechet, 1647): II.290–1. I am indebted to my colleague Dr. Catherine Pascal for drawing my attention to this work.

92. 'Première Partie – Dialogue III Elisabeth d'Angleterre/Le Duc D'Alençon', in Fontenelle, *Nouveaux Dialogues des Morts*, ed. Jean Dagen (Paris: Marcel Didier, 1971), pp. 217, 218.

93. For further discussion, see Monica Pavesio, '*Le Comte d'Essex* di Thomas Corneille e di Claude Boyer: come la tradizione francese si sovrappone a quella ispano-italiana', in Daniela dalla Valle and Monica Pavesio (eds.), *Due storie inglesi, due miti europei. Maria Stuarda e il Conte di Essex sulle scene teatrali* (Alessandria: Edizioni dell'Orso, 2007), pp. 151–65.

94. *La Princesse de Clèves* (vol. II), in Madame de Lafayette, *Romans et Nouvelles*, ed. Émile Magne and Alain Niderst (Paris: Éditions Garnier, 1970), p. 290.

95. Textual references from this play are taken from Thomas Corneille, *Le Comte D'Essex*, ed. Wendy Gibson (Exeter: University of Exeter Press, 2000), p. 48.

96. See *Die Deutsche Schaubühne zu Wienn nach Ulten und Reuen Mustern* (Vienna: Ben John. Paul Krauss, 1749). In the context of German-language renderings of this narrative, see also *Die Geheime Liebes-Geschichte der Welt-befanten Königin Elisabeth und dem Grafen von Essex in Engelland* (Franckfurt/Leipzig: Paul Hammerschmied, 1731, 2nd ed. 1743).

97. 'Au Lecteur', in Claude Boyer, *Le Comte d'Essex. . .* (Paris: Charles Osmont, 1678), A2^{r-v}. All textual references to Boyer's play are from this edition.

98. Anon., *Le Comte D'Essex. Histoire Angloise* (Paris: n. p., 1678), p. 15.

99. (Pietro Piperno?), *Il reo innocente: opera tragica* (Rome: Bartolomeo Lupardi for Michel'Ercole, 1665), A2^r.

100. Niccolò Biancolelli, *La Regina statista d'Inghiltera ed il Conte di Esex, Vita, Successi et Morte* (Bologna: Giosesso Longhi, 1689), p. 35. All textual references are from this edition.

101. In the next century a German student, F. H. Brauer, would draw upon the texts of both Coello and Biancolelli for the playtext *Essex* (1716), written in Strasburg. For further discussion, see Adolphe Rietmann, 'The Earl of Essex and Mary Stuart: Two of John Banks' Tragedies with a Side Reference to Two German Plays on the Same Subjects by Hermann Müller', PhD thesis, Berne University, 1912, esp. p. 26.

102. For further discussion, see Carlo Lanfossi, *Un'opera per Elisabetta d'Inghilterra. La regina Floridea (Milano, 1670)* (Milan: LED, 2009); Maria Grazia Profeti, 'Dal *Conde de Sex* alla *Regina Floridea*', in Maria Grazia Profeti (ed.), *Commedia aurea spagnola e pubblico italiano 4* (Florence: Alinea, 2000), pp. 31–59.

103. All textual references are taken from *La Regina Floridea* (Livorno: Girolamo Suardi, 1679).
104. Carlo Lanfossi has argued that *Floridea* operated as an important source for Tomaso Stanzani's opera *Arsinoe* (1676) which, in turn, was a foundational text for the first English opera all'italiana *Arsinoe, Queen of Cyprus* (1705): music by Thomas Clayton, libretto by Peter Anthony Motteux. See Carlo Lanfossi, 'Elisabetta I, Floridea, Arsinoe: tre regine, un'isola e le vicissitudini di un drama per musica', *Musica e Storia* 17.1 (2009), 197–227.
105. All textual references are taken from *Arsace* (Venice: n. p., 1743).
106. I remain deeply indebted to Professore Giovanni Iamartino for generously sharing his research on Leti's *Vita* with me prior to publication: Giovanni Iamartino, '"La Comediante Politica": On Gregorio Leti's 1693 Life of Queen Elizabeth I', in Donatella Montini and Iolanda Plescia (eds.), *Elizabeth I in Writing: Language, Power and Representation in Early Modern England* (Basingstoke: Palgrave Macmillan, 2018), pp. 145–70.
107. Iamartino, 'La Comediante Politica', p. 151, n.17.
108. Iamartino, 'La Comediante Politica', p. 154.
109. Iamartino, 'La Comediante Politica', p. 160.
110. Iamartino, 'La Comediante Politica', p. 158, n. 22.
111. Thomas Heywood, *An apology for actors* (London: Nicholas Oakes, 1612), E3^r.
112. Rome, Biblioteca Casanatense, MS 1486.
113. All textual references are taken from Biblioteca Casanatense ms. 4186.
114. See 'Lo scenario è tratto dal Gibaldone comico di varii suggetti de comedie, ed opere bellissime copiate da me Antonio Passanti detto Oratio il Calabrese per comando dell'Ecc.mo Sig. Conte di Casamarciano, 1700' (209^r–212^r) anthologised in Elena Liverani and Jesùs Sepúlveda, *Due Saggi sul Teatro Spagnolo nell'Italia del Seicento* (Rome: Bulzoni Editore, 1993). The scenario is preserved in the Naples Biblioteca Nazionale, MS. Cod. AA. XI.
115. Anthologised in Adolfo Bartoli (ed.), *Scenari Inediti della Commedia dell'Arte. Contributo all Storia del Teatro Popolar Italiano* (Florence: G. C. Sansoni, 1880). This scenario is preserved in two manuscripts: Florence Biblioteca Riccardiana MS 2800 fols 35v–47v; Florence Biblioteca Nazionale Centrale MS Magl. II.I.90.
116. All textual references are taken from John Banks, *The unhappy favourite* (London: Richard Bentley & Mary Magnes, 1682).
117. See *The Tatler: or, Lucubrations of Isaac Bickerstaff, Esq.*, IV vols (Dublin: W. Whitestone et al., 1777): I.90. Strikingly, this evaluation is also advertised on the titlepage of Ralph James, *The Fall of the Earl of Essex . . . Alter'd from The Unhappy Favourite of Mr. Banks* (London: W. Meadows, 1731).

118. George Sewell, *The Tragedy of Sir Walter Raleigh* (London: for John Pemberton and John Watts, 1719), A3ʳ. All textual references are taken from this edition.

119. All textual references are taken from James, *The Fall of the Earl of Essex* (1731).

120. All textual references are taken from Henry Brooke, *The Earl of Essex: A tragedy* (Edinburgh: A. Donaldson & J. Reid, 1761).

121. All textual references are taken from Henry Jones, *The Earl of Essex: A tragedy* (London: R. Dodsley, 1753).

122. See, respectively: Voltaire, 'Le Comte D'Essex', Tragédie de Thomas Corneille, 1678. Préface de l'Éditeur', in Voltaire, *The Complete Works of Voltaire*, 55 (Banbury: Voltaire Foundation/Thorpe Mandeville House, 1975), p. 1004; Voltaire, 'Remarques sur *Le Comte D'Essex*', Tragédie', in Voltaire, *Complete Works* 55, p. 1007.

123. Voltaire, *Candide, ou l'Optimisme, première partie* (Paris: Aux Delices, 1763), p. 116.

Conclusion

1. John Dryden, *Troilus and Cressida* (London: Jacob Tonson, 1679), B4ʳ.

2. For further discussion, see Paul Franssen, *Shakespeare's Literary Lives* (Cambridge: Cambridge University Press, 2016), p. 12ff; Paul Franssen and Paul Edmondson (eds.), *Shakespeare and His Biographical Afterlives* (New York: Berghahn, 2020); Andrew Hiscock, '"Shakspeare, s'avançant": A Bard, the Nineteenth Century and a Tale of Two Cities' Theatres', *Shakespeare* 13.4 (2017), 333–50.

3. George Granville (Lord Lansdowne). *The Jew of Venice* (London: Ber. Lintott, Fleet Street, 1701), n. p.

4. Elizabeth Boyd, *Don Sancho* (London: G. Parker, 1739), C₂ʳ.

5. For further discussion, see Andrew Hiscock, '"O, Tom Thumb! Tom Thumb! Wherefore art thou Tom Thumb?": Early Modern Drama and the Eighteenth-century Writer – Henry Fielding and Fanny Burney', *Ben Jonson Journal* 21.2 (2014), 228–63.

6. Alexandre Duval, *Shakespeare Amoureux* (Paris: Vente Librairie, 1830), p. 31 (sc. xi). This comic offering approximates remarkably closely the 1601 anecdote to be found in the diary of John Manningham. See *The Diary of John Manningham...*, ed. and intro. Robert Parker Sorlien (Hanover, NH: University of Rhode Island/University of New England Press, 1976), p. 75.

7. See Franssen, *Shakespeare's Literary Lives*, pp. 42–3.

8. Donald Pippin, *Opera in English: Volume Four: Donizetti* (San Francisco: Donald Pippin's Pocket Opera, 2008), p. 337.

9. Pippin, *Opera in English*, p. 373.

10. See Adolphe Rietmann, *'The Earl of Essex' and 'Mary Stuart': Two of John Banks's Tragedies with a side reference to two German plays on the same subjects by Hermann Müller* (Berne: Wirz, 1915).

11. J. Ancelot, *Élisabeth d'Angleterre* (Paris: J. Bréauté, 1829), p. 70.

12. For further discussion, see Peter Holland, 'Dramatizing the Dramatist', in Peter Holland (ed.), *Shakespeare Survey* 58 (2005), pp. 137–47 (p. 138).

13. Charles A. Somerset, *Shakspeare's Early Days* (London: Dicks' British Drama 792, s. d.), p. 4. See also Hiscock, 'Shakspeare, s'avançant'.

14. Somerset, *Shakspeare's Early Days*, p. 6.

15. See also David Worrall, *The Politics of Romantic Theatricality, 1787–1832* (London: Palgrave Macmillan, 2007), p. 130ff.

16. Somerset, *Shakspeare's Early Days*, p. 14.

17. W. T. Moncrieff, *Shakspeare's Festival* (London: Thomas Richardson, 1831).

18. Moncrieff, *Shakspeare's Festival*, p. 36.

19. J. Stirling Coyne, *This House is to Sold* (London: Nat. Acting Drama Office/ Nassau Steam Press, s.d.), p. 16.

20. George Sand, *Oeuvres Complètes. Théâtre I* (Paris: Calmann Lévy, 1877), p. 133.

21. Sand, *Oeuvres Complètes*, p. 135.

22. Sand, *Oeuvres Complètes*, p. 135.

23. Sand, *Oeuvres Complètes*, p. 138.

24. Sand, *Oeuvres Complètes*, p. 141.

25. Joseph-Bernard Rosier and Adolphe de Leuven, *Le Songe D'une Nuit d'Eté*, in *La Bibliothèque Dramatique: Choix des Pièces Nouvelles Jouées sur Tous les Théâtres de Paris*, vol. XXVII (Paris: Michel Lévy Frères, 1849), p. 73.

26. By the close of the century, William John Dixon would offer *Sir Walter Ralegh: a tragedy* (London: Chiswick Press, 1897), and the new century would see also a new genre accommodating these familiar narratives in the shape of film. French studios produced *L'Anneau du Comte d'Essex* (1910), drawing once again on the details of the return from the Irish campaign, the gift of the ring, the revolt, the executed hero and the dying queen. See *L'Anneau du Comte d'Essex* (Paris: Etablissments Gaumont, 1910), p. 3. Three decades later, Hollywood would take up this narrative in *The Private Lives of Elizabeth and Essex* (1939), featuring Bette Davis, Errol Flynn and Olivia de Haviland. For further discussion, see Lisa Hopkins, 'The Earl of Essex and the Duke of Windsor: Elizabeth and Essex on Film', in Connolly and Hopkins, *Essex: The Cultural Impact of an Elizabethan Courtier*, pp. 279–94.

Select Bibliography

The *Complete Bibliography* can be found online at: www.cambridge.org/9781108830188

Manuscripts and Collations of State Papers

Archivum Venerabilis Collegii Anglorum de Urbe, Scrittore 35/2 'The New Moone'.

CLSP Relating to English Affairs preserved in, or originally belonging to, the Archives of Simancas, vol. IV: Elizabeth, 1587–1603, ed. Martin A. S. Hume (London: Eyre & Spottiswoode, 1899).

CM Bath, vol. II (Dublin: His Majesty's Stationery Office, 1907).

CM Bath, vol. V: Talbot, Dudley and Devereux Papers 1533–1659, ed. G. Dyfnallt Owen (London: Her Majesty's Stationery Office, 1980).

CM Salisbury, pt. III (London: Her Majesty's Stationery Office, 1889).

CM Salisbury, pt. IV (London: Her Majesty's Stationery Office, 1892).

CM Salisbury, pt. V (London: Her Majesty's Stationery Office, 1894).

CM Salisbury, pt. VII (London: Her Majesty's Stationery Office, 1899).

CM Salisbury, pt. X (London: Her Majesty's Stationery Office, 1904).

CM Salisbury, pt. XI (London: Her Majesty's Stationery Office, 1906).

CM Salisbury, pt. XIII (London: Her Majesty's Stationery Office, 1915).

CM Salisbury, pt. XV (London: Her Majesty's Stationery Office, 1930).

CM Salisbury, pt. XVII (London: Her Majesty's Stationery Office, 1938).

CM Salisbury, pt. XX (London: Her Majesty's Stationery Office, 1968).

CSP Col. East Indies, China and Japan, 1513–1616, ed. W. Noël Sainsbury (London: Longman, Green, Longman & Roberts, 1862).

CSP Col. East Indies, China and Japan, 1617–1621, ed. W. Noël Sainsbury (London: Longman, Parker & MacMillan, 1870).

CSP Dom. of the Reign of Elizabeth, 1591–1594, ed. Mary Anne Everett Green (London: Longmans, Green, Reader, and Dyer, 1867).

CSP Salisbury, pt. VI (London: Her Majesty's Stationery Office, 1895).

CSPM, relating to English Affairs, existing in the Archives and Collections of Venice, and in other Libraries of Northern Italy, vol. ix, 1592–1603, ed. Horatio F. Brown (London: Eyre and Spottiswoode, 1897).

CSPM, relating to English Affairs, existing in the Archives and Collections of Venice, and in other Libraries of Northern Italy, vol. xiii, 1613–1615, ed. Allen B. Hinds (London: Eyre and Spottiswoode, 1907).

CSPM, relating to English Affairs, existing in the Archives and Collections of Venice, and in other Libraries of Northern Italy, vol. xiv. 1615–1617, ed. Allen B. Hinds (London: Mackie and Co., 1908).

Florence Biblioteca Nazionale Centrale MS Magl. II.I.90.

Florence Biblioteca Riccardiana MS 2800 fols 35 v–47 v.

Murdin, William (ed.), *A Collection of State Papers relating to affairs in the reign of Elizabeth from 1571 to 1596: transcribed from original papers and other authentic memorials left by W. Cecill Lord Burghley, and reposited in the library at Hatfield House* (London: William Bowyer, 1759).

Naples Biblioteca Nazionale, MS. Cod. AA. XI.

PRO 31/3/29: André Hurault, Sieur de Maisse, *Journal de tout ce qu'a fact Mons'. de Maisse Ambassadeur du Roy en Angleterre vers la Reyne Elisabeth depuis le vingt quatriesme jour de Novembre 1597 qu'il partit de Rouen jusques au 19ᵉ jour du mois de Janvier 1598.*

RM Lord L'Isle, vol. II, ed. C. L. Kingsford (London: His Majesty's Stationery Office, 1934).

RM Viscount L'Isle, vol. V, Sidney Papers, 1611—1626, ed. William A. Shaw and G. Dyfnallt Owen (London: Her Majesty's Stationery Office, 1962).

Rome, Biblioteca Casanatense, MS 1486.

Primary (Select)

Achesone, James, *The military garden* (Edinburgh: John Wreittoun, 1629).

Anon., *The famous victories of Henry the fifth containing the honourable Battell of Agincourt* (London: Thomas Creede, 1598).

Anon., *A lamentable dittie composed vpon the death of Robert Lord Deuereux late Earle of Essex who was beheaded in the Tower of London, vpon Ashwednesday in the morning. 1601. To the tune of Welladay* (London: [Edward Allde] for Margret Allde, 1603).

Anon., *A Lamentable new ballad vpon the Earle of Essex death to the tune of the Kings last good-night* (London: E[dward]. A[llde]., c. 1620).

Anon., *A Myrrour for English Souldiers* (London: V. Sims for Nicholas Ling, 1595).

Anon., *The Secret History of the Most Renowned Queen Elizabeth, and Earl of Essex. By a Person of Quality* (Cologne?: Will of the Wisp, 1681).

Bacon, Sir Francis, *A briefe discourse, touching the happie vnion of the kingdomes of England, and Scotland* . . . (London: R. Read for Felix Norton, 1603).

Bacon, Sir Francis, *A declaration of the demeanor and cariage of Sir Walter Raleigh* . . . (London: Bonham Norton and John Bill, 1618).

Bacon, Sir Francis, *A declaration of the practises & treasons attempted and committed by Robert late Earle of Essex and his complices* . . . (London: Bonham Norton and John Bill, 1601).

Baldwin, William, et al., *The last part of the Mirour for magistrates* (London: Thomas Marsh, 1578).

Banks, John, *The unhappy favourite, or, The Earl of Essex a tragedy* (London: Richard Bentley & Mary Magnes, 1682).

Barlow, William, *A sermon preached at Paules Crosse . . .* (London: R. Read, 1601).

Barnes, Thomas, *Vox Belli, or, An Alarvm to Warre* (London: H. Lownes for Nathanael Newbury, 1626).

Barret, Robert, *The theorike and practike of moderne warres* (London: Richard Field for William Ponsonby, 1598).

Barwick, Humfrey, *A breefe discourse* (London: E. Allde for Richard Oliffe, 1592).

Blandie, William, *The castle, or picture of pollicy shewing forth most liuely, the face, body and partes of a commonwealth* (London: John Daye, 1581).

Bodin, Jean, *The six bookes of a common-weale . . . done into English, by Richard Knolles* (London: Adam Islip, 1606).

Brooke, Henry, *The Earl of Essex. A tragedy* (Edinburgh: A. Donaldson & J. Reid, 1761).

Camden, William, *Annals . . .* (London: Thomas Harper for Benjamin Fisher, 1635).

Camden, William, *Britain, or A chorographicall description . . .* (London: Eliot's Court Press, 1610).

Camden, William, *The historie of the life and reigne of the most renowmed and victorious Princesse Elizabeth, late Queene of England* (London: N. Okes [?] for for Benjamin Fisher, 1630).

Churchyard, Thomas, *Fortunate Farewell to the most forward and noble Earle of Essex* (London: Edmund Bollifant for William Wood, 1599).

Churchyard, Thomas, *A generall rehearsall of warres, called Churchyardes choise* (London: Edward White, 1579).

Clayton, Gyles, *The approoued order of martiall discipline* (London: J. Charlewood, 1591).

Cornwallis, Sir William, *The miraculous and happie vnion of England and Scotland . . .* (London: Edward Blount, 1604).

Crompton, Richard, *The mansion of magnanimitie* (London: Richard Field for William Ponsonby, 1599).

Daniel, Samuel, *The ciuile wars* (London: Humphry Lownes for Simon Waterson, 1609).

de Montaigne, Michel, *Essayes or Morall, Politike and Millitarie Discourses* (London: Melchior Bradwood for Edward Blount and William Barret, 1613).

Devereux, Robert, *An apologie of the Earle of Essex* (London: for J. Smethwick? 1600).

Digges, Leonard and Thomas Digges, *An arithmeticall militare treatise, named Stratioticos* (London: Henry Bynneman, 1579).

Edmondes, Sir Clement, *Obseruations vpon the fiue first bookes of Caesars commentaries* (London: Peter Short, 1600).

Ferne, Sir John, *The blazon of gentrie* (London: John Windet for Andrew Maunsell, 1586).

Fourquevaux, Raimond, *The Practice of Fortification*, trans. Paul Ive (London: Thomas Orwin, 1589).

Foxe, John, *Actes and monuments* (London: John Day, 1583).

Garrard, William, *The arte of warre . . . Corrected and finished by Captaine Hichcock* (London: John Charlewood and William Howe? 1591).

Gates, Geffrey, *The defence of militarie profession* (London: Henry Middleton for John Harrison, 1579).

Gentili, Alberico, *De Iniustitia Bellica Romanorum Actio* (Oxford: Joseph Barnes, 1590).

Gentili, Alberico, *De Iure Belli, Commentatio secunda* (London: John Wolfe, 1589).

Gentili, Alberico, *De Iure Belli, Commentatio tertia* (London: John Wolfe, 1589).

Gibbon, Charles, *Watch-word for War* (Cambridge: John Legat, 1596).

Gibson, Abraham, *Christiana-Polemica, or A preparatiue to warre* (London: Edward Griffin, 1619).

Hakluyt, Richard, *The principal nauigations* (London: George Bishop, Ralph Newberie and Robert Barker, 1599–1600).

Hall, Edward, *The vnion of the two noble and illustre famelies of Lancastre [and] Yorke* (London: Richard Grafton, 1548).

Harington, Sir John, *Nugae Antiquae . . .*, 2 vols. (Bath: W. Frederick, 1769).

Hentzner, Paul, *A Journey into England by Paul Hentzner in the Year MDXCVIII*, ed. Horace Walpole, trans. R. Bentley (London: Strawberry Hill, 1757).

Heywood, Thomas, *An apology for actors* (London: Nicholas Oakes, 1612).

Heywood, Thomas, *The royall king, and the loyall subject . . .* (London: Nicholas & John Okes for James Becket, 1637).

Holinshed, Raphael, *The Second volume of Chronicles* (London: Henry Denham, 1586).

Holinshed, Raphael, *The Third volume of Chronicles* (London: Henry Denham, 1586).

James, Ralph, *The Fall of the Earl of Essex . . . Alter'd from The Unhappy Favourite of Mr. Banks* (London: W. Meadows, 1731).

Jones, Henry, *The Earl of Essex: A tragedy* (London: R. Dodsley, 1753).

Keymis, Lawrence, *A Relation of the Second Voyage to Guiana* (London: Thomas Dawson, 1596).

Lydgate, John, *The auncient historie and onely trewe and syncere cronicle of the warres betwixte the Grecians and the Troyans* (London: Thomas Marshe, 1555).

Machiavelli, Niccolò, *The arte of warre* (London: John Kingston, 1562).

Machiavelli, Niccolò, *Machivael's discourses* (London: G. Bedell/T. Collins, 1663).

Middleton, Thomas, *The Peace-Maker* (London: Thomas Purfoot, 1618).

Munday, Anthony, *A second and third blast of retrait from plaies and theaters* (London: Henry Denham, 1580).

Nashe, Thomas, *Pierce Pennilesse His Supplication to the Devil* (London: Abell Jeffes for J. Busby, 1592).

Naunton, Sir Robert, *Fragmenta regalia, or, Observations on the late Queen Elizabeth, her times and favorits* (London: s. p., 1641).

Petau de Maulette, Geneviève, *Deuoreux Vertues teares . . . paraphrastically translated into English. Ieruis Markham* (London: J. Roberts, 1597).

Plutarch, *The Lives of the Noble Grecians and Romanes ... Translated out of Greeke into French by James Amyot ... and out of French into English by Thomas North* (London: Thomas Vautroullier and John Wright, 1579).

Proctor, Thomas, *Of the Knowledge and Conduct of Warres* (London: Richard Tottel, 1578).

Rainolds, John, *The overthrow of stage-playes* (Oxford: Richard Schilders, 1599).

Ralegh, Sir Walter, *The discouerie of the large, rich, and bewtiful empire of Guiana* (London: Robert Robinson, 1596).

Ralegh, Sir Walter, *The History of the World* (London: Walter Burre, 1617 [1614]).

Ralegh, Sir Walter, *Judicious and select essayes and observations by that renowned and learned knight, Sir Walter Raleigh upon the first invention of shipping, the misery of invasive warre, the Navy Royall and sea-service: with his Apologie for his voyage to Guiana* (London: T. W. for Humphrey Moseley, 1650).

Ralegh, Sir Walter, *The Prerogative of Parliaments in England ...* ('Middleburg' [London]: n. p., 1628).

Ralegh, Sir Walter, *A report of the truth of the fight about the Isles of Açores ...* (London: John Windet for William Ponsonby, 1591).

Ralegh, Sir Walter, *Sir Walter Raleigh's Instructions to his Sonne and to Posterity* (London: Benjamin Fisher, 1632).

Rich, Barnabe, *Allarm to England* (London: Henry Middleton for C. Barker, 1578).

Rich, Barnabe, *A souldiers wishe to Britons welfare* (London: T. Creed for Geoffrey Chorlton, 1604).

Saviolo, Vincentio, *His Practise in two Bookes. The first intreating of the vse of the Rapier and Dagger. The second, of Honor and honorable Quarrels* (London: Thomas Scarlet for John Wolfe, 1595).

[Scott, Thomas] Anon., *Robert Earle of Essex his Ghost; Sent from Elizian: To the Nobility, Gentry, and Communaltie of England* ('Paradise' [London]: J. Beale? 1624).

Scott, Thomas, *Sir Walter Rawleigh's Ghost, or England's Forewarner* (Utrecht [London?]: John Schellem, 1626).

Scott, Thomas, *Vox Populi or Newes from Spayne* (London: n. p., 1620).

Sewell, George, *The Tragedy of Sir Walter Raleigh* (London: for John Pemberton and John Watts, 1719).

Silver, George, *Paradoxes of defence* (London: Richard Field for Edward Blount, 1599).

Smith, John, *A Map of Virginia* (Oxford: Joseph Barnes, 1612).

Smith, Sir Thomas, *The common-welth of England* (London: John Windet for Gregory Seton, 1589).

Smythe, Sir John, *Certain discourses* (London: Thomas Orwin for Richard Jones, 1590).

Sutcliffe, Matthew, *The practice, proceedings, and lawes of armes* (London: deputies of Christopher Barker, 1593).

Tacitus, *Annales of Cornelius Tacitus: The Description of Germanie* (London: Arnold Hatfield, 1598).

Tacitus, *The ende of Nero and beginning of Galba: Fower bookes of the Histories of Cornelius Tacitus. The life of Agricola*, trans. Henry Savile (Oxford: Joseph Barnes, 1591).

Vere, Sir Francis, *The commentaries of Sr. Francis Vere* (London: John Field, 1657).

W. H., *Englands sorrowe or, A farewell to Essex Date* (London: Valentine Sims for Henry Rocket, 1606).

Whetstone, George, *The honorable reputation of a souldier* (London: Richard Jones, 1585).

Williams, Sir Roger, *A briefe discourse of warre* (London: Thomas Orwin, 1590).

Wotton, Sir Henry, *A parallel betweene Robert late Earle of Essex, and George late Duke of Buckingham* (London: s. p., 1641).

Index

282

For EU product safety concerns, contact us at Calle de José Abascal, 56–1°, 28003 Madrid, Spain or eugpsr@cambridge.org.

www.ingramcontent.com/pod-product-compliance
Ingram Content Group UK Ltd.
Pitfield, Milton Keynes, MK11 3LW, UK
UKHW020357140625
459647UK00020B/2520